Migration on the Move

# Immigration and Asylum Law and Policy in Europe

*Edited by*

Elspeth Guild
Valsamis Mitsilegas

VOLUME 42

The titles published in this series are listed at *brill.com/ialp*

# Migration on the Move

*Essays on the Dynamics of Migration*

*Edited by*

Carolus Grütters
Sandra Mantu
Paul Minderhoud

BRILL
NIJHOFF

LEIDEN | BOSTON

Library of Congress Cataloging-in-Publication Data

Names: Grütters, Carolus, editor. | Mantu, Sandra, editor. | Minderhoud, Paul, editor.
Title: Migration on the move : essays on the dynamics of migration / edited by Carolus Grütters, Sandra Mantu, & Paul Minderhoud.
Description: Leiden ; Boston : Brill/Nijhoff, 2017. | Series: Immigration and asylum law and policy in Europe ; volume 42 | Includes bibliographical references and index.
Identifiers: LCCN 2017019546 (print) | LCCN 2017022519 (ebook) | ISBN 9789004330467 (E-book) | ISBN 9789004330450 (hardback : alk. paper)
Subjects: LCSH: Emigration and immigration law--European Union countries. | Emigration and immigration law--European Union countries--History. | Asylum, Right of--European Union countries. | Refugees--Legal status, laws, etc.--European Union countries. | Citizenship--European Union countries. | Freedom of movement--European Union countries.
Classification: LCC KJE6044 (ebook) | LCC KJE6044 .M54 2017 (print) | DDC 342.2408/2--dc23
LC record available at https://lccn.loc.gov/2017019546

Typeface for the Latin, Greek, and Cyrillic scripts: "Brill". See and download: brill.com/brill-typeface.

ISSN 1568-2749
ISBN 978-90-04-33045-0 (hardback)
ISBN 978-90-04-33046-7 (e-book)



This book is printed on acid-free paper and produced in a sustainable manner.

# Contents

## PART 3
## *People's Europe*

# List of Figures

## About the Authors

*Asuncion Fresnoza-Flot*

is a research fellow of the Radboud Excellence Initiative at the Centre for Migration Law at Radboud University Nijmegen (NL). She is also associate researcher at the Migrations and Society Research Unit (URMIS) at Paris Diderot University (France), where she obtained her PhD in Sociology in 2008, and scientific collaborator at the Institute for the Analysis of Change in Historical and Contemporary Societies (IACCHOS) of the Catholic University of Louvain (Belgium). Her recent publications include the co-edited volume *International marriages and marital citizenship. Southeast Asian women on the move* (July 2017 forthcoming, Routledge). Her current research examines marital breakup in "mixed" couples of Filipino migrant women in Europe.

*Kees Groenendijk*

is emeritus professor of Sociology of Law and one of the founders of the Centre for Migration Law at Radboud University Nijmegen (NL). He studied law in Utrecht and learned migration law in Amsterdam while practising as an attorney during the early seventies. In 1982 he was appointed full professor of Sociology of Law (retired in 2008). Prof. Groenendijk was chairman of the Standing Committee of Experts in international immigration, refugee and criminal law (the Meijers Committee). He publishes on regulation of migration and the legal position of migrants in The Netherlands and in Europe.

*Carolus Grütters*

is senior researcher at the Centre for Migration Law at Radboud University Nijmegen (NL). He studied Dutch Law, Criminal Law in particular, at the University of Leiden. After his graduation (1985) he started at Radboud University teaching Law and Information Technology and specialized in building simulation models for policy decisions in the area of asylum law. He holds a doctoral degree awarded by Radboud University in the area of Law as well as Management Sciences (Asylum dynamics – A system dynamics analysis of the Dutch asylum procedure in 1980–2002). In 2009 he moved from Law & IT to the Centre for Migration Law. His research focuses on asylum law, distribution of asylum flows, regularisations (e.g., pardonregeling) and policy guidelines on migration. He is editor in chief of the Newsletter on European Migration Issues (NEMIS) and the Newsletter on European Asylum Issues (NEAIS).

*Elspeth Guild*
is Jean Monnet Professor *ad personam* at Radboud University Nijmegen (NL) as well as at Queen Mary, University of London. She is also partner at the London law firm, Kingsley Napley and an associate senior research fellow at the Centre for European Policy Studies, Brussels. She has published widely in the field of European free movement of persons, asylum and immigration. Professor Guild provides regular advice to the European Parliament, the European Commission, the Council of Europe and other European and international organizations (such as the UNHCR) on free movement of persons, migration and asylum. Professor Guild is also co-editor of the European Journal of Migration and of the book series Immigration and Asylum Law and Policy in Europe (published by Brill | Martinus Nijhoff).

*Betty de Hart*
is professor of Migration Law at the University of Amsterdam (NL) and associate professor at the Centre for Migration Law at Radboud University Nijmegen (NL). She was awarded a doctoral degree by Radboud University on her dissertation on Dutch citizens with foreign partners within the context of nationality law and alien law (2003). In 2007 she received an NWO-Vidi research grant on the project: 'Transnational families between Dutch and Islamic family law'. In 2016 she received a Consolidator Grant from the European Research Council on a research project on 'Regulating mixed intimacies in Europe'. Betty de Hart does interdisciplinary and international comparative research in the area of family law with a sociology of law viewpoint. Her research focuses on gender, ethnicity & diversity and the meaning of law in everyday life.

*Marie-Laure Basilien-Gainche*
is professor of public law at the University Jean Moulin Lyon 3 (France), where she carries out research on constitutional law and European law, political philosophy and fundamental rights. Her research focusses on assessing the legitimacy of the systems and political decisions of the European Union and its Member States. She is member of the Team of Public Law (Centre of Constitutional Law) of the University Lyon 3, as well as associate member of the Centre of research and studies on the fundamental rights CREDOF of the University Paris Nanterre. Marie-Laure Basilien-Gainche is member of the Institut Universitaire de France, where she leads the research project: "La finis et le limes – Reflections on the constitutional identity of the EU with regard to immigration and asylum policy".

*Rahfin Faruk*
is a consultant at FSG, a social impact consultancy. He previously worked at Grameen Bank, the U.S. Department of State, and McKinsey & Company. His research interests include financial inclusion and global migration. He has published in a number of popular press publications, including the Dallas Morning News and the Huffington Post. He has presented at a number of political science conferences and has published original research. He has degrees in economics, political science, public policy and religious studies from SMU (USA). He is a Marshall Scholar and a Harry S. Truman Scholar.

*James Hollifield*
is professor of International Political Economy and director of the John G. Tower Center for Political Studies at SMU (USA). He has worked as a consultant for the U.S. Government, as well as several governmental and intergovernmental organizations, including the United Nations and the OECD and has published widely on international political and economic issues, along with numerous other books and scientific articles. His research looks at how states manage migration for strategic gains. He is the 2016 recipient of the 'Distinguished Scholar Award' for the Ethnicity, Nationalism and Migration section of the International Studies Association. James F. Hollifield has also been the recipient of grants from private foundations and government agencies, including the Social Science Research Council, the Sloan Foundation, and the National Science Foundation.

*Sandra Mantu*
is researcher at the Centre for Migration Law at Radboud University Nijmegen (NL). In 2014, Sandra defended her PhD thesis that dealt with the legal rules and practices of citizenship deprivation in a selection of EU Member States and their link with EU citizenship. She has been involved in several EU funded projects looking at the legal aspects of EU citizenship and EU migration and mobility frameworks. Sandra has participated as European expert in the European Commission's Network of Experts on Free Movement of Workers that was coordinated by the Centre for Migration Law. Her expertise is in the field of non-discrimination in relation to social and tax advantages for EU workers. She has also participated as researcher in a Jean Monnet Multilateral Research project "The Reconceptualization of EU citizenship", looking at access to social and residence rights by mobile EU citizens.

*Paul Minderhoud*
is associate professor at the Centre for Migration Law at Radboud University Nijmegen (NL). His dissertation is a socio-legal study into the differences

between immigrants and native citizens in the implementation of the child benefits and disability insurance legislation in the Netherlands: "Voor mij zijn ze allemaal gelijk", (Amsterdam: Thesis Publishers 1993). His main research interests are the legal and socio-legal aspects of immigration and social security. He was project director of the European Network on Free Movement of Workers and is co-editor of the European Journal of Migration and Law.

*Thomas Spijkerboer*
is professor of Migration Law at the Vrije Universiteit Amsterdam (NL). He is one of the lecturers in the master's track on International Migration and Refugee Law of the Vrije Universiteit Amsterdam. He has worked at Advokatenkollektief Zaanstreek (lawyers' collective), where he specialized in asylum cases and he was a lecturer at the Radboud University (NL). In Nijmegen he wrote his dissertation Gender and Refugee Status (Ashgate, 2000; Praemium Erasmianum 2001), combining qualitative, quantitative and purely legal approaches. At the Vrije Universiteit Amsterdam he established the research group on migration law, which is nowadays one of the largest research groups on the issue worldwide. In 2013, he was awarded a NWO-Vici grant on the project: 'Border Policies and Sovereignty. Human rights and the right to life of irregular migrants'.

*Tineke Strik*
is assistant professor of Migration Law at the Centre for Migration Law at Radboud University Nijmegen (NL). She wrote her dissertation on the decision making process of the Family Reunification Directive and the Procedures Directive and their effects on the national legislation of the Netherlands and Germany. She has participated in European comparative research projects on the transposition of the Family Reunification Directive and the Procedures Directive. She also conducted a comparative research project on integration and language tests and their impact on integration of third country nationals, and a comparative research on family reunification policies and their impact on the integration of the family. Since 2007, Strik is also a member of the Dutch Senate, participating in the Committees on Asylum and Migration, Justice, and Foreign and European Affairs. On behalf of the Dutch Parliament she participates in the Parliamentary Assembly of the Council of Europe, where she chairs the sub-committee on integration.

*Ashley Terlouw*
is professor of Sociology of Law at the Radboud University Nijmegen. She is responsible for the Institute for Sociology of Law and the Centre for Migration

Law (CMR). she wrote her dissertation about cooperation between migration law judges, which was awarded with a doctoral degree by Radboud University in 2003. Her current research is in the area of discrimination and asylum issues and she has supervised several research projects in these fields. She was a full time Commissioner at the former Dutch Equal Treatment Committee (currently: Netherlands Institute for Human Rights) and until recent she was a honorary judge at the District Court of Arnhem. She is Chair of the editorial board of the Journal A&MR (Asylum and Migration Law), and chair of the VSR (Association for Sociology of Law Studies).

*Ozan Turhan*
received his LLM degree from Exeter University (UK) in 2006 and his LL.B from Istanbul Bilgi University in 2003. He was admitted to the Istanbul Bar in 2005. In 2010 Ozan received his PhD in Law from the World Trade Institute at the University of Berne (Switzerland), after which he worked as Assistant Professor of EU law at Yeditepe University (Turkey) (2010–2013) and as vice-dean of the Faculty of Law of Ozyegin University (Turkey) (2013–2016). He also taught law courses at the Turkish Air Force Academy in Istanbul. In February 2016, he joined Fribourg University (Switzerland) as an associated post-doctoral researcher. His research is co-financed by the BMU foundation in Switzerland

*Jens Vedsted-Hansen*
is professor of law at Arhus University (Denmark). His research activities include administrative law, immigration and refugee law and human rights law. Professor Vedsted-Hansen is member of the Management Board of the EU Agency for Fundamental Rights, member of the Odysseus Academic Network for Legal Studies on Immigration and Asylum in Europe and he is member of the editorial board of European Journal of Migration and Law. He has previously worked in Denmark at the University of Aalborg, the faculty of law of the University of Copenhagen and as a senior researcher and research coordinator at the Danish Centre for Human Rights. Jens Vedsted-Hansen is member of the Danish Equal Treatment Board.

*Margarite Helena Zoeteweij*
received her Master's degree in Dutch and International Law from Utrecht University (NL) in 2005, and her LLM in European Union Law from Exeter University (UK) in 2007. After receiving her PhD in European Union Law from Luzern University (Switzerland) in 2010, she spent one year working as legal

councillor at a Turkish law firm, then six years as assistant professor for EU Constitutional and European Human Rights Law at Yeditepe University in Istanbul (Turkey). In February 2016, she returned to Switzerland to work as postdoctoral researcher in EU Migration Law at the University of Fribourg. Her research is co-financed by the BMU foundation in Switzerland.

CHAPTER 1

# Migration on the Move: An Introduction

*Carolus Grütters, Sandra Mantu and Paul Minderhoud*

## 1.1 Background

In the autumn of 1994, a couple of staff members of the Law Faculty of Radboud University (Nijmegen, The Netherlands) organised a meeting to investigate the feasibility of a structured form of cooperation on the issue of migration. At least a dozen or so staff members from different departments within the Law Faculty were working on this topic and were interested in some form of cooperation. As a result, a formal request was sent asking for permission to create a research centre. In January 1996, the Faculty Board approved this idea. Consequently, the informal cooperation became official and the *Centre for Migration Law* (CMR) was founded.[1] In 2016 the Centre for Migration Law celebrated its 20th anniversary. On that occasion the CMR organised an international conference, which testified to the relevance of our research field, its complexity and societal relevance. We were overwhelmed by the interesting and valuable contributions presented during that day and decided to elaborate on the themes discussed there in a book format.

*Migration on the Move* examines the developments of European migration and asylum law over the past two decades. Bringing together experts with different backgrounds, the book sketches the development of European policies and legislation in the field from 1996, the start of negotiations in the EU to grant competence to the EU for immigration and asylum law, to date (2016) including the refugee crisis of 2015/16 and the role of Turkey. The book is divided into three parts representing different angles on the subject. The first part examines the changing focus of immigration and asylum law from a national competence to an EU one, assessing the changing paradigm of law and practice in the area. The second part focuses on Europe in the world, i.e. how does the EU engage with the world on issues of migration and asylum, and with what kinds of consequences. The third part develops the idea of people's Europe: to whom does Europe 'belong'?

1 The Dutch terminology is: Centrum voor Migratierecht (CMR).

 | DOI 10.1163/9789004330467_002

## 1.2 Part One: Changing Focus

Some twenty years ago, two distinct but important measures were taken in Europe that were of profound influence on the issue of migration: (a) the implementation of the 1990 Schengen Implementing Agreement lifting intra-state border controls on the movement of persons (26 March 1995), and (b) the signing of the Treaty of Amsterdam (2 October 1997). The first Schengen Agreement of 1985 was the start of the gradual abolition of border checks between member states and the realisation of one of the 'basics' of Europe: the free movement of people within its borders. The Amsterdam Treaty created a separate body of law: European immigration and asylum law by collapsing the former Third Pillar regarding borders, immigration and asylum into EU law and by incorporating the Schengen acquis. From this perspective, this was a period of transition from nationally oriented intergovernmental cooperation to a common European approach focusing on implementation and compliance with Union Law.

This first part takes its inspiration from the past in order to analyse the major developments that we witness in the field of migration. Particular attention is paid to the Europeanization of migration law and policy, and its consequences on a national level for the legislation, administration, the courts, and the migrants themselves. In that context a diminishing significance of national sovereignty on the one hand and an increased meaning of Union law on the other hand, can be described as the organising principles. The shift in political weight and influence from the national to the European level – and vice versa – has led to different types of adjustment by public bodies or authorities within the administration, legislature, and judicature.

In the first contribution (Chapter 2), Thomas Spijkerboer traces the major shifts that have taken place in respect of migration law and policy in the past decades. He argues that in the framework of the Europeanization of migration law, three distinct developments occurred: proliferation, denationalization, and securitization. The combined effects of these three developments have led to a shift from migration control to migration management: from reactive to pro-active; from an individual orientation towards an orientation on populations; and from a public policy towards a private, commercially oriented approach. Spijkerboer argues that this shift needs to be analysed from the perspective of its effects on the rights of individuals, while taking more seriously the role of individual rights in this process. Moreover, his analysis shows that the shift towards migration management has consequences for how researchers understand and engage with the object of their research. Spijkerboer invites us to think systematically about what is taken into account and what is left out of our analyses, as well as broaden the scope of migration research in terms of geography, social fields and methodology.

Betty de Hart (Chapter 3) addresses the relationship between migrant sexuality and migration policy by relying on a discourse analysis of media reporting in relation to sexual violence supposedly performed by refugees and migrants. The chapter takes as a starting point the manner in which the media have reported on the events of Cologne, Germany, on New Year's Eve (2015) and then goes to discuss the impact of these discourses on the development of migration policy and management in Europe. De Hart's analysis shows that there are similarities between the discourses on sexual assault by asylum seekers in present-day Europe and earlier discourses on black male sexuality in Europe and its colonies, especially those circulating during the interwar period. The representation in several newspapers after the Cologne attacks of the nation and of Europe as a (white) woman under attack by black men elevates the threat stemming from the sexuality of migrant or refugee men to a threat for the nation and for Europe, therefore no longer only a sexual threat, but also a cultural one. The historical analysis undertaken highlights that in several colonies belonging to European states, black male sexuality was perceived as a threat to European white women requiring specific policy measures. Moreover, at the beginning of the 20th century these threats travelled to the metropolis alongside the colonies' struggles for independence. As a result, sexual relations between European women and racialized men were increasingly regulated by the state through laws and reinforced through social norms. De Hart underlines that after the Second World War, racial thinking was rejected as an explanation for social issues. In her view, this makes the resurgence of sexualized and racialized depictions of refugee men remarkable in itself as well as a weak point for EU antiracism and gender equality laws.

Paul Minderhoud's contribution (Chapter 4) discusses the free movement of EU workers from the perspective of recent developments in this field of law. The chapter examines Directive 2014/54, which is a new piece of legislation introduced by the EU Commission to strengthen the rights of EU workers on the ground and ensure the effectiveness of the principle of non-discrimination between national and EU workers. The need for such an instrument was highlighted by the monitoring reports produced by the CMR as part of the network it coordinated in the field of free movement of workers' legislation in all 28 Member States.[2] Minderhoud's analysis identifies a number of weaknesses that have the potential to undermine the Directive's aims. The lack of effective enforcement tools means that the success of the Directive will depend largely

2 See, for an overview of all reports: <http://www.ru.nl/law/cmr/research/projects/fmow-1/>.

on Member States' willingness to take the new legislation seriously – the UK and Dutch examples show this to be a real problem. Moreover, the failure to include posted workers in the Directive's scope is seen as an equally problematic aspect, since it is precisely this group of EU workers that causes great concern for national administrations. Finally, the chapter ends with a discussion on future challenges that the EU and its Member States will have to address. The progressive displacement of (traditional) EU workers by posted EU workers doubled by a changing definition of the notion of EU worker itself bring new challenges for the EU and for the legal framework designed around the fundamental right to freedom of movement. Brexit and the EU response prior to the actual referendum add yet another layer to an already complex discussion.

In the final chapter of this part, Tineke Strik examines (Chapter 5) two decades of EU migration law for third country nationals (TCN) from the perspective of integration, which the EU defines as one of its main policy objectives in relation to legal migration. The chapter questions to what extent the objective of integration has been met in relation to two legislative instruments: (1) the family reunification directive, and (2) the long-term residence directive. Her analysis shows that Member States behave antagonistically towards EU legislation by using the transposition of the two directives to introduce more restrictive policies that have a detrimental effect upon TCNs and their claiming of EU law based statuses. In practice, the procedures designed to implement the two directives and their application by national administrations raise a number of challenges from the perspective of integration as an objective to be met. The overall picture that emerges is one where EU statuses function less as an integration measure and more as proof of the TCN's integration. The chapter highlights that it is at the level of practical implementation where the effectiveness of EU rights is best observed and that more efforts need to be made by all actors involved in this process to ensure that TCNs benefit from the rights they are entitled to. Strik examines several proposals to address the current situation: from the abolition of labour market tests for intra-EU TCN mobility, to the establishment of a full right to free movement for TCNs, and the introduction of a new status resembling the now abandoned concept of 'civic citizenship'.

## 1.3 Part Two: Europe in the World

In this part the changing position of the EU vis-a-vis the rest of the world is under examination. How does the EU develop its policies on migration and asylum, and in light of what international consequences both among states and people? The authors reflect on EU's efforts in the field of asylum, migration and mobility and the extent to which we can describe the EU as a global player in the current asylum and migration crisis. Although migration has been on the agenda for quite some years, current developments regarding the refugee crisis require (more) coherent and effective responses. These responses should cover both the issue of protection of those in need, and the equally important issue of borders and safety. This raises two questions. On the one hand, what is the impact of increasing numbers of asylum seekers and refugees that go to Europe, and what can be said about the selection criteria for relocation of asylum seekers and resettlement of refugees? On the other hand: why has the project on safety of the EU citizen resulted in the reintroduction of controls at the internal and closing of external borders?

Jens Vedsted-Hansen starts this part (Chapter 6) with an analysis of the costs of internal safety in terms of fundamental rights and solidarity. After reviewing where the Common European Asylum System (CEAS) started and where it is now, attention is paid to the complex relations between the two European courts (ECtHR and CJEU). The need to ensure that the two courts are working in tandem has resulted in a very close reading in both courts of the legal reasoning of the other and a high degree of respect for the underlying legal approaches. Subsequently, some legal challenges of the Dublin system are analysed, such as the systemic risk issue in Tarakhel[3] and subsequent cases. The chapter closes with some thoughts on the practical and substantive meaning of the EU-Turkey statement.

Subsequently, this subject is described from an external perspective by James Hollifield and Rahfin Faruk (Chapter 7) focussing on migration in an age of globalization. The authors argue that, while international trade and migration are often looked at in isolation in terms of their impact on development, it is critical to understand the relationship between trade, foreign direct investment, and migration to get a complete picture of globalization. In their view, migration is both a cause and a consequence of political and economic change: a fundamental feature of the post-war liberal order. Throughout the chapter, the authors highlight that although the 'necessary conditions for migration to occur may be social and economic, the necessary conditions are political and legal'. This makes the state an important element of any analysis attempting to understand migration in the 21st century. The authors propose an examination of the role of the state in migration governance from a 'public goods' approach which allows them to engage with questions concerning the effectiveness of international migration regimes. In their view, global migration governance

3 ECtHR 4 November 2014, Appl. 29217/12, GC, *Tarakhel v. Switzerland*, ECLI:CE:ECHR:2014:1104 JUD002921712.

should become a public good regulated through an international migration regime that would be based on a number of generalized principles of conduct. An examination of a number of already existing attempts in this field stemming from the UN, GATS, the EU or NAFTA exposes the underlying difficulties in establishing a truly international migration regime. The authors suggest that the field of migration governance will be shaped by the position of the more powerful liberal states that have the capacity and willingness to act as trend setters.

The topic of 'Europe in the World' is narrowed down to managing migration by selection in the contribution of Marie Laure Basilien-Gainche (Chapter 8). Basilien-Gainche elaborates on the so-called 'Hotspots approach', which – according to the European Commission – provides a platform for the agencies to intervene rapidly and in an integrated manner, in frontline Member States when there is a crisis due to specific and disproportionate migratory pressure at their external borders. She argues that this approach has been presented as a short-term policy response: a quick fix. However, it seems that it does not fix anything and could generate even more critical issues with domino effects in the long term. Her analysis shows how the identification process and the fingerprinting registration lead to the creation of hierarchy between refugees based on their nationality, whereas the relocation and resettlement programmes coupled with an emphasis on improving the effectiveness of return are based on an underlying assumption that all refugees are undesirable. The Hotspot approach proposed by the Commission is seen as failing in its purpose and leading to the return of a large number of refugees to unsafe places without proper consideration of their asylum claims and the encampment of increasing number of refugees in the hotspots of Italy and Greece. In this process, the Member States and the EU institutions are failing in their human rights and non-refoulement related obligations under international, EU and national laws. The designation of Turkey as a safe country and the so-called EU-Turkey deal are seen as part of an EU policy of 'industrialised and institutionalised selection of refugees' that enables the Member States to pick and choose which migrants they want to welcome while also legalizing the refusal to protect all refugees.

This part is closed with a chapter by Margarite Zoeteweij and Ozan Turhan (Chapter 9) in which they analyse the relation between the EU and Turkey. Their focus is on irregular migration to the EU from and through Turkey. Lately, Turkey has been given a central role to play in EU's policies to combat irregular migration. Zoeteweij and Turhan's contribution contends that by entrusting Turkey with the execution of a significant part of the EU migration policy, the EU does not only deliberately make itself dependent on the goodwill of Turkey, it also indirectly takes on responsibility for the migration law and policy of Turkey. Their concern is that this signals a new phase in the management of migration towards the EU, where the EU will rely on Turkey and other third-countries to deal with migration flows while disregarding its human rights obligations. This chapter reviews from the perspective of EU human rights obligations a number of tools that have been agreed as part of EU-Turkey relations, such as: (a) the EU-Turkey readmission agreement and visa liberalization roadmap, (b) the new Turkish asylum and migration law, and (c) the 2016 EU-Turkey deal. These instruments should satisfy on the one hand EU's need to manage migration flows that pass-through Turkey, and on the other hand Turkey's desire for visa free travel to the EU and accelerated EU accession talks. Zoeteweij and Turhan argue that political and legal developments in Turkey make it an ill-chosen partner in the management of EU migration policy since returns to Turkey violate human rights standards and requirements that are fully applicable within the EU and which are required of EU candidate countries. In their view, EU migration management policy should rely on partnerships with third countries in as much as those partnerships and their application stay within the boundaries of human rights protection to which the EU subscribes.

## 1.4 Part Three: People's Europe

The third part elaborates on the question: To whom does Europe belong and how do we identify those people? The people of Europe are not only EU citizens, but also those who are in the process of acquiring rights, claiming rights and contesting state actions to deny them rights. Discussing and differentiating people according to the developing EU law on migration and asylum has also brought with it new cleavages and challenges, which are examined in this part. Citizens, migrants and refugees have been brought within the scope of EU law but more effort is needed in order to understand how the legal framework impacts the experiences and lives of individuals. Along with Brexit, the question then arises what changes are needed in Europe in the wider context of enlargement or the neighbourhood policies of the EU and the sustainability of the EU.

Firstly, Elspeth Guild elaborates (Chapter 10) on the transformation of the objective of free movement: from workers to citizens to people. The chapter starts by examining how workers have gradually extended and consolidated their rights entering into prolonged struggles with some Member States. These struggles have centred around social security and benefit rights, third country national family members and protection from expulsion. Her analysis shows how the choices made at the beginning of the EU in 1957 in respect of the free movement of workers seem strange in light of current thinking on the issue and the increasingly restrictive policies adopted by various states. Yet those choices set the EU on a course that would see the adoption of the status of EU citizenship as a natural continuation. Guild's chapter highlights the struggles that have occurred in law around the emancipation of EU citizenship from nationality of the Member States and the vacillating attempts to confer EU citizenship the same qualities as nationality under international law. She points out that a number of issues remain unsettled as EU citizenship falls short of offering a right to live and enter one's country of nationality, while allowing for its citizens to be expelled. Guild argues that the most important aspect of EU citizenship – the move away from an economic conceptualisation of the rights of the people – may nevertheless turn out to weaken the notion itself, since it is unclear what is the EU response to allegiance as the glue that holds the nation together. The EU adopting its own Charter of Fundamental Rights is examined as another step towards the extension and consolidation of rights in the EU, although the benefits of Charter rights for EU citizens per se are less clear. The attempts that are made to reduce the rights of EU citizens especially in the Brexit context may make the Charter a very valuable instrument for the retention of rights.

The chapter by Sandra Mantu (Chapter 11) takes a closer look at EU citizenship and some of the contradictions inbuilt in its legal framework and their implications for EU citizenship viewed as a fundamental status. Mantu proposes an analysis of EU citizenship and social rights that builds on the notions of the 'Other', biopolitics and difference. The politicized discourse on EU mobility cannot be explained through legal analysis alone, which is why the chapter proposes these alternative frames of reference for understanding what is at stake in discourses that challenge EU mobility. Her analysis of EU citizenship and social rights from the perspective of the 'Other' shows that those who are legally included may nevertheless be symbolically excluded. This opens the path to articulate claims that mobile EU citizens are dangerous 'Others' whose mobility needs to be controlled. The chapter explores how denial of welfare rights for mobile EU citizens is meant to perform something akin migration management for EU citizens, filtering out desirable EU migrants and excluding undesired-able ones (i.e. the unemployed, the poor, the Roma). The chapter argues in favour of seeing EU citizenship as a 'momentum concept' that needs to be constantly reworked to reach its inclusionary potential. Mantu suggests moving beyond economic activity as the only axis of differentiation in the economy of EU citizenship's legal framework and engage with issues such as ethnicity, gender, age, class. Shifting the lens to these issues helps understand why EU citizenship is not experienced in the same way by all those who are mobile. The question of how difference is incorporated in legal rules is an important one and needs to be explored beyond discrimination on the basis of nationality.

Ashley Terlouw's chapter addresses the very topical issue of access to justice or the lack thereof for asylum seekers (Chapter 12). Since the increase of asylum seekers from Syria to Europe, a parallel development of restrictions on rights can be detected. By using a sociology of law approach to the issue of access to justice, Terlouw points towards the need to develop a specific access to justice theory for asylum seekers that takes into account the following elements: (a) access to territory, (b) access to an asylum procedure, and (c) access to a fair and durable solution. These three issues are used as entry points to highlight the obstacles that asylum seekers face when attempting to find justice in Europe while seeking protection against persecution. Although in her view the EU is – currently – 'not in the mood' for solidarity or accepting the need for closer cooperation, access to justice can and needs to be improved. This would require ensuring that asylum seekers can safely reach Europe though legal pathways and that they have access to a fair procedure. The latter requires from Member States closer collaboration, acceptance of solidarity and of responsibilities that stem from the externalisation of EU policies. The chapter also identifies a number of promising options, such as the joint processing of claims within the EU and the strengthening of humanitarian and development assistance to respond to large movements of people.

The chapter by Asuncion Fresnoza-Flot (Chapter 13) investigates migrants' experiences of and interactions with state policies and provides insights into how state policies structure individual lives and aspirations as well as how individuals respond to such policies. The chapter urges us to view the relationship between people and state as neither static nor straightforward, but rather mutually constructed. The case studies presented focus on Filipino and Thai migrants in Europe and are broken down into 3 micro-level studies of maternal migration, marriage migration and children's migration. The analysis of migrants' responses to state governmentality is part of a growing literature that examines migrant agency as an important element of migration regimes. It shows that despite EU States investing in the creation of 'immobility regimes' and 'enclave societies', migrants are not passive actors; they can live with, navigate or contest migration policies designed to keep them out as well as use a number of tactics, including 'legal consciousness', to find alternative ways to realize their own migration projects. The groups investigated by Fresnoza-Flot – undocumented Filipino mothers in France, Thai women who migrate to Belgium using the 'intimate route' and Filipino children who migrate to unite with their parents in Europe – all navigate migration laws, both 'here' and 'there' and rely on alternative migration channels to reach Europe. Often this leads to expensive migration fees, family separation and long periods of irregular status in their destination countries in Europe. The chapter argues that policy makers should pay more attention to the ways in which the subjects of migration policies react to the laws and policies that are supposed to discipline them, and to the long-term effects of such policies on migrants.

In the final contribution of the book, Kees Groenendijk discusses Brexit and its consequences for the free movement of Union citizens and the rights of third-country nationals (Chapter 14). He focuses on the Decision that the Heads of State and Government agreed on prior to the British vote on Brexit. This agreement is, according to Groenendijk, an informal agreement between the 28 Member States aiming at changing elements of Union law without amending the Treaties. Thus, the Decision is a piece of international law not an instrument of Union law. The chapter examines in detail the changes proposed by the Decision in the area of social rights and free movement: the introduction of an emergency brake on in-work benefits and the indexation of child benefits for EU workers; limiting EU citizen's security of residence by expanding the interpretation of the public policy exception in allowing for expulsion; and the reduction of the right to family reunification for EU citizens with TCN family members. Groenendijk shows that for the first time since 1961, the Member States had agreed to reduce the right to free movement of Union citizens, which will also have consequences for the interpretation of the rights of TCNs and Turkish nationals due to increasing interlinkages between these legal regimes. The manner chosen by the Member States to deal with UK demands – the intergovernmental method – lacked transparency, ignored constitutional arrangements concerning the changing of EU law, and minimized the role of the European Parliament. Although, as a result of the Brexit vote, the Decision will never enter into force, both its preparation and contents raise fundamental questions on the reduction of rights of Union citizens and TCNs, and highlight attempts to 'renationalize' the free movement of persons.

# PART 1

## *Changing Focus*

CHAPTER 2

# Changing Paradigms in Migration Law Research

*Thomas Spijkerboer*

## 2.1 Introduction

Over the past 25 years, regulation of migration has changed. To use two contrasting images: whereas in 1990, the regulation of migration was embodied by the border guard (a state agent who waited for people to turn up at the border in order to be admitted to the territory), in 2016 the regulation of migration is embodied by drones (hovering over North Africa mapping populations whose movement might be reason for evoking a policy response from European states). Migration regulation has become proactive (and not merely reactive), focused on populations (instead of individuals), extra- and intraterritorial (in addition to a renewed focus on the physical border), with security as the central lens (instead of public administration), and administered by an assemblage of public, private and intermediate actors (instead of by domestic civil servants). In Europe, this transformation has taken shape within the context of the European Union. This invites a reflection on the ways in which this fundamental transformation of the research object 'migration law' has necessitated a parallel transformation of the academic study of migration law.

First of all, I want to express my gratitude for having been invited to speak at this birthday party. The people who initiated the work of the CMR, Kees Groenendijk and Roel Fernhout, have provided me with one of the contexts within which I have developed as an academic, and I am very grateful for that. For many of us, the existence of the CMR is really something to celebrate. And although it may be a bit early in the day for that, I also want to say that this is a moment in which we acutely miss a number of people – Hanneke, Bert, Cathelijne, Sarah. They should have been here, they would have loved to be here, and this meeting would have been better in content and definitely more fun if they had been able to participate. Let us at least make this into an event in which they would have liked to have been a part.

In this chapter, I wish to do three things. First, I want to sketch in very broad strokes what I think are the major changes in European migration law and

 | DOI 10.1163/9789004330467_003

policy over the past decades. Then, I will give a concrete example of how these changes manifest themselves in everyday reality – I will share my experiences at the migrant smuggling conference in Amsterdam in January 2016 which I think illustrate these changes very well. And finally, I will suggest ways in which the changes in European migration law and policy have affected our work. But these reflections are tentative and incomplete, and I hope to invite you to join me in thinking through what it is that we are up against in these deeply troubling days.

## 2.2 Proliferation, Denationalization and Securitization of Migration Law and Policy

Since World War II, European states have put in place modern bureaucratic systems to deal with immigration: they have introduced new legislation, introduced a system of residence permits and entry visas, distinguished between admission at the border and residence on the territory, created links between residence and access to the labour market and social security, set up asylum procedures and allowed immigration to be subject to judicial review. When this happened in the late 1950s and 1960s, the aim was to regulate labour migration to north-western Europe (guest workers).[1] This enormous undertaking, which took place in all western European states between 1950 and 1980, despite regional and national particularities, did not necessarily have the desired effect of controlling migration.[2] However, it did create a specialised bureaucracy, with the personnel, the conceptual framework and the legal tools that constituted the regulation of migration as a policy field. These policies allowed European states to deal bureaucratically with their migrant labour force. When in the mid-1970s labour immigration policies were halted, the system was adapted, but did not need to change to be able to deal with the 'new' forms of migration (family and asylum) that became dominant after the end of formal labour immigration policies.[3]

---

1 Castles, S. & M.J. Miller (2009), *The age of migration*, Basingstoke: Palgrave, pp. 96–108; Castles, S. & G. Kosack (1973), *Immigrant workers and class structure in Western Europe*, Oxford: Oxford University Press.

2 Castles & Miller (2009), p. 205; Andrijasevic, R. (2010), *Migration, agency and citizenship in sex trafficking*, Basingstoke: Palgrave, pp. 124–144.

3 On this period in the Netherlands, see: Jones, G.R. (2007), *Tussen onderdanen, rijksgenoten en Nederlanders: Nederlandse politici over burgers uit Oost en West en Nederland, 1945–2005*,

Around 1990, several developments coincided and changed both migration and migration policies. The Iron Curtain fell, which made borders in Europe more permeable. Long distance air traffic increased dramatically, accompanied by larger volumes of long distance migration. After the 1986 Single European Act (the first major reform of the European Communities since the founding Rome Treaty of 1957) European integration in the field of migration took form (1985 and 1990 intergovernmental Schengen Agreements; the 1992 Maastricht Treaty; 1997 Amsterdam Treaty; 2007 Lisbon Treaty).

In all sub-projects of the *Transnationality and Citizenship: New Approaches to Migration Law* research project, carried out by the migration law research groups of the Vrije Universiteit Amsterdam and the – then still – Katholieke Universiteit Nijmegen between 2001 and 2006, the researchers found two turning points: 1973 (followed by the end of Keynesian socio-economic policies; shift from labour migration to family and asylum migration), and 1990 (end of the Cold War; Europeanization).

Three developments have occurred within the framework of this Europeanization:

(1) Proliferation
Policies are increasingly aimed at creating effects outside as well as inside the territories of Europe; examples are legislation obliging airlines to check passports and visas before embarkation ("carrier sanctions"); agreements with third countries obliging them to keep migrants away from their territory, and to take back undocumented migrants when they have succeeded in reaching Europe; sea patrols with third countries in their territorial waters or on the high seas; employer sanctions; the linkage principle; combat of "marriages of convenience" and suchlike in private, administrative and criminal law; the reintroduction of internal border controls and the re-fencing of borders we are witnessing these

Amsterdam: Rozenberg; Bem, K. (2007), *Defining the refugee: American and Dutch case-law 1975–2005*, dissertation Vrije Universiteit Amsterdam; Lange, T. de (2007), *Staat, markt en migrant*, Den Haag: Boom Juridische Uitgevers; Walsum, S.K. van (2008), *The family and the nation. Dutch family migration policies in the context of changing family norms*, Cambridge: Cambridge Scholars Publishing; Pool, C. (2011), *Migratie van Polen naar Nederland in een tijd van versoepeling van migratieregels*, Den Haag: Boom Juridische Uitgevers; Hart, B. de (2012), *Een tweede paspoort. Dubbele nationaliteit in de Verenigde Staten, Duitsland en Nederland*, Amsterdam: Amsterdam University Press.

days suggests that these developments should not be understood as externalization (because internalization takes place as well), nor as delocalization (because borders themselves are enforced as well), but as a process of proliferation.

(2) Denationalization
Policies are increasingly being implemented through non-state actors; examples are private enterprises being involved in detention, policing, border control, the development and everyday running of databases of illegal migrants, in the development and deployment of high tech systems for the surveillance of land and sea borders; migration law being enforced through the obligation for employers, banks, insurance companies, transportation companies, health care providers to check legal residence. But humanitarian actors are involved as well – think of the UNHCR, the Red Cross and the Jesuit Refugee Service running asylum seeker reception centres in the Balkans and elsewhere, MOAS/MSF engaging in search and rescue in the Mediterranean in a way that is very similar to that of the Italian navy; the role of the IOM in debriefing boat migrants; the way in which European states seek to instrumentalize third countries to do their border work.[4]

(3) Securitization
Policies rely increasingly on criminal sanctions, high tech equipment and militarized means; examples are criminal sanctions against airlines, against human smuggling and trafficking (Palermo Protocol), against employers, the use of huge databases, as well as the interoperable radar, infrared and video systems through which computer networks can give information used by air force, navy and coast guard (such as Eurosur); the deployment of EUNavFor (aka Operation Sophia) on the basis of UNSC Resolution 2240(2015) of 9 October 2015, and the deployment of NATO in the Aegean decided on 11 February 2016.[5]

4 Alpes, M.J. (2015), 'Airport casualties: non-admission return risks at times of externalised and internalised migration control', *Social Sciences,* 4(3) pp. 742–757. Also think of the agreements between the EU and Turkey in 2015–2016, and of the introduction of visa obligations for Syrians after 2011 by North African states, possibly under pressure from the EU.

5 <www.nato.int/cps/en/natohq/news_127981.htm?selectedLocale=en>.

The Europeanization,[6] as well as the externalization,[7] internalization,[8] denationalization[9] and securitization[10] of migration policies as well as border policies[11] are emerging as objects of research.

Together, these three developments suggest that a shift has occurred in migration law and policy. Instead of dealing with individual migrants who have

6 Meijers, H. *et al.* (1997), *Democracy, migrants and police in the European Union: The 1996 IGC and beyond*, Utrecht: Forum 1997; Boeles, P. *et al.* (2009), *European migration law*, Antwerp: Intersentia.

7 Maes, M., M.C. Foblets & Ph. de Bruycker (eds) (2011), *External dimensions of EU migration and asylum Law and policy*, Brussels: Bruylant; Ryan, B. & V. Mitsilegas (eds) (2010), *External immigration control: legal challenges*, Leiden/Boston: Martinus Nijhoff; Cuttitta, P. (2005), *Delocalization of migration controls to North Africa*, paper for the workshop 'The Europeanization of national immigration policies – varying developments across nations and policy areas', European Academy, Berlin, 1–3 September 2005; Heijer, M. den (2011), *Europe and extraterritorial asylum*, dissertation Leiden University; Scholten, S. (2015), *The privatization of immigration control through carrier sanctions*, Leiden: Brill.

8 Slingenberg, L. (2014), *The reception of asylum seekers under international law. Between sovereignty and equality*, Oxford: Hart Publishers.

9 Gammeltoft-Hansen, T. (2011), *Access to asylum: International refugee law and the globalization of migration control*, Cambridge: Cambridge University Press; Gammeltoft-Hansen, T. & N.N. Sørensen (eds) (2012), *The migration industry and the commercialization of international migration*, Routledge: London. See generally on privatization and human rights: Law & Ethics of Human Rights 5 (2011), pp. 1–423. On the role of technology see: Dijstelbloem, H. & A. Meijer (eds) (2009), *De Migratiemachine. De rol van technologie in het migratiebeleid*, Amsterdam: Van Gennep, p. 233; Wisman, T. (2012), *Function creep by design*, paper for the 4th Bergen aan Zee Seminar on Migration and law, VU University, 9 & 10 February 2012.

10 Brouwer, E. (2008), *Digital borders and real rights. Effective remedies for third-country nationals in the Schengen information system*, Leiden/Boston: Martinus Nijhoff; Baldaccini, A. & E. Guild (eds) (2006), *Terrorism and the foreigner*, Leiden/Boston: Martinus Nijhoff; Guild, E. & P. Minderhoud (eds) (2006), *Immigration and criminal law in the European Union*, Leiden/Boston: Martinus Nijhoff; Zureik, E. & M.B. Salter (2005), 'Global surveillance and policing: borders, security, identity – introduction', in: Zureik, E. & M.B. Salter (eds) (2005), *Global surveillance and policing. Borders, security, identity*, Cullompton: Willan Publishing, pp. 1–10; Mallia, P. (2009), *Migrant smuggling by sea: Combating a current threat to maritime security through the creation of a cooperative framework*, Leiden: Martinus Nijhoff.

11 Rijpma, J.J. (2009), *Building borders: the regulatory framework for the management of the external borders of the European Union*, Doctoral thesis, San Domenico di Fiesole: European University Institute.

already turned up at European border crossing points (reactive migration control), the aim has become to influence *potential* migrant populations, in order to prevent unwanted migrants from leaving their country of origin for Europe or, having left, from reaching the border (proactive migration management).

One might say that the changes in migration law and policy (proliferation, denationalization, securitization) have led to a shift from migration control (reactive, orientation on individuals) to migration management (proactive, orientation on populations) constituting a new migration regime.[12] The post-war period during which the immigration bureaucracy was constructed was characterized by Keynesian socio- economic policies aiming at full employment and at reducing social inequality. One of the reasons for these policies was to prevent large sectors of the population being expelled from society and becoming vulnerable to recruitment by fascism. The period since 1990 has been characterised by privatisation of the welfare state. Socioeconomic policies now aim at competitiveness of countries, companies and individuals. Inequality is considered as a way to stimulate competition and therefore as something good.[13] During the Keynesian period, migration policy was a secondary policy field. In ways that we still have to comprehend, the present post-Keynesian phase has seen the rise of migration policy as one of the dominant rationales for state policy. The linkage principle is a clear illustration: previously, social security was granted to people even if they had no legal residence, because welfare logic prevailed over immigration logic. This relation of dominance between the two logics has now been reversed: the grant of social security to people without a residence permit is considered an anomaly.

The change from migration control to migration management calls for analysis of the effects of this on the rights of individuals,[14] as well as of the role of individual rights in this process.[15]

---

12 Geigner, M. & A. Pecoud (eds) (2012), *The new politics of international mobility: migration management and its discontents*, IMIS Beiträge 40/2012; Geigner, M. & A. Pecoud (eds) (2010): *The politics of international migration management*, Basingstoke: Palgrave.

13 Sassen, S. (2008), *Territory, authority, rights. From medieval to global assemblages*, Princeton: Princeton University Press.

14 Compare in the context of detention; Cornelisse, G. (2010), *Immigration detention and human rights*, Leiden: Brill.

15 Compare Perugini, N. & N. Gordon (2015), *The human right to dominate*, Oxford: Oxford University Press.

### 2.3 An EU Presidency Conference on Human Smuggling

So we need to look at the relationship between migration management and individual rights. But before we continue at the macro level, it is useful to consider the micro level. I want to share with you the experience I had when attending a conference on human smuggling organized by the Dutch EU Presidency in January 2016. At the suggestion of Theodore Baird I approached this conference as an ethnographer. Following academic literature on "event ethnography", I understood the conference as "venues where epistemic communities align and can be tracked, and where their ideological work is partly done. Meetings can be read as spectacles, orchestrated and structured to facilitate a renegotiated 'order'".[16] I took the conference to be an opportunity to test the hypothesis that the dominant perspective on human smuggling is a repressive one. The dominant perspective holds that combating smuggling and prosecuting smugglers will make things better – will reduce irregular migration as well as exploitation and even death of migrants. My personal view is that this is a form of tunnel vision: the repressive approach has not worked in the past 25 years, but the dominant conclusion is that more of same is needed.[17] But was my hypothesis correct to begin with?

The title of the conference was *Promoting the Multidisciplinary Approach in Addressing Migrant Smuggling.* A multidisciplinary approach meant that different kinds of actors had to work together (Member States and EU institutions; European and non-European states; law enforcement and immigration and asylum agencies; public and private actors). Equally, it meant that different social fields had to be realigned so as to jointly combat migrant smuggling: not just policing, but also the financial sector, social media, and transportation. As one speaker said: "We're not going to arrest our way out of this problem". Another element of the multidisciplinary approach was "dealing with legal issues", which invariably meant making law enforcement operate more smoothly by allowing for data exchange and suchlike.

An element that functioned as the glue for the different elements of the multidisciplinary approach was the emphasis on the tragic element in human smuggling and the consistent vilification of smugglers. The conference was

16 Brosius, J.P. & L.M. Campbell (2010), Collaborative event ethnography: conservation and development trade-offs at the fourth world conservation congress, *Conservation and Society* 8, pp. 245–255.

17 See: Spijkerboer, T.P. & T.K. Last (2015), 'EU border plan is a textbook example of tunnel vision', *Border Criminologies* 16 December 2015, <www.law.ox.ac.uk/research-subject-groups/centre-criminology/centreborder-criminologies/blog/2015/12/eu-border-plan>, [1 March 2016].

opened by the Dutch minister for Security and Justice Ard van der Steur. His opening words were (according to my notes): "We need a multidisciplinary approach in our fight against migrant smuggling. We all have seen the images of women, children and men. More than one million of them entered the European Union in 2015, through ruthless networks taking advantage of their despair. They are seeking only profit, disregarding whether they can deliver and whether the migrants will arrive alive. We have seen death on the seas, on our highways, on the side of the road. The International Organization for Migration calculated there were 3.500 deaths in 2015, but we do not even know the precise numbers. These deaths were caused by criminals. This is why we should all work together and find new ways to stop these atrocities". Other terms used were "ugly business", "human beings whose need to improve their life is exploited by criminals", "a period of unprecedented catastrophes and disasters", "tragic deaths", "the horrific crime of human smuggling", and "one of the most deadly forms of transport". Law enforcement officials (public prosecutors, police) tended to emphasise the role of "rape, murder, extortion". One argued that smuggling for high prices equalled trafficking because the excessive price was indicative of exploitation of vulnerability.

I noted four forms of counter-narrative. Two participants from humanitarian NGOs *explicitly* opposed the dominant narrative. They articulated European migration policy as a way of maintaining global inequality and criticized the politics of non-entrée. Researchers and representatives from international humanitarian organizations formulated *implicit* counter-narratives, i.e. they said things that were clearly at odds with the dominant narrative, such as: combating smuggling leads to higher prices and higher risks, not to less smuggling. However, they did not explicitly flag that these statements stood in opposition to the narrative dominating the conference. A third counter-narrative was *warped*, in the sense that some speakers clearly dissented from the dominant narrative but then quickly incorporated it into their narrative – as in speakers who pleaded for legal channels for migration, and immediately before or after that referred to "interdicting migrant smuggling and smugglers" and to national sovereignty and national security.

The final, and as far as I was concerned most interesting, variety of counter-narrative I had some problem in putting my finger on, and ended up labelling as *despair*.[18] During one plenary session, there was a remarkable contrast between speakers. One European official gave an energetic and lively presentation

18 The label is inspired by Nathaniel Berman's article '"But the alternative is despair". European nationalism and the modernist renewal of international law', *Harvard Law Review* 106 (1993), pp. 1793–1903.

on how much the EU and the Member States were doing to combat smuggling, and emphasized the results that had been achieved. The other three speakers, also European officials, spoke in a flat voice, dutifully went through their slides, adding only technical details. The reflections I noted immediately after this session ended mentioned that the one energetic speaker "is the only one who is cheerfully catching criminals". Falling back on a very factual presentation, often with many technical details, was in this case an expression of a lack of faith, of despair.

Explicit counter-narrative was met with ridicule on several occasions. But mostly counter-narratives were either ignored, or incorporated. Of this incorporation, the consistent vilification of smugglers was a clear example – the emphasis on the suffering and death of migrants, initiated by critics of European migration policy, was used to support intensification of European migration policy.

What this teaches us is that the shift from control to management is not just a theoretical construct, but something that is made to actually happen. Human smuggling is to be dealt with in third countries, throughout European territories, on social media. It is seen as crucial that different agencies (law enforcement, migration, financial) at the level of Member States, the EU and third states cooperate, together with humanitarian organizations, civil society and private actors including banks. And the increasing use of criminal law, military means and institutions (NATO, EUNavFor) was a prominent theme at the conference.

## 2.4 Consequences for Our Work

We have to be very much aware of the frame within which we perform legal analysis – not in the sense of frame analysis but in the filmic sense: what is within the frame and what is not, what is on screen and off screen, what is the camera position and what are the camera movements, what does all this imply? Let me give three examples to clarify what I mean by this.

(1) Twitter

On Twitter, we can follow in "near real-time" (to borrow Frontex lingo) the use of state violence against migrants in Calais and at the Greek-Macedonian border.[19] Teargas grenades are fired at groups of people including young children. If we analyse the legality of the use of

19 This relates to events on 29 February 2016. See: <www.theguardian.com/world/2016/feb/29/teargas-fired-as-refugees-try-to-breach-greece-macedonia-border> and <www.

force, we should be aware that it makes a difference whether we limit our analysis to the question of whether the state agents firing at people followed their rules of engagement and suchlike – i.e. whether we analyse this case of state violence as any other one. Or whether we include in the analysis that the people who are being fired at have been put in a desperate position by conscious European laws and policies and do not merely misbehave, do not merely disobey, but in a meaningful way rebel against their position, and consequently against the failure of – in this case – the "Common European Asylum System". This is reminiscent of the opening sentences of Camus' *Man in Revolt:* "Mais s'il refuse, il ne renonce pas: c'est aussi un homme qui dit oui, dès son premier mouvement".[20] These people are trying to protect their bidonville because it is the best they have, or they are trying to create a DIY version of a humanitarian corridor because the international community has failed to do so. Shooting at people who protest against the desperate position they have been put in by the very state that does the shooting, is a bit harder to justify than shooting at people who merely refuse to obey a police order to move on.

(2) Basic welfare provisions

On 26 November 2015, two different Dutch highest administrative courts ruled on the right of irregular migrants to basic welfare provisions.[21] They side-lined the view of the European Committee on Social Rights on this issue. At a crucial point, they ruled that the relevant provisions of the European Social Charter were not directly applicable in the Dutch legal order – a position which was far from self-evident in light of standing case law of both courts. One of the two courts previously had a more liberal position than the other one. In the decisions of 26 November, this liberal court relinquished its jurisdiction in future irregular migrant cases in favour of the more governmentalist court. These court decisions are part of a larger context. If we analyse these decisions, we choose to what extent we take that context into account. Do we take into account that these cases have come out of the Dutch *sans-papiers* movement? Do we take into account that they are the combined effect of the linkage principle and an asylum procedure which produces "wasted lives", i.e. people

---

theguardian.com/world/video/2016/feb/29/calais-shelters-on-fire-refugees-police-clash-jungle-break-up-video>, [both: March 8, 2016].

20 Albert Camus (1965), *L'homme révolté*, Paris: Gallimard (Pléiade edition), p. 423.

21 Afdeling bestuursrechtspraak van de Raad van State 26 November 2015, 201500577/1/V1 (Dutch: Council of State, Administrative Division); Centrale Raad van Beroep 26 November 2015, 15/4189WMO (Dutch: Central Appeals Tribunal).

who have been illegalized but who cannot be deported? Do we take court rulings on direct applicability for granted or do we problematize them? Do we take into account the intricate institutional politics which led the more progressive court to abdicate its jurisdiction in favour of the more governmentalist court?

(3) Naturally Occurring Illness
In *N. v. UK*, the European Court of Human Rights held that removal of an HIV positive person to Uganda did not constitute inhuman treatment even though it was likely that the woman would die of AIDS within two years.[22] Crucial in the Court's judgment was that HIV was labelled as a naturally occurring illness, and the suffering resulting from that could only in very exceptional circumstances lead to a prohibition on removal. A legal analysis of that judgment requires us to choose whether or not the analysis is limited to the words of the judgment. One might decide that, indeed, HIV is a naturally occurring illness, but the problem N. had with removal to Uganda (the lack of HIV medication) was not a naturally occurring circumstance but a result of the Ugandan government's preference for purchasing arms over medicine. For the initiated: we have to choose whether or not to naturalize or denaturalize the distinction between the *Sufi & Elmi* test and the *N. v. UK* test.

Migration law and policy over the past 20 years has been characterised by proliferation, denationalization and securitization. In our analyses, it makes sense to move with our object of study, and to multiple perspectives (domestic, European, international law; core and periphery perspective), disciplines (law, social sciences, technology) and fields (migration, social security, family, police, military, banking, transport) as well as the relationship between these fields. Because we cannot do all things all the time, we have to choose and it would be good to do so conscious of the consequences of these choices.

I am not saying anything revolutionary here. And this is what we have been doing. The work being done here in Nijmegen and elsewhere is increasingly characterised by a broadening of the scope of research, in geographical terms, in terms of the social fields that are covered, and in methodological terms. If we are aware that we are adapting our research in order to keep up with our object of research, can this awareness be helpful? I think it can be in three ways.

First, I think we have a tendency to err on the side of lack of self-awareness. We can hardly be conscious enough of the choices we make in how we

22 ECtHR 27 May 2008, 26565/05, *N. v. United Kingdom*, ECLI:CE:ECHR:2008:0527JUD 002656505.

approach our research and teaching topics. Our choices have consequences for what it is that we are saying to our peers, to our students and to the wider public. The quality of our work will improve if we try to make our choices explicit and to motivate them.

Second, our perspective tends to be very Eurocentric, and to ignore perspectives from the "periphery". To give one example from my own work on border deaths: a special issue of the New African magazine in November 2014 on the issue focused not on the role of European states, but on the question of what it is African States did to their citizens that so many of them were prepared to die on their way out of these states. I have to admit that the question had never occurred to me before, and that I have hardly been able to develop it because of my lack of contact with counterparts in Africa. This is not just political correctness. Our limited perspective results in analyses with substantive limitations.

Third, we should work more to not always *a priori* assume the state. I do not mean to suggest that we should think of "free migration", i.e. of migration without any state regulation, which I doubt would be a good idea. But we should not assume that it is necessarily the state which is doing the regulating. When we see extensive high tech systems provided by the defence industry being incorporated into the regulation of migration, shouldn't we begin to question whether it is the state making these policies; isn't it business, or maybe the notion of the deep state would be useful? And when in the Dutch *Wet Modern Migratiebeleid* we see that sponsors and employers are to a large extent mandated to take migration decisions, doesn't that mean that the state rubber stamps the outcome of family and market relations? Is this something to welcome, or do we perhaps want the state to intervene in such relations in order to repair imbalances instead of affirming them?

Therefore, I think it is very useful to look back and reflect on the manner in which we as academics approach our object. For this, I think we need another 20 years, and I look forward to doing that with our Nijmegen colleagues.

## References

Albert Camus (1965), *L'homme révolté*, Paris: Gallimard (Pléiade edition).

Alpes, M.J. (2015), 'Airport casualties: non-admission return risks at times of externalised and internalised migration control', *Social Sciences*, 4(3): 742–757.

Andrijasevic, R. (2010), *Migration, agency and citizenship in sex trafficking*, Basingstoke: Palgrave.

Baldaccini, A. & E. Guild (eds) (2006), *Terrorism and the foreigner*, Leiden: Martinus Nijhoff.

Bem, K. (2007), *Defining the refugee: American and Dutch case-law 1975–2005*, dissertation Vrije Universiteit Amsterdam.

Berman, N. (1993), '"But the alternative is despair". European nationalism and the modernist renewal of international law', *Harvard Law Review* 106, pp. 1793–1903.

Boeles, P. *et al.* (2009), *European migration law*, Antwerp: Intersentia.

Brosius, J.P. & L.M. Campbell (2010), 'Collaborative event ethnography: conservation and development trade-offs at the fourth world conservation congress', *Conservation and Society* 8, pp. 245–255.

Brouwer, E. (2008), *Digital borders and real rights. Effective remedies for third-country nationals in the Schengen information system*, Leiden: Martinus Nijhoff.

Castles, S. & G. Kosack (1973), *Immigrant workers and class structure in Western Europe*, Oxford: Oxford University Press.

Castles, S. & M.J. Miller (2009), *The age of migration*, Basingstoke: Palgrave.

Cornelisse, G. (2010), *Immigration detention and human rights*, Leiden: Brill.

Cuttitta, P. (2005), 'Delocalization of migration controls to North Africa', paper for the workshop 'The europeanization of national immigration policies – varying developments across nations and policy areas', European Academy, Berlin, 1–3 September 2005.

Dijstelbloem, H. & A. Meijer (eds) (2009), *De Migratiemachine. De rol van technologie in het migratiebeleid*, Amsterdam: Van Gennep.

T. Gammeltoft-Hansen, (2011), *Access to asylum: International refugee law and the globalization of migration control*, Cambridge: Cambridge University Press.

T. Gammeltoft-Hansen, & N.N. Sørensen (eds) (2012), *The migration industry and the commercialization of international migration*, Routledge: London.

Geigner, M. & A. Pecoud (eds) (2010), *The politics of international migration management*, Basingstoke: Palgrave.

Geigner, M. & A. Pecoud (eds) (2012), 'The new politics of international mobility: migration management and its discontents', *IMIS Beiträge* 40/2012.

Guild, E. & P. Minderhoud (eds) (2006), *Immigration and criminal law in the European Union*, Leiden: Martinus Nijhoff.

Hart, B. de (2012), *Een tweede paspoort. Dubbele nationaliteit in de Verenigde Staten, Duitsland en Nederland*, Amsterdam: Amsterdam University Press.

Heijer, M. den (2011), *Europe and extraterritorial asylum*, dissertation Leiden University.

Jones, G.R. (2007), *Tussen onderdanen, rijksgenoten en Nederlanders: Nederlandse politici over burgers uit Oost en West en Nederland, 1945–2005*, Amsterdam: Rozenberg.

Lange, T. de (2007), *Staat, markt en migrant*, Den Haag: Boom Juridische Uitgevers.

Maes, M., M.C. Foblets & Ph. de Bruycker (eds) (2011), *External dimensions of EU migration and asylum law and policy*, Brussels: Bruylant.

Mallia, P. (2009), *Migrant smuggling by sea: combating a current threat to maritime security through the creation of a cooperative framework*, Leiden: Martinus Nijhoff.

Meijers, H. *et al.* (1997), *Democracy, migrants and police in the European Union: the 1996 IGC and beyond*, Utrecht: Forum.

Perugini, N. & N. Gordon (2015), *The human right to dominate*, Oxford: Oxford University Press.

Pool, C. (2011), *Migratie van Polen naar Nederland in een tijd van versoepeling van migratieregels*, Den Haag: Boom Juridische Uitgevers.

Rijpma, J.J. (2009), *Building borders: the regulatory framework for the management of the external borders of the European Union*, Doctoral thesis, San Domenico di Fiesole: European University Institute.

Ryan, B. & V. Mitsilegas (eds) (2010), *External immigration control: legal Challenges*, Leiden: Martinus Nijhoff.

Sassen, S. (2008), *Territory, authority, rights. From medieval to global assemblages*, Princeton: Princeton University Press.

Scholten, S. (2015), *The privatization of immigration control through carrier sanctions*, Leiden: Brill.

Slingenberg, L. (2014), *The reception of asylum seekers under international law. Between sovereignty and equality*, Oxford, Hart Publishers.

Spijkerboer, T.P. & T.K. Last (2015), 'EU border plan is a textbook example of tunnel vision', *Border Criminologies* 16 December 2015, <www.law.ox.ac.uk/research-subject-groups/centre-criminology/centreborder-criminologies/blog/2015/12/eu-border-plan>, [1 March 2016].

Walsum, S.K. van (2008), *The family and the nation. Dutch family migration policies in the context of changing family norms*, Cambridge: Cambridge Scholars Publishing.

Wisman, T. (2012), 'Function creep by design', paper for the 4th Bergen aan Zee Seminar on Migration and law, VU University, 9 & 10 February 2012.

Zureik, E. & M.B. Salter (eds) (2005), *Global surveillance and policing. Borders, security, identity*, Cullompton: Willan Publishing.

CHAPTER 3

# Sexuality, Race and Masculinity in Europe's Refugee Crisis

*Betty de Hart*

## 3.1 Introduction[1]

After the large-scale sexual assaults on women in Cologne, Germany, on New Year's Eve 2015, Europe was in shock. The sexual assaults by – allegedly – asylum seekers were widely reported by news media across Europe and beyond. What actually happened is, at the time of writing in August 2016, still being studied by a parliamentary inquiry in the *Land* Nordrhein-Westfalen. What is clear is that there were 1,182 criminal reports relating to New Year's Eve in Cologne, of which 497 were about sexual violence, made by 648 victims. 284 persons reported being the victim both of sexual violence and theft. Five criminal reports involved rape (pushing fingers into the vagina of the woman). 183 men were suspected of committing the crimes, of which 55 were Moroccan, 53 Algerian, 22 Iraqi, 14 Syrian, and 14 German (which totalled 158 suspects). 73 of the suspects were asylum seekers, 36 did not have a residence status, and 11 had a residence permit. The residence status of the rest is unknown.[2]

This contribution does not aim to describe these events in Cologne, or to minimize their gravity. Its aim is to understand how they were reported and why they were reported in this way; in other words: the discourses that were produced. A further aim is to understand the impact of these discourses on policy development: if and how the discourses on sexual violence by asylum seekers were related to calls for a different migration management in Europe. What role did the perceptions of the Cologne sexual assaults play in changing understanding of asylum policy in Europe? Thus, this contribution is an analysis of discourses that employ notions of difference, gender and sexuality to make its case for a politics of migration and border control. In such discourses

1 I am very much indebted to Marga Altena, who has taught me to understand and analyse images and who commented on this contribution.

2 *Die Zeit* 23 June 2016, 'Was geschah wirklich? Die Silvesternacht von Köln wurde zur Projektionsfläche in der Flüchtlingsdebatte. Eine Frage blieb unbeantwortet'.

 | DOI 10.1163/9789004330467_004

notions of dangerous, patriarchal migrant masculinity are often employed to articulate the dangers of migration if it is not governed correctly.[3]

To understand how notions of dangerous migrant masculinity are used in discourses on migration management in Europe, insight into the historical trajectories of the images employed is necessary. This contribution will demonstrate that these images are not incidents, but part of a larger historical pattern in which the masculinity of racialized others has been perceived as a threat to European culture and European women. Racialization refers to the process by which a certain group's social position is attributed to 'racial' characteristics; it starts with the assumption that 'race' is a social construct. It does not necessarily involve only people who are considered visibly 'black' but also other groups, such as migrants, asylum seekers or Muslims, who can become racialized in certain times and places.[4]

To gain insight into the historical trajectories, this chapter looks back at the historical period of the interbellum, in which – alleged – mass sexual assaults by 'black' men caused uproar, both in the colonies and the metropole. In both the colonies and Europe after World War I, alleged mass sexual assaults led to campaigns for legal and other measures in which labour unions, intellectuals, politicians and women's organisations were involved.

This contribution is structured as follows. First, the images that were produced after the New Year's Eve events in Cologne will be discussed. Then, it will be demonstrated that claims of sexual assault, or the fear thereof, by asylum seekers did not start with New Year's Eve 2015. Sexual assaults by asylum seekers had been an issue in the media months earlier, in August and September 2015, when the reporting on the 'European refugee crisis' became particularly intensive. This will be based on an analysis of Dutch media reports. Subsequently, the historical roots of the discourses produced during the 'refugee crisis' will be explored, going back to the interbellum period. It will be argued that European images of 'black' and migrant male sexuality are built on colonial images of black sexuality, that travelled to the European metropole and were reproduced there, specifically in the European-wide debate on the 'black' French troops that occupied the German Rhineland. First, the theoretical

---

3 Scheibelhofer, P. (2016) 'How would you react if you learned that your son was gay? Racialized sexualities and the production of migrant others in Europe', in: Amelina, A., K. Horvath & B. Meeus (eds.), *An anthology of migration and social transformation*, Frankfurt: Springer, pp. 295–306.

4 Castles, S. & A. Davidson (2000), *Citizenship and migration: globalization and the politics of belonging*, Hove: Psychology Press.

framework will be set out on how to understand the relation between migrant sexuality and migration policy.

## 3.2 Migrant Sexuality and Migration Policy

Numerous scholars have demonstrated that migration policy is shaped in fundamental ways by norms about gender, family and family relationships. Modern-day migration and integration policies may seem gender-neutral at face value, but are in fact informed by norms about what the roles of women and men ought to be, what marriage ought to be, what parenting ought to be and what family ought to be.[5] This counts not only for family migration policies, but also for labour migration and asylum policies.[6] LGTB/queer studies have drawn attention to the impact of norms on sexuality on migration policies.[7]

Overall, much of this academic work has focussed on discourses on migrant women's gender roles and sexuality. Discourses on the gender roles and sexuality of migrant men and their impact on migration policies have remained relatively understudied.[8] However, gendered images of men are ever present – although hardly made explicit – in the gendered images of women. Indeed, the

5 Bonjour, S. & B. De Hart (2013), 'A proper wife, a proper marriage: constructions of 'us' and 'them' in Dutch family migration policy', *European Journal of Women's Studies* 20:1, pp. 61–76. Strasser, E., *et al.* (2009), 'Doing family: responses to the constructions of "the migrant family" across Europe', *The History of the Family* 14:2, pp. 165–176. Van Walsum, S. (2008), *The family and the nation: Dutch family migration policies in the context of changing family norms*, Newcastle upon Tyne: Cambridge Scholars Publishing. Wray, H. (2011), *Regulating marriage migration into the UK: A stranger in the home*, Franham: Ashgate Publishing, Ltd.

6 Spijkerboer, T. (1999) *Gender and refugee status*, thesis Radboud University Nijmegen. De Lange, T. (2008), 'Ongehuwd en kinderloos: Regels, sekseonderscheid en arbeidsmigratie naar Nederland 1945–2006', *Tijdschrift voor Sociale en Economische geschiedenis* 5:1, pp. 75–100.

7 Luibheid, E. (2002), *Entry denied: controlling sexuality at the border*, Mineapolis/London: University of Minnesota Press. Luibheid, E. (2013), *Pregnant on arrival*, Mineapolis/London: University of Minnesota Press.

8 See however: Charsley, K. & H. Wray (2015), Special Issue 'The invisible (migrant) man', *Men and Masculinities* 18:4, pp. 403–423. De Hart, B. (2015), 'Superdads migrant fathers' right to family life before the European court of human rights', *Men and Masculinities* 18:4, pp. 448–467. Scheibelhofer, P. (2012), 'From health check to Muslim test: the shifting politics of governing migrant masculinity', *Journal of Intercultural Studies* 33:3, pp. 319–332. Bilge, S. & P. Scheibelhofer (2012), Special Issue 'Unravelling the new politics of racialised sexualities: introduction, *Journal of Intercultural Studies* 33:3, pp. 255–259.

image of migrant women as victims of Muslim patriarchy rests on the image of migrant men as the perpetrators and oppressors.[9] Furthermore, the academic literature has largely limited itself to the question of how imageries of oppressive gender relations *within* migrant communities have impacted migration and integration policies rather than the perceived threat of migrant men *towards non-migrant European women*. Keskinen is one of the few who have explored the importance of gender and rhetoric of sexual violence and rape of Finnish white women by migrants in anti-immigration sentiments and its impact on migration policy.[10] She explores how in Finland unrelated incidents of rape and sexual assault allegedly by men 'who looked like migrants' – the wrongdoers were never caught – were related to each other in a discourse on mass rape of Finnish white women by migrant men. It was a debate used by right-wing political parties in their attacks on Finnish migration policies.

As Scheibelhofer has pointed out, such images of threatening migrant male sexuality are not just images per se, but instigate specific policy actions. He also explains that these gender discourses serve not only the male domination of men over women, but also power struggles among men over what constitutes normative, hegemonic masculinity.[11]

This chapter builds on this literature, but also moves beyond it. First, it explores specifically discourses on migrant men's sexuality as a *threat to European white women*. Secondly, it looks not only at discourses on migrant men's sexuality in the national context, but within the European context, in observing how the perception of the sexual threat of migrant Muslim men has travelled across borders within Europe. We now turn to the images that were produced in response to the Cologne attacks.

## 3.3 Sexual Assault in Cologne and European Magazine Covers

Two months after Cologne, Dutch extreme right-wing politician Geert Wilders tweeted the image of a girl (half-woman), seemingly half-naked, huddled, covering her face with her hands as if protecting herself, in shame or sadness

---

9 Bonjour & De Hart 2013. Wray 2011.

10 Keskinen, S. (2011), 'Borders of the Finnish nation: media, politics and rape by 'foreign' perpetrators', in: Eide, E. & K. Nikunen (eds.), *Media in motion. Cultural complexity and migration in the Nordic region*, London: Routledge, pp. 107–124.

11 Scheibelhofer 2016.

FIGURE 3.1 *'What is YOUR daughter worth?'.*
SOURCE: TWITTER ACCOUNT OF GEERT WILDERS: <TWITTER.COM/GEERTWILDERSPVV/STATUS/702814577772392448/PHOTO/1?REF_SRC=TWSRC%5ETFW> [15 AUGUST 2016].

(figure 3.1). It was accompanied by the text: 'Islamic immigration is raping our civilisation one girl at a time' and spoke directly to the audience: 'What is YOUR daughter worth?'

The picture is meant to evoke emotion and shock, to feel for the young girl being assaulted and provoke rage about the perceived wrongdoers: Islam and Muslims. It speaks to a specific audience: the parents of the girl, the parents of all girls. Herewith, Muslim migrants are accused not only of raping women, but raping children. Furthermore, it connects the rape of 'our' girls by Muslim migrants directly to the rape of 'our' civilisation. Wilders had taken the image from UKIP (United Kingdom Independence Party) that shares with Wilders a strong anti-immigrant stance. This means we can assume that 'our' civilisation in its first use by UKIP meant British civilisation. Now that the image has come to be used across borders, it has come to mean 'our' European civilisation. Thus, it is about much more than 'just' the chance of girls being sexually assaulted. It is suggested that Europe is being assaulted by Muslim migration, symbolized by the rape of the girl, who we can then assume to be European. The existence and future of Europe is at stake. Asking the question *What is your daughter worth?* seems to imply that action is needed, to protect the daughters of Europe, and in this manner, Europe itself.

The image and text not only exclude Muslims as the others that European civilisation needs protection from. By presenting male Muslim migrants as the ultimate rapists, sexual violence is constructed as a new phenomenon that entered Europe with Muslim migration and was absent from European civilisation before that. Secondly, it excludes rape by white European men as well as sexual violence against Muslim women and girls. In this respect, it is in line with historical discourses on rape of white women within the context of slavery and colonialism. Such discourses ignored rape by white men of colonized, enslaved women, which was much more widespread and a structural part of the colonial and slavery order, by pointing to the alleged sexual threat of black men to white women.

Of course, one may want to discard the picture tweeted by Wilders as racist imagery employed by extreme right-wing politicians; just what one would expect of them. However, the image of white European women assaulted by 'other' men representing an attack on Europe was not limited to extreme right-wing groups or politicians. On the contrary, it was found on the covers of mainstream and even progressive magazines and newspapers across Europe. Figures 3.2–3.4 show the covers of three opinion magazines, a Polish, a German, and a Dutch one. The Polish *wSieci* is a mass-market conservative magazine, the German *Focus* is considered conservative, and the Dutch *Vrij Nederland* is considered a progressive opinion magazine. The three covers present different versions of very similar imageries: white blond women being attacked by racialized migrant (Muslim) men. The Polish one is the most extreme, both in image and text. The woman is draped in the European flag, thus clearly and explicitly representing Europe. Although this is not clear, it could be assumed that she is naked underneath. The flag is torn from her body in the assault by black and brown hands, representing migrant men. She (the white woman, Europe) cries out in fear against this act of violence. The accompanying text says: *Islamski Gewalt na Europie* which means: Islamic Rape of Europe. Thus, as in the image tweeted by Wilders, the white woman's rape represents the rape of the entire European Union.

The German *Focus* cover is less violent, but it is part of the same imagery. First of all, the white blond woman is fully naked, covering her breasts and private parts with her hands. She stands still and is silent, remains passive against the attack by migrant men's hands. We cannot see all of her face, as the upper part (her eyes) is covered by the magazine title. The black and brown hands are painted on her naked body, herewith more indirectly than on the Polish cover representing the assault by migrant men. The accompanying text says: *Frauen klagen an. Nach den Sex-attacken von Migranten. Sind wir noch tolerant oder schon blind?* (Women impeach: after the sexual assaults by migrants. Are we still tolerant or already blind?) That the woman is naked is meaningful. As on the Polish cover, she embodies symbolically and materially the battleground

FIGURE 3.2 *Cover, 'Islamski Gwalt Na Europie',* wSieci *(Journal, Poland), February 2016.*

on which group struggles, in this case between 'Europeans' and 'migrants' take place.[12] That her eyes are covered by the magazine title may be significant, in combination with the question *are we already blind* in the cover text.

12 McClintock, A. (1995), *Imperial leather. Race, gender and sexuality in the colonial contest,* New York/London: Routledge.

FIGURE 3.3 *Cover, 'Frauen klagen an,'* Focus *(Journal, Germany), 8 January 2016.*

The Dutch cover is the most moderate, but still builds on the same imagery. At least the woman is fully clothed, and the accompanying text is not about a 'we' under attack, but says *The Muslim man and I*, thus individualizing the issue. Still, this woman is also being groped by several anonymous brown hands, including her breasts, as in the other two images. One of these hands is covering her mouth as if preventing her from speaking out. Like the covering of eyes on

FIGURE 3.4 *Cover, 'De Moslimman en Ik',* Vrij Nederland *(Journal, The Netherlands), 5 February 2016.*
PHOTO OF MARTIN DIJKSTRA, ILLUSTRATION BY PAUL FAASSEN.

the *Focus* cover, this is meaningful as there was a lot of talk about the media or police 'covering up' the sexual violence in Cologne committed by asylum seekers and Muslim men.

Image 3.5 presents the cover of Dutch quality newspaper *NRC* showing part of a nineteenth century painting and an obvious product of 'Orientalism'. Edward

FIGURE 3.5 *Cover, 'Is dat van alle tijden?'* NRC Handelsblad *section Opinie & Debat, (Newspaper, The Netherlands), 9/10 January 2016.*
PART OF A PAINTING BY OTTO PILNY (THE SLAVE MARKET, 1910).

Said defined Orientalism as ways of speaking, thinking and writing that offers the West an 'other' in order to be able to determine the own identity.[13]

The image shows two Arab men, each groping a white woman, one practically naked, the other covered in harem dress; the Arab men are grinning. The

13 Said, E. (1978) *Orientalism*, New Delhi: Penguin.

accompanying text says: 'Is this of all times? (and all cultures?)'. The cover relates to two opinion articles in the *NRC*, one by Dutch-Moroccan writer Hafid Bouazza who claims that sexual violence against women is part of Muslim culture, while the second article by Mieke van der Linden argues that male sexual aggression is of all times (without going into the question whether it is of all cultures). The image refers specifically to the stereotype of Arab men as sexually aggressive, while the other cover images do not refer to a specific group of 'other' men, other than that they are apparently 'coloured', as signified by the brown groping hands. By using the early twentieth century orientalist painting of Arab male sexual aggression as a comment on present-day events, the continuity of such imageries becomes obvious.[14]

What these images have in common is that they present women as objects of sexual desire by 'other' men. Marga Altena has argued that in analysing images, we should take into account the motives and understanding of their makers and the editors that used the images.[15] Although I have not done that, it seems definitely an interesting question how the editorial boards made the choice for these particular covers. Both the Polish and the German images were criticised by the public (on social media across Europe) and the German magazine apologised. The Dutch covers were not criticised on social media, and the editors did not apologize, but the covers have been criticised on various weblogs.[16]

The discussed covers were published in the weeks after the Cologne events. However, the events in Cologne were not the cause of the media attention to the sexual threat of asylum seekers. Months earlier, when the media reported extensively on the European 'refugee crisis', they had also reported on the alleged sexual threat by asylum seekers, as Dutch media reports demonstrate.

## 3.4 Short Skirts and Asylum Seekers in Dutch Media

In September 2015, a Dutch newspaper published an article under the heading: 'Fear of asylum seekers is growing. Can I still wear my short skirt?'[17] The same

14 De Jong, S., 'Keulen: ook in de opinies schieten er voetzoekers langs', *NRC* 19 January 2016.

15 Altena, M. (2012), *A true history full of romance. Mixed marriages and ethnic identity in dutch art, news media, and popular culture (1883–1955)*, Amsterdam: Amsterdam University Press.

16 See e.g. a weblog that critically analyses the representation of women in the media, <lezeresdesvaderlands.wordpress.com> January 2016, criticising the NRC cover. De Jong, S., 'Keulen: ook in de opinies schieten er voetzoekers langs', *NRC* 19 January 2016.

17 *AD* 18 September 2015.

newspaper wrote a few weeks later: 'Concerns about asylum seekers' centre. Girls no longer out to play hockey in a short skirt'.[18] In the same period, TV news showed Dutch white men protesting the placement of asylum seekers in their neighbourhood, claiming that their women and daughters would no longer be able to cycle home at night as they had to pass the asylum seekers' centre. A regional newspaper *De Gelderlander*, had researched these fears, but found no indication of a rising number of rapes as a result of the influx of asylum seekers.[19] Time and again, the press mentioned that the neighbourhoods close to asylum seekers' centres had nothing against the placement of refugee families, but did not want – a large number of – young single refugee men.

It was also in this period that extreme right-wing politician Geert Wilders criticised the Dutch asylum policy for letting 'walking testosterone bombs' into the country. Although he was criticised severely for using this term, the 'short skirt' issue is built on similar assumptions of uncontrollable migrant male sexuality. Municipalities and local politicians were determined to take the concerns of the people in the neighbourhoods seriously, especially after some violent rioting in one town had demonstrated what the anger and fear of local populations could lead to. At times, this led to discussions about measures to protect women and girls, as will be discussed in more detail below.

At this point, it is important to note that the discourses on the perceived sexual threat of asylum seekers not only construct racialized male sexuality, but also gendered images of the (white) women involved. Although the discourses are about women and girls, this has little to do with women-friendliness, gender equality or feminism. First of all, in these discourses, women and girls are at least partly held responsible for behaviour that invites male sexual aggression: wearing short skirts and cycling at night, is apparently dangerous behaviour for women that may lure men into sexual aggression. After the Cologne events, the mayor of Cologne was criticised for advising women to keep men always at arm's length. Such discourses reproduce historical ones on sexual violence, in which women are at least partly to blame for its cause and rape is connected to sex. This often leads to policing of women's behaviour, as the examples mentioned demonstrate.

Secondly, sexual violence is made into something that happens in the public sphere, outside on the streets, by complete strangers, although it is well known that sexual violence is more common in the private sphere of families, friends and colleagues or acquaintances. After the Cologne events, this discourse was severely critiqued by German feminist organisations that started a petition

---

18 *AD* 6 October 2015, 'Zorgen om azc. Meisjes niet meer in rokje naar hockey' (Girls no longer in skirts to field hockey).

19 *De Gelderlander* 10 October 2015, 'Verkrachtende vluchtelingen? Onzin!' (Raping refugees? Nonsense!).

under the hash tag *#Ausnamhslos*.[20] They repeated the demands that they had had for many years, amongst others for a change in German criminal law that holds the victim responsible for resisting a sexual attack. They also expressly rejected the use of feminism for racism, stating sexual violence should be a priority every day because it is omnipresent. They referred to EU statistics reporting that one in three women over the age of fifteen had experienced physical and/or sexualized violence.[21] Other feminists, in the Netherlands and elsewhere, have put forward similar arguments in response to the reactions on the Cologne events.[22]

To further understand this link between gendered and racialized discourses, the next paragraph goes into the question of why and how sexual violence against women by racialized men is linked to representations of nation and Europe.

## 3.5 Europe as a Woman

The covers of the opinion magazines described above show blond white women representing Europe. For anyone familiar with the relation between gender and nation, this is hardly surprising. Women have always represented the nation, as they in particular embody the national boundaries and carry the burden of representing national honour and identity.[23]

Although the European Union has always presented itself as a supranational project that transcends the nation, it is constructed on the same symbols as the 'old' nation-states, including flags, coins, anthems and passports. It has been argued that the European Union in fact continues the nationalist project of nation-states, but as a collective effort by a number of nation-states instead of individual nation-states.[24]

20 <ausnahmslos.org/english> [14 August 2016].

21 Fundamental Rights Agency, Violence against women, a EU-wide survey, 2014, <fra.europa.eu/sites/default/files/fra-2014-vaw-survey-at-a-glance-oct14_en.pdf>, [14 August 2016].

22 *Lover* 26 January 2016, Annelies van Doornbos & Tim de Visser, 26 jan 2016, <www.tijdschriftlover.nl/politiek_en_maatschappij/keulen_toont_hoe_racisme_en_seksisme_elkaar_versterken#sthash.xjcmCKJv.dpuf> [14 August 2016]. Renee Romkens, 'De Keulse kwestie: over de culturalisering van geweld en genderongelijkheid', *Sociologie* 2015 (11) 3/4.

23 McClintock 1995. Yuval-Davis, N. (1997), *Gender and nation*, London: Sage Publishing. Stoler, A.L. (2002), *Carnal knowledge and imperial power: race and the intimate in colonial rule*, Berkeley: University of California Press.

24 Shore, C. (1996), 'Imagining the new Europe: identity and heritage in European Community discourse', in: Graves-Brown, P., S. Jones & C.S. Gamble (eds.), *Cultural identity and archaeology: the construction of European Communities*, London: Routledge, pp. 96–115.

In its symbolic imagery, the European Union has been frequently represented as a woman, starting with its founding myth. Representations of the European Union often refer to the Greek mythology of Europa abducted by Zeus disguised as a bull, who rapes her or, in other versions, seduces her, after which she founds a new, European civilisation. This founding myth is commonly referred to in news media representations, cultural objects, public expressions by EU officials, and European law textbooks.[25] A sculpture by artist Leon de Pas, *Europe en avant* of a woman riding a bull, has been placed in front of the Justus Lipsius building, where the EU Council of Ministers is housed. And on the coin that was designed to commemorate the 70 years existence of peace in Europe in 2015, Europe is represented as a woman with stars in her hair (fig. 3.6).[26]

The covers of the opinion magazines build on this imagery of Europe as a female. This embodiment of Europe by women is also at least partly the explanation for the extensive media attention after the Cologne events. During the so-called 'refugee crisis', the media often claimed that the crisis was not only

FIGURE 3.6
*Coin of 50 Euro, at the occasion of 70 years of Peace in Europe, 2015 (Monnaie de Paris, France).*

25 Manners, I., (2010), 'Global Europa: mythology of the European Union in world politics'. JCMS: *Journal of Common Market Studies* 48:1, pp. 67–87. For a European law textbook representing the myth of Europe see: Chalmers, D., G. Davies & G. Monti (2010), *European Union law: cases and materials*, Cambridge: Cambridge University Press, cover and p. XIX. See further on the imagery of Europe: Wintle, M. (2004), *Europa and the bull, Europe, and European studies: visual images as historical source material*, Amsterdam: Amsterdam University Press.

26 <www.monnaiedeparis.fr/en/shop/coins/70-years-of-peace-in-europe-70-years-of-peace-in-europe> [16 August 2016].

about the refugees, but also about a crisis in Europe more generally. The sexual assaults on women, in this manner, represent the weakness of the European Union, of a Europe in crisis, confronted with violence and flooded by uncontrollable outsiders. As women are under attack, Europe is under attack. This representation of sexual violence against European white women, shows continuity in how sexual violence has been represented in earlier times, including in colonial discourses, to which we turn next.

## 3.6 Masculinity and Sexuality in the Colonies

Black feminists have long since problematized the ways in which black men were presented as the ultimate rapists in order to maintain white privilege.[27] Studies of colonialism and imperialism have similarly demonstrated the role of imageries of savage, dangerous and/or seductive otherness in rationalizing and legitimizing conquest and exploitation.[28] The colonial order was built on race and the need to keep the 'Europeans' and 'natives' apart. Discourses on the sexuality of colonized men functioned to maintain this colonial order. Colonized men were seen as having a heightened sexuality, primitive sexual urges and uncontrollable lust. This lust was assumed to be always directed at European white women who, consequently, needed to be protected from black men.[29] In periods of crisis in the colonies, this translated into the introduction of laws and regulations that were supposed to offer this protection. In the 1920s and 1930s, in the colonies of Rhodesia and Kenya, this resulted in the establishment of civil militias and women's rifle clubs. In Australian New Guinea (the Southern part of what is now Papua New Guinea), the 1926 *White Women Protection Ordinance* was put in place, introducing the death penalty for any person who was convicted of rape or attempted rape of white women – and only white women. In 1934 on the Solomon Islands, public flogging was introduced for crimes against white women.[30]

As historian Ann Stoler explains in her discussion of such colonial regulations, they shared several similarities. First, there was no correlation between

27 hooks, b. (1981), *Ain't I A woman. Black women and feminism*, Boston: South End Press.

28 MacClintock 1995. Stoler 2002.

29 El Tayeb, F. (1999), '"Blood is a very special juice": racialized bodies and citizenship in twentieth-century Germany', *International Review of Social History* 44:7, pp. 149–169.

30 Inglis, A. (1975), *The white women's protection ordinance: sexual anxiety and politics in Papua*, St. Martin's Press.

the rhetoric on sexual assault and the actual attacks by colonized men on white women. Not that sexual assault never happened, but they were incidents, not part of a pattern of mass rape or sexual assault. Furthermore, there was no relation between these incidents and the increased anxiety at specific moments in time. Stoler puts forward the argument that they were not caused by the fact of rape itself, but by a period of more general, political crisis within the colonial order, e.g. because of increased civil rights and nationalist activities by colonized subjects. Hence, it was not coincidental that these anxieties about sexual violence occurred at the beginning of the twentieth century, when in the European colonies nationalism and independence struggles were intensifying. The regulations also often followed periods of tension within the European community in the colony itself, such as labour strikes. An example Stoler mentions is that in the late 1920s, corporations on Sumatra in Indonesia intensified the activities of vigilante groups in response to labour protests by Indonesian and European employees, arguing that is was necessary to ensure that 'their women were safe and workers kept in place'.[31]

A second commonality was that the rape laws were race specific, as it was only rape of white women that was criminalised, not that of colonized women – although the rape of colonized and enslaved women by white men was much more large-scale and part of the colonial order. The laws made all colonized men into potential transgressors, as just being found in the vicinity of the house of a European woman could be enough to be considered 'attempted rape'.[32]

Third, these anxieties led not only to the increased surveillance and punishment of colonized men, but also of European white women. The European women were often held responsible for instigating the assault by their 'loose' behaviour and voluntary sexual relations with colonized men were just as reproachable (or even more) as rape. Hence, in Rhodesia a law was put in place prohibiting European women from making an 'indecent gesture' towards native men. And if not by introducing laws, their behaviour became subject to increased surveillance by social norms and etiquette regulating their behaviour.

31 Stoler, A.L. (1989), 'Making empire respectable: the politics of race and sexual morality in 20th-century colonial cultures', *American Ethnologist* 16:4, pp. 634–660.

32 As was also often the case in lynching practices of black men in the United States. For instance, in 1955 in Mississippi, African-American youngster Emmet Till (14) was lynched for allegedly flirting with a white woman.

As Cooper and Stoler have pointed out, such discourses did not remain confined to the colonies but travelled to the metropole in Europe.[33] In twentieth century Europe there were numerous periods of increased anxiety about sexual relations between European women and racialized men, including sexual violence.[34] At one particular time, during the interwar period, such relations caused uproar across Europe, that is: during the occupation of the German Rhineland by French colonial troops after World War I.

## 3.7 The 'Black Shame'

After the First World War, France sent its colonial soldiers to occupy the German Rhineland. This occupation caused anxiety that spread across Europe, about the alleged mass rape of white German women by these colonial soldiers. Across Europe, the news media reported on the so-called 'Black Shame' and

FIGURE 3.7 *Coin, 'Die Wacht am Rhein/Die schwarze Schande' (The Watch on the (river) Rhein / The Black Shame), by Karl Goetz 1920.*

---

33 Cooper, F., and A.L. Stoler (1997), *Tensions of empire: colonial cultures in a bourgeois world*, Berkeley: University of California Press.

34 Bland, L. (2005), 'White women and men of colour: miscegenation fears in Britain after the great war', *Gender & History* 17:1, pp. 29–61. Schrover, M. (2011), *Om de meisjes, voor de meisjes. Een historisch perspectief op problematisering en bagatellisering van onderwerpen die te maken hebben met migratie en integratie*, Leiden: Universiteit Leiden. Stovall, T. (1998), 'The color line behind the lines: racial violence in France during the great war', *The American Historical Review* 103:3, pp. 737–769.

campaigns called for the withdrawal of these 'black' troops (consisting mainly of Moroccans, Tunisians and Senegalese) from the German Rhineland. Feminist organisations across Europe, including the Netherlands, were involved in these campaigns.[35] They considered it an opportunity to put sexual violence on the political agenda, and used the racist discourses on the 'Black Shame' to achieve their goal. Dutch newspapers wrote about the events in the Rhineland under the heading 'the Black Shame' often without putting into question the information about 'black bands that violate helpless German women and girls'.[36] Across Europe, images were being produced referring to the 'Black Shame', such as those in the Dutch left-wing magazine *De Notenkraker* (The Nutcracker, fig. 3.8) and the German magazine *Simplicissimus* (fig. 3.9).

As is obvious, these images are not only highly racialized, but also highly sexualized, portraying defenceless white women, violated and threatened by ape-like black male figures representing the colonial French soldiers. As Iris Wigger has pointed out in her work on the 'Black Shame' propaganda, the images employed were often (close to) pornographic, and they were about the fantasies of its makers, offering them an opportunity to put a naked woman on the cover, and imagine what sexual violence by black men against white women would look like.[37] It could be argued that this is exactly what the editors of the opinion magazines covers did after Cologne.

Years after the media hype about the 'Black Shame', research demonstrated that there had been no mass rape, and that the international media had fallen for German propaganda. They did so because, as we have seen, the stereotyping of black men as sexual aggressors on white women was familiar to many European countries that were colonial powers at the time. At the beginning of twentieth century Europe, racial thinking was common and mainstream, and scientific racism and eugenics were at their peak. It was only after the Second World War had demonstrated – again – the disastrous consequences of race thinking, that it was rejected as an explanation for social issues. This makes the media representations and images after Cologne, although familiar, all the more remarkable. After Cologne, unrelated incidents of sexual violence by migrant men continued to make the headlines, wherever in Europe they

35 Van Galen Last, D. (2012), *De zwarte schande: Afrikaanse soldaten in Europa*, Amsterdam-Antwerpen: Atlas Contact.

36 E.g.: *De Grondwet*, 21 December 1920, 'De zwarte schande'. *Limburger Koerier*, 15 December 1921, 'De zwarte schande'.

37 Wigger, I. (2010), '"Black shame" – the campaign against "racial degeneration" and female degradation in interwar Europe', *Race & Class* 51:3, 33–46. Wigger, I. (2002), '"Against the laws of civilisation": race, gender and nation in the international racist campaign against the "black shame"', *Berkeley Journal of Sociology*, pp. 113–131.

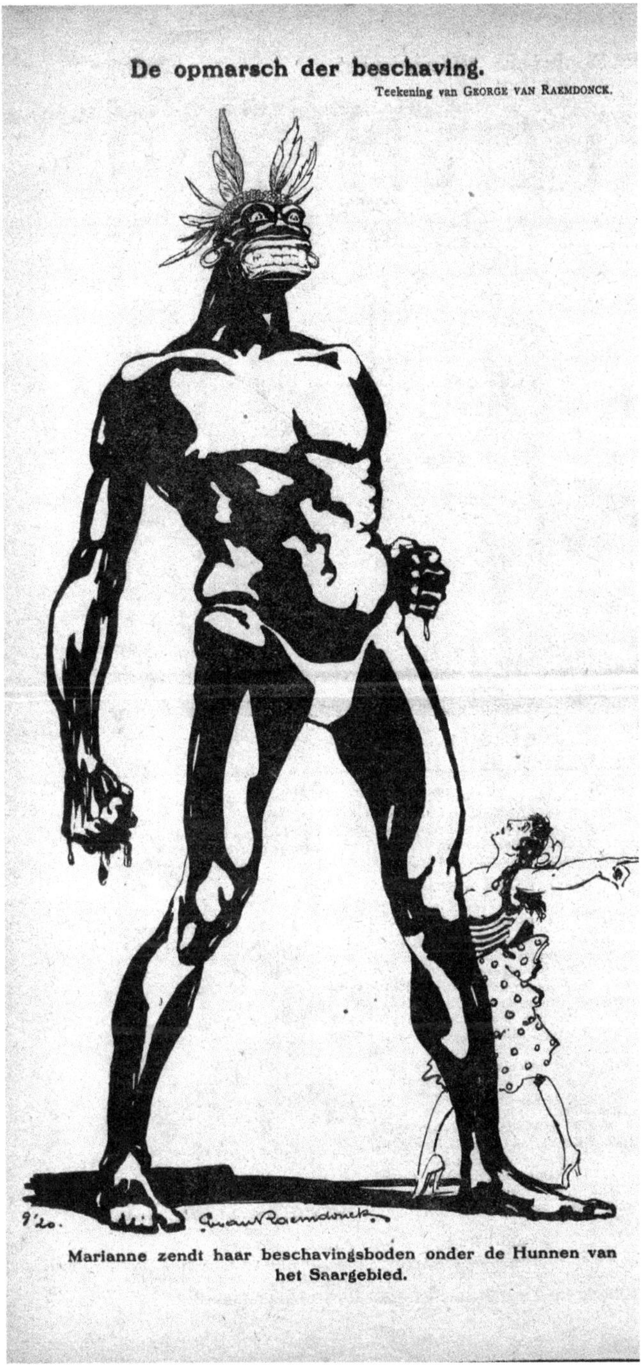


FIGURE 3.8 *Drawing by George van Raemdonck, 'De Opmarsch Der Beschaving' (The Advance of Civilization), in:* Notenkraker *(Journal, The Netherlands), 4 September 1920; original in the collection of the International Institute of Social History (Amsterdam).*

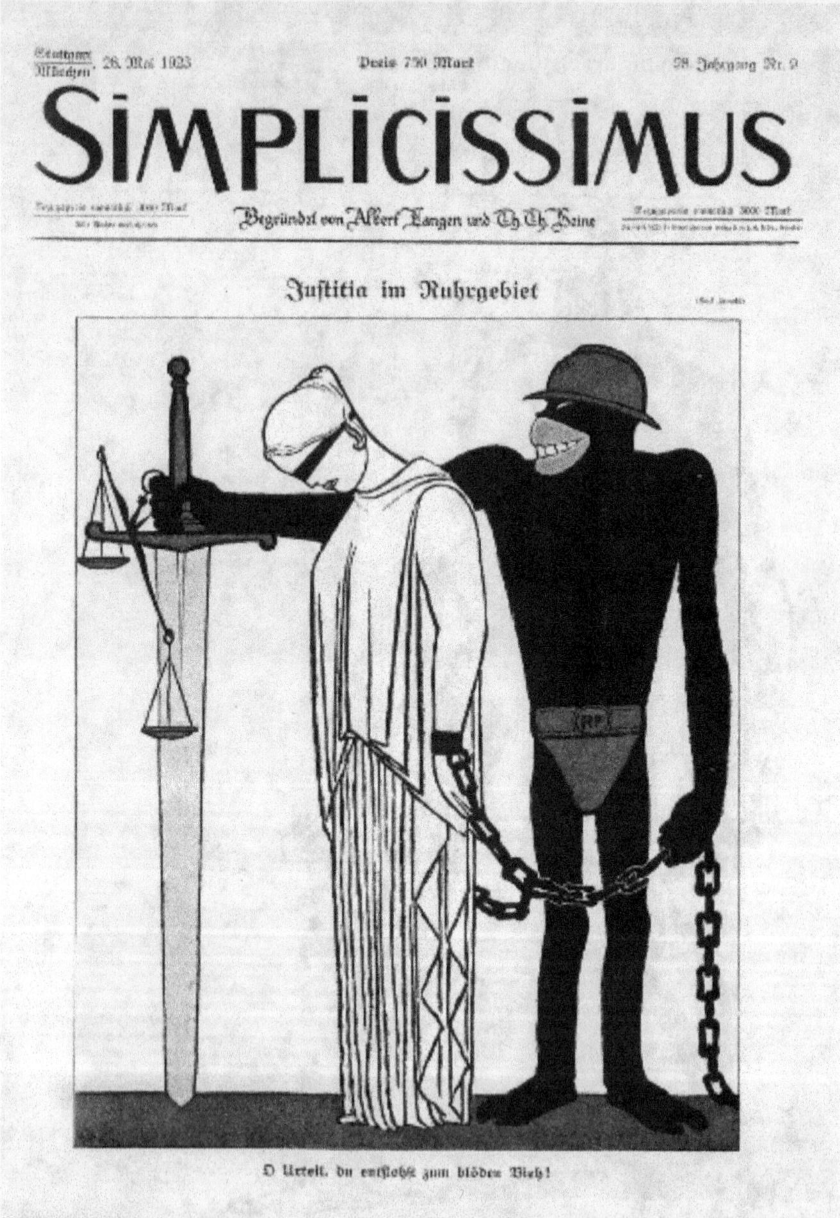


FIGURE 3.9 *Cover, 'Justitia im Ruhrgebiet' (Justice in the Ruhr Region; subtitle: Oh Judgment, you've absconded with the stupid brute),* Simplicissimus *(Journal Germany), 28 May 1923.*

occurred, suggesting, as Keskinen has observed, a pattern of continuous sexual violence and rape by migrants.[38] The main message remained that mass sexual violence by migrants towards European white women happened and that there had to be consequences. It is to these consequences that we now turn.

## 3.8 Changing Migration Policy and Policy Measures

After the Cologne events, commentators claimed that German Chancellor Merkel's position of *Wir schaffen das* had weakened within her own party, at national level, and at European level. So far, there has been little indication of measures or changing asylum policies at European level. EU Commissioner Avrampoulos condemned the sexual violence in Cologne in a speech before the European Parliament, but denied that all refugees were a threat to public order. His talk was on the refugee crisis and herewith he connected the two issues, even in his denial.[39]

At a national level, there are some signs of changing policies in migration law and other fields of law. In Germany, one week after the Cologne events, Angela Merkel announced that asylum seekers who had committed crimes would be expelled more rapidly. This required a change in legislation, which was submitted to the *Bundestag* in February 2016.[40] Referring to the German bill, the Dutch did the same a few months later, making it possible to reject or withdraw an asylum residence status in cases of criminal acts, including sexual crimes.[41]

Outside the context of migration law, the German legislation on sexual assault and rape was amended. According to this amendment, submitted in February and accepted by a large majority in the Bundestag on July 7, 2016, it is enough to prove rape or sexual assault where the victim makes it clearly known that there is no consent to the sexual act, for instance just by saying 'no'. Before this amendment, proof was required that the victim had clearly resisted the sexual act, for instance if the perpetrator had used violence. Groping has also become criminally punishable, and persecuting such acts committed by

38 *Telegraaf* 5 July 2016, 'Massa-aanranding schokt Zweden'; *NOS* 18 August 2016, 'Nine arrest for group-rape on NewYears Eve in Vienna'.

39 <europa.eu/rapid/press-release_SPEECH-16-215_en.htm> [14 August 2016].

40 Entwurf eines Gesetzes zur erleichterten Ausweisung von straffälligen Ausländern und zum erweiterten Ausschluss der Flüchtlingsanerkennung bei straffälligen Asylbewerbern, 16 February 2016, *Drucksache* 18/7537.

41 *Second Chamber* 2015–2016, 19 637, 1288 (Dutch Parliament). These measures had already been proposed earlier, in October 2015, but now came to be framed in the context of the Cologne events by some parties.

groups has become easier.[42] German women's organizations had been lobbying for such a change in the law for years, but earlier bills submitted in 2014 and 2015 had not been accepted by the Bundestag.[43] Apparently, the Cologne events changed the position of German political parties.

The fear of sexual assault by asylum seekers also had consequences at a local level. In the Netherlands, some local authorities became reluctant to host asylum seekers because of the concerns of the local population who feared that 'our women and daughters' would no longer be safe. Some of the municipalities decided to host smaller groups of asylum seekers, others not to host any asylum seekers at all, such as the town of Steenbergen after riots that threatened the safety of the members of the local board.

Furthermore, some local authorities announced measures to protect women and children. In one Dutch town, municipal authorities offered to arrange for volunteers to accompany children who had to cycle past an asylum seekers' centre to arrive at their local primary school. It made the free nationwide newspaper *Metro* and national radio.[44] The alderman explained that they had not succeeded in convincing the parents that their 'feelings of insecurity' were not justified. Just a few days later it was reported that the measure had been dropped because of a lack of demand. Elsewhere in the media, it was reported that the municipality of Enschede (a midsize town in the east of the Netherlands) had suggested that women should no longer wear short skirts. After a member of the public mentioned this to a regional newspaper, the alderman denied that the municipal authorities had ever made such a suggestion, at least not in an official capacity.[45]

Finally, there has been some indication of vigilante activities to 'protect' European women. Geert Wilders distributed pepper spray (labelled as 'resistance spray') to Dutch women to protect themselves from the so-called testosterone

---

42 *Focus online* 7 July 2015, Bundestag stimmt für Verschärfung des Sexualstrafrechts. On the same date, an Integration Act for refugees was adopted. It was not explicitly linked to the Cologne events, with the exception of the alternative bill, by Bundnis/die Grünen, that connected the sexual assaults to lack of integration of the wrongdoers. *Drucksache* 18/7651, p. 4.

43 Grieger, K., C. Clemm, A. Eckhardt & A. Hartmann (2014), *Was ihnen widerfahren ist, ist in Deutschland nicht strafbar, Fallanalyse zu bestehenden Schutzlücken in der Anwendung des deutschen Sexualstrafrechts bezüglich erwachsener Betroffener*, Berlin. <www.frauen-gegen-gewalt.de/fallanalyse-zu-schutzluecken-im-sexualstrafrecht.html>, [29 July 2016].

44 *Metro* 20 December 2015, 'Leerlingen met rugzakje begeleid langs azc'.

45 *Tubantia* 6 November 2015, 'Wethouder Hatenboer: Kort rokje is niet uit den boze na komst azc Enschede'.

bombs. When a group of Dutch feminists organised a demonstration against this use of racism to fight sexism, they were sexually harassed by Wilders' supporters and arrested by the police.[46] Sexual harassment also occurred at town hall meetings, against women speaking out in favour of the placement of asylum seekers (groups of Dutch white males shouting: she needs to have a penis inserted (*daar moet een piemel in*)). In Finland, the extreme right-wing group *Soldiers of Odin* was established, with factions in other European countries, including the Netherlands. In a Dutch town, members of this group were reported to have made a citizen's arrest of an asylum seeker who had, allegedly, sexually harassed women.[47] The media also reported on the surge in weapon sales, especially pepper spray, in Germany after the Cologne events.[48]

## 3.9 Concluding Remarks

In this contribution, I have suggested that there are similarities between the discourses on sexual assault by asylum seekers in present-day Europe and earlier discourses on black male sexuality in Europe and its colonies, specifically in the interwar period.

First, it was demonstrated that there was no correlation between the rhetoric on sexual assault and the actual attacks by asylum seekers. As was illustrated by the discussion in Dutch media debates, discourses on the dangerous sexuality of refugee men had started months before the Cologne events, although Cologne certainly intensified such discourses.

Second, the anxiety about dangerous male refugees' sexuality emerged in a period of more general perceived crisis or even threatening collapse of the European Union, as has been observed by many commentators. The attacks on European white women have come to represent this feeling of crisis in Europe, and exemplify what the crisis is about. We have also seen that the anxiety about male asylum seekers has resulted in increased surveillance of European (white) women, who were held partly responsible for instigating the alleged attacks, by wearing short skirts, or cycling at night.

---

46 Annelies van Doornbios en Tim de Visser, 'Keulen' toont hoe racisme en seksisme elkaar versterken: <www.tijdschriftlover.nl/politiek_en_maatschappij/keulen_toont_hoe_racisme_en_seksisme_elkaar_versterken#sthash.itOporut.dpuf>, *Lover* 26 January 2016.

47 *Volkskrant* 21 July 2016, 'Asielzoeker niet mishandeld door burgerwacht Soldiers of Odin'.

48 *Tageschau* 8 February 2016, 'Sprunghafter Anstieg seit November "Kleiner Waffenschein" hat Konjunktur'.

Third, in response to the Cologne events measures specifically targeting asylum seekers were taken. The anxiety about sexual assault by asylum seekers, preceding the Cologne events had resulted in asylum seekers not being placed in certain towns or neighbourhoods in the Netherlands, or placed in smaller numbers. Expulsion of asylum seekers has become easier in Germany and the Netherlands, at least partly in response to the Cologne events. lastly, the women's movements demand for the amendment of German rape laws, finally met with success. Although feminist organisations expressly resisted the connection between racism and sexism, it seems that the Cologne events offered a window of opportunity to finally achieve their goals. On the other hand, the Cologne events have also drawn attention to sexual assaults committed during other large-scale public events such as the *Oktober fest*.

Self-evidently, this is not to suggest that we can draw a straight line from the colonies to modern-day Europe in terms of discourses on the sexuality of racialized men. The use of racialized stereotypes by the media discussed in this contribution has been severely criticised by feminists, anti-racists and others, editors have apologized and reflected on their own reporting. However, such critical comments are mainly found on opinion pages, weblogs and social media.

It still raises questions about the state of European anti-racism and gender equality that the events in Cologne were able to produce this age-old stereotypical imagery within the mainstream media.

## References

*AD* 6 October 2015, 'Zorgen om azc. Meisjes niet meer in rokje naar hockey'.

*AD* 18 September 2015, 'Angst voor vluchtelingen groeit: 'Kan ik m'n rokje nog wel aan?'.

Altena, M. (2012), *A true history full of romance. Mixed marriages and ethnic identity in Dutch art, news media, and popular culture (1883–1955)*, Amsterdam: Amsterdam University Press.

Bilge, S. & P. Scheibelhofer (2012), Special Issue 'Unravelling the new politics of racialised sexualities: introduction', *Journal of Intercultural Studies* 33:3, pp. 255–259.

Bland, L. (2005), 'White women and men of colour: miscegenation fears in Britain after the great war', *Gender & History* 17:1, pp. 29–61.

Bonjour, S. & De Hart B. (2013), 'A proper wife, a proper marriage: constructions of "us" and "them" in Dutch family migration policy', *European Journal of Women's Studies* 20:1, pp. 61–76.

Castles, S. & A. Davidson (2000), *Citizenship and migration: globalization and the politics of belonging*, Hove: Psychology Press.

Chalmers, D., G. Davies & G. Monti (2010), *European Union law: cases and materials*, Cambridge: Cambridge University Press.

Charsley, K. & H. Wray (2015), Special Issue 'The invisible (migrant) man', *Men and Masculinities* 18:4, pp. 403–423.

Cooper, F. & A.L. Stoler (1997), *Tensions of empire: colonial cultures in a bourgeois world*, Berkeley: University of California Press.

*De Gelderlander* 10 October 2015, 'Verkrachtende vluchtelingen? Onzin!'.

*De Grondwet*, 21 December 1920, 'De zwarte schande'.

De Hart, B. (2015), 'Superdads migrant fathers' right to family life before the European court of human rights', *Men and Masculinities* 18:4, pp. 448–467.

De Jong, S. (2016), 'Keulen: ook in de opinies schieten er voetzoekers langs', *NRC* 19 January 2016.

De Lange, T. (2008), 'Ongehuwd en kinderloos: Regels, sekseonderscheid en arbeidsmigratie naar Nederland 1945–2006', *Tijdschrift voor Sociale en Economische geschiedenis* 5:1, pp. 75–100.

*Die Zeit* 23 June 2016, 'Was geschah wirklich? Die Silvesternacht von Köln wurde zur Projektionsfläche in der Flüchtlingsdebatte. Eine Frage blieb unbeantwortet'.

Doornbos, A. van & T. de Visser (2016), *Lover* 26 January 2016, <www.tijdschriftlover.nl/politiek_en_maatschappij/keulen_toont_hoe_racisme_en_seksisme_elkaar_versterken#sthash.xjcmCKJv.dpuf> [14 August 2016].

El Tayeb, F. (1999), '"Blood is a very special juice": racialized bodies and citizenship in twentieth-century Germany', *International Review of Social History* 44:7, pp. 149–169.

*Focus online* 7 July 2015, 'Bundestag stimmt für Verschärfung des Sexualstrafrechts'.

Fundamental Rights Agency (2014), *Violence against women, a EU-wide survey*, 2014, <fra.europa.eu/sites/default/files/fra-2014-vaw-survey-at-a-glance-oct14_en.pdf>, [14 August 2016].

Grieger, K., C. Clemm, A. Eckhardt & A. Hartmann (2014), *Was ihnen widerfahren ist, ist in Deutschland nicht strafbar, Fallanalyse zu bestehenden Schutzlücken in der Anwendung des deutschen Sexualstrafrechts bezüglich erwachsener Betroffener*, Berlin.

hooks, b. (1981), *Ain't I a woman. Black women and feminism*, Boston: South End Press.

Inglis, A. (1975), *The white women's protection ordinance: sexual anxiety and politics in Papua*, St. Martin's Press.

Keskinen, S. (2011), 'Borders of the finnish nation: media, politics and rape by "foreign" perpetrators', in: Eide, E. & K. Nikunen (eds.), *Media in motion. Cultural complexity and migration in the Nordic region*, London: Routledge, pp. 107–124.

*Limburger Koerier*, 15 December 1921, 'De zwarte Schande'.

Luibheid, E. (2002), *Entry denied: controlling sexuality at the border*, Mineapolis/London: University of Minnesota Press.

Luibheid, E. (2013), *Pregnant on arrival*, Mineapolis/London: University of Minnesota Press.

Manners, I., (2010), 'Global Europa: mythology of the European Union in world politics', *Journal of Common Market Studies* 48:1, pp. 67–87.

McClintock, A. (1995), *Imperial leather. Race, gender and sexuality in the colonial contest*, New York/London: Routledge.

*Metro* 20 December 2015, 'Leerlingen met rugzakje begeleid langs azc'.

*NOS* 18 August 2016, 'Nine arrest for group-rape on NewYears Eve in Vienna'.

Romkens, R. (2015), 'De Keulse kwestie: over de culturalisering van geweld en genderongelijkheid', *Sociologie* 2015 (11) 3/4.

Said, E. (1978), *Orientalism*, New Delhi: Penguin.

Scheibelhofer, P. (2012), 'From health check to Muslim test: the shifting politics of governing migrant masculinity', *Journal of Intercultural Studies* 33:3, pp. 319–332.

Scheibelhofer, P. (2016), 'How would you react if you learned that your son was gay?' Racialized sexualities and the production of migrant others in Europe', in: Amelina, A., K. Horvath & B. Meeus (eds.), *An anthology of migration and social transformation*, Frankfurt: Springer, pp. 295–306.

Schrover, M. (2011), *Om de meisjes, voor de meisjes. Een historisch perspectief op problematisering en bagatellisering van onderwerpen die te maken hebben met migratie en integratie*, Leiden: Universiteit Leiden.

Shore, C. (1996), 'Imagining the new Europe: identity and heritage in European Community discourse', in: Graves-Brown, P., S. Jones & C.S. Gamble (eds.), *Cultural identity and archaeology: the construction of European Communities*, London: Routledge, pp. 96–115.

Spijkerboer, T. (1999), *Gender and refugee status*, dissertation Radboud University Nijmegen.

Stoler, A.L. (2002), *Carnal knowledge and imperial power: race and the intimate in colonial rule*, Berkeley: University of California Press.

Stoler, A.L. (1989), 'Making empire respectable: the politics of race and sexual morality in 20th century colonial cultures', *American Ethnologist* 16:4, pp. 634–660.

Stovall, T. (1998), 'The color line behind the lines: racial violence in France during the great war', *The American Historical Review* 103:3, pp. 737–769.

Strasser, E. *et al.* (2009), 'Doing family: responses to the constructions of "the migrant family" across Europe', *The History of the Family* 14:2, pp. 165–176.

*Tageschau* 8 February 2016, 'Sprunghafter Anstieg seit November "Kleiner Waffenschein" hat Konjunktur'.

*Telegraaf* 5 July 2016, 'Massa-aanranding schokt Zweden'.

*Tubantia* 6 November 2015, 'Wethouder Hatenboer: Kort rokje is niet uit den boze na komst azc Enschede'.

Van Galen Last, D. (2012), *De zwarte schande: Afrikaanse soldaten in Europa*, Amsterdam/Antwerpen: Atlas Contact.

Van Walsum, S. (2008), *The family and the nation: Dutch family migration policies in the context of changing family norms*, Newcastle upon Tyne: Cambridge Scholars Publishing.

*Volkskrant* 21 July 2016, 'Asielzoeker niet mishandeld door burgerwacht Soldiers of Odin'.

Wigger, I. (2002), '"Against the laws of civilisation": race, gender and nation in the international racist campaign against the "black shame"', *Berkeley Journal of Sociology*, pp. 113–131.

Wigger, I. (2010), '"Black shame" – the campaign against "racial degeneration" and female degradation in interwar Europe', *Race & Class* 51:3, 33–46.

Wintle, M. (2004), *Europa and the bull, Europe, and European studies: visual images as historical source material*, Amsterdam: Amsterdam University Press.

Wray, H. (2011), *Regulating marriage migration into the UK: a stranger in the home*, Farnham: Ashgate Publishing, Ltd.

Yuval-Davis, N. (1997), *Gender and nation*, London: Sage Publishing.

CHAPTER 4

# Free Movement of Workers: Some Reflections

*Paul Minderhoud*

## 4.1 Introduction

This chapter will focus on the issue of Free Movement of Workers and give some reflections on recent developments. Developments regarding the Free Movement of Persons and European Citizenship can be found in the contributions of Elspeth Guild (Chapter 10) and Sandra Mantu (Chapter 11) to this book. The essay starts with a brief reflection on the Network on Free Movement of Workers, followed by a discussion on the new Directive 2014/54, which provides measures facilitating the exercise of workers' rights within the context of freedom of movement for workers. Then some challenges ahead are dealt with: the ongoing displacement of workers by posted workers, the changing concept of workers and the Brexit proposals regarding the reform of social security rights for workers.

## 4.2 The Network on Free Movement of Workers

Free movement of workers is one of the four fundamental freedoms in the EU Treaty, enshrined now in Article 45 TFEU and further developed in Regulation 492/2011 and Directive 2004/38. Free movement of workers has always been an important research issue for the Centre for Migration Law (CMR).

Twenty years ago, in the early beginning of the CMR, Kees Groenendijk wrote every year a report on the state of implementation of free movement of workers legislation in the Netherlands. Once a year he met with some officials from DG Employment of the European Commission in Brussels to present this report and then the report more or less disappeared into one of the desk drawers of these officials and everyone proceeded to the order of the day. But in 2003 the Commission established a network of independent experts, which was coordinated by the Centre for Migration Law to monitor in a systematic way the implementation of free movement of workers legislation in all Member States and to detect still existing or new developed legal obstacles. In 2013 this network consisted of a CMR coordination team and legal experts from all

 | DOI 10.1163/9789004330467_005

28 Member States. The network was engaged in a long list of activities. It did not only produce annually a European report on the state of implementation of the free movement of workers legislation, based on national reports of all Member States. It also produced several analytical reports on issues such as language requirements, retention of EU worker status, social and tax advantages, developments on free movement in the public sector, obstacles to free movement of young workers, breaches of Union law by private parties and the follow-up of relevant case law in the Member States. Experts answered legal requests from the Commission. From 2006 onwards an annual conference and seminars in various Member States were organised.

In 2014, however, the network was forced to merge with the existing TReSS network on EU Social Security Coordination into one larger network, which was called FreSsco: Free movement of workers and Social security coordination, which is now coordinated by the University of Ghent.[1] This merger was partly influenced by the fact that Free Movement of Workers and Social Security Coordination belonged to the same organisational unit of the Commission at that time. This merger also meant the end of one of the most successful products of our network: The *Online Journal of Free Movement of Workers* within the European Union, which only consists of 7 issues. The last issue was published in February 2014.

Its aim was to develop academic interest and stimulate debate on this fundamental area of European law. It is still online on the internet and it shows that it has had between 2,000 and 8,000 downloads per issue so far.[2] Issue 3, published in December 2011, contained a contribution by Koen Lenaerts, now the President of the Court of Justice of the EU, in which he explored how the Court had determined the existence of a cross-border element in the light of the landmark cases *Rottmann*, *Ruiz Zambrano*, and *McCarthy*. This issue has even been downloaded more than 14,000 times.[3] Of course downloading does not automatically mean the same as reading it, but as a scholar I would be very satisfied if my articles were just downloaded so frequently.

A number of articles published in this Online Journal are still frequently cited or referred to, especially the articles which deal with such topical issues as the retention of the status of EU workers, who have worked in another Member State and the right of residence and access to social benefits for jobseekers

1 See <ec.europa.eu/social/main.jsp?catId=1098>.

2 See <ec.europa.eu/social/main.jsp?catId=475>.

3 See <ec.europa.eu/social/main.jsp?catId=737&langId=en&pubId=6193>.

seeking work in another Member State or economically inactive EU citizens. All online journal issues and other publications of the Network on Free Movement of Workers are also available on the website of the CMR.[4]

In my opinion the choice of one integrated network has weakened the effectiveness of a monitoring system dedicated only to the issue of free movement of workers. Only a minority of the activities of the new FreSsco network deals with free movement of workers issues, while the rest of the activities are social security coordination related. In 2015, within DG Employment the units of social security coordination and free movement of workers were separated from each other. Free movement of workers has become an independent unit, together with EURES (the European labour office) falling under EMPL D1. And social security coordination is now an independent unit falling under EMPL D2.[5] This organizational separation could be a reconsideration to split the current FreSsco network in two as well.

Two reports of the Network on Free Movement of Workers deserve special attention here, because they provided the basis for the Commission to come up with a proposal to strengthen the enforcement of the free movement of workers, which led to the adoption of Directive 2014/54 (see below).[6] The first report, finalised in January 2011, focused on the existing legal framework in each Member State and the guarantees and supporting measures they offer to EU workers. The second one, submitted in October 2011, presented an overview of the main problems related to the application of EU rules that had been identified in each Member State. These reports showed that protection against discrimination on the ground of nationality and support offered to workers varied from one Member State to another.

## 4.3 Directive 2014/54

In 2014 the EU adopted new legislation, Directive 2014/54/EU, aimed at facilitating the uniform application and enforcement in practice of the already existing rights conferred on workers by Article 45 TFEU and by Regulation (EU) 492/2011 in the context of freedom of movement for workers.[7] Thus, the scope

4 <www.ru.nl/law/cmr/research/projects/fmow-1>.

5 DG Employment, Social Affairs and Inclusion Organization Chart see: <ec.europa.eu/social/main.jsp?langId=en&catId=656>.

6 Proposal for a Directive of the European parliament and of the Council on measures facilitating the exercise of rights conferred on workers in the context of freedom of movement for workers, 26 April 2013, COM(2013)236.

7 OJ 2014 L126/8.

of this Directive is identical to that of Regulation (EU) 492/2011 and it applies to Union workers and members of their families. The right of free movement of workers includes the right not to be discriminated against on grounds of nationality as regards access to employment, pay and other working conditions. Regulation 492/2011 details the rights derived from free movement of workers and defines specific areas where discrimination on grounds of nationality is prohibited, in particular as regards:

- access to employment
- working conditions
- access to social and tax advantages
- access to training
- membership of trade unions and eligibility for workers' representative bodies
- access to housing
- access to education apprenticeship and vocational training for the children of Union workers
- assistance given by employment offices

Although all these rights exist, there is a difference between formal equality (equal rights before the law) and material equality (equal outcomes, results). From a sociology of law perspective, this is described as the difference between *law in the books* and *law in action*. Directive 2014/54 aims to remove existing obstacles to the free movement of workers, such as the lack of awareness of EU rules among public and private employers and the difficulties faced by mobile citizens in obtaining information and assistance in the host Member States. To overcome these barriers and prevent discrimination, the Directive requires Member States to:

- create national contact points providing information, assistance and advice so that EU migrant workers, and employers, are better informed about their rights
- provide appropriate means of redress at national level
- allow labour unions, NGOs and other organisations to launch administrative or judicial procedures on behalf of individual workers in cases of discrimination
- give better information for EU migrant workers and employers in general

These measures should ensure better application of EU law on people's right to work in another Member State and make it easier for people to exercise their rights in practice. The Directive does not create any new rights for workers, but according to the Commission will help to ensure real and effective application of the existing legislation. A crucial part of the Directive is the obligation for Member States to:

> designate one or more structures or bodies ('bodies') for the promotion, analysis, monitoring and support of equal treatment of Union workers and members of their family without discrimination on grounds of nationality, unjustified restrictions or obstacles to their right to free movement and shall make the necessary arrangements for the proper functioning of such bodies.

Member States shall ensure that the competences of those bodies include:

(a) providing or ensuring the provision of independent legal and/or other assistance;
(b) acting as a contact point *vis-à-vis* equivalent contact points in other Member States in order to cooperate and share relevant information;
(c) conducting or commissioning independent surveys and analyses concerning unjustified restrictions and obstacles to the right to free movement, or discrimination on grounds of nationality;
(d) ensuring the publication of independent reports and making recommendations on any issue relating to such restrictions and obstacles or discrimination;
(e) publishing relevant information on the application at national level of Union rules on free movement of workers. (Article 4)

Those bodies may form part of existing bodies at national level which have similar objectives. In that case the Member State must ensure allocation of sufficient resources to the existing body for the performance of additional tasks (Recital 18). Where bodies provide assistance in legal proceedings, such assistance shall be free of charge to persons who lack sufficient resources in accordance with national law or practice.

## 4.4 What are Still the Main Obstacles?

The following five issues can be distinguished as providing the main obstacles regarding free movement of workers:

- Tension between free movement of workers law and national immigration law

- Equality of treatment
- Access to employment in the public service
- Language requirements and recognition of diplomas and qualifications
- Frontier workers

### 4.4.1 *Tension Free Movement of Workers Law and National Immigration Law*

One of the obstacles in the application of the EU rules on free movement is the lack of separation between national immigration law and the implemented free movement rules. The privileged position of EU nationals is disregarded in practice because free movement rules are integrated into general immigration law and applied by immigration officers with these national immigration rules in mind. EU workers are required to prove sufficient income (which is not correct), they are required to present documents routinely requested from third-country nationals but not required under EU law, they have to wait for their cases to be dealt with because immigration authorities give preference to other (e.g. asylum) cases, and sometimes national rules on expulsion on public order grounds are applied rather than the stricter EU public order exception.

### 4.4.2 *Equality of Treatment*

As a result of the economic crisis and austerity measures, national authorities have become increasingly interested in limiting access to social assistance and benefits, including stricter scrutiny to end residence for workers. Social benefits are subject to conditions more easily met by nationals than by EU citizens (e.g. a residence condition). The Netherlands for instance introduced in 2016 a language requirement as a condition for eligibility for social assistance. Although the new requirement in theory applies to "everyone", there is an exemption for recipients of social assistance who have had eight years of education in the Netherlands. This clause exempts practically all indigenous (=non-immigrant) Dutch nationals.[8]

### 4.4.3 *Access to Employment in the Public Service*

There are still problems for EU workers in accessing employment in the public service in many EU Member States both in law and practice. Article 45(4) TFEU allows for a restriction of access to certain posts in the public service to its own nationals, but the Court of Justice of the European Union (CJEU) has consistently held that this exception is to be interpreted restrictively and covers only

---

8 *Stb* 2015, 136 and 194. See also: Groenendijk, K. & P. Minderhoud, 'Taaleis in de bijstand: discriminerend, disproportioneel en onnodig', *NJB* 2016/91, afl. 3, pp. 183–189.

posts which involve direct or indirect participation in the exercise of powers conferred by public law and duties designed to safeguard the general interests of the State or of other public authorities.

#### 4.4.4 *Language Requirements and Recognition of Diplomas and Qualifications*

There are continuing restrictions in some Member States regarding access to posts in several sectors (for instance academic and maritime sector) caused by strict language requirements. Another problem is that professional qualifications and experience acquired in other Member States is not taken into account or is taken into account in a different way.

#### 4.4.5 *Frontier Workers*

Special problems can still be recognised for frontier workers, who live in one Member State and work in another.[9] They often encounter difficulties with access to social entitlements and labour market support and tax issues, caused by provisions which use a direct or indirect residence requirement as a condition for eligibility. Other reported obstacles are linguistic differences, lack of information and knowledge pertaining to the legal status of frontier workers and the implications thereof, lack of mutual recognition of professional and academic qualifications and lack of cooperation between competent authorities and administrations in the various Member States.[10]

### 4.5 What Impact and Added Value Can be Expected from the Directive?

A good sign is that the Directive underlines the importance of the issue of free movement of workers, even in times when this is under pressure, and faces the reality that there are still problems to be tackled, despite the fact that equality of rights has already been formally established. But it is an illusion to think that all existing problems can be removed by a legal instrument like the Directive itself. The Directive is not some kind of magical remedy.

---

9 Frontier workers are defined as EU citizens who work in one Member State, yet reside in another, and who return to the Member State of residence on a daily or weekly basis (Article 1(f) Reg. 883/2004).

10 Jorens, Y., P. Minderhoud & J. De Coninck (2015), *Comparative report: frontier workers in the EU*, FreSsco, European Commission.

In my view there are three main factors which can influence the effectiveness of the Directive in a negative way. The first problem is that the Directive, which is modelled on other Equality Directives, suffers from the same weaknesses as those Directives, and moreover lacks their enforcement tools. Secondly, the success of the Directive is highly dependent on the willingness of Member States to take it seriously. Thirdly, it is not applicable to posted workers, while this is an area in which some of the most structural problems regarding discrimination on nationality occur.

### 4.5.1 *Same Weaknesses as Other Equality Directives*

The structure and text of the provisions of Directive 2014/54 are highly similar to that of, for instance, the Race Directive 2000/43 *which implements the principle of equal treatment between persons irrespective of racial or ethnic origin.*[11] An important difference is that neither the Race Directive, nor any of the other equal treatment Directives covers the ground of nationality, and the Race Directive stipulates specifically in its Recital 13 and Article 3(2) that "This prohibition of discrimination should also apply to nationals of third countries, but does not cover differences of treatment based on nationality…".

The text of Article 3 on defence of rights is highly similar to the text of Article 7 of the Race Directive on defence of rights. The same applies to Article 5 on dialogue which corresponds partly with Article 11 Race Directive on social dialogue and Article 12 Race Directive on dialogue with non-governmental organizations. Article 7 on minimum requirements corresponds with Article 6 Race Directive (minimum requirements). Article 6 on access to and dissemination of information corresponds with Article 10 Race Directive (dissemination of information), but here an extra provision can be found in Article 6(2) of Directive 2014/54, which says that:

> Member States shall provide, in more than one official language of the institutions of the Union, information on the rights conferred by Union law concerning the free movement of workers that is clear, free of charge, easily accessible, comprehensive and up-to-date. This information should also be easily accessible through Your Europe and EURES.

However, there are two important provisions which are incorporated into the Race Directive but which are lacking in the new Directive 2014/54. First, there

11 Council Directive 2000/43/EC of 29 June 2000 implementing the principle of equal treatment between persons irrespective of racial or ethnic origin OJ L 180, 19/07/2000 pp. 22–26.

is no article similar to Article 8 of the Race Directive on the burden of proof, which stipulates that Member States shall take measures necessary to ensure that it shall be for the respondent to prove that there has been no breach of the principle of equal treatment. This provision can be seen as a key element necessary for ensuring the correct handling of discrimination.

And, second, there is no article similar to Article 15 of the Race Directive on sanctions, which stipulates that Member States shall lay down the rules on sanctions applicable to infringements of the national provisions adopted pursuant to this Directive and shall take all measures necessary to ensure that they are applied. These sanctions, which may comprise the payment of compensation to the victim, must be effective, proportionate and dissuasive, according to the Race Directive.

Therefore the Directive can be characterized as a kind of symbolic legislation which will probably suffer from a serious lack of effectiveness in advance.[12] On the one hand, this legislation seeks to strengthen the rights of workers, but on the other hand, it does not provide the proper tools for enforcement of the objectives the Directive wants to achieve.

A related problem is that reports monitoring the implementation of the Race Directive, which has more tools than Directive 2014/54, underline that the main challenge identified in many Member States is still the lack of enforcement of anti-discrimination laws in practice, particularly with regard to access to justice.[13] There is still a problem of lengthy procedures, evidence, high costs, failures in the provision of legal aid, ineffective sanctions, barriers in the form of language, issues relating to legal standing and legitimate interest.[14] For effective claiming it is necessary to have adequate access to justice, which is not always available. In this context we can refer to the so-called naming, blaming and claiming problem.[15] EU workers first have to become conscious of the fact that they are being discriminated against and to define the acts as such. Therefore they need knowledge not only of the equal treatment rules but also of the facts, the context and the ability to compare their situation with the situation of others. As a second step they have to hold someone responsible

12 Aubert, V. (1966), 'Some social functions of legislation', *Acta Sociologica* Vol. 10, No. 1/2, Contributions to the Sociology of Law, pp. 98–120.

13 Report of the European Commission on the application of 2000/43 and 2000/78, 17 January 2014, COM(2014)2, p. 16.

14 Equinet, Equality law in practice; report on the implementation of the race and general framework directives, 2013, <www.equineteurope.org/Report-on-the-Implementation-of>.

15 Felstiner, W.F.L., R.L. Abel & A. Sarat, 'The emergence and transformation of disputes: naming, blaming, claiming', *Law & Society Review* 1981, pp. 613–654. See also the contribution of Terlouw in this book, Chapter 12.

for the act of discrimination (blaming) and thirdly, they have to start a legal procedure, which could be difficult because of fear of retaliation or worsening of the relations.

### 4.5.2 *Willingness of Member States to Take This Directive Seriously*

The Directive has to be implemented in national legislation by 21 May 2016. Some Member States, such as the UK and the Netherlands, have indicated that they do not have to take many measures because all the rights of EU workers have already been secured. The British government stated: "These rights are already enforceable in the UK before the national courts and the Government considers the likely impacts of the Directive to be minor in practice". According to the government the Directive will not significantly affect the balance of competence.[16]

The Dutch Minister of Social Affairs said in Parliament that the Directive would not lead to many legal changes. According to the Minister and the Parliament, the Netherlands was already doing a good job and the Directive would not add anything new.[17] He emphasized that the scope of the Directive was limited to the scope of Regulation 492/2011. Some members of parliament even questioned the necessity of the Directive in light of the own responsibility of the EU migrant workers themselves.[18] In order to fulfil the obligation to implement the Directive the Dutch government only issued one ministerial decree in which a part of the Ministry of Social Affairs was designated with the competence to coordinate the activities of existing bodies which deal with equal treatment of Union workers, like the Dutch legal advice centres, the ombudsman, local anti-discrimination organisations and the Netherlands Institute for Human Rights (the Dutch Equality Body).[19]

According to the Dutch government the extra provision of Article 6(2) on access to and dissemination of information does not need special implementation because there is already sufficient information available on the website of the national government (www.rijksoverheid.nl) and through a leaflet, entitled: Nieuw in Nederland (New in the Netherlands). This leaflet of 20 pages provides information on the rights of workers (like labour conditions and

16 <www.niassembly.gov.uk/globalassets/documents/raise/publications/2015/ofmdfm/13515.pdf>.

17 Tweede Kamer, vergaderjaar 2012–2013, 33 635, nr. 4, pp. 8–9 (Dutch Parliament).

18 Tweede Kamer, vergaderjaar 2012–2013, 33 635, nr. 4, p. 4 (Dutch Parliament).

19 Wijziging OMV-besluit ivm implementatie richtlijn 2014/54 vergemakkelijken uitoefening vrij verkeer van werknemers *Official publication: Staatscourant (Journal Officiel néerlandais)*; Number: 23600; Publication date: 10/05/2016 pp. 1–6.

rules on working hours), and also on membership of a trade union, education, learning the Dutch language and on the possibilities for housing. This leaflet has been translated into most EU languages and is given to EU migrant workers when they receive their Citizen Service Number, which is a necessary document to enable them to work legally in the Netherlands. See www.newinthenetherlands.nl. It can be questioned whether this minimalist approach will be seen as sufficient for implementing the Directive. For instance it is not clear which body in the Netherlands is competent to deal with the issue of nationality discrimination as regards social and tax advantages.

Lithuania, on the other hand, wants to use this Directive to also strengthen the rights of their own Lithuanian workers in other Member States. Given the fact that more Lithuanian workers leave, than other EU workers enter Lithuania, this is an understandable desire. With regard to their own legislation, Lithuania has a problem in that much of its legislation contains a permanent residence requirement which is a condition for accessing most of the social benefits. This requirement discriminates against EU workers from other Member States and will need to be adapted.[20] The fact that Lithuania has amended 66 different Acts in the implementation process of this Directive raises the presumption that they have dealt with this adaptation of the residence requirement in a structural way.[21]

### 4.5.3 *Not Applicable to Posted Workers*

The new Directive will only apply to situations which fall within the scope of Article 45 TFEU and Regulation 492/2011. At the moment for instance in the Netherlands the more structural problems occur with Polish and Portuguese workers, who work as "posted workers" and fall within the scope of Article 56 TFEU (freedom of services) and Directive 96/71, concerning the posting of workers (within the framework of the provision of services), which gives these workers a much lower set of rights than Article 45 TFEU and Directive 492/2011 do.

A worker is a "posted worker" when he is employed in one EU Member State but sent by his employer on a temporary basis to carry out his work in another Member State. There is an employment relationship between the undertaking making the posting and the worker during the period of the posting. The core of mandatory rules on posting covers issues such as payment of minimum wages, maximum work periods and minimum rest periods, minimum

20 See presentations FreSsco seminar Latvia-Lithuania, Riga, 16 September 2015 <ec.europa.eu/social/main.jsp?langId=nl&catId=88&eventsId=1042&furtherEvents=yes>.

21 <eur-lex.europa.eu/legal-content/en/NIM/?uri=celex:32014L0054>.

paid annual leave, equal treatment between men and women and issues such as health and safety at work and includes protective measures in the terms and conditions of employment of pregnant women, children and young people. These workers are much cheaper because they do not have to be paid the higher wages based on collective labour agreements and they fall within the lower social security and pensions systems of their country of origin, like Portugal or Poland. The issue of posting of workers seems to have created more structural difficulties at this time than the issue of free movement of workers. Posting has become one of the channels for cross-border recruitment of "cheap" labour without reference to the rights that can be derived from EU law on genuine labour mobility.[22] Main problems are evasion of payment of minimum wages, abuse of payment of social security contributions and evasion of abiding by collective agreements.

This is an issue which is getting more attention in the Netherlands at the moment: An anecdotal example is the building of a tunnel in 2013 in Maastricht in the southern part of the Netherlands which led to scandalous exploitation of mainly Polish and Portuguese construction workers. They were working under the posting of workers regime and were paid the obligatory minimum wage and therefore at first sight this seemed to be in line with Directive 96/71. But it appeared that they had to pay back 965 Euro per month for so-called "logistic costs" to the company which hired them out. This amount of money was half of their salary. According to the company, these costs were meant to cover the costs of housing and transportation. But in fact these workers were sleeping three persons to a room in several old flats, which would be demolished because of the construction of the tunnel. The construction site itself was only 100 metres away from their accommodation. In the end the Polish and Portuguese workers got part of their money back under pressure of action from the largest trade union in the Netherlands, FNV, which supported them in a lawsuit.[23]

In another situation, posted workers who were building an energy plant in the Northern part of the Netherlands (also mainly Polish and Portuguese workers) were not paid the obligatory minimum wage. The Dutch trade union, FNV, tried to mobilize these workers and challenged their structural underpayment and succeeded in the end by winning a court procedure. But the trade union had to overcome a lot of resistance not only from the employers, who did not allow FNV to visit the site of the plant itself, but also from the Portuguese and

---

22 Cremers, J. (2016), 'Economic freedoms and labour standards in the European Union', *Transfer*, pp. 149–162.

23 <www.l1.nl/algemeen/237605-dossier-misstanden-arbeiders-a2-maastricht>.

Polish workers, who were actually content with their underpayment, because they still earned more than double the amount of money they could have earned in their home country (if they had had a job at all).[24]

## 4.6 Challenges Ahead

This issue of posted workers brings us to the challenges ahead for the free movement of workers in the near future. In my view there are three important challenges. Firstly, there is a progressive displacement of workers by posted workers, which will lead to serious risks of erosion of labour standards and downward pressure on pay. Secondly, there is the changing concept of workers, which can undermine the position of EU migrants and, thirdly, the Brexit proposals, which were accepted by the other Member States, affecting the principles of free movement of workers in an unprecedented way.

### 4.6.1 *Progressive Displacement of Workers by Posted Workers*

In 2014 there were 1.9 million posted workers in the EU. The number of posted workers increased by 44.4% between 2010 and 2014. The total number of EU workers who live and work or look for a job in another EU Member State is 8.3 million. The concentration of posted workers in some sectors is high. The construction sector, for example, comprises about 43.7% of the total posted workers. Such concentration is especially high in Belgium, Luxembourg and Austria.[25] In the Netherlands the amount of A1 declarations which register that workers are posted and fall within the social security system of another Member State (like Poland or Portugal) doubled last year to 100,000. In 2016 the Netherlands is the fifth EU country per number of received posted workers.

A concentration of posted workers in the lower echelons of the labour market carries the risk of an erosion of labour standards and an evasion of mandatory rules. In low skills sectors, such as construction, wage gaps of up to 30% have been observed between posted workers and local national workers.[26]

To strengthen the practical application of the rules on posting of workers by addressing issues related to fraud, circumvention of rules, and exchange of information between the Member States, in 2014 Directive 2014/67 (the so-called

24 <ec.europa.eu/social/contentAdmin/BlobServlet?docId=9983&langId=en>.

25 <ec.europa.eu/social/BlobServlet?docId=15181&langId=en>.

26 Cremers, J. (2016), 'Economic freedoms and labour standards in the European Union', *Transfer*, pp. 149–162.

Enforcement Directive) was adopted.[27] This Enforcement Directive aims to guarantee better protection of posted workers and a more transparent and predictable legal frame work for service providers.[28]

But the Commission feared that this Enforcement Directive would not be enough to tackle the phenomenon of social dumping and therefore introduced in March 2016 a proposal to revise the 1996 Posting of Workers Directive.[29] The main change concerns the *rates of pay* to which a posted worker is entitled. The current Directive only requires that posted workers are subject to the *minimum* rates of pay. The new proposal foresees that the *same* rules on remuneration in the host Member State will apply, as laid down by law or by universally applicable collective agreements. Posted and local workers will therefore be subject to the same rules when it comes to remuneration. Another important proposed change is that workers posted for longer than two years will at least be covered by all the mandatory rules of protection of the labour law of the host Member State. A comparable 24-month rule already exists in the social security coordination legislation.[30]

Ironically, there is resistance from the Central and Eastern European Member States to this principle, because they fear that the competitive position of their own citizens working in another EU country will diminish. The national parliaments of 11 Member States (Bulgaria, Croatia, Czech Republic, Denmark, Estonia, Hungary, Latvia, Lithuania, Poland, Romania and Slovakia) have therefore used the yellow card procedure to stop this proposed legislation. In July 2016 the Commission concluded that the proposal for a revision of the Directive does not constitute a breach of the subsidiarity principle and it will be maintained.[31] But given the fierce resistance, the process of adoption is very unpredictable.

### 4.6.2 *Changing Concept of Who is a Worker*

A second challenge concerns the changing concept of who is a worker. According to the settled case law of the CJEU, "worker" has a European definition: "services performed under supervision of another in return for remuneration, so long as such activities are genuine and effective and not on such a small

27 *OJ* L 159, 28 May 2014, pp. 11–31. Transposition date was 18 June 2016.

28 <europa.eu/rapid/press-release_MEMO-16-467_en.htm>.

29 COM(2016)128.

30 See: Article 12(1) Regulation 883/2004.

31 Communication on the proposal for a Directive amending the Posting of Workers Directive, with regard to the principle of subsidiarity, in accordance with Protocol No 2, COM(2016)505.

scale as to be marginal and ancillary". The consequences of being found to be or not to be a worker are increasingly significant for residence rights and social entitlements for the worker and his/her family. For instance, workers have an unconditional right to reside without a requirement for resources or comprehensive health insurance, the right to equal treatment in relation to most matters including welfare assistance, the right to education for children etc. As part-time work and atypical contracts are on the increase, the borderlines of the worker concept are becoming more crucial for an increasing number of people.

Working patterns are changing. As said previously, part-time and atypical employment are on the increase, and different forms of working relationships such as para-subordination (a mix between self-employment and employment) are emerging. Also working forms like apprenticeships, volunteering, bogus self-employment, and other fringe work – such as rehabilitative/sheltered work and participation in workfare programmes – raise the important question: Are they workers?

EU migrants are often concentrated in lower paid, less stable positions and atypical work relationships and are incoherently, inconsistently treated by different States – both during their activities, and during the inevitable gaps between the activities where contracts are short-term, or "on-call". This significantly undermines the protections that are otherwise afforded to those in "typical", stable employment relationships whilst also threatening the effectiveness of the free movement of workers provisions.

The CJEU has never set a fixed amount of hours of work for the definition of being a worker. Verschueren reconstructs the answer of the CJEU to the question of how many hours a week a person has to work for his/her employment to be considered as "real and genuine" and not as "purely marginal and ancillary" as follows:[32]

> In Kempf, the CJEU accepted 12 hours a week as sufficient, in Megner and Scheffel even 10 hours.[33] In Genc, concerning the EEC-Turkey Association Agreement, the CJEU did not rule out that 5.5 hours a week might be considered as "real and genuine", following an overall assessment of the

---

32 Verschueren, H. (2016), 'Being economically active: how it still matters', in: Verschueren, H. (ed.), *Residence, employment and social rights of mobile persons. On how EU law defines where they belong*, Cambridge: Intersentia, p. 194 e.v.

33 CJEU 3 June 1986, C-139/85, *Kempf*, ECLI:EU:C:1986:223; and CJEU 14 December 1995, C-444/93, *Megner & Scheffel*, ECLI:EU:C:1995:442.

> employment relationship in question.[34] Part-time working students,[35] trainees[36] or au pairs[37] could also be "workers". However, the low threshold the CJEU applies may also lead to situations in which persons are very close to being economically inactive, as a result of which different rules on the right to reside and the right to equal treatment apply, leading to seemingly arbitrary outcomes.[38] Therefore, Member States may be tempted to apply a strict test and give a narrow interpretation to what is "real and genuine" with a view to excluding certain migrants, such as part-time migrants, from the "worker" status and hence from the rights which this entails.

Verschueren also discusses the fact that some new forms of labour and non-standard work could also run the risk of not being covered by the concept of "worker".[39] This was illustrated by the *Raulin* case in 1992. In that case the CJEU had to decide on the question of whether a worker employed under a so-called "on-call" contract (sometimes also called a "zero-hours" contract) could be regarded as a worker. Such a contract is a means of recruiting workers in sectors where the volume of work is subject to seasonal or other variations. Under such a contract, no guarantee is given as to the hours to be worked and, often, the person involved works only a few days a week or hours a day. The employer is held to pay wages and grant social advantages insofar as the worker has actually performed work. Such contracts normally mean that there is no obligation for employers to offer work, or for workers to accept it. The CJEU did not exclude that workers under such an "on-call" contract could be regarded as migrant workers within the meaning of the Treaty. However, it also said that the national court might, when assessing the effective and genuine nature of the activity in question, take account of the irregular nature and limited duration of the services actually performed under a contract for occasional employment. The fact that the person concerned worked only a very limited number

---

34 CJEU 4 February 2010, C-14/09, *Genc*, ECLI:EU:C:2010:57, para. 28.

35 CJEU 21 February 2013, C-46/12, *L.N.*, ECLI:EU:C:2013:97.

36 CJEU 26 February 1992, C-3/90, *Bernini*, ECLI:EU:C:1992:89; CJEU 17 March 2005, C-109/04, *Kranemann*, ECLI:EU:C:2005:187; and CJEU 9 July 2015, C-229/14, *Balkaya*, ECLI:EU:C:2015:455, para. 50.

37 Case C-294/06, *Payir*, ECLI:EU:C:2008:36.

38 Thym, D. (2015), 'The elusive limits of solidarity: residence rights of and social benefits for economically inactive union citizens', 52 *CML Rev*, 43.

39 Verschueren, H. (2016), 'Being economically active: how it still matters', in: Verschueren, H. (ed.), *Residence, employment and social rights of mobile persons. On how EU law defines where they belong*, Cambridge: Intersentia, p. 196.

of hours in a labour relationship might be an indication that the activities exercised were purely marginal and ancillary.[40]

A recent FreSsco study found that some Member States establish formal or informal earnings or hours thresholds to assess whether someone is a worker.[41] Falling below the threshold creates a presumption of marginality, which must be refuted by the claimant. This can place a heavy burden of proof on the worker.

In the UK a worker must earn £156 per week (the equivalent of approximately 22 hours per week at the national minimum wage) for three months before automatically being considered a worker. Falling below the threshold creates a presumption of marginality and claimants are required to prove that their work is genuine and effective while being given little guidance on how to do this.

In Belgium there is a 12 hour per week threshold for determining whether work is genuine and effective. Denmark uses a 10–12 hour per week threshold and Finland 18 hours per week or 80 hours in four weeks as well as an earnings threshold of € 1165 a month. In the Netherlands the individual concerned must either receive an income which exceeds 50% of the social assistance standard or must work at least 40% of the normal working time to be considered a "worker" anyway.[42] The effect of this statement is that in the Netherlands in practice often EU nationals working less than 40% of the normal working time are not considered to be workers and the free movement rights of that person or his family members are denied or disregarded on that ground or because of the lack of sufficient income.

There is a significant risk that in all Member States where the threshold is not achieved, it is up to the claimant to adduce evidence to refute a presumption of marginality.

### 4.6.3 *Proposals to Prevent a BREXIT*

The third challenge is the proposals the Member States formulated to prevent a Brexit. On 19 February 2016 the European Council made an agreement

40 CJEU 26 February 1992, C-357/89, *Raulin*, EU:C:1992:87, paras. 11–14.

41 O'Brien, C., E. Spaventa & J. De Coninck, 'The concept of worker under Article 45 TFEU and certain non-standard forms of employment', FreSsco Comparative Report 2015, <www.ec.europa.eu/social/BlobServlet?docId=15476>. See also: O'Brien, C. (2016), 'Civis capitalist sum: class as the new guiding principle of EU free movement rights', 53 *CML Rev*, p. 955 e.v.

42 See chapter B10/3.2.1 of the Dutch Aliens Act Implementation Guidelines <cmr.jur.ru.nl/cmr/vc/vc2013/wbv.2013.05.pdf>.

regarding the demands of the UK necessary to keep them in the EU.[43] On 23 June the UK held a referendum where the British people, despite this agreement, voted to leave the EU. It was only if they had voted to remain in the EU that the proposals of the deal would have been further elaborated.[44] But the proposals reflect the opinion of a lot of other Member States as well.

I will deal here with two proposals which touch upon the social security position of workers, challenging the principle of free movement of workers fundamentally: the emergency brake on in-work benefits and the limiting of the export of child benefits.

### 4.6.4 *'Emergency brake' on in-work Benefits*

The first one concerns the introduction of the so-called "emergency brake". This is a proposal to amend Regulation (EU) No 492/2011, which will provide for an alert and safeguard mechanism that responds to situations of inflow of workers from other Member States of an exceptional magnitude over an extended period of time, including as a result of past policies following previous EU enlargements, taking into account a pull factor arising from a Member State's in-work benefits regime.

This emergency brake would allow the UK to limit the access of newly arriving EU workers to non-contributory in-work benefits for a total period of up to four years from the commencement of employment. For the UK, this concerns the supplementary fiscal benefits for those EU workers who earn a low wage. These are Tax Benefits, Child Tax Benefits and Housing Benefits. The limitation would be graduated, from initial complete exclusion but gradually increasing access to such benefits to take account of the growing connection of the worker with the labour market of the host Member State. The authorisation would have limited duration and apply to newly arriving EU workers for a period of seven years.

This emergency brake does not apply exclusively to the UK. Any Member State wishing to avail itself of the mechanism could notify the Commission and the Council that such an exceptional situation exists on a scale that affects essential aspects of its social security system, including the primary purpose of

43 European Council (2016), Conclusions of the European Council meeting, 18–19 February, EUCO 1/16.

44 European Council (2016); No 4 of the Conclusion of the European Council Meeting of February 18/19 states: "It is understood that, should the result of the referendum in the United Kingdom be for it to leave the European Union, the set of arrangements referred to in paragraph 2 above will cease to exist".

its in-work benefits system, or which leads to difficulties which are serious and liable to persist in its employment market or are putting an excessive pressure on the proper functioning of its public services. On a proposal from the Commission after having examined the notification and the reasons stated therein, the Council could authorise the Member State concerned to restrict access to non-contributory in-work benefits to the extent necessary.

From a legal point of view, I think this proposal is extremely problematic for those benefits which are defined as social security benefits, like the UK Child Tax Benefits.[45] In these cases just adapting Regulation 492/2011 would not provide enough legal basis for this exclusion, because it would be in breach of the equal treatment provision of Article 4 of Regulation 883/2004.[46]

This proposal means for the first time in the history of the EU that some kind of unequal treatment between EU nationals and own nationals in the field of free movement of workers has been introduced (except for the restriction on access to the public service for a limited category of posts and the transitional arrangements restricting the free movement of workers of new accession States for a limited period of time).

A UK scholar, Ruhs, has advocated in this regard that if a choice has to be made, the unrestricted movement of workers within the EU is a more important asset than fully equal access to EU Member States' welfare states. The freedom to move and take up employment in other EU countries generates very large economic and other gains for workers and their families in lower-income Member States. Protecting this freedom and these gains is, in his view, worth the price of more (temporary) restrictions on access to national welfare states, especially to noncontributory benefits.[47] In my opinion this is a crucial fallacy because the moment equal access to benefits between own nationals and EU nationals is restricted there is no longer a full principle of free movement of workers. Moreover, abandoning the equal principle will only fuel the suspicion that EU migrant workers are taking jobs from the 'native' workers, not assuage it.

---

45 See: Neville Harris (2016), 'Demagnetisation of social security and health care for migrants to the UK', *European Journal of Social Security*, pp. 130–163.

46 Article 4 of Regulation 883/2004: "Unless otherwise provided for by this regulation, persons to whom this regulation applies shall enjoy the same benefits and be subject to the same obligations under the legislation of any member state as the nationals thereof". This Regulation is based on Article 48 TFEU which is explicitly designed to prevent that restrictions in the field of social security would hinder the free movement of workers.

47 Ruhs, M. (2013), *The price of rights: Regulating international labour migration*, Princeton (NJ) and Oxford: Princeton University Press.

### 4.6.5 *Limiting the Export of Child Benefits*

Second there was a proposal to amend Regulation 883/2004 on the coordination of social security systems in order to give Member States, with regard to the exportation of child benefits to a Member State other than that in which the worker resides, an option to index such benefits to the living conditions of the Member State in which the child resides. This measure was not only limited to the UK, but could be applied by the other Member States as well. The restriction was that initially this measure should only apply to new claims made by EU workers in the host Member State. But, as from 1 January 2020, all Member States would be given the possibility to extend indexation to existing claims to child benefits already exported by EU workers. The Commission delicately notes that it does not intend to propose that this future system of optional indexation of child benefits be extended to other types of exportable benefits, such as old-age pensions.

The question arises as to whether such an amendment of Regulation 883/2004 would stand the test of the case law of the CJEU on this issue. Already in 1986 the CJEU decided in the *Pinna* case that this kind of limitation on the export of child benefits had to be seen as a form of unjustified covert discrimination.[48] However, the content of the *Pinna* case was not completely similar to the now proposed changes. In that case the old coordination Regulation 1408/71 (the predecessor of Regulation 883/2004) permitted France to not export child benefits for children living in other EU countries at all. The children of an Italian worker in France who in that case lived in Italy were only entitled to the much lower Italian child benefits. The Court found this provision invalid (in so far as it precluded the award to employed persons subject to French legislation of French family benefits for members of their family residing in the territory of another Member State) and contrary to (now) Article 45 TFEU on the free movement of workers.

The introduction of this indexation of the amount of the exported child benefits will above all be a matter of principle. The financial consequences will be minimal. There are no exact figures known, but the British government estimated it would save around € 38 million. This concerns only a very small percentage of the overall benefits paid for children.[49] The same goes for the

48 CJEU 15 January 1986, C-41/84, *Pinna v Caisse d'allocations familiales de la Savoie*, ECLI:EU:C:1986:1.

49 Only 0.26% of the total UK child benefits was paid to EU migrants whose children live in another Member State in December 2013, and 0.09% UK child tax benefits were claimed by families with children in another Member State. See: <bruegel.org/2016/02/child-benefits-for-eu-migrants-in-the-uk>.

Netherlands, where the savings would be around € 8 million (which represents 0.25% of the total amount of money paid in child benefits). It is only in Germany, which pays child benefits for 83,000 children living in the Central and Eastern European Member States that the adaptation would lead in absolute terms to a more substantial saving of € 100 million.[50] In this context the reasoning of the Advocate General in the above-mentioned *Pinna* case is still valid. He did not see any justification for the contested provision, because the finances of (in that case) France did not seem to be threatened to such an extent as to warrant this special rule.[51]

## 4.7 Conclusion

It is good to emphasize that free movement of workers is one of the four fundamental freedoms in the EU Treaty. Developments of the last decade show that this freedom cannot just be taken for granted but has to be cherished actively every day. The fact that there is still a need for a special Directive to enforce the rights of EU workers, which have existed for almost 50 years, is a sign that these rights should not be watered down. But it is also useful to remember that there will always be a gap between formal equality and material equality and that legalisation is not a panacea in this respect. The success of the new Directive 2014/54 will be determined to a large extent by the efforts and activities of governments, and also of trade unions and national Equity Bodies.

An example of good practice is a report published in March 2013 by the Netherlands Institute for Human Rights (the Dutch Equity Body), entitled *Polish migrant workers from a human rights perspective,* based on a literature study and interviews with stakeholders and Polish labour migrants.[52] This report gives an inventory of the problems and obstacles with which Polish migrant workers are confronted in the Netherlands and formulates 11 recommendations addressed to the Minister of Social Affairs.

The effectiveness of Directive 2014/54 and the ability to obtain rights as EU workers deserves a good monitoring system.

The preparedness of the Member States to find a balance between the rights of EU mobile workers and those of posted workers will influence the direction

50 *Elsevier* 5 March 2016, pp. 48–49.

51 Opinion of Advocate General Mancini, point 7, ECLI: EU:C:1985:215.

52 The report is in Dutch with a summary in English and can be found on the website of the Netherlands Institute for Human Rights: <mensenrechten.nl> under the header *Publicaties.*

on terms and conditions of employment within the EU in the near future. What is important in this respect will be answering the question of who can be seen as a worker. Time will tell whether the Brexit deal had to be seen as an incidental solution to keep a Member State aboard or a harbinger of the development of new proposals to restrict the free movement of workers in a more structural way in an ever closer Union.

## References


Aubert, V. (1966), 'Some social functions of legislation', *Acta Sociologica* Vol. 10, No. 1/2, Contributions to the Sociology of Law, pp. 98–120.

Cremers, J. (2016), 'Economic freedoms and labour standards in the European Union', *Transfer*, pp. 149–162.

Felstiner, W.F.L., R.L. Abel & A. Sarat (1981), 'The emergence and transformation of disputes: naming, blaming, claiming', *Law & Society Review*, pp. 613–654.

Groenendijk, K. & P. Minderhoud (2016), 'Taaleis in de bijstand: discriminerend, disproportioneel en onnodig', *NJB* 2016/91, afl. 3, pp. 183–189.

Harris, N. (2016), 'Demagnetisation of social security and health care for migrants to the UK', *European Journal of Social Security*, pp. 130–163.

Jorens, Y., P. Minderhoud & J. De Coninck (2015), *Comparative report: frontier workers in the EU*, FreSsco, Brussels: European Commission.

O'Brien, C. (2016), 'Civis capitalist sum: class as the new guiding principle of EU free movement rights', 53 *CML Review*, p. 955.

O'Brien, C., E. Spaventa & J. De Coninck (2015), *The concept of worker under article 45 TFEU and certain non-standard forms of employment*, FreSsco Comparative Report 2015, <www.ec.europa.eu/social/BlobServlet?docId=15476>.

Ruhs, M. (2013), *The price of rights: regulating international labour migration*, Princeton (NJ): Princeton University Press.

Thym, D. (2015), 'The elusive limits of solidarity: residence rights of and social benefits for economically inactive union citizens', 52 *CML Review*, 43.

Verschueren, H. (2016), 'Being economically active: how it still matters', in: Verschueren, H. (ed.), *Residence, employment and social rights of mobile persons. On how EU law defines where they belong*, Cambridge: Intersentia, pp. 187–214.

CHAPTER 5

# Two Decades EU Migration Law for Third Country Nationals

***Are There any Integration Challenges Left?***

*Tineke Strik*

## 5.1 Introduction

As the current Migration Agenda of the Commission has been dominated by asylum and irregular migration, the political and public debate on legal migration seems almost absent. At the same time, in European societies integration of third country nationals has been hotly debated, fuelled by the emerging populist right wing parties and the threat of terrorism. Integration has been one of the main objectives of EU policy on legal migration, which started to develop twenty years ago. It is therefore relevant to assess the extent to which the EU legal migration instruments have contributed to the integration of third country nationals: the Family Reunification Directive and the Long-Term Residents Directive. To what extent do Member States use the directives to maximise their chances for integration, and what more steps are needed?

### 5.1.1 *History*

At the time the Centre for Migration Law was established, the competence for regulating the rights of third country nationals was still at the national level. However, the Council had already defined some principles. In 1985, when it became clear that the residence of third country nationals had acquired a more permanent character, the Council called on the Member States to cooperate in order to promote their integration and participation.[1] It referred to its resolution, adopted in 1974, which emphasized the importance of equal treatment between EU citizens and third country nationals including their family members regarding their life and work circumstances. The Council explicitly intervened in the rights of legally residing third country nationals, but operated cautiously regarding the admission policy of third country nationals.[2] At

1 Resolution of the Council 16 July 1985 on Guidelines for a communitarian Migration Policy, *Pb* C 186, 26 July 1985, pp. 0003–0004.

2 Resolution of the Council 21 January 1974 regarding a Social Action Programme, *Pb* C 013, 12 February 1974, pp. 0003–0004.

DOI 10.1163/9789004330467_006

that time, a clear competence was absent from the Treaties.[3] Until the Treaty of Maastricht entered into force, cooperation on admission remained outside the institutional framework of the EEC. In mid-1997 the Commission introduced a proposal for a Treaty on admission. This proposal served as a model for the legal migration instruments based on the Treaty of Amsterdam, especially the Family Reunification Directive and the Long-Term Residents Directive.[4]

The content of both directives was guided and inspired by the Tampere conclusions in which the European leaders declared that a vigorous integration policy would need to grant third country nationals rights and obligations comparable to those of EU citizens. According to the conclusions, enhancement of the non-discrimination of third country nationals in economic, social and cultural life should be part of this policy.[5] The preambles of both directives make reference to these Tampere conclusions.[6] So besides harmonization of national policies, integration has always been an important goal of the European rules on family reunification and long-term residents.

### 5.1.2 *Equal Rights?*

This firm objective of equal treatment, however, did not prevent the Member States from retaining clear distinctions between third country nationals and EU citizens in both directives. Just to mention a few differences: for family reunification, Member States are allowed to impose material conditions and to limit the scope to core family members. During the first five years after admission, the rights and status of admitted family members remain dependent on the sponsor fulfilling the requirements.

The regime of intra-EU mobility for long-term residents is still a long way from the right of free movement for Union citizens. Economic activity is insufficient for settlement in another Member State; instead a minimum income is required and the second Member State can apply a labour market test, prioritizing Union citizens. Furthermore, the free movement is limited to one other Member State. Any onward settlement is only permitted after five years of residence in the second Member State.

Despite the remaining distance from Union citizens, both directives have clearly strengthened the rights of third country nationals in most Member States. The EU Court of Justice has made clear that family reunification and the granting of a long-term residence status are subjective EU rights and that

---

3 The legal basis for policies on integration was Article 177 EC Treaty.

4 Articles 63(3) and (4) EC Treaty.

5 Conclusion no. 18.

6 Recital no. 3 of Directive 2003/86 and recital no. 2 of Directive 2003/109.

the discretion of the Member States is limited to the requirements in the directives. Both directives entered into force a decade ago, which enables us to assess their impact.[7] To what extent have they enhanced the harmonization of national policies and the integration of third country nationals? I will highlight the main results below.

## 5.2 Family Reunification

The comparative studies on the transposition of the Family Reunification Directive show a mixed picture of the impact the directive has had on national policies.[8] On the one hand, the directive led to a liberalisation of the national policies: some Member States needed to raise their standards, some had to restrict their national discretion by introducing the right to family reunification in their national legislation.[9] This result was achieved despite, rather than thanks to, the actual aims of the Member States. An analysis of the negotiations shows that they did not negotiate with a view to harmonization or integration, but to defend their national legislation and preferably their discretion.[10] It is therefore no surprise that some Member States used the adoption of the directive as a vehicle for restricting their policies, although the directive in no way condones to lowering certain standards. Those governments negotiated restrictive measures into the directive and legitimized them on the national level by presenting them as transposition. This strategic use of

7 The Family Reunification Directive entered into force on 3 October 2005, the Long Term Residence Directive entered into force on 23 January 2006.

8 Groenendijk, C.A., R. Fernhout, D.P.L.M. van Dam, R. van Oers & M.H.A. Strik (2007), *The family reunification directive in EU member states. The first year of implementation*, (report, Nijmegen Migration Law Working Papers Series, no. 2007/01). Nijmegen: Radboud University Nijmegen. Labayle, H. & Y. Pascouau (2008), *Directive 2003/86/EC on the right to family reunification, synthesis report, in the framework of the 'conformity checking of the transposition by member states of 10 EC directives in the sector of asylum and immigration'*, Odysseus Network. Pascouau, Y. & H. Labayle (2011), *Conditions for family reunification under strain. A comparative study in nine EU member states*, European Policy Centre. Strik, T., B. De Hart & E. Nissen (2013), *Family reunification: a barrier or facilitator of integration? A comparative study*, Nijmegen: Wolf Legal Publishers.

9 Groenendijk, C.A., R. Fernhout, D.P.L.M. van Dam, R. van Oers & M.H.A. Strik (2007), *The family reunification directive in EU member states. The first year of implementation*, Centre for Migration Law, Nijmegen: Wolf Legal Publishers, 2007, paragraph 11.1.

10 Strik, T. (2011), *Besluitvorming over asiel- en migratierichtlijnen. De wisselwerking tussen nationaal en Europees niveau*, Den Haag: Boom Juridische Uitgevers, section 3.2.2, 3.2.3 and 3.7.2.

Europeanization however outweighed the liberal changes that Member States were forced to make.

Although the transposition has been subject to several studies, less is known about the impact of the directive and the case law of the Court of Justice after the transposition process. Can we observe certain tendencies in national policy changes related to the directive? And does it lead to adjustments in the decision making practice?

### 5.2.1 *Policies*

As the directive limits national discretion and possibilities for regression, Member States rely on the optional clauses to make their policy more restrictive. A lobby for a standstill clause in the directive, prohibiting regressive changes at national level, had failed.[11] The case of the Netherlands exemplifies the impact: after an unsuccessful attempt to persuade the Commission to propose a more restrictive directive, it decided in 2010 to apply most of the optional clauses of the directive to restrict the right to family reunification.[12] Since these policy changes, the directive has been functioning as standard setting for the Dutch family reunification policies instead of being the bare minimum. This result is in contrast to the formal position the Dutch government communicated to its parliament at the start of the negotiations on the directive that it aimed at the highest protection level and insisted on the possibility to deviate from the norms in the directive in a positive sense.[13] As in other countries, the government's attitude towards family reunification reversed from perceiving it as a chance to integrate migrants to a threat to social cohesion and integration.

Many governments have used the optional clauses of the directive to adopt policies from the Netherlands (f.i. the pre-entry test, minimum age level of 21 for spouses, three-month time limit for family reunification for refugees), and also from other countries. Hence, the search for possibilities to reduce the number of family migrants within the limits of the directive has had a harmonizing effect, albeit not in the upward sense that the directive was initially meant to create. An analysis of the political debates demonstrates huge similarities in the arguments Member States use to justify their restrictions: these

11 Strik, T. (2011), *Besluitvorming over asiel- en migratierichtlijnen. De wisselwerking tussen nationaal en Europees niveau*, Den Haag: Boom Juridische Uitgevers, section 3.2.1.

12 'Kabinetsaanpak gezinsmigratiebeleid', 2 October 2009, *Kamerstukken II* 2009–2010, 32.175, no 1 (Dutch Parliament); The Coalition Agreement VVD-CDA, "Vrijheid en Verantwoordelijkheid" Chapter 6, 30 September 2010.

13 *Kamerstukken II* 1999–2000, 23.490, nr. 154, p. 13 and nr. 158, p. 10 (Dutch Parliament).

are, apart from promoting integration, protecting the national economy and preventing fraud.[14]

### 5.2.2 *Response to Refugees*

Recital no. 8 of the Family Reunification Directive recognizes that the situation of refugees requires special attention due to the compelling reasons for their flight, which has prevented them from leading a normal family life in their own country. For this reason, they are entitled to more favourable rules, laid down in Chapter 5. However, in response to the recent increase in the number of refugees, many Member States have restricted the right to family reunification. With regard to those persons with subsidiary protection, the Austrian government has suspended their right to family reunification for two years (an increase from one to three years), and Germany has introduced a suspension of two years. The Swedish government has suspended family reunification for all protection categories, suggesting that it will lift the suspension for convention refugees after three years.

Those with subsidiary protection are not covered by the Family Reunification Directive, as most Member States rejected the initial Commission's proposal to include them, arguing that at that time there was no common definition of subsidiary protection. The Commission excluded them in its second proposal, but announced that it would insert a *rendez-vous* clause in order to review this decision after adoption.[15] Member States now benefit from this legal loophole, not only by introducing these suspension mechanisms, but also by granting the subsidiary protection status more frequently than before (for instance to Syrian refugees). It however remains doubtful if such different treatment between convention refugees and those with subsidiary protection, who are in an analogous situation, is allowed, as Article 14 ECHR requires very high standards for justification and proportionality.[16]

With regard to convention refugees, Belgium has reduced the time limit for application to three months and Sweden has introduced a minimum age limit of 21 years for both spouses. In several countries the waiting period has or will be introduced or existing periods extended. The Dutch government has published a legislative proposal to expand the time limit for deciding on family

---

14 Strik, T., B. De Hart & E. Nissen (2013), *Family reunification: a barrier or facilitator of integration? A comparative study*, Nijmegen: Wolf Publishers, Chapter 4.

15 See COM(1999)638, Council document no. 6504/00 MIGR 24, 16 March 2000 and COM(2000)624, 10 October 2000. See Art. 19 of the directive for the *rendez-vous* clause.

16 See also "Information note on family reunification for beneficiaries of international protection in Europe" ECRE/ELENA, June 2016.

reunification for refugees to nine months, which is the minimum norm in the directive.[17]

These changes, if at all allowed, clearly run counter to the objective of integration. In earlier research, family members often described their lives during the application procedure as being on hold. Delay in the process means that the family members live separately, and thus, focus on the process and not on the host society.[18] These conclusions contrast with the objective of integration, formally used by governments to introduce restrictive admission rules. The emotional impact is especially strong when refugee parents are separated from their children, as the constant worrying about the safety of the family members left behind are detrimental to the wellbeing of the refugee. The delay therefore also affects the refugees' ability to recover from the traumatic experiences of persecution and war and their capacity to benefit from existing integration support and learn a new language, search for a job and adapt to their country of asylum. In a research report on the Netherlands, a Burundian refugee woman whose family reunification process with her five children took more than four years stated: '*I came as a young and healthy woman and now I am a wreck*'.[19] Other research confirms that the psychological effect especially hampers integration, and that the longer the period of separation, the harder it is to regain the balance within the family.[20] These outcomes relate to the primary aim of refugees: reuniting with their family members.[21]

17 *Kamerstukken II*, 2016–2017, 34 544 (Dutch Parliament).

18 Strik, T., B. De Hart & E. Nissen (2013), *Family reunification: a barrier or facilitator of integration? A comparative study*, Nijmegen: Wolf Publishers.

19 Strik, De Hart & Nissen (2013), paragraph 6.5.

20 Marsden, R. & C. Harris (2012), *We started life again: integration experiences of refugee families reuniting in Glasgow*, Glasgow: British Red Cross/Scottish Refugee Council, with reference to RASNZ (2012), *Refugee family reunification, mental health and resettlement outcomes in Aotearoa New Zealand*; McDonald-Wilmsen, B. & S. Gifford (2009), 'Refugee resettlement, family separation and Australia's humanitarian programme', *New Issues in Refugee Research* Paper No. 178R; Schweitzer, R. *et al.* (2006), 'Trauma, post-migration living difficulties, and social support as predicators of psychological adjustment in resettled Sudanese refugees', *Australian and New Zealand Journal of Psychiatry*, 40, pp. 179–187; Derluyn, I. *et al.* (2009), 'Mental health problems in separated refugee adolescents', *Journal of Adolescent Health*, 44, pp. 291–297; A. Smith, *et al.* (2004), 'Serial migration and its implications for the parent–child relationship: a retrospective analysis of the experiences of the children of Caribbean immigrants', *Cultural Diversity Ethnic Minority Psychology*, 10:2, pp. 107–22.

21 UNHCR (2013), *A new beginning: refugee integration in Europe*, September 2013, p. 127, <www.refworld.org/docid/522980604.html>.

### 5.2.3 *Practice*

In all Member States, however, it is not only legislation that determines the extent to which migrants can exercise a right to family reunification. The way requirements are applied or assessed and procedures are organized are equally important for their possibilities to bring their families.[22] Jurisprudence has made clear that the Family Reunification Directive not only impacts the policy level but also the practical implementation. The Court of Justice has imposed clear requirements for the examination of individual applications, whether it concerns admission or the renewal of the residence permit of family members. The EU principles on effectiveness and proportionality oblige national authorities to assess the application in light of the aim to further family reunification, taking into account all individual circumstances, interests and rights of the Charter. These requirements are not easy to reconcile with the transformation of immigration authorities in many countries in the past decade, from a *street-level bureaucracy* (with daily face to face contact with applicants) to a *system-level* (*screen-level*) *bureaucracy* (with a computerized, standardized procedure), which seems to have certain drawbacks for individual applicants in terms of being able to tell their story.[23]

In a research study on the impact of the family reunification procedures, family members mentioned the faceless procedure as a problem, specifically in the Netherlands and the United Kingdom. The respondents complained that they could not contact the official who handled their application to provide information, ask questions or be informed about the state of affairs.[24] In the case of the Netherlands the consistent emphasis on the individual assessment by the Court, has finally compelled the central organized Immigration and Naturalization Service to transform its practice from a mechanical assessment of the requirements into a full 'EU-proof' examination, taking a more individual and active approach. For years the government managed to retain its practice by framing categorical exemptions as an individual approach. However, when the national courts became more critical, encouraged by the Court of Justice, the authorities had no other option than to comply with Union law on an individual level.

---

22 Strik, T., B. De Hart & E. Nissen (2013), *Family reunification: a barrier or facilitator of integration? A comparative study*, Nijmegen: Wolf Publishers, p. 109.

23 Böcker, A. & B. De Hart, 'Wat zijn de bedoelde en onbedoelde effecten van het migratierecht?', in: Hertogh & Weyers (eds), *Recht van onderop. Antwoorden uit de rechtssociologie*, pp. 409–426, 2011, Nijmegen: Ars Aequi Libri.

24 Strik, De Hart & Nissen (2013), paragraph 3.8.

This example shows that governments tend to (fully) adjust to the case law of the Court only if they are forced to on a national level. One-way pressure, however, is not always sufficient. According to Van der Vleuten, compliance by governments that do not intend to comply only occurs if there is pressure from both national and European level.[25] As the possibility for the Court of Justice to come up with a decisive ruling depends on an action from the Commission or national judges, the extent to which national governments are being compelled to adjust their legislation to European case law largely depends on the position and perseverance of national actors.

### 5.2.4 *Disconnecting Objectives*

The negotiation results reached thirteen years ago still determine where the race to the bottom ends. The harsher the climate towards migrants grows, the more visible and relevant these boundaries become. Different national strategies can be observed: restricting policies to the minimum standards, circumventing the directive or not complying with its obligations and waiting to see if courts overturn this decision. The objectives of furthering family reunification, harmonization and integration, or the principle that the optional clauses should be interpreted strictly (and not in a manner that undermines the objectives),[26] do not seem to be part of the considerations when defining these strategies.

The more lenient approach at the front door of family reunification, enforced by case law, seems to trigger two efforts to regain sovereignty. First, many Member States have intensified their methods to verify family members' identity or relationship or the genuineness of the marriage or partnership. These methods, applied on the basis of a wide range of indicative criteria, cause delays and frustration amongst the applicants. From empirical research it emerges that many applicants (both the sponsor and the spouse) feel that they are treated with suspicion, which impedes their feeling of belonging to the country in which they want to reunite. Nationals of 'nonwestern' countries feel discriminated against because they are faced with extra authentication procedures and with more requirements, like the pre-entry test.

Second, there seems to be a tendency towards a more restrictive policy and practice at the back door. At least in the Netherlands, family members lose their residence permit more easily when all requirements are no longer fulfilled or

25 Van der Vleuten, A. (1998), 'Two-level interaction as source of influence: the European Union and equal treatment policies', in: Reinalda, B. & B. Verbeek (eds), *Autonomous policy making by international organizations*, London: Routledge, pp. 62–78.

26 See CJEU 4 March 2010, C-578/08, *Chakroun*, ECLI:EU:C:2010:117, paragraph 43.

when they fail to inform the authorities of changes in their situation. This fuels their insecurity of residence and hence affects their integration as well.

The overall reluctant attitude of Member States and national immigration authorities is quite in contrast with the principles of the Family Reunification Directive, emphasizing the importance of family reunification as a fundamental right and its positive impact for the whole society. Pressure will remain necessary to align the national policies and practices with these principles. In response to the Dutch lobby to restrict the Family Reunification Directive, the Commission announced in 2014 that the directive should not be re-opened. Instead, it should ensure the full implementation of the existing rules, open infringement procedures where necessary and produce guidelines on identified issues.[27] National courts feel encouraged by the guidelines to critically scrutinize the decisions of the immigration authorities, but they are cautious in asking for a preliminary ruling. Until now the Commission has refrained from infringement procedures, but it may be time to conclude that they have become necessary. Further research on the implementation by street-level bureaucrats and its impact on family members and their integration process, could provide substantive information for these judicial steps.

## 5.3 Long Term Residents

The Long-Term Residents Directive (2003/109) adopted in 2003 applies to third country nationals who have been residing in a Member State for five years or more. The Court of Justice has confirmed several times now that the directive has established a subjective right to the long-term residence status once the third country national has fulfilled the requirements.[28] Recital no. 6 expresses that the duration of residence in a Member State should be the main criterion for acquiring the status of long-term resident. Peers describes the directive as an accomplishment as it facilitates the security of residence, equal treatment and free movement of third-country nationals.[29] Security of residence, being a central element of the directive, forms the basis for the integration of the third country national in his or her country of residence. Integration is described as

---

27 Communication on guidance for application of Directive 2003/86/EC on the right to family reunification, COM(2014)210, 4 April 2014, p. 2.

28 CJEU 8 November 2012, C-40/11, *Iida*, ECLI:EU:C:2012:691; CJEU 26 April 2012, C-508/10, *Commission v The Netherlands*, ECLI:EU:C:2012:243.

29 Peers, S. (2011), *EU justice and home affairs law*, 3rd edition, Oxford: OUP, pp. 478–485.

a key element in promoting economic and social cohesion, which is anchored in the Treaty as a fundamental objective of the Union.[30]

### 5.3.1 *Policies*

Despite this emphasis on integration as an objective of the directive, fourteen Member States require applicants to fulfil integration conditions before they grant EU status.[31] They include knowledge of the language of the host country (at varying levels) and knowledge about the host society – mainly history, legal order and values. Some Member States require the third country national to pass an exam after following compulsory courses (which may be expensive) while others only require attendance at integration courses. In this way the EU status functions as proof rather than as a tool for integration. At the time the Commission launched the proposal for the EU Long-Term Residence Directive, only Germany had a language requirement for its national permanent status. This shows that Member States, as we saw before with the Family Reunification Directive, used the discretion the directive allowed them to restrict the right to EU status, by adopting policies from other states. Several national experiences have shown that an integration requirement reduces the number of applications for a permanent status as well as the number of permits issued.[32] More third country nationals thus remain with a temporary, more conditional, status, which is in general not beneficial for their integration.

The directive foresees intra-Member State mobility for long-term residents with the possibility of work or residence in a second Member State. Article 14 paragraph 3 of the directive allows the second Member State to apply the labour market test prioritizing Union citizens in cases of admission for economic activities. The restricted access to the labour market can remain during the first year of residence (Article 21 paragraph 2). Only seven Member States exempt long-term residence status holders from the labour market test.[33] This means that the large majority doesn't treat labour migrants with a long-term residence status differently from those entering directly from outside the EU. Italy and Romania apply a national quota and they also (together with France)

30 See the preamble of the directive, recital nr. 4, and Article 3(3) TEU.

31 COM(2011)585, 28 September 2011. These Member States are Austria, the Czech Republic, Germany, Estonia, Greece, France, Italy, Lithuania, Luxembourg, Latvia, Malta, the Netherlands, Portugal and Romania.

32 Strik, T., A. Böcker, M. Luiten & R. Van Oers (2012), 'The INTEC project, synthesis report. integration and naturalisation tests. The new way to European citizenship', in: Pascouau, Y. & T. Strik (eds) (2012), *Which integration policies for migrants? Interaction between the EU and its member states*, Nijmegen: Wolf Legal Publishers.

33 Belgium, Cyprus, Hungary, Latvia, Poland, Portugal and Sweden, COM(2011)585, p. 7.

impose a higher income requirement than for the acquisition of a long-term residence permit.[34]

### 5.3.2 *Practice*

The introduction of the subjective right to the EU long-term status seems difficult to reconcile with the huge variety between the Member States in the number of holders of a long-term residence permit. In its evaluation report in 2011, the Commission pointed out that 80 per cent of the LTR status holders lived in only four Member States: Estonia, Italy, Austria and the Czech Republic.[35] In 2014 there were almost 7 million holders of a permanent residence permit in the EU, but less than 3 million of them have the EU permit. Austria and Italy have large numbers: more than 200,000 in Austria and more than 2 million in Italy. But in Germany and France compared to their high number of third country nationals, only a handful have been granted LTR status.[36]

It is likely that these huge differences reflect national policy choices rather than the choices of the individual migrants. For some countries specific explanations can be given. Estonia and Slovenia granted the permit to long-term residents who did not naturalise after the disintegration of the USSR and Yugoslavia, in order to avoid large-scale statelessness. This explains why many of the EU permit holders are nationals of Russia, Ukraine, Serbia and Bosnia. Other Member States have de facto replaced the national permanent residence permit with the EU permit (Austria), or have introduced the EU permit as the first permanent permit.

But these reasons still don't explain why the permit is not applied and granted in other Member States. Groenendijk points to the relationship between the EU status and the national permanent residence status. In the Member States with low numbers of EU permit holders, long-term residents have to choose between the national permanent status and the EU long-term residence status, causing a threshold for migrants to invoke their EU rights. In other countries, the possession of a national permit is a condition for the granting of the EU permit.[37] The less migrants are aware of their rights under EU law and the benefits of the EU status, the less likely it will be that they will insist on the granting of the EU permit without unlawful requirements.

---

34 The Commission mentions Italy, Romania and Slovenia.

35 COM(2011)585, 28 September 2011, p. 10.

36 Source: Eurostat.

37 Groenendijk, C.A. (2012), 'Chapter 10, long-term residents', in: Peers, S. *et al.* (2012), *EU immigration and asylum law. Text and commentary, second revised edition, volume 2: EU immigration law*, Leiden-Boston: Nijhoff, pp. 327–330.

Another reason for differences in numbers might be the national accessibility to citizenship. If the requirements are more or less the same, then naturalization has the advantage of acquiring all the rights of a Union citizen. If naturalization implies the loss of the original nationality, migrants might still prefer to opt for a strong residence permit. In 2014, the number of naturalizations in Austria was only 6,000, while in Germany it was 90,000. Despite the different national situations, the figures imply at least that the local authorities in certain states do not actively promote the EU status, or are even not aware that migrants are entitled to the permit. In Italy and the Netherlands, public campaigning by migrant organisations and lawyers was necessary to enforce effective access to the status. Again this shows that correct transposition is only the first step, as implementation at the practical level determines the effectiveness of the transposition. But EU compliance also needs knowledge and awareness by other actors, like lawyers, courts and migrant organisations in order to create pressure at national and European level.

The lack of awareness among third country nationals might also concern the added value of the EU permit, especially the intra-EU mobility right, due to the labour market test and the restricted access to the labour market in most Member States. The Commission observed in 2011 that only small numbers of LTR third country nationals had made use of this mobility right within the EU: less than fifty per Member State.[38] The labour market test most Member States apply is probably the main cause of this disappointing number. Jesse refers specifically to this provision while questioning the harmonization purpose through EU law when the same EU law allows so much discretion that national implementation can lead to fundamentally different legal situations.[39] The provisions on intra-EU mobility and their transposition have clearly not bridged the gap between TCNs and Union citizens. Besides using the discretion the directive allows, a number of Member States do not comply with the requirements of a second Member State, like granting equal treatment and giving full access to the labour market after one year of residence.

#### 5.3.3 *New Perspectives*

The Commission mainly blames the many deficiencies in the transposition of the directive and the lack of awareness of the directive for its limited impact. It however also admits that as the instrument itself is insufficient in promoting

38 COM(2011)585, p. 10.

39 Jesse, M. (2012), 'Integration, access to employment and occupation under EU law', in: Morano-Foadi, S. & M. Malena (eds), *Integration for third country nationals in the European Union. The equality challenge*, Cheltenham (UK): Edward Elgar, pp. 145–166.

mobility, it should be amended by facilitating access to the labour market and further simplifying the acquisition of LTR status in the second Member State. As the Commission was dissatisfied with the thresholds for mobility, which the Member States had established in the directive, it laid down a *rendez-vous* clause in Article 24 in which it gave priority to amending Chapter 3 of the directive. In its evaluation report of 2011 the Commission repeated that it would propose amendments to the directive in order to further promote intra-EU mobility.[40] Five years later, no such amendment has been tabled.

But the number of reasons not to wait any longer to enhance intra-EU mobility is only growing. First, the number of third country nationals living in the EU on a permanent basis is rapidly increasing, especially since refugees and those with subsidiary protection have gained access to the permit. On 1 January 2015 almost 20 million third country nationals lived in the 28 EU Member States.[41] Second, as long as third country nationals are locked up in their Member State, no real participation in the internal market or integration into European society as such will be attained. This hampers the achievement of economic and social cohesion. Third, as the labour market test has created a de facto higher threshold with the enlargement of the EU in 2004 and later on, the prioritization of EU citizens has led to more exclusion of TCNs. Even citizens from Norway, Iceland, Liechtenstein and Switzerland have a privileged position over migrants who have lived in the EU for many years. Fourth, the accession and economic crisis has led to more competitiveness for third country nationals in their country of residence. Facing discrimination in the labour market, they end up jobless more frequently. Enlarging the scope of job opportunities would at least increase their perspective on participation. Lastly, employers as well as the national welfare systems would benefit from a better chance for a match in the labour market. The current restrictions on access to the labour market, although heavily defended, don't favour the Member States either, while 'isolated labour markets remain unattractive for foreign professionals'.[42] Demographic changes will make this match even more urgent.

Abolishing the labour market test in the second Member State, however, will not equalise the rights of LTRs and Union citizens. A more far reaching

40 COM(2011)585, p. 11.

41 Source: Eurostat.

42 Jesse, M. (2012), 'Integration, access to employment and occupation under EU law', in: Morano-Foadi, S. & M. Malena (eds), *Integration for third country nationals in the European Union. The equality challenge*, Cheltenham (UK): Edward Elgar, pp. 145–166; Kocharov, A. (2008), 'What intra-community mobility for third-country workers?', *European Law Review*, 33, pp. 913–926.

but also more effective step would be to grant them the right of free movement, for instance by enlarging the personal scope of the Union Citizens Directive. Article 45 of the Charter offers a legal basis for this. However, the current negative perception of the free movement of EU citizens makes the political feasibility of widening the scope within the short or medium term rather unlikely.

## 5.4 Conclusions

We have seen antagonistic behaviour by the Member States. The Court contributes to coherence by taking the Member States' aims of equal rights seriously. But the Member States themselves try to limit the consequences of the jurisprudence, with as one of the results that the gap with EU citizens remains large. The tendency to minimize the application of certain granted rights also creates more different categories among third country nationals, leading to a further fragmentation of their rights. All categories have a different set of rights: Turkish nationals, long-term residents, Blue Card holders, students and researchers, other types of workers, family members, refugees, and those with subsidiary protection. This provokes questions on the justification for all those differences, and compatibility with the non-discrimination principle, as enshrined in Article 18 TFEU and Article 14 ECHR. The objective of the Single Permit Directive to achieve more equal treatment, has failed due to the many derogation clauses. And so its impact is again dependent on its use by Member States, which until now have shown merely reluctance to strengthen the legal position of migrants, except with regard to the most wanted ones: the Blue Card holders. According to Jesse the privileges of the highly skilled third country nationals exactly concern the lifting of optional restrictions applied to other TCNs, like waiting periods, pre-entry tests, labour market tests etc. It is therefore legitimate to question the real purpose of those optional requirements, if they have to be removed to attract the wanted immigrants. Preventing immigration of unwanted immigrants or furthering their integration?[43]

These restrictions, leading to unequal treatment, are especially problematic as regards the ones who have settled in the EU permanently, many of them family members or long-term residents. Their rights are based in European legislation, they live in European societies, hence they de facto belong to the

43 Jesse, M. (2012), 'Integration, access to employment and occupation under EU law', in: Morano-Foadi, S. & M. Malena (eds), *Integration for third country nationals in the European Union. The equality challenge*, Cheltenham (UK): Edward Elgar, pp. 145–166.

European integration as a whole. The European Council endorses the objective that long-term legally resident third country nationals be offered the opportunity to obtain the nationality of the Member State in which they are resident. But as access to EU citizenship remains a national competence, integration of TCNs could be promoted by making nationality less determining of their rights and participation within the EU. The Commission invented the concept of 'civic citizenship', inspired by the Charter of Fundamental Rights, which would enhance successful settlement into society.[44] The Commission relaunched this initiative in 2003 and although it was supported by the European Parliament, the idea was abandoned in further Communications.[45] It is time to think of a new, similar concept, like membership. This EU membership would still be based on criteria for inclusion and exclusion, but not along the lines of nationality, and not to be determined or granted by individual Member States. Membership could be directly linked to a European rather than a national society, and safeguard full integration and mobility. Such a concept would reflect the Tampere objectives of equal rights as well as the promotion of economic and social cohesion at EU level.

There are numerous remaining research challenges regarding the evolution of the position of third country nationals within the EU. Academic research could contribute to gaining insight into the strategic use of the directives by the Member States and finding explanations for it. Multi-disciplinary research on the impact of the directives is necessary to conclude to what extent they have led to harmonization and integration of TCNs or to other, unintended effects. It could contribute to a much needed evidence-based and rational approach to European immigration policy furthering harmonization and integration. Nowadays facts are widely ignored in the politicized and polarized debate on integration. If researchers also look into explanations of the impact of the directives, they could formulate recommendations on the necessary steps required to further the aimed integration. In finding ways to reconnect the objectives of the directives, on the one hand, and the Member States on the other hand, the reluctance of the latter to reduce their discretion should be taken into account. Perseverance by the Commission is however indispensable, because of its competence to start infringement procedures and to propose legislative changes.

---

44 Communication of the Commission on a Community Immigration Policy, COM(2000)757, 22 November 2000.

45 Acosta, D. (2011), *The long-term residence status as a subsidiary form of EU citizenship. An analysis of directive 2003/109*, Leiden-Boston: Martinus Nijhoff Publications, p. 84.

## References

Acosta, D. (2011), *The Long-term residence status as a subsidiary form of EU citizenship. An analysis of directive 2003/109*, Leiden-Boston: Martinus Nijhoff Publications.

Böcker, A. & B. De Hart (2011), 'Wat zijn de bedoelde en onbedoelde effecten van het migratierecht?', in: Hertogh & Weyers (eds), *Recht van onderop. Antwoorden uit de rechtssociologie*, Nijmegen: Ars Aequi Libri, pp. 409–426.

Derluyn, I. a.o. (2009), 'Mental health problems in separated refugee adolescents', *Journal of Adolescent Health*, 44, pp. 291–297.

ECRE (2016), *Information note on family reunification for beneficiaries of international protection in Europe*, ECRE/ELENA, June 2016.

Groenendijk, C.A. (2012), 'Chapter 10, long-term residents', in: Peers, S. *et al.*, *EU immigration and asylum law. Text and commentary, second revised edition, volume 2: EU immigration law*, Leiden-Boston: Nijhoff, pp. 327–330.

Groenendijk, C.A., R. Fernhout, D.P.L.M. van Dam, R. van Oers & M.H.A. Strik, (2007), *The family reunification directive in EU member states. The first year of implementation*, (report, Nijmegen Migration Law Working Papers Series, no 2007/01). Nijmegen: Radboud University Nijmegen.

Jesse, M. (2012), 'Integration, access to employment and occupation under EU law', in: Morano-Foadi, S. & M. Malena (eds), *Integration for third country nationals in the European Union. The equality challenge*, Cheltenham, UK-Northampton: Edward Elgar, pp. 145–166.

Kocharov, A. (2008), 'What intra-community mobility for third-country workers?', *European Law Review*, 33, pp. 913–915.

Labayle, H. & Y. Pascouau (2008), *Directive 2003/86/EC on the right to family reunification, synthesis report, in the framework of the conformity checking of the transposition by member states of 10 EC directives in the sector of asylum and immigration*, Odysseus Network.

Marsden, R. & C. Harris (2012), *We started life again: integration experiences of refugee families reuniting in Glasgow*, Glasgow: British Red Cross/Scottish Refugee Council.

McDonald-Wilmsen, B. & S. Gifford (2009), 'Refugee resettlement, family separation and Australia's humanitarian programme', *New Issues in Refugee Research* Paper No. 178R.

Pascouau, Y. & H. Labayle (2011), *Conditions for family reunification under strain. A comparative study in nine EU member states*, European Policy Centre.

Peers, S. (2011), *EU justice and home affairs law*, 3rd edition, Oxford: OUP, pp. 478–485.

RASNZ (2012), *Refugee family reunification, mental health and resettlement outcomes in Aotearoa New Zealand*, Research Unit New Zealand.

Schweitzer, R. *et al.* (2006), 'Trauma, post-migration living difficulties, and social support as predictors of psychological adjustment in resettled Sudanese refugees', *Australian and New Zealand Journal of Psychiatry*, 40, pp. 179–187.

Smith, A. a.o. (2004), 'Serial migration and its implications for the parent–child relationship: a retrospective analysis of the experiences of the children of Caribbean immigrants', *Cultural Diversity Ethnic Minority Psychology*, 10:2, pp. 107–22.

Strik, T. (2011), *Besluitvorming over asiel- en migratierichtlijnen. De wisselwerking tussen nationaal en Europees niveau*, Den Haag: Boom Juridische Uitgevers.

Strik, T., A. Böcker, M. Luiten & R. Van Oers (2012), 'The INTEC project, synthesis report. Integration and naturalisation tests. The new way to European citizenship', in: Pascouau, Y. & T. Strik (eds), *Which integration policies for migrants? Interaction between the EU and its member states*, Nijmegen: Wolf Legal Publishers.

Strik, T., B. De Hart & E. Nissen (2013), *Family reunification: a barrier or facilitator of integration? A comparative study*, Nijmegen: Wolf Legal Publishers.

UNHCR (2013), A new beginning: Refugee integration in Europe, September 2013, p. 127, <www.refworld.org/docid/522980604.html>.

Van der Vleuten, A. (1998), 'Two-level interaction as source of influence: the European Union and equal treatment policies', in: Reinalda, B. & B. Verbeek (eds), *Autonomous policy making by international organizations*, London: Routledge, pp. 62–78.

# PART 2

## *Europe in the World*

CHAPTER 6

# Current Protection Dilemmas in the European Union

*Jens Vedsted-Hansen*

## 6.1 Introductory Remarks on Topic and Context

The ongoing migratory movements call for academic attention and reflection, not only because they are the crucial reality of life for thousands of forcibly displaced persons, at times creating serious challenges for their host societies in Europe and, more often, beyond Europe. In addition, the recent increase of the numbers of persons on the move – not least due to the protracted conflict in Syria and the overburdening of protection capacities in the countries neighbouring that conflict – and the changes of the composition of migration flows also represent a significant transformation of the migratory landscape in and around Europe that necessitates rethinking of the challenges posed by reality for research on issues of migration and asylum law and policy. This is not least the case as regards the current situation for the Common European Asylum System.

Whereas the recast instruments constituting the second phase of the Common European Asylum System had formally come into place by the middle of 2013 and were due to be implemented by Member States in 2014 and 2015,[1]

1 Qualification II Directive: Directive 2011/95/EU of the European Parliament and of the Council of 13 December 2011 on standards for the qualification of third-country nationals or stateless persons as beneficiaries of international protection, for a uniform status for refugees or for persons eligible for subsidiary protection, and for the content of the protection granted, *OJ* 2011 L 337, p. 9;
Asylum Procedures II Directive: Directive 2013/32/EU of the European Parliament and of the Council of 26 June 2013 on common procedures for granting and withdrawing international protection, *OJ* 2013 L 180, p. 249;
Reception Conditions II Directive: Directive 2013/33/EU of the European Parliament and of the Council of 26 June 2013 laying down standards for the reception of applicants for international protection, *OJ* 2013 L 180, p. 96;
Dublin III Regulation: Regulation (EU) No. 604/2013 of the European Parliament and of the Council 26 June 2013 establishing the criteria and mechanisms for determining the Member State responsible for examining an application for international protection lodged

 | DOI 10.1163/9789004330467_007

developments on the ground during 2014 and 2015 illustrated the need to take initiatives for developing further this European system. Thus, if the Common European Asylum System is genuinely meant to be able to form the basis of the European Union's joint efforts to prevent displaced persons from suffering or dying, the EU legislative instruments and not least their transposition and application in the Member States need to be subject to further revision aiming to level, if not eradicate the differences in the treatment of protection seekers existing so far. Similarly, if there is a sincere intention of alleviating the burden of overstretched southern Member States and to assist their recovery from the continuing and probably enhanced risk of malfunctions within their asylum systems, there is a need for fundamental rethinking of the protective structures underlying the Common European Asylum System, in particular the distributive and protective challenges inherent in the Dublin Regulation.

In addition, it seems inevitable to rethink the enforcement strategy hitherto practised by the European Commission so as to secure that Member States actually comply with their obligations under EU law in the area of asylum and refugee protection.

In this chapter, I shall first identify the dysfunctional structures and tendencies of the Common European Asylum System that have become ever clearer during the asylum crisis emerging since 2014 (section 6.2). The following sections will focus on some legal implications of these deficiencies and the attempts to remedy them in law and policy: The notion of 'mutual trust' and the ensuing legal presumption of compliance with EU legal obligations that have played a significant role in the construction and development of this system as an element of the broader Area of Freedom, Security and Justice, and the protective shortcomings of this notion and its alleged status of a 'principle' of EU law will be discussed (section 6.3). The varying emphasis on and direction of the external dimensions of EU migration control and asylum policy will then be pointed out with a special focus on the EU-Turkey arrangements concluded in 2016 (section 6.4). The potential of upholding and strengthening the positive protection developments, that were to an appreciable extent brought about by the Common European Asylum System, shall be discussed in the light of developments in asylum law and policy and the challenges represented by recent legislative proposals (Sections 6.5 and 6.6).

---

in one of the Member States by a third-country national or a stateless person, *OJ* 2013 L 180, p. 31;

Eurodac II Regulation: Regulation (EU) No. 603/2013 of the European Parliament and of the Council of 26 June 2013 on the establishment of 'Eurodac' for the comparison of fingerprints for the effective application of Regulation (EU) No. 604/2013, *OJ* 2013 L 180, p. 1.

The activities of the CMR over the past 20 years reflect the prevailing diversity within the sub-discipline of migration law, encompassing both legal, sociological and more policy-oriented studies. While the CMR has traditionally held a particularly strong position in the studies of intra-EU free movement rights for workers and other economically active persons, and later on for Union citizens in general, the Centre has also conducted significant research on issues pertaining to third country nationals' residence rights under EU law, either derived from Union citizens' residence rights, on the basis of the EU-Turkey association agreement or pursuant to EU legislation adopted under the common asylum and immigration policy that has got an ever more solid Treaty basis, in particular since the entry into force of the Treaty of Amsterdam in 1999. During that same period the CMR has also been very active in the study of various aspects and legislative elements of the Common European Asylum System that will be the main focus of this chapter, reflecting on the current protection dilemmas in the EU. Importantly, though, the developments that have been challenging the harmonisation of EU asylum law and policy, and thus framing the current dilemmas of refugee protection, have also proven to be challenges to the wider system of intra-EU free movement rights.

## 6.2 Dysfunctional Structures and Tendencies of the Common European Asylum System

### 6.2.1 *The Initial Aspirations – From Tampere to Stockholm*

As a starting point for the discussion of protection dilemmas in the European Union, we shall note the basic features of the evolving EU asylum system as these may point to important factors underlying these dilemmas. Notwithstanding the fact that the current asylum crisis was sparked off by the significant increase of the number of arrivals of asylum seekers and migrants during the past couple of years, some basic causes of the asylum crisis can be identified by looking back on the origins of the EU asylum system in order to identify the apparent shortcomings of this system and, in particular, its interaction with the various asylum systems of EU Member States.

The still incomplete nature of the Common European Asylum System becomes specially clear when taking into account that it has been the aspiration ever since the entry into force of the Treaty of Amsterdam, as witnessed by the European Council's 1999 Tampere Conclusions setting the directions for the first phase of the evolving Common European Asylum System. Here it was 'agreed to work towards establishing a Common European Asylum System, based on the full and inclusive application of the Geneva Convention, thus ensuring that nobody is sent back to persecution, i.e. maintaining the principle of non-refoulement'.[2]

As to the elements of the prospective Common European Asylum System, the European Council continued:

> This System should include, in the short term, a clear and workable determination of the State responsible for the examination of an asylum application, common standards for a fair and efficient asylum procedure, common minimum conditions of reception of asylum seekers, and the approximation of rules on the recognition and content of the refugee status. It should also be completed with measures on subsidiary forms of protection offering an appropriate status to any person in need of such protection (…)[3]

Ten years later, the 2009 Stockholm Programme reaffirmed the principles adopted the previous year in the European Pact on Immigration and Asylum[4] and recalled the basic commitments here set out. In addition to organising legal migration to take account of Member States' priorities, needs and reception capacities, as well as encouraging integration, controlling illegal immigration and making border controls more effective, the 2008 European Pact had set out the commitment to constructing 'a Europe of asylum'. Under this heading the European Council had 'solemnly reiterated' that any persecuted foreigner is entitled to obtain aid and protection in the territory of the European Union in application of the Geneva Convention and other relevant treaties, and stressed that the necessary strengthening of European border controls 'should not prevent access to protection systems by those people entitled to benefit under them'.[5]

Against this background, the Stockholm Programme declared the European Council's commitment to the objective of 'establishing a common area of protection and solidarity based on a common asylum procedure and a uniform status for those granted international protection'. The Common European

2 European Council: Presidency Conclusions, Tampere European Council, 15–16 October 1999, para. 13.

3 European Council: Presidency Conclusions, Tampere European Council, 15–16 October 1999, para. 14.

4 European Council: European Pact on Immigration and Asylum, 24 September 2008 (Council doc. 13440/08 ASIM 72, not published in the Official Journal).

5 European Council: European Pact on Immigration and Asylum, 24 September 2008 (Council doc. 13440/08 ASIM 72, not published in the Official Journal), Section IV, p. 11.

Asylum System (CEAS) should be based on high protection standards while 'due regard should also be given to fair and effective procedures capable of preventing abuse'.[6] As regards the ambition of harmonising standards, the European council stated:

> It is crucial that individuals, regardless of the Member State in which their application for asylum is lodged, are offered an equivalent level of treatment as regards reception conditions, and the same level as regards procedural arrangements and status determination. The objective should be that similar cases should be treated alike and result in the same outcome.[7]

Realising that there were still significant differences between national provisions and their application, the Stockholm Programme further proclaimed the aim to 'achieve a higher degree of harmonisation'. For this reason:

> the establishment of CEAS, should remain a key policy objective for the Union. Common rules, as well as a better and more coherent application of them, *should prevent or reduce secondary movements* within the Union, and *increase mutual trust* between Member States.[8]

Notably, the European Council at the same time emphasised that 'The Dublin System remains a cornerstone in building the CEAS, as it clearly allocates responsibility for the examination of asylum application'.[9] The rather unexplored relationship between the Dublin System and the legislative intention of effective harmonisation of asylum rules as well as the actual application of such harmonised rules may, however, have been laying the ground – or at least the 'cornerstone' – for subsequent dilemmas and functional problems within the Common European Asylum System. Therefore, these programmatic statements call for reconsideration of the specific elements of the CEAS.

### 6.2.2 *The Dublin System as a Source of Protective Failure?*

When considering the Dublin System with its underlying assumption of 'mutual trust' the notion, first expressed in the Tampere Conclusions, of a 'clear

6 The Stockholm Programme – An open and secure Europe serving and protecting citizens, adopted by the European Council in December 2009, *OJ* 2010 C 115, p. 1, para 6.2.

7 The Stockholm Programme, *OJ* 2010 C 115, p. 1, para. 6.2.

8 The Stockholm Programme, *OJ* 2010 C 115, p. 1, para. 6.2.1 (italics added).

9 The Stockholm Programme, *OJ* 2010 C 115, p. 1, para. 6.2.1.

and workable determination of the State responsible for the examination'[10] of asylum applications springs to mind inasmuch as the basic features and developments of the Dublin System may be seen as symbolic of the more general dysfunctions of the EU asylum system. The various problems stemming from the Dublin System can be identified at least at three different, yet interconnected levels: First, the *distribution of responsibilities* and corresponding burdens of protection in terms of reception conditions, asylum procedures and the actual protection of those found in need thereof. Second, the *structure of incentives* for Member States as well as asylum seekers in terms of compliance or non-compliance with the CEAS standards supposed to govern their conduct. Third, the impact of the Dublin System on the *level of protection* of asylum seekers and refugees in compliance with the existing standards under international law and EU law.

If the Dublin System may from the very outset, by way of its design, have had unfair or unjust distributive implications because of its impact on the sharing of the responsibilities and burdens of protection among Member States,[11] in any event this inherent quantitative imbalance has gradually acquired new qualities of protective dysfunction. This has resulted in the failure to uphold and respect the most central fundamental rights of the asylum seekers whose right to protection it was meant to secure, as amply demonstrated by realities on the ground in a number of Member States and, yet with some reluctance and consequent delay, as recognised by domestic courts and not least the European courts.[12] This development is closely linked to the legal meaning and application of the notion of 'mutual trust' within the CEAS that shall be further discussed below in section 6.3.

10 European Council: Presidency Conclusions, Tampere European Council, 15–16 October 1999, para. 14 (quoted above at note 3).

11 For an extensive discussion of the Dublin System from the perspective of burden sharing and solidarity between EU Member States, see: Madeleine Garlick (2016), *Solidarity under strain. Solidarity and fair sharing of responsibility in law and practice for the international protection of refugees in the European Union* (Dissertation, Nijmegen), pp. 151–168.

12 See, as significant case examples from the two European courts: ECtHR 21 January 2011, Appl. no. 30696/09, GC, *M.S.S. v. Belgium and Greece,* ECLI:CE:ECHR:2011:0121; CJEU 21 December 2011, Joined cases C-411/10 and C-493/10, *N.S. v. Secretary of State for the Home Department* and *M.E. and Others v. Minister for Justice, Equality and Law Reform,* ECLI:EU:C:2011:865; cf. Jens Vedsted-Hansen (2015), 'Reception Conditions as Human Rights: Pan-European Standard or Systemic Deficiencies?', in: V. Chetail, P. De Bruycker & F. Maiani (eds.), *Reforming the common european asylum system: the New European refugee law*, Leiden: Brill, pp. 317–352.

It is to be noted, though, that the rulings of the European Court of Human Rights and, at least to some extent, the Court of Justice of the European Union are likely to have created incentives for asylum seekers and Member States not to act in accordance with CEAS standards. Instead, asylum seekers were induced to escape dysfunctional asylum systems by way of secondary movements to other Member States, while Member States in charge of such dysfunctional systems were rewarded for their failure to comply with the relevant CEAS standards due to the judicial protection of asylum seekers against being returned to those Member States under the Dublin Regulation.

In addition to the distributive aspects of the Dublin System, likely to have played a crucial role in exacerbating the asylum crisis in southern Member States, the gradually increased dysfunctions of the Common European Asylum System are inextricably linked to the fact that the Dublin and Eurodac Regulations, aiming to relocate asylum seekers according to the criteria for responsibility between Member States for the examination of asylum applications, were adopted and entered into force as far more complete regulatory instruments than the CEAS legislation intended to harmonise the procedural and substantive standards of protection. Thus, the very premise of forcibly relocating asylum seekers to other Member States under the Dublin System sits ill with the fact that the protective elements of the CEAS have been subject to only gradual harmonisation with vague standards set by the EU legislature and with incomplete implementation of these standards by a number of Member States.

While it would obviously go beyond the limits of this chapter to account in any detail for the regulatory flaws of each of the asylum instruments adopted during the first phase of the Common European Asylum System, and how these flaws were not completely remedied by the recast instruments of the second phase, a few examples could be mentioned in order to illustrate the point that forcible relocation under the Dublin System did make crucial differences for the affected asylum seekers in terms of the protective standards they were offered as well as the likelihood of obtaining protection altogether.

Perhaps most importantly, the plethora of optional clauses of the first generation of asylum Directives have allowed Member States to go to a lower level of protection. That was particularly clear for the 2005 Asylum Procedures Directive[13] that contained numerous exception or derogation clauses allowing Member States to have procedural rules or practices below the 'minimum

13 Council Directive 2005/85/EC of 1 December 2005 on minimum standards on procedures in Member States for granting and withdrawing refugee status, *OJ* 2005 L 326, p. 13.

standards' purportedly adopted by the Directive.[14] Even the recast Qualification Directive has retained certain optional clauses, both in the context of the definition of beneficiaries of protection and in the standards on the content of international protection.[15] Thus, it is still permissible for Member States to reduce the level of social assistance for beneficiaries of subsidiary protection, which is indeed an example of weak harmonisation that is likely to negatively impact on a considerable part of the beneficiaries of international protection, and hard to reconcile with the principle of non-discrimination.[16] In addition, the option of differential treatment given to Member States by such a Directive provision may eventually in itself contribute to the unwanted secondary movements of asylum seekers.

Given the currently enhanced efforts to combat this phenomenon, it may seem counterproductive to uphold optional provisions that cannot but exacerbate asylum seekers' predisposition to move to those Member States where prospects of protection are better or protection standards higher. Interestingly, it appears that the optional clause in the Qualification Directive, permitting the grant of lower social assistance to subsidiary protection holders has in fact not been used as extensively by Member States as one might have expected. Even so, however, the very existence of the optional clause constitutes a problem not only as a matter of principle, but indeed also in terms of a potential harmonisation problem given the fact that many Member States' strategy during the past year has been to respond to the increased arrivals by reducing protection standards to the legally possible minimum and possibly even beyond in order to reduce their relative attractiveness as an asylum country. In this light, optional clauses are likely to be utilised more widely in the future with a view to creating such deterrent effects on asylum seekers.

---

14 For a critical examination of the 'optionalist' Asylum Procedures Directive, see: Jens Vedsted-Hansen (2012), 'Common EU standards on asylum – optional harmonisation and exclusive procedures?', in: Elspeth Guild & Paul Minderhoud (eds.), *The first decade of EU migration and asylum law,* Leiden: Martinus Nijhoff, pp. 255–271, in particular pp. 257–261.

15 Directive 2011/95 (see note 1). Examples of optional provisions are Article 5(3) on protection needs arising *sur place* in cases of subsequent applications and Article 28(2) on derogation from the general rule on equal treatment of the two categories of beneficiaries as regards the right to social assistance.

16 Cf. recital 17 of the Directive 2011/95, referring to obligations under international law, including in particular those prohibiting discrimination, with respect to the treatment of persons falling within the scope of the Directive; see also the Commission proposal for a recast Qualification Directive, COM(2009)551 final/2, 23 October 2009, Explanatory Memorandum, p. 8.

One may speculate whether more efficient enforcement measures could have been taken by the European Commission, and whether that might have remedied the situation and prevented the tendencies towards collapse of asylum systems in an increasing number of Member States. The Commission itself seems to be aware of the need for more efficient enforcement of the EU asylum legislation, as reflected in its statement in May 2015 that '[t]he priority is to ensure a full and coherent implementation of the Common European Asylum System. This will be supported by *a new systematic monitoring process*, to look into the implementation and application of the asylum rules and foster mutual trust'.[17] Against this background, it is hard to ignore the possibility that the Commission's somewhat reluctant enforcement strategy may be part of the explanation of the actual collapses that have caused the gradual dissolution of the Dublin System that some would welcome and others regret, depending on their basic position towards the legitimacy and operability of this distributive system.

## 6.3 From Mutual Trust to Mutual Frustration

### 6.3.1 *Varying Thresholds for Rebuttal of Mutual Trust*

The increasingly successful legal challenges of the Dublin System during the past few years are arguably reflecting the inherent dichotomy between the basic assumptions underlying the Common European Asylum System, as described above. This CEAS dichotomy is inextricably linked to the assumption of *mutual trust* that is now being considered a 'principle of mutual trust between the Member States ... of fundamental importance in EU law, given that it allows an area without internal borders to be created and maintained'.[18] While the notion of mutual trust is of general importance to the implementation and application of EU legislative instruments within the Area of Freedom, Security and Justice, and thus also to EU harmonisation of asylum law, it plays a particular role within the Dublin System, due to the potential of this system

17 European Commission, Communication on *A European Agenda on Migration*, COM(2015)240 final, 13 May 2015, p. 12. In particular, the Commission here stated its intention to 'prioritise transposition and implementation in practice' of the recently adopted recast Directives on Asylum Procedures and on Reception Conditions in the context of infringement procedures.

18 Cf. CJEU Opinion 18 December 2014, *Opinion 2/13 on the Accession of the European Union to the ECHR*, para. 191, referring to CJEU judgment 21 December 2011 *N.S. and Others* (C-411/10 and C-493/10, ECLI:EU:C:2011:865 see above note 12) paras. 78–80.

of forcibly relocating asylum seekers to the Member State responsible for their case in accordance with the criteria for responsibility for the examination of applications laid down in the Dublin Regulation. Thus, the rationale of the Dublin System is the legislatively established confidence in all other Member States' willingness and ability to provide adequate protection to persons claiming to need it, in compliance with the various CEAS instruments on reception conditions, examination procedures and definitions of persons in need of international protection as well as the standards of treatment for such persons.[19]

The mutual presumption of compliance with CEAS standards has been subject to significant modification as a result of proceedings before the two European courts that have maintained that such a presumption cannot be conclusive, but must be subject to rebuttal.[20] At the same time, however, these courts have not been unequivocal as regards the threshold that has to be met in order to rebut the presumption of compliance in order to modify the mutual trust that is supposed to be the point of departure. Subsequent to the two landmark rulings in 2011 from the European Court of Human Rights and the Court of Justice of the European Union there was quite considerable legal uncertainty as to whether the criteria for rebutting the presumption of compliance should be the ordinary 'real risk' test under Article 3 ECHR or rather the finding of 'systemic deficiencies' in the asylum system of the Member State normally responsible for the examining of the application.[21]

The European Court of Human Rights settled the issue of the requisite threshold for rebuttal of the mutual trust presumption when delivering its judgment in 2014 in the *Tarakhel* case which upheld, or perhaps rehabilitated, the 'real risk' test and thereby apparently abandoned any requirement of

19 Cf. Battjes, H. (2006), *European asylum law and international law*, Leiden: Martinus Nijhoff, pp. 418–421; Noll, G. (2001), 'Formalism v. empiricism: some reflections on the Dublin convention on the occasion of recent European case law', *Nordic Journal of International Law* 70, pp. 161–182, in particular pp. 162–164 and pp. 181–182; Boeles, P., M. den Heijer, G. Lodder & K. Wouters (2014), *European migration law*, 2. Ed., Cambridge: Intersentia, pp. 260–261.

20 See, in particular, the ECtHR and CJEU judgments mentioned in note 12.

21 For an analysis of the aforementioned judgments from the ECtHR and the CJEU and their interrelation, as well as the subsequent line of ECtHR cases on similar issues, see: Jens Vedsted-Hansen (2015), 'Reception conditions as human rights: pan-european standard or systemic deficiencies?' (note 12), in particular pp. 331–338 and pp. 342–347; see also Cathryn Costello (2012), 'Courting access to asylum in Europe: recent supranational jurisprudence explored', *Human Rights Law Review* 12, pp. 287–339; Violeta Moreno-Lax (2012), 'Dismantling the Dublin system: M.S.S. v. Belgium and Greece', *European Journal of Migration and Law* 14, pp. 1–31; Cathryn Costello (2016), *The human rights of migrants and refugees in European law*, Oxford: Oxford University Press, pp. 255–275.

'systemic' flaw or deficiency under Article 3 ECHR in order to attract protection against *refoulement* in connection with Dublin transfers.[22] In this case, the Grand Chamber referred to the possibility that, given the current situation in the Italian reception system, a significant number of asylum seekers transferred to Italy might be left without accommodation or accommodated in overcrowded or even insalubrious or violent conditions. It was therefore incumbent on the Swiss authorities to obtain assurances that on arrival in Italy the applicants would be 'received in facilities and in conditions adapted to the age of the children' and that the family would be kept together. The Italian Government had only made rather general statements about the treatment of asylum seeking families with children in the reception system. In the absence of 'detailed and reliable information concerning the specific facility, the physical reception conditions and the preservation of the family unit', the Court considered that the Swiss authorities did not possess *sufficient assurances* that the applicants would be taken charge of in a manner adapted to the age of the children in case of transfer to Italy. Without having first obtained *individual guarantees* of reception conditions adapted to the children's age and keeping the family together, transfer of the family to Italy would be in violation of Article 3 ECHR.[23]

### 6.3.2 *Individual Guarantees in Generalised Terms?*

The 'assurance' terminology introduced by the European Court of Human Rights in *Tarakhel* provided little detail on the contents and enforcement of the necessary guarantees, and the judgment had no indication of the criteria for the reception conditions to be considered adequate. Nonetheless, all asylum seeking children, whether alone or accompanied by parents,[24] would in consequence of this judgment be entitled to have concrete guarantees on the prospective reception conditions in Italy issued in each individual case as a precondition for any transfer decision. Here again, however, the Court's clarification has proven to be only a temporary solution to the legal problems raised in the context of challenging Dublin transfers to Member States with deficient asylum systems.

In the first two *post-Tarakhel* cases on transfer to Italy before the European Court of Human Rights, the Court accepted the respondent State's decision to

22 ECtHR 4 November 2014, Appl. no. 29217/12, GC, *Tarakhel v. Switzerland*. See: Jens Vedsted-Hansen (2015), 'Reception Conditions as Human Rights: Pan-European Standard or Systemic Deficiencies?' (note 12), pp. 347–350.

23 ECtHR 4 November 2014, Appl. no. 29217/12, GC, *Tarakhel v. Switzerland*, paras. 120–122.

24 ECtHR 4 November 2014, Appl. no. 29217/12, GC, *Tarakhel v. Switzerland*, para. 99.

transfer single applicants who were in personal situations entirely different from the *Tarakhel* family.[25] The first applicant was an able young man with no dependents.[26] In the second case the applicant was a young man invoking the risk of inadequate medical treatment in Italy and the consequent serious deterioration of his mental health status, and the Court noted the medical information confirming that he had severe symptoms of post-traumatic stress disorder, but held – in the light of its findings in the *Tarakhel* judgment that deficiencies of the Italian reception system could not in themselves act as a bar to all removals of asylum seekers to that country – that his condition did not meet the threshold of 'very exceptional circumstances' normally applied in Article 3 cases concerning health condition as a barrier to removal.[27]

In the meantime, the Italian Ministry of Interior sent a 'circular letter' to the Dublin Units in all other Member States, providing a brief description of the system of SPRAR reception centres as well as a generally phrased statement according to which 161 'specific places' in 29 specified SPRAR centres had been 'reserved for family groups in the framework of the implementation of local reception projects'.[28] Whereas the European Court of Human Rights quoted the letter in two decisions from November 2015, these decisions cannot be seen as expressing general acceptance of the information here provided as a sufficient alternative to the individual guarantees that the Court in *Tarakhel* considered a necessary precondition to Dublin transfers to Italy of families with children. Notably, in one of these cases the Italian Ministry of Interior had already before the issuance of the circular letter sent a letter to the Netherlands' Dublin Unit titled '*Tarakhel Garanzie*' with an enclosed note detailing a reception project regarding the transfer of the applicant and her child.[29] This letter could therefore reasonably be understood as an individual guarantee in the sense of the *Tarakhel* judgment. In the other case, the applicants were a mother and

25 In addition to the cases mentioned below, the ECtHR has decided to strike out the applications in cases where the respondent State had accepted to carry out the examination of the asylum seeker's application for protection or granted protection, so that there was no longer a risk of removal to Italy, see: ECtHR decision 2 June 2015, Appl. no. 7149/12, *K.O.J. v. Netherlands*; ECtHR decision 7 July 2015, Appl. no. 50165/14, *T.A. et autres c. Suisse*; ECtHR decision 17 November 2015, Appl. no. 288686/14, *L.N.T. v. Netherlands and Italy*.

26 ECtHR decision 13 January 2015, Appl. no. 51428/10, *A.M.E. v. Netherlands*.

27 ECtHR judgment 30 June 2015, Appl. no. 39350/13, *A.S. v. Switzerland*, paras. 31–33 and 35–38.

28 Circular letter of 8 June 2015 from the Italian Ministry of Interior; the letter is quoted in the ECtHR decision 28 June 2016, Appl. no. 15636/16, *N.A. and others v. Denmark*, para. 11.

29 ECtHR decision 17 November 2015, Appl. no. 54000/11, *A.T.H. v. Netherlands*, para. 22; the Court referred to the letter of 4 May 2015 in para. 38 of the decision.

two daughters aged 16 and 18 years at the time of the Court's decision, and thus markedly different from the situation of the *Tarakhel* family.[30] Uncertainty could, however, be caused by the following statement in the Court's inadmissibility decision:

> 'The Court has noted the applicants' concern that the 161 places earmarked so far will be insufficient but, *in the absence of any concrete indication in the case file*, does not find it demonstrated that the applicants will be unable to benefit from such a place when they arrive in Italy'.[31]

Whereas this statement was somewhat unclear, and not necessarily easy to reconcile with the Court's own line of reasoning in *Tarakhel*, the Court appears to have dissociated itself more clearly from that precedent in a case that was declared inadmissible in the summer of 2016. Here the applicants were a 23-year-old mother and her three children aged one and two years whose transfer from Denmark to Italy under the Dublin Regulation had initially been conditioned on the provision of an individual guarantee meeting the criteria set out in the *Tarakhel* judgment. However, in the light of the Italian circular letter of 8 June 2015 and statements by the Italian Government at a meeting in the EU 'Dublin Contact Committee' on 24 June 2015, the Danish Immigration Service later decided to transfer the family to Italy without any further assurances as to their reception conditions. The modified transfer decision was upheld by the Danish Refugee Appeals Board.

When the case was brought before the European Court of Human Rights, the Court accepted this decision in a manner that may seem to presuppose some kind of assurance of adequate reception conditions in the concrete case without insisting on the existence of any individual guarantee. As to the applicant's personal situation, the Court first noted that, similar to the applicants in *Tarakhel*, the applicant was a single mother with two young children. However, unlike the situation in *Tarakhel*, the Danish authorities – as regards transfers to Italy under the Dublin Regulation – would decide in consultation with the Italian authorities how and when the transfer of an asylum seeker to the competent Italian authorities would take place. In particular, where it concerned a family with children, 'prior notice of transfer' would be given to the Italian authorities, thus 'allowing the latter to identify where adequate accommodation

30 ECtHR decision of 3 November 2015, Appl. no. 21459/14, *J.A. and others v. Netherlands*.

31 ECtHR decision of 3 November 2015, Appl. no. 21459/14, *J.A. and others v. Netherlands*, para. 31 (italics added).

is available'.[32] The Court then took issue with the requirement of obtaining pre-transfer individual guarantees:

> The Court accepts that for *efficiency* reasons the Italian authorities cannot be expected to keep open and unoccupied for an extended period of time places in specific reception and accommodation centres reserved for asylum-seekers awaiting transfer to Italy in accordance with the Dublin Regulation and that, for this reason, *once a guarantee of placement in a reception centre has been received by the State requesting transfer, transfer should take place as quickly as practically possible.*
>
> The Court notes that the Refugee Appeals Board's decision of 3 February 2016 was based, among other things, on the circular letter of 8 June 2015 from Italy and Italy's subsequent assurances on the appropriate standard of its reception capacity at the meeting of the Contact Committee on 24 June 2015 … It was thus a *prerequisite for the applicants' removal* to Italy that they would be *accommodated in one of the said reception facilities earmarked* for families with minor children, that those facilities satisfied the requirements of suitable accommodation which could be inferred from Tarakhel and, in addition, that the Italian Government would be notified of the applicants' particular needs before the removal.[33]

Thus, while apparently still requiring a 'guarantee of placement' and considering it a 'prerequisite' for the transfer that the applicants be accommodated in one of the earmarked reception centres, the Court goes on pointing out that it 'understands from the two circular letters … that the applicant and her children will be placed together in one of the reception facilities in Italy which have been earmarked for families with minor children'.[34] Thus, it may seem that the circular letters and other *general*(*ised*) information are more or less being accepted as replacing the *individual* guarantees that were formally required by the Court in its *Tarakhel* judgment.

---

32 ECtHR decision 28 June 2016 *N.A. and others v. Denmark* (Appl. no. 15636/16), para. 28.

33 ECtHR decision 28 June 2016 *N.A. and others v. Denmark* (Appl. no. 15636/16), paras. 29–30 (italics added).

34 ECtHR decision 28 June 2016 *N.A. and others v. Denmark* (Appl. no. 15636/16), para. 31; reference is here made to a second circular letter from the Italian Ministry of Interior, dated 15 February 2016, cf. para. 19.

### 6.3.3 *Judicial Pragmatism vs. Legal Certainty*

There may indeed be good reasons for the shift towards a more pragmatic approach in this regard, insofar as the requirement of individual pre-transfer guarantees might actually have rather unfortunate practical implications in terms of reducing the efficiency of the administration of scarce reception conditions. It is not beyond doubt, however, that solving problems of administrative efficiency by this kind of judicial approach may be obtained at the expense of individual asylum seekers being left without effective remedy against transfers that eventually may not be implemented in compliance with the Court's assumptions. At the same time, this pragmatic approach is not necessarily helpful towards a sustainable solution to the burden sharing problems underlying the deficiencies of the Italian reception system.

In any event, the judicial responses so far from the European Court of Human Rights concerning the Dublin Regulation are unlikely to prevent future challenges in terms of political controversies over the overall distributive fairness of the existing system towards both Member States and asylum seekers, as well as legal disputes due to the inherent problem of enforcing the distribution of asylum seekers as long as fundamental rights compliance has not yet been secured in a genuinely Common European Asylum System harmonising reception conditions, asylum procedures, determination of persons in need of international protection and the standards of treatment of the persons who are found to be in need of protection.

## 6.4 External Dimensions of Current EU Asylum Law and Policy

While the increased arrivals at the borders of southern EU Member States during the past few years are inextricably linked to the deterioration of human rights conditions in a number of Middle Eastern and African countries, part of the explanation for the increased numbers during 2014 and 2015 may arguably have been the tendency towards shifting interception strategies in the Mediterranean. In particular since the shipwrecks off the island of Lampedusa in October 2013, causing the death of probably close to 400 persons, the Italian Government redirected the efforts of its coast guard to having a stronger emphasis on search and rescue operations. Thus, the costly Italian operation *Mare Nostrum* contributed to reducing the deterrent or deflective elements of the border controls hitherto carried out in the Mediterranean.

The EU's response to this may be characterised as somewhat ambiguous, as was illustrated by the less protective operation *Triton*, replacing *Mare Nostrum* since November 2014 and coordinated by the EU border control agency Frontex. More recently, this was supplemented by the operation *EUNAVFOR MED*, an anti-migrant smuggling operation established by the EU in May 2015 with the mission of 'contributing to the disruption of the business model of human smuggling and trafficking networks',[35] later renamed operation *Sophia* and gradually developing through different phases and with additional tasks such as training the Libyan coast guard.[36]

In addition to these military operations, apparently re-establishing the extraterritorial enforcement of immigration control at the external borders of southern Member States, the EU entered into negotiations with Turkey in order to step up cooperation on the prevention of 'illegal migration flows … in view of the situation in Syria and Iraq'.[37] Leaving the details of the rather interesting negotiation process aside,[38] it resulted in the much debated agreement on a statement – as such not formally considered an international 'agreement' for the purposes of Articles 216–218 TFEU, and therefore not governed by the rules on procedures and competences laid down in these provisions – between the EU and Turkey in March 2016.[39]

Three elements in the statement should be mentioned as being of particular significance to the current protection dilemmas of the EU:

- Point (1) according to which 'All new irregular migrants crossing from Turkey into Greek islands … will be returned to Turkey … in full accordance with EU and international law, thus excluding any kind of collective expulsion', and

35 Council Decision (CFSP) 2015/778 of 18 May on a European Union military operation in the Southern Central Mediterranean (EUNAVFOR MED), OJ 2015 L 122, p. 31, Article 1, cf. recital (5); for an analysis of the legal issues arising in the context of this operation, see: Graham Butler & Martin Ratcovich (2016), 'Operation Sophia in uncharted waters: European and international law challenges for the EU naval mission in the Mediterranean sea', *Nordic Journal of International Law* 85, pp. 235–259.

36 See: Thierry Tardy (2015), 'Operation Sophia: tackling the refugee crisis with military means', *Brief Issue* 30/2015, EU Institute for Security Studies, Paris.

37 Statement from the special meeting of the European Council on migratory pressures in the Mediterranean, 23 April 2015.

38 For an overview of the preparatory process and its likely outcome, see: Steve Peers & Emanuela Roman (2016), 'The EU, Turkey and the refugee crisis: what could possibly go wrong?' blog post at *EU Law Analysis*, 5 February 2016.

39 EU-Turkey statement, 18 March 2016, Press release 144/16 from the European Council, 18 March 2016.

- Point (2) on the resettlement from Turkey to the EU of one Syrian refugee for every Syrian being returned to Turkey from the Greek islands according to the first point.
- Point (3) stating the Turkish promise to take 'any necessary measures to prevent new sea or land routes for illegal migration opening from Turkey to the EU'.

From a legal perspective, point (1) raises the most straightforward, yet rather difficult question of the permissibility of returning asylum seekers to a third country without having examined their request for international protection. In this case, the difficulty in considering Turkey as a 'safe third country' – the most likely legal justification of the immediate return of asylum seekers to Turkey as apparently intended by the EU-Turkey arrangement – is increased by the fact that Turkey is not a full party to the UN Refugee Convention as it has limited its protection obligation to refugees from Europe, in accordance with Article 1 B of the Convention. The question is not immediately answered by the Asylum Procedures Directive which stipulates that in order to consider an application as inadmissible under the 'safe third country' clause in Article 33, the applicant must be treated in accordance with the prohibition of direct and indirect *refoulement*, and the possibility must exist in the relevant non-Member State to request refugee status and, if found to be a refugee, to receive 'protection in accordance with the Geneva Convention'.[40] Although the wording does not explicitly require the third country to be a party to the Refugee Convention, it would seem very difficult, if not impossible, for a Member State to establish the existence of the adequate possibility of protection – in both the procedural and the substantive sense – with a sufficient degree of certainty to fulfil the requirement laid down in the Directive, if the third country in question has not undertaken the legal commitments under the Refugee Convention or equivalent international obligations.[41] Similarly, the refugee protection standards under international law would, as a general rule, also require a 'safe

40 Asylum Procedures Directive (see note 1), Article 38(1)(a)–(e), cf. Article 33(2)(c).

41 Cf. James C. Hathaway (2005), *The rights of refugees under international law,* Cambridge: Cambridge University Press, pp. 328–333; Rainer Hofmann & Tilmann Löhr (2011), 'Introduction to chapter V: requirements for refugee determination procedures', in: Andreas Zimmermann (ed.), *The 1951 convention relating to the status of refugees and its 1967 protocol. A commentary,* Oxford: Oxford University Press, pp. 1110–1114; Jens Vedsted-Hansen (2016), 'Asylum procedures directive 2013/32/EU', in: Kay Hailbronner and Daniel Thym (eds.), *EU immigration and asylum law,* 2nd Ed., Munich/Oxford/Baden Baden: C.H. Beck/ Hart/Nomos, p. 1363.

third country' to be bound by the Refugee Convention and to comply with the Convention in actual practice.

Criticism along similar lines as those indicated above has been levelled against the EU-Turkey arrangement from various sides, including the UNHCR.[42] In preparation of the conclusion of the cooperation agreement with Turkey, the political desirability of introducing Turkey as a 'safe third country' had been expressed by the EU Commission in a somewhat ambiguous manner with significant provisos on the legal prerequisites, yet with a clear intention as regards the policy direction.[43] The political intention has been reflected in the Commission's statements of impatience with the Greek asylum authorities' application of the inadmissibility rules in order to return asylum seekers to Turkey as a 'safe third country' and the emphasis of the urgent need for further efforts to build a 'substantially increased and sustained capacity to return arriving migrants' which, according to the Commission, is considered to be the 'key deterrent factor for irregular migrants and smugglers'.[44]

This notwithstanding, it still has to be seen under which conditions and to which extent the rejection of asylum applications as inadmissible and the consequent return of asylum seekers without any substantive examination of their application for protection will be considered legally tenable. While the Greek asylum appeals bodies have apparently been skeptical towards such inadmissibility decisions, at least during the period until June 2016 when the composition and structure of the Asylum Appeals Committees were modified,[45] the legal questions briefly outlined and discussed above are unlikely to become finally answered until either the Court of Justice of the European Union or the European Court of Human Rights, or probably both European courts, have decided on the adequacy of the concrete protection conditions in Turkey and on the compatibility of applying this country as a 'safe third country' with EU law, respectively.

---

42 UNHCR, *Legal considerations on the return of asylum-seekers and refugees from Greece to Turkey as part of the* EU-*Turkey Cooperation in Tackling the Migration Crisis under the safe third country and first country of asylum concept*, 23 March 2016.

43 European Commission, Communication on *Next operational steps in* EU-*Turkey cooperation in the field of migration*, COM(2016)166 final, 16 March 2016, para. 2.1.

44 European Commission, Communication *Third Report on the Progress made in the implementation of the* EU-*Turkey Statement*, COM(2016)634 final, 28 September 2016, p. 5.

45 See: Mariana Gkliati (2016), 'Greece creates new asylum committees after decisions blocking returns under the EU-Turkey deal', blog entry at *Leiden Law Blog*, 5 August 2016.

## 6.5 Revision of EU Asylum Legislation

Referring to the record number of 600,000 applicants for asylum in EU Member States in 2014, the European Commission already in the spring of 2015 announced the need to revise the legislative instruments establishing the EU asylum system. With a view to ensuring a 'coherent implementation of the Common European Asylum System' and strengthening this system, the Commission suggested that practical cooperation should be stepped up, and that a more effective approach should be taken against abuses in that too many applications for protection were unfounded.[46] The objective was still for Europe to continue to be a safe haven for those fleeing persecution, and the duty to protect those in need was emphasised as the 'immediate imperative'.[47]

In its subsequent Communication on reform of the Common European Asylum System, the Commission restated the objective of ensuring a humane and efficient asylum policy, while putting stronger emphasis on the *fight against abuse* of the asylum system and not least against asylum seekers' *secondary movements* within the EU.[48] At the same time, the Commission quite openly conceded the *inherent weaknesses* of the EU asylum standards hitherto adopted and not least their outcomes in terms of varying recognition rates, lack of convergence in the granting of either refugee or subsidiary protection status and variations in reception conditions, the duration of residence permits, access to social assistance and family reunification.[49]

Despite these concessions, it may seem questionable whether the ensuing Commission proposals for revised legislative acts will effectively tackle these important root causes of secondary movements. The proposals, in particular those concerning asylum procedures, generally appear more persistent in expanding the scope of inadmissibility rules and accelerated procedures and introducing other restrictive measures towards asylum seekers than in limiting Member States' possibilities to uphold varying practices on substantive and procedural matters. Not least importantly, the strong emphasis on

46 European Commission, Communication on *A European agenda on migration*, COM(2015)240 final, 13 May 2015, Section III.3, pp. 12–14.

47 European Commission, Communication on *A European agenda on migration*, COM(2015)240 final, 13 May 2015, Section III.3, p. 2.

48 European Commission, Communication *Towards a reform of the common European asylum system and enhancing legal avenues to Europe*, COM(2016)197 final, 6 April 2016, pp. 2, 5 and 11–12.

49 European Commission, Communication *Towards a reform of the common European asylum system and enhancing legal avenues to Europe*, COM(2016)197 final, 6 April 2016, pp. 4–5.

*inadmissibility procedures* and *accelerated examination* is reflected in the proposal to merge the examination procedure and the Dublin procedure – or, to some extent, reverse the order of the two distinct procedures – by requiring Member States to examine the admissibility of applications under the 'safe third country' and 'first country of asylum' rules, as well as the merits of applications in accelerated procedures under the 'safe country of origin' rule, before determining the Member State responsible for the examination in accordance with the rules in the (amended) Dublin Regulation.[50]

While any detailed account of the Commission proposals would fall outside the framework of this chapter, it should be noted that the proposed replacement of the Qualification Directive and the Asylum Procedures Directive by Regulations[51] will indeed in itself have the effect of reducing Member States' implementing discretion, given that such Regulations on qualification and content of protection and on asylum procedures, respectively, will have direct effect and therefore not be subject to transposition legislation that may be differing between Member States. Nonetheless, the mandatory restrictions and sanctions against asylum seekers' secondary movements proposed in these Regulations are only to a limited extent accompanied by the abandonment of such optional rules that may have the potentially significant effect of creating incentives for asylum seekers to commit the very same secondary movements that are supposed to be prevented or punished by the mandatory restrictive measures. For instance, while it is proposed that the application of 'safe third country' and 'safe country of origin' rules will be mandatory, it will still be left within Member States' discretion to limit the social assistance for beneficiaries

---

50 Cf. Article 3(3)–(5) of the Commission Proposal for a Regulation establishing the criteria and mechanisms for determining the Member State responsible for examining an application for international protection lodged in one of the Member States by a third-country national or a stateless person, COM(2016)270 final, 4 May 2016; see: Explanatory Memorandum, pp. 14–16, as well as the Explanatory Memorandum of the Proposal for Asylum Procedures Regulation (note 51), pp. 15–16.

51 Commission Proposal for a Regulation of the European Parliament and of the Council on standards for the qualification of third-country nationals or stateless persons as beneficiaries of international protection, for a uniform status for refugees or for persons eligible for subsidiary protection and for the content of the protection granted and amending Council Directive 2003/109/EC of 25 November 2003 concerning the status of third-country nationals who are long-term residents, COM(2016)466 final, 13 July 2016; Proposal for a Regulation of the European Parliament and of the Council establishing a common procedure for international protection in the Union and repealing Directive 2013/32/EU, COM(2016)467 final, 13 July 2016.

of subsidiary protection to 'core benefits',[52] and there will still be no binding rules of EU law stipulating a legal right to reunification with family members of persons having been granted subsidiary protection.

Thus, the harmonisation strategy so far pursued by the Commission seems to be fraught with a notable imbalance between the regulatory measures addressing Member States and asylum seekers. Both the substantive and the procedural harmonisation proposals are to a considerable degree focusing on the aforementioned restrictive elements, in particular making 'safe country' rules mandatory, expanding the 'safe third country' notion and sanctioning asylum seekers' abuse and secondary movements. Even while such legislative measures may be understandable and indeed desirable for policy makers, the combined effect may end up being harmonisation that stresses disproportionately those elements of the examination procedure which Member States would be prepared to restrict at their own motion, regardless of the existence of mandatory EU standards. The consequent risk is that harmonisation of the eligibility criteria and of the examination procedures, and not least of the implementation and application of these standards in Member States' practice will remain ineffective and insufficient, resulting in highly different examination procedures and similarly different outcomes of applications for asylum across Member States.

## 6.6 Final Observations

Despite the dilemmas outlined in the preceding sections of this chapter and the fact that the Common European Asylum System is currently undergoing a potentially fatal crisis, it should not be ignored that the very introduction of the CEAS aspirations following the entry into force of the Amsterdam Treaty in 1999 and the adoption of gradually evolving legislation with harmonised standards on both substantive and procedural aspects of asylum is in itself to be considered as a promising development of EU law and policy pertaining to international protection. Similarly, a number of positive protection developments have been occurring in Member State practice under the first and second phase of the CEAS.

As a significant example of such evolutive protection measures it could be mentioned that, in comparison with the pre-Amsterdam intergovernmental harmonisation, the Qualification Directive has resulted in relatively wide recognition of the protection needs of groups of asylum seekers whose eligibility

52 Cf. Article 34 of the proposed Qualification Regulation (note 51).

for protection was not beyond doubt before harmonisation was becoming adopted by way of binding instruments of EU law. Not least thanks to the impact of generally recognised rules of treaty interpretation and of international human rights standards on the eligibility criteria, the impact of certain distorted definitional perceptions appears to have been reduced as a result of EU harmonisation. In a similar vein, the harmonised standards on examination procedures are likely to have had quite a significant impact in (at least some of) the new Member States that did not, at the time of EU accession, have well-established traditions or robust structures for examining asylum applications and granting protection to those in need thereof.[53]

What remains dilemmatic, however, is the apparent reluctance towards genuinely common standards on central substantive and procedural issues pertaining to international protection at a point in time where incomplete harmonisation has proven to be a significant reason for dysfunctions of the Common European Asylum System while, on the other hand, EU policy initiatives aiming to remedy the dysfunctions – such as strengthened enforcement of EU legislation, relocation of protection seekers or revision of the standards affecting burden sharing the most – do not appear to address these underlying reasons sufficiently. This is even more disturbing inasmuch as the objective regulatory dysfunctions are being supplemented, and potentially reinforced, by subjective resistance against EU harmonisation that may affect Member States' sovereign competences. The dilemma is a particular reality in certain Member States where national sovereignty tendencies are on the increase and may therefore seem to undermine even the protective structures and standards that had been introduced as a result of the first phase of CEAS legislation.

## References

Battjes, H. (2006), *European asylum law and international law*, Leiden: Martinus Nijhoff.

Boeles, P., M. den Heijer, G. Lodder & K. Wouters (2014), *European migration law*, 2. ed., Antwerp: Intersentia.

Butler, G. & M. Ratcovich (2016), 'Operation Sophia in uncharted waters: European and international law challenges for the EU naval mission in the Mediterranean Sea', *Nordic Journal of International Law* 85, pp. 235–259.

53 Cf. Rosemary Byrne, Gregor Noll & Jens Vedsted-Hansen (eds.) (2002), *New asylum countries? Migration control and refugee protection in an enlarged European union*, The Hague: Kluwer.

Costello, C. (2012), 'Courting access to asylum in Europe: recent supranational jurisprudence explored', *Human Rights Law Review* 12, pp. 287–339.

Costello, C. (2016), *The human rights of migrants and refugees in European law*, Oxford: Oxford University Press.

Garlick, M. (2016), *Solidarity under strain. Solidarity and fair sharing of responsibility in law and practice for the international protection of refugees in the European union* (Dissertation, Nijmegen).

Hathaway, J.C. (2005), *The rights of refugees under international law*, Cambridge: Cambridge University Press.

Hofmann, R. & T. Löhr (2011), 'Introduction to chapter V: requirements for refugee determination procedures', in: A. Zimmermann (ed.), *The 1951 convention relating to the status of refugees and its 1967 protocol. A commentary* Oxford: Oxford University Press, pp. 1081–1128.

Moreno-Lax, V. (2012), 'Dismantling the Dublin system: M.S.S. v. Belgium and Greece', *European Journal of Migration and Law* 14, pp. 1–31.

Noll, G. (2001), 'Formalism v. empiricism: some reflections on the Dublin convention on the occasion of recent European case law', *Nordic Journal of International Law* 70, pp. 161–182.

Peers, S. & E. Roman (2016), 'The EU, Turkey and the refugee crisis: what could possibly go wrong?' (blog post at) *EU Law Analysis*, 5 February 2016.

Tardy, T. (2015), 'Operation Sophia: tackling the refugee crisis with military means', *Brief Issue* 30/2015, EU Institute for Security Studies, Paris.

Vedsted-Hansen, J. (2012), 'Common EU standards on asylum – optional harmonisation and exclusive procedures?' in: Elspeth Guild & Paul Minderhoud (eds.), *The first decade of EU migration and asylum law*, Leiden: Martinus Nijhoff, pp. 255–271.

Vedsted-Hansen, J. (2015), 'Reception conditions as human rights: pan-European standard or systemic deficiencies?', in: V. Chetail, P. De Bruycker & F. Maiani (eds.), *Reforming the common European asylum system: the New European refugee law*, Leiden: Brill, pp. 317–352.

Vedsted-Hansen, J. (2016), 'Asylum procedures directive 2013/32/EU', in: K. Hailbronner & D. Thym (eds.), *EU immigration and asylum law*, 2nd Ed., C.H. Beck/Hart/Nomos, Munich/Oxford/Baden Baden, pp. 1284–1380.

CHAPTER 7

# Governing Migration in an Age of Globalization

*James Hollifield and Rahfin Faruk*

## 7.1 Introduction

To understand the impact of international migration on world politics we must know how states try to shape and control migration. Since 1945 immigration in liberal democracies has been increasing, although there was a slight leveling off of the numbers in the wake of the 2008–09 financial crisis and ensuing recession. Immigration into member states of the Organization for Economic Cooperation and Development (OECD) is down about 7 percent since 2009, not counting refugees and asylum seekers. The overall rise in immigration in the last half of the twentieth century is partly a function of market forces (demand-pull and supply-push) and kinship networks, which reduce the transactions costs of moving from one society to another. These economic and sociological forces are the necessary conditions for migration to occur, but the sufficient conditions are legal and political. The OECD states with highly developed industrial and service-based economies reap enormous economic gains from migration – new sources of human capital and manpower, more flexible labor markets, more entrepreneurial activity, lower levels of inflation in periods of high growth, and so forth. But to get the benefits of migration states must be willing to accept certain costs – principally the long term costs of social integration and the short term fiscal burdens of concentrated immigrant populations in certain regions and localities. Liberal states also must deal with the issue of rights (legal status) for migrants, including legalization, naturalization, and citizenship, otherwise they risk undermining the social contract. Hence economic needs for openness are pitted against political and legal pressures for closure – what I have called elsewhere the "liberal paradox".[1]

It is not enough to look just at the receiving (OECD) countries of the industrialized north. Migration also has important costs (brain drain) and benefits (remittances and brain gain) for less developed countries (LDCs) in the south. International trade is a well-established determinant for income and growth. In addition to the classic gains from specialization (comparative advantage) for all trading partners, international trade provides access to technological

1 Hollifield 1992.

 | DOI 10.1163/9789004330467_008

know-how and capital, thus giving less developed countries (LDCs) a chance to reduce the development gap at a faster pace. The impact of international migration on the welfare of both source and recipient countries is less well understood. Receiving countries benefit, *inter alia*, from immigrant workers, both skilled and unskilled. Sending countries benefit, *inter alia*, from the remittances sent back home by migrant workers, an important source of foreign exchange in many LDCs. While international trade and migration are often looked at in isolation in terms of their impact on development, it is critical to understand the relationship between trade, foreign direct investment (FDI), and migration to get a complete picture of globalization.[2]

Alongside trade and FDI, migration is a defining feature of the international political economy – the third pillar of globalization – and states struggle to regulate migration and mobility. Here we argue that rights are essential to migration governance – to protect the social contract – as modern states strive to fulfil three key functions: maintaining security, building trade and investment regimes, and regulating migration.

Migration and mobility raise a host of security concerns for states in the north and the south. The garrison state was linked with the trading state in the eighteenth and nineteenth centuries. The twentieth and twenty-first centuries have seen the emergence of *the migration state*, where regulation of international migration is important in providing for the security of the state and the well-being of the population.

## 7.2 The Politics of Migration and Mobility

International migration has been steadily increasing in every region of the globe since the end of the Second World War. At the beginning of the twenty-first century over 231 million people resided outside of their country of birth and over the past half century individual mobility has increased at a steady pace (see figure 7.1). Tens of millions of people cross borders on a daily basis, which adds up to roughly two billion annually. International mobility is part of a broader trend of globalization, which includes trade in goods and services, investments and capital flows, greater ease of travel, and a veritable explosion of information. While trade and capital flows are seen as the twin pillars of globalization, migration often is overlooked, especially among scholars of international relations.[3]

2 Hollifield, Orrenius & Osang 2006; Martin, Martin & Weil 2006; Peters 2014.

3 Hollifield 2012.

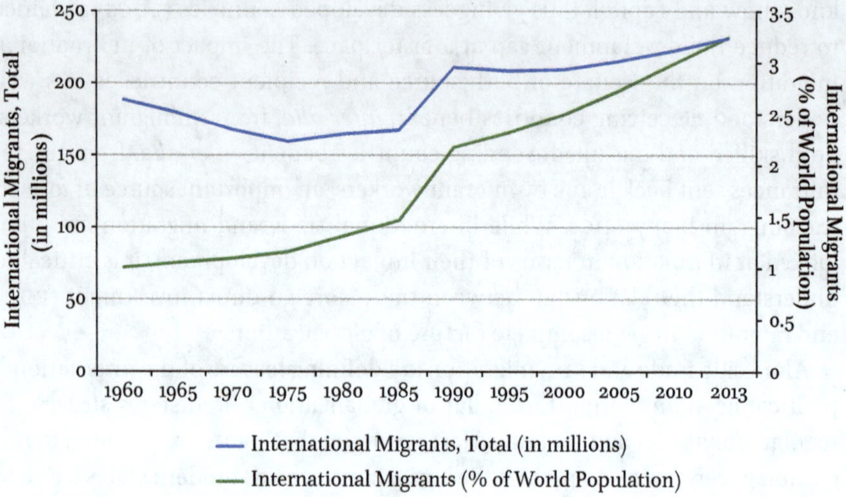


FIGURE 7.1 *International migrants (1960–2013).*
SOURCE: WORLD BANK DATA BANK

Yet migration is a defining feature of the global era in which we live; and, although it is connected in many ways to trade and investment, it is profoundly different. Some clever person once observed that "people are not shirts", which is another way of saying that labor is not a pure commodity. Unlike goods and capital, individuals can become actors on the international stage (they have agency) whether through peaceful transnational communities or violent terrorist/criminal networks. Migration and mobility can be a threat to the security of states. Immigrants bring new ideas and cultures (diversity) to their host societies and in liberal societies they come with a basic package of (human and civil) rights that enables them to settle and become members of society, if not citizens, of their adoptive countries. Conversely they may return to their countries of origin where they can have a dramatic impact on economic and political development.[4] And lest we forget, not all migration is voluntary – in any given year millions of people move to escape political violence, hunger, and deprivation, becoming refugees, asylum seekers, or internally displaced persons. In 2015 the number of people 'of concern' to UNHCR was 59.5 million, including 19.5 million refugees, 1.8 million asylum seekers, and 38.2 million internally displace people. Wars in the Middle East (especially Syria and Iraq), East and West Africa, and South Asia continue to feed a growing population of

4 Hollifield, Orrenius & Osang 2006; Martin, Martin & Weil 2006.

forced migrants.[5] Europe (the EU) and Germany in particular have struggled to cope with the latest waves of forced migration – over 1 million asylum seekers arrived in Germany alone in 2015. Because it is so complex and multi-faceted, migration of all types poses a regulatory challenge for individual states, for the European Union, and for the international community.[6]

Migration, increasingly, is linked to issues of security. Myron Weiner (1995) argued that the increase in international migration in the postwar period posed a threat to international stability and security, especially in those areas of the globe where nation-states are most fragile – South Asia, the Middle East, North and Sub-Saharan Africa. Weiner extended his argument to the western democracies, pointing out that the rise in xenophobic and nationalist politics in Western Europe (and we now could add the U.S.) showed that even the most advanced and tolerant democracies risk being destabilized politically by an influx of unwanted migrants. The terrorist threat and the rise of radical Islam have added to these security concerns. Weiner – like Paul Collier (2013) in a more recent book – postulated that there are limits on how many foreigners a society can absorb. Samuel Huntington of the "clash of civilizations" fame argued that failure to control American borders is the single biggest threat to the national security of the United States.[7] Weiner and Huntington echo the sentiments of Arthur Schlesinger and others,[8] who fear that immigration and multiculturalism will lead to the "disuniting of America". The fear of immigrants has been echoed by many others in the West, such as Thilo Sarrazin (2010), the German economist and politician who wrote a provocative and best-selling book entitled *Germany does away with itself: how we put our country at risk* (*Deutschland schafft sich ab: Wie wir unser Land aufs Spiel setzen*) in which he argues that Germany has failed to integrate its large Muslim population.

National security, the institutions of sovereignty and citizenship (rights), and economics (markets) are all part of a multi-dimensional game (figure 7.2) in migration policymaking. In 'normal' times the debate about immigration control in liberal democracies revolves around two poles: markets (numbers) and rights, or how many immigrants to admit and with what status? Should they be temporary (guest) workers, or should they be allowed to settle, bring their families, and get on a 'path to citizenship?' Is there a tradeoff between rights and numbers (markets) as Martin Ruhs (2013) suggests? All good questions but cultural concerns (where should the immigrants come from, which

5 Betts 2013.

6 Hollifield, Martin & Orrenius 2014; Geddes 2003; Betts 2009a; Peters 2015.

7 Huntington 1996; 2004.

8 Schlesinger, Jr. (1992); Brimelow 1995.

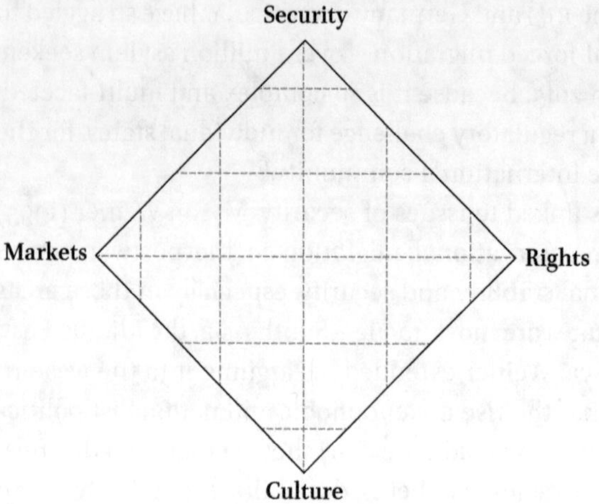


FIGURE 7.2 *Four factors influence migration politics.*

regions of the globe, and with which ethnic characteristics) almost always intrude in immigration politics, and they are more intense in some periods and in some countries than in others. Throughout most of U.S. history, for example, immigrants were selected on the basis race (and cultural compatibility), from the Chinese Exclusion Act of 1882 to the National Origins Quota Act of 1924. It was only in the 1950s and '60s that the U.S. moved away from selection by race – the definitive break came with the repeal of the national origins quota system and the passage of the Hart-Celler immigration act of 1965.[9] With the September 11th attacks and again with the November 13th attacks in Paris, immigration and refugee policymaking has been dominated by a national security dynamic (with a cultural subtext) and the fear that relatively open borders poses a serious threat to the nation and to civil society. In times of war and political crises, the normal dynamic of markets and rights is replaced by a culture-security dynamic and finding equilibrium (compromise) in the policy game is much harder – this is the challenge facing leaders across the Western world, and the German Chancellor, Angela Merkel, is in the forefront of this struggle. As if this domestic game is not complicated enough, it is compounded by the fact that immigration control has important foreign policy implications, and it can affect the balance of power. Hence politicians are always engaged in a two-level game to use the language of Robert Putnam (1988) in which they seek to build domestic coalitions to maximize electoral support for policy but always with one eye on the foreign policy consequences. To use the example of the U.S.,

9 King 2000; Fitzgerald & Cook-Martín 2014.

whether it is refugee policy in the cold war that was geared to the fight against communism, or the repeal of the national origins quota system, designed to bring U.S. policy into line with rapidly shifting values on race and ethnicity, and to help win the ideological battles of the cold war[10] foreign policy plays an important role in immigration and refugee policy.

If we accept the Weberian definition of sovereignty – which flows more or less directly from the Treaty of Westphalia of 1648 – a state can exist only if it has a monopoly of the legitimate use of force in a given territorial area. In this way, states have some protection from interference in their internal affairs[11] and it is easier to manage religious conflicts (*cuis regio eus religio*). It would then follow that the ability or inability of a state to control its borders and hence its population must be the *sine qua non* of sovereignty.[12] With some notable exceptions – such as the international refugee regime created by the 1950 Geneva Convention in the aftermath of World War II,[13] the right of a state to control entry and exit of persons to and from its territory is an undisputed principle of international law.[14] But this principle, which is one of the cornerstones of the international legal system, immediately raises another question or puzzle: Why are some states willing to accept rather high levels of immigration (or emigration) when it would seem not to be in their interest to do so and when public opinion is hostile?[15] The refugee crisis in Europe in 2015–16 is a case in point.

It might be tempting to argue, as some have, that international migration is simply a function of the inexorable process of globalization.[16] Demand for labor – both skilled and unskilled – is high in the principal receiving countries of North America, Europe, and Australia, and the supply of workers in Asia, Latin America and Africa, willing to fill this demand is virtually unlimited. Demand-pull and supply-push forces seem to account rather well for the surge in international migration over the past fifty years. Yet we know that individuals are risk averse and migration is fraught with risks – the transaction costs alone should be enough to deter most people from moving, and indeed this is the case. Two hundred and thirty one million immigrants represent a little

10 Again see: Fitzgerald & Cook-Martín 2014, but also: Rudolph 2006; Zolberg 2006; Adamson, Triadafilopoulos & Zolberg 2011; Joppke 2010.

11 Weber 1947; Krasner 1999; Hollifield 2005.

12 Hollifield 2005, 2012.

13 Goodwin-Gill 1996; Betts 2009b, 2013.

14 Shaw 1997.

15 Hollifield, Martin & Orrenius 2014; Freeman 1995; Joppke 1998b.

16 Sassen 1996.

over three percent of the world's population. But despite efforts to restrict immigration, people are moving in increasing numbers, and there is a sense of crisis and loss of control, quite apart from the current refugee crisis in Europe. Sociologists and anthropologists have helped us to understand how individuals reduce the risks associated with migration.[17] Individuals are more likely to migrate if they have friends or relatives in the destination country willing to provide support (social capital) and ease the process of transition. Social networks lower the transaction costs associated with emigration, making it less risky and connecting supply and demand, like a cable between two poles of a battery.

Is this the end of the story? If so there would be little room for the state in managing migration, and 'migration governance' would be a moot point in a world of pure agency where structure does not matter. Policy, some say,[18] may be irrelevant, playing at best only a marginal role in the migration process, and the institutions of sovereignty and citizenship are increasingly outdated.[19] According to this logic, we are entering a post-national era, and migration is increasingly a transnational phenomenon. We shall argue that it is a mistake to eliminate the state (and politics) from our analysis.[20] *The necessary conditions for migration to occur may be social and economic, but the sufficient conditions are political and legal.* States must be willing to open their borders to the movement of people, and as people move they can acquire rights. Politics matters and states are critical in shaping migration outcomes, whether negative (more exploitation and deprivation) or positive (greater freedom and human development). But the questions remain: Why are some states more willing to open their borders than others, to what extent can states cooperate in managing migration, and what is the future of global migration governance?

## 7.3 A Public Goods Approach to Migration Governance

Because migrants have agency – that is they are not inanimate commodities subject to strict controls – it is difficult for states to regulate flows of people in the same way they regulate the movement of goods, services, and capital. As with trade and FDI, however, there are great obstacles to cooperation in migration governance. One state's policies to control or regulate migration inevitably affect another state's, and externalities in migration governance abound. If

17 Massey *et al.* 2002; Fitzgerald 2014; Brettell 2014.

18 Sassen 1996.

19 Soysal 1994.

20 Hollifield & Wong 2014.

anything, interdependence with respect to migration is even greater than with trade and investment, making unilateral approaches to regulation extremely difficult. Short of autarky states have little choice but to cooperate in migration governance, even though a truly multilateral migration regime has proven elusive. Levels of (migration) interdependence vary considerably from one region to another, and states' interests in migration often diverge, leading to beggar-thy-neighbor policies and making global governance difficult. One way to see this is to plot migration dependence on two axes, remittances as a percentage of GDP and migrant stock as a percentage of population, which produces an 'L-Curve' (figure 7.3) and shows that states tend to array on one of two poles: either sending or receiving, with some states in the transition category, neither sending nor receiving societies. When thinking about the migration state (more on this below) we can see the empirical underpinning of the concept, with some developing states, like the Philippines, Bangladesh and Morocco, highly dependent on remittances. Whereas the 'nations of immigrants', like the U.S., Canada, and Australia, along with countries of immigration, like Germany, France, and other West European states, are dependent on immigrants for economic and demographic growth.[21] How can these states come together through a multilateral process to cooperate in managing migration? And what are the prospects for 'global governance' of migration, including refugees?

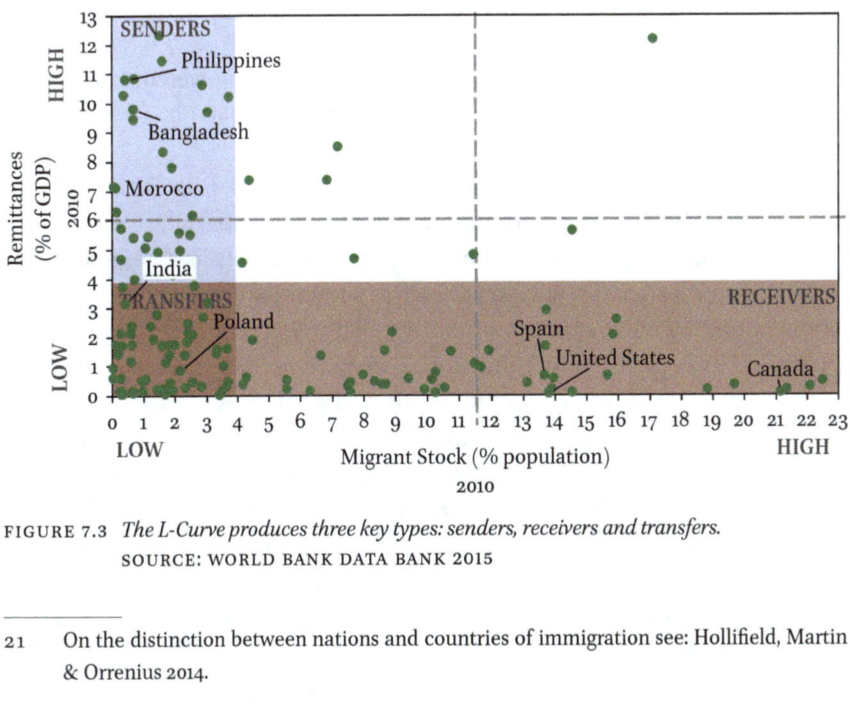


FIGURE 7.3 *The L-Curve produces three key types: senders, receivers and transfers.*
SOURCE: WORLD BANK DATA BANK 2015

21 On the distinction between nations and countries of immigration see: Hollifield, Martin & Orrenius 2014.

Following the work of John Ruggie,[22] we can identify three tenets of multilateralism. The first is *indivisibility*, which is another way of saying the object of a multilateral process should take the form of a global public good (the benefits of an international migration regime would have to be non-excludable and non-rivalrous). A single state or even a small group of states cannot provide migration governance for the international community. The costs and benefits of governance and its provision must be shared relatively equally among states, and there must be some mechanism for dealing with externalities and free riding – this problem is very much in evidence in the current European crisis. The second tenet of multilateralism is *principles,* or *norms of conduct*, which can alter the behavior of states. The fewer principles or norms there are, the greater the likelihood that states will adhere to them and change their behavior. The most difficult problem in any multilateral regime is to find a single compelling principle (or at least a very small number of interrelated norms or principles) "around which actor expectations can converge". Third, Ruggie points to *diffuse reciprocity*, meaning that states must be convinced that all the players will respect the rules of the game, making it possible for governments to persuade a skeptical or even hostile public to accept the short-term political and economic costs of establishing the regime in order to reap the long-term gains, access to much-needed labor (manpower), human capital, and orderly (legal) movement of people across borders.

Using this liberal/public goods framework, we can ask: What are the possibilities of building effective international migration regimes? What would be the incentives to participate in such a regime? Can states overcome their misgivings, which may include loss of sovereignty, threats to national security and identity, and changes in the composition of the citizenry?[23]

On the first point, indivisibility, we must ask if migration can be defined as a global public good. As noted earlier, this is problematic, especially if we compare migration and trade. During the postwar period, a consensus emerged – based on American leadership and the principle of comparative advantage – that an open trading regime would promote global welfare and advance the cause of peace. The motto of the immediate postwar period was "peace through trade". The General Agreement on Tariffs and Trade (GATT) system was created, based on the principle of comparative advantage, to ensure that the costs and benefits of free trade would be shared equally, and this allowed the leading liberal states (especially the U.S.) gradually to overcome collective action problems. Free trade would lead not only to specialization in production, increased

22 Ruggie 1993, pp. 3–47.

23 Joppke 1998a; Betts 2011; Martin 2014.

output, and Pareto-optimal outcomes it also would promote interdependence and a more peaceful world – the Kantian dream. And even before the creation of the multilateral trade regime, the leading liberal states – in this case the U.S. and the U.K. – moved to stabilize the international monetary system, through the Bretton Woods process, creating a relatively fixed exchange rate regime, to provide exchange rate stability, liquidity and structural adjustment. The purpose of these international regimes was clear and compelling.

This type of economic reasoning, however, does not work well in the area of migration because the asymmetry of interests between developed and developing countries is too great. It is only at certain points in time (such as the turn of the century in America, and the period of reconstruction in Europe – what the French call *les trente glorieuses* after World War II – or the period of very high growth in Asia in the 1970s and '80s) that the interests of developing and developed states converge. Developing states more often than not have an incentive to export surplus populations, whereas developed states only periodically have an interest in admitting large numbers of foreign workers. The history of south-to-north migration has tended to be one of fits and starts, of peaks and valleys that follow the business cycle. But there is strong evidence that this cyclical dynamic may have been broken in the postwar period, at least for certain "core" liberal states in America and Europe.[24] We can see this in the rates of world migration, which have been rising continuously since 1945 (figure 7.1), albeit at a steady, not alarming pace.

So, if migration does not follow the business cycle, what is driving it? The answer, in a word, is rights. As the world becomes more open, more democratic, and more liberal, people are freer to move than ever before. This has placed great strains on liberal states, especially on the institutions of sovereignty and citizenship. Liberal states (and by extension the EU) are caught on the horns of a dilemma or, a liberal paradox.[25] In liberal political and economic systems, there is constant tension between markets and rights; but we argue that this is not a straight tradeoff between numbers and rights as Martin Ruhs (2013) contends. Rules of the market require openness and factor mobility, whereas rules of the liberal polity, especially citizenship, require some degree of closure, mainly to have a clear definition of the citizenry (who is in and who is out) and to protect the social contract – the legal cornerstone of every liberal polity. Equal protection and due process cannot be extended to everyone without undermining the legitimacy of the liberal state itself. How can states solve this dilemma, avoid falling into the trap of numbers (markets) versus rights, and

24 Hollifield, Martin & Orrenius 2014; Hollifield & Wilson 2011.

25 Hollifield 1992a; Weiner 1995; Hollifield, Martin & Orrenius 2014.

escape from the paradox? Constructing an international migration regime, as European Union members have done, is one way; but as we have seen a high degree of openness and mobility comes with risks, especially when terrorists and other criminals are able to slip across borders (again see figure 7.1 for the tradeoffs); and the danger of moral hazard is ever present. Even a slight opening or change in policy can lead to a flood of migrants.

One way out of the dilemma (short of establishing a federal union with common external borders and a single citizenship regime) is to build an international migration regime and to make global migration governance a public good. But, assuming such a regime could meet the criteria of non-excludability and non-rivalry – where the benefits of governance could not be denied to any state, all could benefit equally, all would share the costs, and there would be no free riding – it could not be defined purely in economic terms (*homo economicus* is a non-starter), even though mobility of productive factors is recognized to be welfare improving and Pareto optimal.[26] To regulate migration on a unilateral basis, liberal states must adopt draconian (illiberal) policies that can threaten the foundations of the liberal state itself, violating the rights of individuals. It is not efficient or desirable in a liberal state to close or seal borders – growth and prosperity depend on openness. Sealing borders would be the ultimate strategy for external control[27] and it would resolve the dilemma of immigration control but at a very high cost. Likewise, strategies for internal control, including heavy regulation of labor markets, limiting civil rights and liberties for foreigners and citizens, and tampering with founding myths (for example, weakening birthright citizenship in the U.S.) also would threaten the founding principles of the liberal state.[28] Illiberal measures can fan the flames of racism and xenophobia by further stigmatizing foreigners, leading to a surge in nationalism and right-wing populism. Establishing a multilateral process for regulating and controlling immigration offers one way out of this dilemma, but to accomplish this, control must be done on a multilateral basis with a core organizing principle, "orderly movement of people".[29] Orderly movements imply respect for the rule of law and state sovereignty, which are fundamental principles in every liberal state,[30] and they require close cooperation between sending, transit and receiving states. And most difficult, political coalitions must be (re)built at the domestic level to support such regimes.[31]

---

26 Clemens 2011; Bhagwati 1983, 2004.

27 Freeman 1995.

28 Hollifield 1999.

29 Ghosh 2000.

30 Hollifield 2005.

31 See for example: Hollifield, Hunt & Tichenor 2008.

The problem remains of how to set up generalized principles of conduct in the area of migration. Various conventions exist, many put forward by the UN and its agencies[32] to safeguard the rights of refugees,[33] migrant workers and their families.[34] Likewise, Mode 4 of the General Agreement on Trade in Services (GATS) includes provisions for labor migration.[35] But none of these agreements has achieved the status of a full-blown international migration regime capable of altering the behavior of states. Moreover, economic migration, whether low-skilled or high-skilled, is a private (not a public) good and states have the option of competing in a relatively open marketplace for basic labor (manpower) and human capital. It is only with asylum and refugees that a quasi-effective international regime, which approximates a global public good, has emerged in the postwar period, with a single guiding norm/principle – a well-founded fear of persecution.[36] The freedom-of-movement clauses of the various European Union treaties have resulted in the construction of a regional migration regime for EU member states, and the Schengen group has developed rules (the Dublin Agreement) for dealing with the migration of third-country nationals, specifically asylum seekers (Uçarer 1997; Geddes 2008). This regime has broken down with the massive wave of asylum seekers that reached one million in 2015, and the terrorist attacks of 13 November, 2015 in Paris have placed enormous pressure on individual states to close their borders and on the EU to seek new mechanisms and policies for external border control. At this writing the Schengen system itself hangs in the balance, showing once again how strong security concerns can override all other considerations in immigration and refugee policy (see figure 7.2 above).

Nonetheless, in a regional context, where the asymmetry is less pronounced than in the international system, it is easier to solve the problems of reciprocity and collective action, and pursue a migration regime that more closely approximates a club good (with benefits limited to a defined group of states and costs equally shared) than a true global good. In the European Union, for example, rules can be adopted and formalized through already established institutional procedures that discourage free riding. At the international level, what we have seen instead is a proliferation of very weak rules, norms, and procedures, resulting in a kind of fragmented and ineffective regime,[37] and the

---

32 UNHCR, IOM, and ILO.

33 The 1951 Refugee Convention and the 1967 Protocol.

34 The 1990 Convention on the Protection of the Rights of All Migrant Workers and Members of Their Families.

35 Bhagwati 1998; Ghosh 2000; Martin 2014.

36 Betts 2009; Martin 2014.

37 Ghosh 2000.

proliferation of bilateral agreements for migration control has resulted in what trade experts would call a "spaghetti bowl" effect. Moreover, the primary concern of the most powerful liberal states is not to facilitate the orderly movement of people (even tourists) or to promote international factor mobility. Rather, the concern is for control *tout court*, which has as many different meanings as there are states.[38] The challenge for any state or organization attempting to construct an international migration regime will be to define control in such a way that it is indivisible, can serve as a generalized norm or principle of conduct, and can lead to diffuse reciprocity. This is no mean feat because, heretofore, international migration has been regulated largely on a unilateral or bilateral basis, if not through some type of imperial hierarchy (like the old British Commonwealth with its principle of *Civis Britannicus Sum*) – the EU is a notable exception. In fact, we still see both regulatory systems at work today. It is only among the OECD states that freedom of movement through visa waiver systems (but not settlement) has been more or less achieved, especially for the highly skilled. Between the core liberal states in the international system and the less developed countries, movement of populations is still governed by a system of imperial hierarchy (based largely on power relations), which is in many ways more one-sided today than it was during the colonial era.

To illustrate the difficulties of international cooperation in regulating migration, we have constructed a simple typology of international regimes. This typology, depicted in figure 7.4, points to a clear distinction between the regulation of capital, goods, and services on one hand and migrant labor or refugees (people) on the other.

Of the two "regimes" dealing with migration, one for labor migrants and the other for refugees, clearly the refugee regime, which is institutionalized through UNHCR, is the more effective and comes closer to a global public good. The rules for entry and exit of economic migrants are controlled by nation-states, not by international organizations like the UN, IOM, or ILO.[39] Again, the major exception is the EU, but the EU regime for international labor migration functions only for nationals of the member states (it is a club good), not (or at least not yet) for third-country nationals.[40] Even for the Schengen states – referred to in the British press derisively as Schengenland – third-country nationals do not have freedom of movement. Only Schengen nationals have this right. The EU through the Dublin Agreement has constructed a multilateral regime for refugees, which requires asylum seekers to register and request asylum in the

---

38 Hollifield, Martin & Orrenius 2014.

39 Joppke 1998a; Martin 2014.

40 Guiraudon 1998.

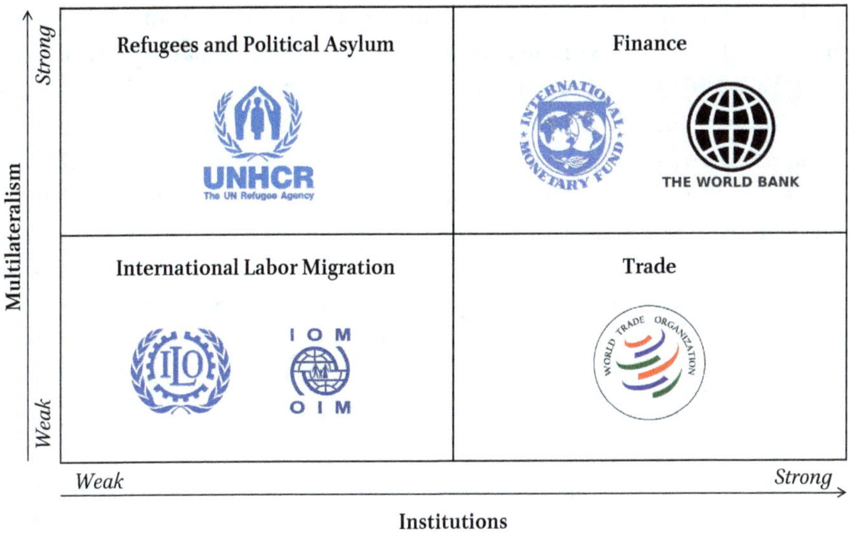


FIGURE 7.4 *Global governance and the missing regime.*

first 'safe country' in which they arrive. This arrangement is designed to help member states restrict refugee migration and prevent "asylum shopping", but it has broken down completely in the face of the massive wave of refugees that arrived in 2015.[41] The Dublin system was consistent with the Geneva Convention. If an individual transits through a 'safe' third country, they can be *refoulés* (sent back to that third country). The result was to turn many of the states along the EU's southern and southeastern borders into buffer states, forced to accept large numbers of asylum seekers. Spain and Italy initially bore the brunt of movements across the Mediterranean with Greece becoming the primary point of entry for migrants and refugees in the 2010s. At the beginning of 2016 roughly 800,000 asylum seekers were awaiting 'processing' in Greece. The European states, together with the U.S. and other liberal democracies, are respecting the letter, if not the spirit, of international refugee law. Although the principles of the refugee regime are widely recognized, UNHCR as an institution remains weak and heavily dependent on a few "client states", especially Sweden, The Netherlands, and other small European social democracies.[42] The Japanese contribute a lot of money to UNHCR, and the Americans support it and use it as a tool for managing refugee crises around the world, especially when American national interests are involved.

41 Thielemann 2003.

42 Loescher *et al.* 2008; Gibney 2004; Betts 2009; Martin 2014.

The regime for international labor migration is weakly institutionalized (depicted on the x axis) with no central norm, and its principal organs, ILO and IOM, based in Geneva, have little regulatory or institutional capacity. For developed states in particular, the costs of participating in a regime for international labor migration outweigh the benefits, and a short-term strategy of unilateral or bilateral regulation of migration is preferred to a long-term, multilateral strategy. This is less true for the refugee regime because the more powerful liberal states need this regime for situational exigencies – to manage massive refugee flows that can destabilize governments and, in some cases, entire regions, as is happening in the Middle East in the 2010s. When such crises strike close to home, as in Europe in 2015, the utility of the refugee regime goes up exponentially. But when the crisis is past, it drops again.

To date, unwanted labor migrations might be considered more of a nuisance, especially from a political and security standpoint. They are not fundamentally threatening and, therefore, can be handled unilaterally and on an ad hoc basis. The payoff from international cooperation in the area of unwanted labor migration is negative, and opportunities for defection are numerous. The possibilities for monitoring, enforcing, or developing some principle of nondiscrimination are minimal at this point. That brings us back to the domestic level in our search for an explanation of why states risk migration. The four factors driving migration policies – security, cultural and ideational concerns, economic interests, and rights – must be studied on a case-by-case basis. Yet an international market for labor exists and is growing. If the first rule of political economy is that markets beget regulation, some type of a stronger regime is likely to develop. What will be the parameters of such a regime, and how will it evolve? International relations theory, especially liberal/rationalist arguments, offers some clues.

## 7.4 Suasion and Regional Migration Regimes

One of the principal effects of economic interdependence is to compel states to cooperate.[43] Increasing international migration is one indicator of interdependence, and it shows no signs of abating. From figure 7.5 we can see that North America and Europe are among the most migration interdependent regions in the world, with the Middle East and the 'Arab world' not far behind. As the international market for skilled and unskilled labor grows in the coming decades, pressures to create an international regime will increase. Following

43 Keohane & Nye 1977; Milner 1988.

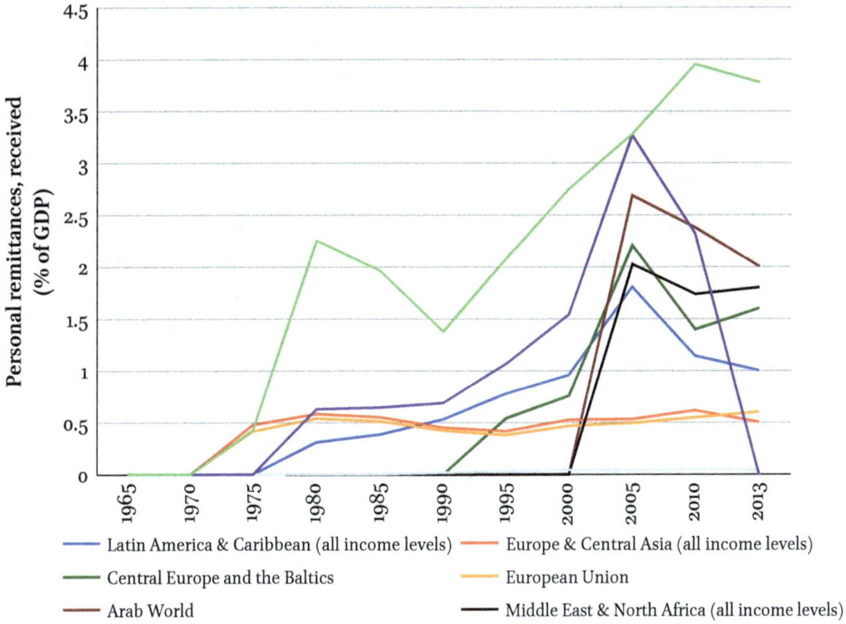


(a)

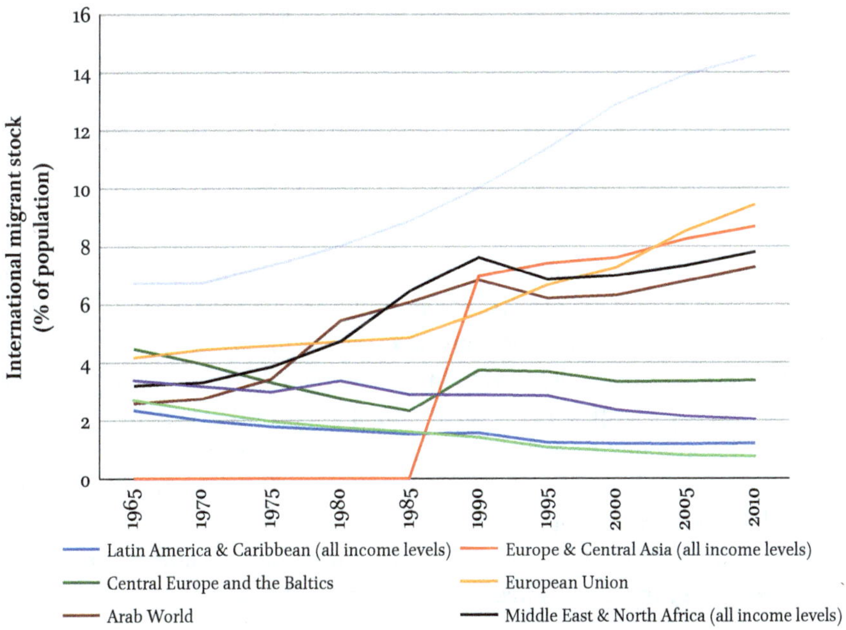


(b)

FIGURE 7.5 *(a) Migration interdependence. Remittances by region, 1960–2013.*
*(b) Migration interdependence. International migrant stock (% of population) by region.*
SOURCE: WORLD BANK DATA BANK 2015

the work of Lisa Martin (1993, 91–121) we can identify two ways in which states can overcome coordination problems in the absence of trust and reciprocity (developed states do not trust less developed states to help control borders and deter irregular migration): (1) through the centralization of regulatory power and pooling of sovereignty, and (2) suasion or, as Lisa Martin puts it, 'tactical issue linkage'.[44]

We already have seen an example of the first strategy at the regional level in Europe. The EU and, to a lesser extent, the Schengen and Dublin regimes were built through processes of centralization and pooling of sovereignty. But this was easy to do in the European context because of the symmetry (of interests and power) within the EU and the existence of an institutional framework (the various treaties of European Union). It would be much more difficult to centralize control of migration in the Americas or Asia, for example, where the asymmetry (of interests and power) is much greater, and levels of political and economic development vary tremendously from one state to another.[45] It is unlikely that regional trade regimes like the North American Free Trade Agreement (NAFTA) or Asia-Pacific Economic Cooperation (APEC) will lead quickly to cooperation in the area of migration. But the beginnings of collaborative arrangements are there, just as they were with the European Coal and Steel Community (ECSC) in the early 1950s. The regional option – multilateralism for a relevant group of states where migration governance can be defined as a club good – is one way to overcome collective-action problems and to begin a process of centralization. Most international regimes have had a long gestation period, beginning as bilateral or regional agreements. It is unlikely, however, that an international migration regime could be built following the example of the International Trade Organization/GATT/WTO. It is too difficult to fulfil the prerequisites of multilateralism: indivisibility, generalized principles of conduct, and diffuse reciprocity. The norm of nondiscrimination (equivalent of MFN) does not exist, and there are no mechanisms for punishing free riders and no way of resolving disputes. In short, as depicted in figure 7.4, the basis for multilateralism is weak, and the institutional framework is very weak.

With the asymmetry of interests and power between developed (migration receiving) and less developed (migration sending) countries, *suasion* is the only viable strategy for overcoming collective-action problems, whether at the regional or international level. Lisa Martin points to a number of ways in which suasion can help to solve coordination problems.[46]

44 Martin 1993a, p. 104.

45 Fields 1994; Sadiq 2009.

46 Martin 1993a, pp. 104–106.

Step one is to develop a *dominant strategy*, which can be accomplished only by the most powerful states, using international organizations to persuade or coerce smaller and weaker states. From the standpoint of receiving countries, the orderly movement of people, defined in terms of rule of law and respect for state sovereignty, would be the principal objective of the powerful liberal states. From the standpoint of the sending countries, migration for development, taking advantage of remittances and returns (brain gain) or circular migration, would be the principle upon which an international regime could be based.[47]

Circular migration encompasses a wide range of migrants: low-skilled seasonal workers, medium and high-skilled professionals, students, researchers and entrepreneurs. Several countries in Europe have experimented with circular migration on the assumption that it will stimulate trade, enterprise networks and investments by diaspora, often called co-development schemes. These agreements have taken the form of 'Mobility Partnership Pacts'. For example, Cape Verde has adopted a mobility partnership program focused on better visa policy and border control. India has initiated discussions with the EU to negotiate new labor mobility agreements. These agreements are biased based on exporting high skilled professionals in the health care sectors, information technology, biotechnology, hospitality. They are quite different than those that Spain has signed with Ecuador, Senegal, Morocco and Mauritania. Nonetheless these mobility partnership pacts point to the fact that states are interested in promoting international labor mobility in specific sectors and geographical regions.

Little analysis of these labor mobility agreements has been done with the exception of Sweden. In July 2009, the Swedish Government appointed an independent Parliamentary Committee to examine the connection between circular migration and development. Proposals and impact assessments were presented in a final report in March 2011. Sweden has set new rules for labor migration in December 2008. Under the new rules, an employer who is not able to meet his or her labor needs through recruitment in Sweden or in other EU/EEA countries is able to recruit labor form a third country. The migrant first gets a temporary permit for the duration of the employment or for a maximum of two years, renewable for two additional years, at which time a permanent residence permit can be issued.

Step two is to persuade other states to accept the dominant strategy. This will necessitate *tactical issue linkage*, which involves identifying issues and interests not necessarily related to migration (such as MFN, for example) and

47 Russell 1986; Faini 2007; Martin, Martin & Weil 2006; Ratha 2007.

using these as leverage to compel or coerce states to accept the dominant strategy. This is, in effect, an "international logroll". Such tactics will have only the appearance of multilateralism, at least initially. Tactical issue linkage was considered in negotiations between the U.S. and Mexico over the NAFTA agreement, and migration issues have figured prominently in negotiations between the EU and prospective EU members in East Central Europe, and more recently with Turkey. At the EU summit in Seville in 2002, for example, the British and Spanish delegates attempted to link official development aid (ODA) and trade concessions for African states to migration control, but this initiative was blocked by the French and the Swedes.

In such instances, reciprocity is specific rather than diffuse. Individual states may be rewarded for their cooperation in controlling migration, as Turkey was for its willingness to cooperate in stemming the flow of refugees from the Middle East in 2015. Again, we have seen many bilateral examples of this type of strategic interaction between the states of Western and Eastern Europe. The post-unification German governments have cut a number of deals with East Central European states to gain their cooperation in the fight against irregular migration. In the case of Poland, this has involved investments and debt relief as well as greater freedom of movement for Polish nationals in Germany. But liberal-democratic states may face a problem of credibility in pursuing these types of strategies. They need international organizations to give them greater credibility (cover) and facilitate these logrolls. With respect to forced migration the UNHCR often has played this role.

The third step for hegemonic states is to move from what is an essentially one-sided, manipulative game to a multilateral process, and eventually to *institutionalize this process*. The long-term benefits of such a strategy for receiving states are obvious. It will be less costly to build an international regime than to fight every step of the way with every sending state, relying only on unilateral or bilateral agreements. This may entail some short-term loss of control (such as larger numbers of visas, or higher quotas for the sending states, the case of Turkey in 2015 comes to mind) in exchange for long-term stability and more orderly/regular migration. The ultimate payoff for liberal states is the establishment of a liberal world order based upon rule of law, respect for state sovereignty, ease of travel, and the smoother functioning of international labor markets. The payoff for sending states is greater freedom of movement for their nationals, greater foreign reserves and a more favorable balance of payments (thanks to remittances), increased prospects for return (brain gain) migration, and increases in cultural and economic exchange, including technology transfers – potentially a "win-win-win" for sending and receiving states, as well as the migrants themselves.[48] Terrorist attacks can upset this delicate equilibrium and lead to defections. The U.S. is considering the suspension of its visa-waiver program with European states because of the terrorist attacks in Paris, which were perpetrated by EU nationals.

However, changes in the international system with the end of the Cold War have altered this game in several ways. First, it has made defection easier. Since 1990, states have been more likely to pursue beggar-thy-neighbor policies by closing their borders and not cooperating with neighboring states in the making of migration and refugee policies. The Schengen process itself is a kind of beggar-thy-neighbor policy on a regional scale. Second, the new post-Cold War configurations of interests and power, both at the international and domestic levels, make it more difficult to pursue a multilateral strategy for controlling international migration. Rights-markets coalitions have been breaking apart in the dominant liberal states, increasing polarization and politicization over immigration and refugee issues. Yet liberalization and democratization in formerly authoritarian states to the east and south have dramatically reduced the transaction costs for emigration.[49] Initially, this caused panic in Western Europe, where there was a fear of mass migrations from east to west. Headlines screamed "The Russians are Coming!" Even though these massive flows did not materialize, Western states began to hunker down and search for ways to reduce or stop immigration. The time horizons of almost all Western democracies suddenly were much shorter because of these changes in domestic and international politics, and the terrorist attacks of the 2000s have exacerbated these fears, as migration and mobility have come to be perceived as greater threats to national security, especially in the post-9/11 strategic environment.

If the U.S. or the EU were to defect from the liberal refugee and migration "regimes", such as they are, it could mean the collapse of these regimes. In game theoretic terms, such defections would fundamentally alter the equilibrium outcome, and it would be very costly to all states and to the international community. The process of globalization of exchange and increased mobility could be quickly and dramatically reversed. To prevent the collapse of liberal migration and refugee regimes the U.S. and other liberal states must pursue an aggressive strategy of multilateralism, taking the short-term political heat for long-term political stability and economic gain, much as Angela Merkel and Germany have done in the face of the refugee crisis of 2015–16. This happened in the areas of international finance, with the collapse of the Bretton Woods

48 Russell 1986; Hollifield *et al.* 2007; Ratha 2007; Faini 2007.

49 Hollifield & Jillson 1998; Geddes 2003; Koslowski 2005; Kessler & Rother 2016.

system in the early 1970s and the creation of the G-7, and in trade, with the Latin debt crisis of the 1980s and Asian crisis of the 1990s. Without the kind of leadership exhibited in international trade and finance, irregular migrations will increase and become ever more threatening, leading more states to close their borders.

## 7.5 The Emerging "Migration State"

International migration is likely to increase in coming decades, unless there is some cataclysmic international event, like war or economic depression. Despite the 9/11 terrorist attack on the United States and various attacks in Europe, the liberal democracies have remained relatively open to international migration. Global economic inequalities mean that supply-push forces remain strong, while at the same time demand-pull forces are intensifying.[50] The growing demand for highly skilled workers and the demographic decline in the industrial democracies create economic opportunities for migrants. Transnational networks have become more dense and efficient, linking the sending and receiving societies. These networks help to lower transaction costs and reduce the risks of migration, making it easier for people to move across borders and over long distances. Moreover, when legal migration is not an option, migrants have increasingly turned to professional smugglers, and a global industry of migrant smuggling – often with the involvement of organized crime – has sprung up, especially in the last decade of the twentieth century.[51] Hardly a week passes without some news of a tragic loss of life associated with migrant smuggling.[52]

But migration, like any type of transnational economic activity (such as trade and foreign investment), cannot and does not take place in a legal or institutional void. As we have seen, states have been and still are deeply involved in organizing and regulating migration and the extension of rights to nonnationals has been an extremely important part of the story of international migration in the post-World War II period. For the most part, rights that accrue to migrants come from the legal and constitutional protections guaranteed to all "members" of society.[53] Thus if an individual migrant is able to establish some claim to residence on the territory of a liberal state, his or her chances of being able to remain and settle will increase. At the same time, developments

50 Martin, Abella & Kuptsch 2006.

51 Sadiq 2009.

52 Kyle & Koslowski 2000.

53 Layton-Henry 1990; Hollifield 1992a, 1999; Joppke 2001.

in international human rights law have helped to solidify the position of individuals vis-à-vis the nation-state, to the point that individuals (and certain groups) have acquired a sort of international legal personality, leading some analysts to speculate that we are entering a post-national era, characterized by 'universal personhood',[54] the expansion of 'rights across borders',[55] and even 'transnational citizenship'.[56]

Others have argued that migrants have become transnational, because so many no longer reside exclusively on the territory of one state,[57] opting to shuttle between a place of origin and destination. This line of argument gives priority to agency as a defining feature of contemporary migrations; but it ignores the extent to which state policies continue to shape the choices that migrants make. The migration state is almost by definition a liberal state, inasmuch as it creates a legal and regulatory environment in which migrants can pursue individual strategies of accumulation.

But regulating international migration requires liberal states to be attentive to the (human or civil) rights of the individual; because if rights are ignored or trampled upon the *liberal* state risks undermining its own legitimacy and *raison d'être*.[58] As international migration and transnationalism increase, pressures build upon liberal states to find new and creative ways to cooperate, to manage flows. The definition of the national interest and *raison d'Etat* have to take this reality into account, as rights become more and more a central feature of domestic and foreign policy. New international regimes will be necessary if states are to risk more openness, and rights-based (international) politics will be the order of the day.[59]

Some politicians and policymakers, as well as international organizations, continue to hope for market-based/economic solutions to the problem of regulating international migration. Trade and foreign direct investment – bringing capital and jobs to people, either through private investment or official development assistance – it is hoped, will substitute for migration, alleviating both supply-push and demand-pull factors.[60] Even though trade can lead to factor-price equalization in the long term, as we have seen in the case of the European Union,[61] in the short and medium term exposing LDCs to market forces results

54 Soysal 1994.

55 Jacobson 1996.

56 Bauböck 1994.

57 Glick-Schiller 1999; Levitt 2001.

58 Hollifield 1999.

59 Hollifield 1992b, 1994b, 2000b, 2000c; Hollifield, Martin & Orrenius 2014.

60 Bhagwati 1983; Martin, Martin & Weil 2006; Martin, Abella & Kuptsch 2006; Hollifield, Martin & Orrenius 2006.

61 Straubhaar 1988.

in increased (rather than decreased) migration, as is evident with NAFTA and the US-Mexican relationship.[62] Likewise, trade in services can stimulate more "high end" migration, because these types of products cannot be produced or sold without the movement of the individuals who make and market them.[63]

In short, the global integration of markets for goods, services and capital entails higher levels of international migration; therefore, if states want to promote freer trade and investment, they must be prepared to manage higher levels of migration. Many states (like Canada, Australia, and Germany) are willing, if not eager, to sponsor high-end migration, because the numbers are manageable, and there is likely to be less political resistance to the importation of highly skilled individuals. However, mass migration of unskilled and less educated workers is likely to meet with greater political resistance, even in situations and in sectors, like construction or health care, where there is high demand for this type of labor. In these instances, the tendency is for governments to go back to the old guest worker models, in hopes of bringing in just enough temporary workers to fill gaps in the labor market, but with strict contracts between foreign workers and their employers that limit the length of stay and prohibit settlement or family reunification.[64] The alternative is illegal immigration and a growing black market for labor – a Hobson's choice.

The most basic function of the modern state, providing security for the territory, the population, and the government has not changed much since the creation of the garrison state and the evolution of the Westphalian system of nation-states in the sixteenth and seventeenth centuries (see figure 7.6). But the eighteenth and nineteenth centuries saw the rise of what Richard Rosecrance (1986) has labeled the *trading state*, where economic considerations (free trade and a stable international monetary system) often take precedence over crude power maximization. The latter half of the twentieth century has given rise to the *migration state*, where states are constrained by 'embedded liberalism' and rights based politics. In fact, from a strategic, economic and demographic standpoint, trade and migration go hand in hand; because the wealth, power and stability of the state is now more than ever dependent on its willingness *to risk both trade and migration*.[65] In launching a new "blue card" program to attract highly skilled foreign workers, the European Union is clearly seeking to emulate the United States and Canada, on the premise that global competitiveness, power, and economic security are closely related to a willingness to accept immigrants. Europeans are somewhat reluctantly following the American and

62 Martin 1993b; Massey, Durand & Malone 2002; Hollifield & Osang 2005; Rosenblum 2006.

63 Bhagwati 1998; Ghosh 2000.

64 Miller & Martin 1982; Rogers 1985.

65 Lusztig 1996; Hollifield 1998, 2004; Hatton & Williamson 1998.

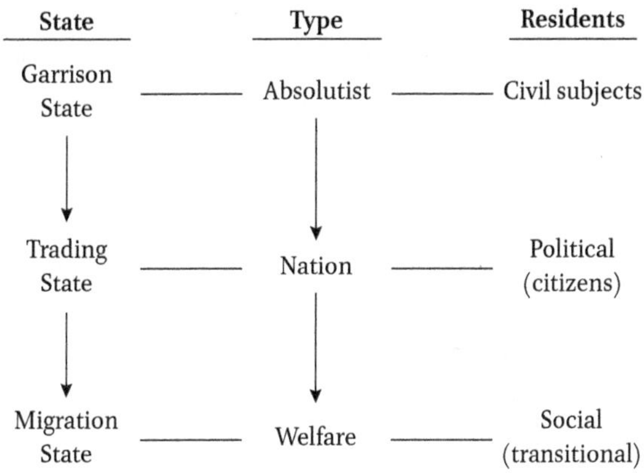


FIGURE 7.6 *The modern state: 3 functions.*

Canadian examples in order to enhance their material power and wealth. But, in one important respect, Europe has an advantage over the United States, and Canada or Australia. Europe is a regional economic enterprise, which is not only creating a free trade zone, but also a free migration area.

Now more than ever, *international security and stability are dependent on the capacity of states to manage migration.* It is extremely difficult, if not impossible, for states to manage or control migration either unilaterally or bilaterally. Some type of multilateral/regional regime is required, similar to what the EU has constructed for nationals of the member states. The EU model, as it has evolved from Rome to Maastricht to Amsterdam and beyond, points the way to future migration regimes, because it is not based purely on *homo economicus*, but incorporates rights for individual migrants and even a rudimentary citizenship, which continues to evolve.[66] The problem, of course, in this type of regional migration regime is how to deal with third country nationals (TCNs). As the EU expands and borders are relaxed, the issue of TCNs, immigrants, and ethnic minorities becomes ever more pressing, and new institutions, laws and regulations must be created to deal with them.[67]

In the end, the EU, by creating a regional migration regime and a kind of supra-national authority to deal with migration and refugee issues, allows the member states to finesse, if not escape, the liberal paradox.[68] Playing the good cop/bad cop routine and using symbolic politics and policies to maintain the illusion of border control help governments fend off the forces of closure, at

66 Geddes 2003; Lahav 2004.

67 Guiraudon 1998.

68 Geddes 2003.

least in the short run.[69] In the end, however, it is the nature of the liberal state itself and the degree to which openness is institutionalized and (constitutionally) protected from the "majority of the moment", that will determine whether states will continue to risk trade and migration.[70]

Regional integration reinforces the trading state and acts as a mid-wife for the migration state. In the EU, migrants are gradually acquiring the rights that they need in order to live and work on the territory of the member states.[71] Regional integration blurs the lines of territoriality, lessening problems of integration and national identity. The fact that there is an increasing disjuncture between people and place – which in the past might have provoked a crisis of national identity and undermined the legitimacy of the nation-state – is less of a problem when the state is tied to a regional regime, like the EU. This does not mean, of course, that there will be no resistance to freer trade and migration. Protests against globalization and nativist or xenophobic reactions against immigration have been on the rise throughout the OECD world.[72] Nonetheless, regional integration – especially when it has a long history and is deeply institutionalized as it is in Europe – makes it easier for states to risk migration and for governments to construct the kinds of political coalitions that will be necessary to support and institutionalize greater openness.

Mexican leaders, like former Presidents Raul Salinas de Gortari and Vicente Fox, looked to Europe as a model for how to solve problems of regional integration, especially the very delicate political issue of illegal Mexican immigration to the United States. Their argument is that freer migration and a more open (normalized) border are logical extensions of the North American Free Trade Agreement (NAFTA). The government of Ernesto Zedillo moved to grant dual nationality to Mexican nationals living north of the border, thereby taking a big step towards consolidating and extending the rights of Mexicans in the US. But, the US government under George W. Bush was reluctant to move so fast with economic and political integration, especially after the attack of September 11, 2003, preferring instead to create new guest worker programs, or to continue with the current system, which tolerates high levels of unauthorized migration from Mexico.[73] Clearly, however, North America is the region that is closest to taking steps towards an EU-style regional migration regime, and the U.S. is facing the prospect of another amnesty comparable to the one carried out as part of the 1986 Immigration Reform and Control Act. In the long run,

69 Rudolph 2006.

70 Hollifield 2000a, 2008; Hollifield *et al.* 2008.

71 Layton-Henry 1990; Groenendijk *et al.* 2000; Geddes 2003; Hollifield 1992b & 2000b.

72 Bhagwati 2004.

73 Massey, Durand & Malone 2002; Fitzgerald 2009.

it is difficult for liberal states, like the U.S., to sustain a large, illegal population. For this reason, amnesties, legalizations, or regularizations have become a common feature of the migration state.

Even though there are large numbers of economic migrants in Asia, this region remains divided into relatively closed and often authoritarian societies, with little prospect of granting rights to migrants and guest workers.[74] The more liberal and democratic states, like Japan, Taiwan and South Korea, are the exceptions; but they have only just begun to grapple with the problem of immigration, on a relatively small scale.[75] In Africa and the Middle East which have high numbers of forced migrants and refugees, there is a great deal of instability as a result of civil wars, diasporas abound, and states are fluid with little institutional or legal capacity for dealing with international migration.[76]

## 7.6 Conclusion

Migration is both a cause and a consequence of political and economic change. International migration, like trade, is a fundamental feature of the postwar liberal order. But, as states and societies become more liberal and open, migration has increased. Will this increase in migration be a virtuous or a vicious cycle? Will it be destabilizing, leading the international system into greater anarchy, disorder and war; or will it lead to greater openness, wealth and human development? Much will depend on how migration is managed by the more powerful liberal states, because they will set the trend for the rest of the globe. To avoid a domestic political backlash against immigration, the rights of migrants must be respected and states must cooperate in building an international migration regime. We have argued that the first, halting steps towards such a regime have been taken in Europe, and that North America is likely to follow.[77] As liberal states come together to manage this extraordinarily complex phenomenon, it may be possible to construct a truly international regime, under the auspices of the United Nations. But we are not sanguine about this possibility, because the asymmetry of interests, particularly between the developed and the developing world, is too great to permit states to overcome problems of coordination and cooperation. Even as states become more dependent on trade and migration, they are likely to remain trapped in a liberal paradox, needing to be economically open and politically closed, for decades to come.

---

74 Fields 1994; Sadiq 2009.

75 Cornelius, *et al.* 2004.

76 Lischer 2005; Adamson 2006; Salehyan 2009; Betts 2009a.

77 Hollifield 1997b; 2004.

## References

Adamson, F. (2006), 'Crossing borders: international migration and national security', *International Security* 31(1), pp. 165–199.

Bauböck, R. (1994), *Transnational citizenship: membership and rights in international migration,* Aldershot (UK): Edward Elgar.

Betts, A. (2013), *Survival migration: failed governance and the crisis of displacement,* Ithaca (NY): Cornell University Press.

Betts, A. (2009a), *Forced migration and global politics,* Oxford: Wiley-Blackwell.

Betts, A. (2009b), *International protection by Persuasion: international cooperation in the refugee regime,* Ithaca (NY): Cornell University Press.

Bhagwati, J. (2004), *In defense of globalization,* New York: Oxford University Press.

Bhagwati, J. (1998), *A stream of windows: unsettling reflections on trade, immigration, and democracy,* Cambridge (MA): MIT Press.

Bhagwati, J. (1983), *International factor mobility,* Cambridge (MA): MIT Press.

Brettell, C.B. (2014), 'Theorizing migration in anthropology: the cultural, social, and phenomenological dimensions of movement', in: C.B. Brettell & J.F. Hollifield (eds.), *Migration theory: talking across disciplines,* New York: Routledge.

Brimelow, P. (1995), *Alien nation: common sense about America's immigration disaster,* New York: Random House.

Brubaker, R. (1992), *Citizenship and nationhood in France and Germany* Cambridge (MA): Harvard University Press.

Brubaker, R. (1996), *Nationalism reframed nationhood and the national question in the new Europe,* Cambridge: Cambridge University Press.

Calavita, K. (1992), *Inside the state: the bracero program, immigration and the INS,* New York: Routledge.

Castles, S. & G. Kosack (1985), *Immigrant workers and class structure in Western Europe,* New York: Oxford University Press.

Castles, S. & A. Davidson (2000), *Citizenship and migration: globalization and the politics of belonging,* New York: Routledge.

Castles, S. & M. Miller (2009), *The age of migration: international population movements in the modern world,* New York: Guilford.

Clemens, M.A. (2011), 'Economics and emigration: trillion dollar bills on the sidewalk?', *Journal of Economic Perspectives* 25(3) pp. 83–106.

Collier, P. (2013), *Exodus: how migration is changing our world,* Oxford: Oxford University Press.

Cornelius, W.A., Ph.L. Martin & J.F. Hollifield (eds.), (1994), *Controlling immigration: a global perspective 1st edn,* Stanford (CA): Stanford University Press.

Faini, R. (2007), 'Remittances and the brain drain: do more skilled migrants remit more?', *The World Bank Economic Review* 21(2) pp. 177–191.

Fields, G. (1994), 'The migration transition in Asia', *Asian and Pacific Migration Journal* 3(1) pp. 7–30.

FitzGerald, D. (2009), *A nation of emigrants: how Mexico manages its migration*, Berkeley: University of California Press.

FitzGerald, D. (2014), 'The sociology of international migration', in: C.B. Brettell & J.F. Hollifield (eds.), *Migration theory: talking across disciplines*, New York: Routledge.

FitzGerald, D.S. & D. Cook-Martín (2014), *Culling the masses: the democratic origins of racist immigration policy in the Americas*, Cambridge (MA): Harvard University Press.

Freeman, G.P. (1995), 'Modes of immigration politics in liberal democratic states', *International Migration Review* 29(4) pp. 881–902.

Freeman, G.P. (1998a), 'The decline of sovereignty? Politics and immigration restriction in liberal states', in: Christian Joppke (ed.), *Challenge to the nation-state*, Oxford: Oxford University Press.

Freeman, G.P. (1998b), '*Toward a theory of the domestic politics of international migration in Western nations*', South Bend (IN): Nanovic Insititute, University of Notre Dame.

Freeman, G.P. (2004), 'Immigrant incorporation in Western democracies', *International Migration Review* 38(3) pp. 945–969.

Gabaccia, D. (2014), 'Time and temporality in migration studies', in: C.B. Brettell & J.F. Hollifield (eds.), *Migration theory: talking across disciplines*, New York: Routledge.

Geddes, A. (2003), *The politics of migration and immigration in Europe*, London: Sage Publications.

Ghosh, B. (ed.), (2000), *Managing migration: the need for a new international regime*, Oxford: Oxford University Press.

Ghosh, B. (1997), *Gains from global linkages: trade in services and movement of persons*, London: Macmillan.

Gibney, M.J. (2004), *The ethics and politics of asylum: liberal democracy and the response to refugees*, Cambridge: Cambridge University Press.

Glick Schiller, N. (1999), 'Transmigrants and nation-states: something old and something new in the U.S. immigrant experience', in: Charles Hirschman, Philip Kasinitz & Josh DeWind (eds.), *The handbook of international migration: the American experience*, New York: Russell Sage, pp. 94–119.

Goldstein, J. (1993), 'Creating the GATT rules: politics, institutions, and American policy', in: John G. Ruggie (ed.), *Multilateralism matters: the theory and practice of an institutional form*, New York: Columbia University Press.

Goodwin-Gill, G.S. (1996), *The refugee in international law*, Oxford: Clarendon.

Groenendijk, K., E. Guild & R. Barzilay (2000), *The legal status of third country nationals who are long-term residents in a member state of the European union*, Nijmegen: University of Nijmegen Centre for Migration Law.

Guiraudon, V. (1998), 'Third country nationals and European law: obstacles to rights' expansion', *Journal of Ethnic Studies* 24(4) pp. 657–674.

Guiraudon, V. & G. Lahav (2000), 'A reappraisal of the state sovereignty debate: the case of migration control', *Comparative Political Studies.*

Hatton, T.J. & J.G. Williamson (1998), *The age of mass migration: causes and economic impact,* New York: Oxford University Press.

Hobsbawm, E. (1990), *Nations and nationalism since 1780,* Cambridge: Cambridge University Press.

Hollifield, J.F. (2012), 'Migration and international relations', in: M.R. Rosenblum & D.J. Tichenor (eds.), *The oxford handbook of the politics of international migration,* Oxford: Oxford University Press.

Hollifield, J.F. (2010), 'Should countries liberalize immigration policies? yes' in: P.M. Haas, J.A. Hird & B. McBratney (eds.), *Controversies in globalization: contending approaches in international relations,* Washington: CQ Press.

Hollifield, J.F. (2005), 'Sovereignty and migration', in: M.J. Gibney & R. Hansen (eds.), *Immigration and asylum from 1900 to the present, volume two,* Santa Barbara (CA): ABC-CLIO.

Hollifield, J.F. (2004), 'The emerging migration state', *International Migration Review* 38 pp. 885–912.

Hollifield, J.F. (2000a), 'Migration and the "new" international order: the missing regime', in: B. Gosh (ed.), *Managing migration: time for a new international regime,* Oxford: Oxford University Press.

Hollifield, J.F. (2000b), 'Immigration and the politics of rights', in: M. Bommes & A. Geddes (eds.), *Migration and the welfare state in contemporary Europe,* London: Routledge.

Hollifield, J.F. (2000c), 'Immigration in two liberal republics', *German Politics and Society,* 18/1, Spring, pp. 76–104.

Hollifield, J.F. (1999), 'Ideas, institutions and civil society: on the limits of immigration control in liberal democracies', *IMIS-Beiträge* 10/January, pp. 57–90.

Hollifield, J.F. (1998), 'Migration, trade and the nation-state: the myth of globalization', *UCLA Journal of International Law and Foreign Affairs* 3(2) pp. 595–636.

Hollifield, J.F. (1997a), *L'Immigration et L'Etat-Nation à La Recherche d'un Modèle National,* Paris: L'Harmattan.

Hollifield, J.F. (1997b), 'Immigration and integration in Western Europe: a comparative analysis', in: E. Uçarer & D. Puchala (eds.), *Immigration into Western societies: problems and policies,* London: Pinter.

Hollifield, J.F. (1994), 'Entre droit et marché', in: B. Badie & C Wihtol de Wenden (eds.), *Le défi migratoire: Questions de relations internationales,* Paris: Presses de la Fondation Nationale des Sciences Politiques.

Hollifield, J.F. (1992a), *Immigrants, markets and states: the political economy of postwar Europe,* Cambridge (MA): Harvard University Press.

Hollifield, J.F. (1992b), 'Migration and international relations: cooperation and control in the European Community', *International Migration Review* 26(2) pp. 568–595.

Hollifield, J.F. & T.K. Wong (2014), 'The politics of international migration: how can "bring the state back in?"' in: C.B. Brettell & J.F. Hollifield (eds.), *Migration theory: talking across disciplines,* New York: Routledge.

Hollifield, J.F., P.M. Orrenius & Ph.L. Martin (eds.), (2014), *Controlling immigration: a global perspective, 2nd edn,* Stanford (CA): Stanford University Press.

Hollifield, J.F. & C.J. Wilson (2011), 'Rights-based politics, immigration and the business cycle, 1890–2008', in: B. Chiswick (ed.), *High-skilled immigration in a global labor market,* Washington, DC: American Enterprise Institute Press.

Hollifield, J.F., V.F. Hunt & D.J. Tichenor (2008), 'Immigrants, markets and the American state: the United States as an 'emerging migration state', *Washington University Journal of Law & Policy* 27 pp. 7–44.

Hollifield, J.F. & C. Jillson (eds.), (1999), *Pathways to democracy: the political economy of democratic transitions,* New York: Routledge.

Hollifield, J.F. & Th. Osang (2005), 'Trade and migration in North America: the role of NAFTA', *Law and Business Review of the Americas* 11(3–4) pp. 327–360.

Hollifield, J.F., P. Orrenius & Th. Osang (eds.), (2006), *Trade, migration and development* Dallas: Federal Reserve Bank of Dallas.

Huntington, S.P. (1996), 'The West: unique, not universal', *Foreign Affairs* 75(6) pp. 28–46.

Huntington, S.P. (2004), *Who are we? The challenges to America's identity,* New York: Simon & Schuster.

Jacobson, D. (1996), *Rights across borders: immigration and the decline of citizenship,* Baltimore (MD): Johns Hopkins University Press.

Joppke, Ch. (ed.), (1998a), *Challenge to the nation-state: immigration in Western Europe and the United States,* Oxford: Oxford University Press.

Joppke, Ch. (1998b), 'Why liberal states accept unwanted migration', *World Politics* 50(2) pp. 266–293.

Joppke, Ch. (2001), 'The legal-domestic sources of immigrant rights: the United States, Germany and the European Union', *Comparative Political Studies* 34(4) pp. 339–366.

Joppke, Ch. (2005), *Selecting by origin: ethnic migration in the liberal state,* Cambridge (MA): Harvard University Press.

Keohane, R.O. & H.V. Milner (1996), *Internationalization of domestic politics,* New York: Cambridge University Press.

Keohane, R.O. & J.S. Nye (1977), *Power and interdependence: world politics in transition,* Boston: Little, Brown.

Kessler & Rother (2016), *Democratization through migration?: political remittances and participation of Philippine return migrants*, Lanham (MA): Lexington Books.

King, D.S. (2000), *Making Americans: immigration, race and the diverse democracy*, Cambridge (MA): Harvard University Press.

King, D.S. (2005), *The liberty of strangers: making the American nation*, New York, NY: Oxford University Press.

Kohn, H. (1962), *The age of nationalism: the first era of global history*, New York: Harper &Row.

Koslowski, R. (2000), *Migrants and citizens: demographic change in the European system*, Ithaca (NY): Cornell University Press.

Koslowski, R. (2005), *International migration and the globalization of domestic politics*, London: Routledge.

Krasner, S.D. (1999), *Sovereignty: organized hypocrisy*, Princeton (NJ): Princeton University Press.

Kyle, D. & R. Koslowski (2001), *Global human smuggling: comparative perspectives*, Baltimore (MD): Johns Hopkins University Press.

Lahav, G. (2004), *Immigration and politics in the new Europe*, Cambridge: Cambridge University Press.

Layton-Henry, Z. (ed.), (1990), *The political rights of migrant workers in Western Europe*, London: Sage.

Levitt, P. (2001), *The transnational villagers*, Berkeley and Los Angeles (CA): University of California Press.

Lischer, S. (2005), *Dangerous sanctuaries: refugee camps, civil war and the dilemmas of humanitarian aid*, Ithaca: Cornell University Press.

Loescher, G., A. Betts & J. Milner (2008), *UNHCR: the politics and practice of refugee protection into the 21st century*, London: Routledge.

Lusztig, M. (1996), *Risking free trade: the politics of trade in Britain, Canada, Mexico and the United States*, Pittsburgh (PA): University of Pittsburgh Press.

Martin, L. (1993a), 'The rational state choice of multilateralism', in: J.G. Ruggie (ed.), *Multilateralism matters: the theory and practice of an institutional form* New York: Columbia University Press.

Martin, Ph.L. (1993b), *Trade and migration: NAFTA and agriculture*, Washington (DC): Institute for International Economics.

Martin, Ph.L., M. Abella & Ch. Kuptsch (2006), *Managing labor migration in the twenty-first century* New Haven (CT): Yale University Press.

Martin, Ph.L., S.F. Martin & P. Weil (2006), *Managing migration: the promise of cooperation*, Lanham (MD): Lexington Books.

Martin, Ph.L. & J. Widgren (1996), 'International migration: a global challenge', *Population Bulletin* 51(1) pp. 1–48.

Martin, S.F. (2014), *International migration: evolving trends from the early twentieth century to the present*, New York: Cambridge University Press.

Massey, D.S. (1987), *Return to Aztlan: the social processes of international migration from Western Mexico,* Berkeley and Los Angeles: University of California Press.

Massey, D.S., J. Durand & N.J. Malone (2002), *Beyond smoke and mirrors: Mexican immigration in an era of economic integration,* New York: Russell Sage Foundation.

Messina, A. (2007), *The logics and politics of Post-WWII migration to Western Europe,* New York: Cambridge University Press.

Miller, M.J. & Ph.L. Martin (1982), *Administering foreign worker programs,* Lexington (MA): D.C. Heath.

Milner, H.V. (1988), *Resisting protectionism: global industries and the politics of international trade,* Princeton (NJ): Princeton University Press.

Milner, H.V. (1997), *Interests, institutions and information: domestic politics and international relations,* Princeton (NJ): Princeton University Press.

Moch, L.P. (1992), *Moving Europeans: migration in Western Europe since 1650,* Bloomington (IN): Indiana University Press.

Moravcsik, A. (1997), 'Taking preferences seriously: a liberal theory of international politics', *International Organization* 51(4) pp. 513–553.

Mundell, R.A. (1957), 'International trade and factor mobility', *American Economic Review* 47 pp. 321–335.

Nugent, W., (1992), *Crossings: the great transatlantic migrations, 1870–1914,* Bloomington (IN): Indiana University Press.

Peters, M.E. (2015), 'Open trade, closed borders: immigration policy in the era of globalization', *World Politics* 67(1) pp. 114–154.

Peters, M.E. (2014), 'Trade, foreign direct investment, and immigration policy making in the United States', *International Organization* 68(4) pp. 811–844.

Piore, M.J. 1979, *Birds of passage: migrant labor in industrial societies*, Cambridge: Cambridge University Press.

Portes, A. (1996), 'Transnational communities: their emergence and significance in the contemporary world-system', in: R.P. Korzeniewidcz & W.C. Smith (eds.), *Latin America in the world economy* Westport, Conn: Greenwood.

Putnam, R. (1988), 'Diplomacy and domestic politics: the logic of two-level games', *International Organization* 42 pp. 427–460.

Putnam, R. (2007), '*E Pluribus unum*: diversity and community in the 21st century', *Scandinavian Political Studies* 30(2) pp. 137–174.

Ratha, D. (2007), 'Leveraging remittances for development', in: J.F. Hollifield, P. Orrenius & Th. Osang (eds.), *Trade, migration and development,* Dallas: Federal Reserve Bank of Dallas.

Robertson, R., 'Globalization and Mexican labor markets', in: Hollifield, J.F., P. Orrenius & Th. Osang, *Trade, migration and development,* Dallas: Federal Reserve Bank of Dallas.

Rogers, R. (ed.), (1985), *Guests come to stay: the effects of European labor migration on sending and receiving countries*, Boulder, Colo: Westview.

Rosecrance, R. (1986), *The rise of the trading state*, New York: Basic Books.

Rosenau, J.N. (1990) *Turbulence in world politics: a theory of change and continuity*, Princeton (NJ): Princeton University Press.

Rosenblum, M.R. (2004), *The transnational politics of U.S. immigration policy*, La Jolla (CA): University of California-San Diego, Center for Comparative Immigration Studies.

Rosenblum, M.R. (2006), 'US-Mexican migration cooperation: obstacles and opportunities', in: Hollifield, J.F., P. Orrenius & Th. Osang (eds.), *Trade, migration and development* Dallas: Federal Reserve Bank of Dallas.

Ruhs, M. (2013), *The price of rights: regulating international labor migration* Princeton (NJ): Princeton University Press.

Ruggie, J.G. (ed.), (1993), *Multilateralism matters: the theory and practice of an institutional Form*, New York: Columbia University Press.

Ruggie, J.G. (1998), *Constructing the world polity: essays on international institutionalization*, New York: Routledge.

Rudolph, Ch. (2006), *National security and immigration: policy development in the United States and Western Europe since 1945*, Stanford: Stanford University Press.

Russell, S.S. (1986), 'Remittances from international migration a review in perspective', *World Development* 41(6) pp. 677–696.

Sadiq, K. (2009), *Paper citizens: how illegal immigrants acquire citizenship in developing countries*, New York: Oxford University Press.

Salehyan, I. (2009), *Rebels without borders: transnational insurgencies in world politics*, Ithaca: Cornell University Press.

Sassen, S. (1991), *The global city: New York, London, Tokyo*, Princeton (NJ): Princeton University Press.

Sassen, S. (1996), *Losing control? Sovereignty in an age of globalization*, New York: Columbia University Press.

Sassen, S. (2006), *Territory, authority, rights: from medieval to global assemblages*, Princeton (NJ): Princeton University Press.

Schlesinger, A. Jr (1992), *The disuniting of America*, New York: W.W. Norton.

Shaw, M.N. (1997), *International law*, Cambridge: Cambridge University Press.

Simon, J. (1989), *The economic consequences of immigration*, Oxford: Blackwell.

Soysal, Y.N. (1994), *Limits of citizenship: migrants and postnational membership in Europe*, Chicago: University of Chicago Press.

Stolper, W.F. & P.A. Samuelson 1941, 'Protection and real wages', *Review of Economic Studies* 9 pp. 58–73.

Straubhaar, Th. (1988), *On the economics of international labor migration*, Bern: Haupt.

Teitelbaum, M.S. (1984), 'Immigration, refugees and foreign policy', *International Organization* 38(3) pp. 429–450.

Thielemann, E. (2003), 'Between interests and norms: explaining burden-sharing in the European Union', *The Journal of Refugee Studies* 16(3) pp. 253–273.

Tilly, Ch. (ed.), (1975), *The formation of national states in Western Europe*, Princeton (NJ): Princeton University Press.

Torpey, J. (2000), *The invention of the passport: surveillance, citizenship, and the state* New York: Cambridge University Press.

Uçarer, E.M. (1997), 'Europe's search for policy: the harmonization of asylum policy and European integration', in: E.M. Uçarer & D.J. Puchala (eds.), *Immigration into Western societies: problems and policies*, London: Pinter.

Waever, O., B. Buzan, M. Kelstrup & P. Lemaitre (1993), *Identity, migration, and the new security agenda in Europe*, New York: St Martin's Press.

Waldinger, R. & D. Fitzgerald (2004), 'Transnationalism in question', *American Journal of Sociology* 109(5) pp. 1177–1195.

Wallerstein, I. (1976), *The modern world system*, New York: Academic Press.

Waltz, K.N. (1979), *Theory of international politics*, Reading (MA): Addison-Wesley.

Weiner, M. (1995), *The global migration crisis: challenge to states and to human rights*, New York: HarperCollins.

Weiner, M. (ed.), (1993), *International migration and security*, Boulder (CO): Westview.

Weiner, M. & S.S. Russell (eds.), (2001), *Demography and national security*, New York: Berghahn Books.

Weiner, M. & M.S. Teitelbaum (2001), *Political demography, demographic engineering*, New York: Berghahn Books.

Wendt, A. (1999), *Social theory of international politics*, Cambridge: Cambridge University Press.

Williamson, J.G. (2006), 'Inequality and schooling responses to globalization forces: lessons from history', in: Hollifield, J.F., P. Orrenius & Th. Osang, *Trade, migration and development*, Dallas: Federal Reserve Bank of Dallas.

Zolberg, A.R. (1981), 'International migration in political perspective', in: M.M. Kritz, C.B. Keely & S.M. Tomasi (eds.), *Global trends in migration: theory and research in international population movements* New York: Center for Migration Studies.

Zolberg, A.R., A. Suhrke & S. Aguayo (1989), *Escape from violence: conflict and the refugee crisis in the developing world*, New York.

CHAPTER 8

# Hotspots, Cold Fact. Managing Migration by Selecting Migrants

*Marie-Laure Basilien-Gainche*

## 8.1 Introduction

The 'Hotspots' approach is one of the immediate actions that has been taken to counter the improperly so-called refugee crisis the Commission announced in May 2015 in the *European Agenda on Migration*.[1] According to the Commission's *Explanatory note on the hotspot approach,* which Statewatch published in July 2015,[2] "the aim of the 'Hotspot' approach is to provide a platform for the agencies to intervene, rapidly and in an integrated manner, in frontline Member States when there is a crisis due to specific and disproportionate migratory pressure at their external borders".[3] This initiative has been presented to provide frontline States with "a comprehensive and targeted support by the EU Agencies" in order "to swiftly identify, register and fingerprint incoming migrants".[4] Therefore, the 'Hotspots' approach entails a genuine cold fact: the European Union and more precisely its Member States has provided a sparse reception to refugees in order to establish a global rejection of migrants, even though the legal obligations that the international, European, and national laws impose on them are thus violated (in particular the right to life and the right to asylum). The expression 'Cold Fact' can be used in the present chapter, because the European approach to the refugee arrivals endorses an uncaring policy built upon deeply concerning indifference and disregard for the human dignity of such third country nationals. Furthermore, one can consider that the risk the current European approach to migration poses is to create a regional 'apartheid' between 'them' and 'us'.[5] Indeed, as Bridget Anderson puts

---

1 COM(2015)240 final, 13 May 2015, p. 6.

2 Document available at: <www.statewatch.org/news/2015/jul/eu-com-hotsposts.pdf>

3 Commission, *Explanatory note on the hotspot approach*, p. 2.

4 COM(2015)240 final, 13 May 2015, p. 6.

5 One must be reminded that 'Cold Fact' is precisely the title of Sixto Rodriguez's first album which became in South Africa the music of the fight against apartheid (particularly the single "Establishment blues"). On the opposition the EU migration law establishes between 'them' and

 | DOI 10.1163/9789004330467_009

it, "what the world is witnessing is not a refugee crisis facing Europe, but a European crisis facing refugees".[6]

Before examining further what the 'Hotspots' approach produces and triggers, it is necessary to determine what exactly hotspots are. According to the Commission, they are sections of European external borders that are "characterised by specific and disproportionate migratory pressure, consisting in mixed migratory flows, which are largely linked to the smuggling of migrants, and where the Member States concerned request support and assistance to better cope with the migratory pressure".[7] Yet every element of such an assertion raises questions. First, though Italian and Greek shores have experienced since Spring 2015 huge migration pressure due to significant refugee maritime arrivals, one could wonder whether such "migratory pressure" could be considered "specific and disproportionate": the refugee maritime arrivals on European shores are forced migration flows among all the others that are spreading all over the globe; perhaps its specificity lies in considering EU territory as a separate entity; and, with regard to its disproportion, it appears that the Commission has omitted to provide a yardstick for measuring it; meanwhile Turkey, Lebanon and Jordan actually welcome incomparable numbers of refugees.[8] Second, the position the Commission adopts in regarding migration flows as mixed needs to be questioned, in so far as it admits that "there is an exponential increase in the number of persons seeking international protection, notably from Syria, Iraq and Afghanistan", that "90% of those using the Eastern Mediterranean route come from one of these three countries":[9] the words that the Commission chooses to encapsulate the situation seem therefore quite misleading, adopting terms that are inappropriate to genuinely qualify the legal issue at stake, that of significant refugee arrivals. Third, by asserting

---

'us', see my analysis developed upon Paul Ricoeur's reflexion in his book *Oneself as another*, Marie-Laure Basilien-Gainche, "Leave and let die. The EU *banopticon* approach of migrants at sea", in: Violeta Moreno-Lax & Eftymios Papastavridis (2017), *Boat refugees' and migrants at sea: a comprehensive approach integrating maritime secutiry in human rights*, Brill.

6 "Why the EU-Turkey migrant deal is a moral disaster", *Fortune*, 17 March 2016, available at: <fortune.com/2016/03/17/eu-turkey-migrant-crisis-deal-disaster>.

7 Commission, *Explanatory note on the hotspot approach*, p. 3.

8 According to the UNHCR, there were at the beginning of August 2016 2,724,937 registered Syrian refugees in Turkey, 1,033,513 in Lebanon, 656,198 in Jordan, 249,395 in Iraq, 114,911 in Egypt. Such numbers don't of course include all the unregistered refugees. Information is available at: <data.unhcr.org/syrianrefugees/regional.php>.

9 Commission, Joint communication on addressing the refugee crisis in Europe. The role of EU external action, JOIN(2015)40 final, 9 September 2015, p. 2.

that these refugee flows "are largely linked to the smuggling of migrants",[10] the Commission tends to overlook the fact that the real and essential causes of such migration flows lie in the fear of the conflict and persecution refugees have experienced in their home countries (Syria, Iraq, Afghanistan, Eritrea), the impossibility of obtaining real and effective protection in the transit countries through which they have passed and the difficulty they face in using legal migration pathways into Europe.

No matter what, the sections of European external borders where 'Hotspots' have been installed are understandably situated in Italy (Lampedusa, Pozzallo, Porto Empedocle, Augusta, Taranto and Trapani) and in Greece (Samos, Lesbos, Chios, Kos and Leros). In these areas, the national authorities benefit from personnel and equipment from EU agencies (Frontex, EASO, Europol, Eurojust), their functions being coordinated by Migration Management Support Teams, along with the EU Regional Task Force (EURTF). The following are the five main aims the 'Hotspots' approach is called to fulfil:

(1) registration and screening of irregular migrants, which Frontex is supposed to ensure in conjunction with the competent national authorities;
(2) briefing of migrants to understand migratory routes and modus operandi, for which Frontex has responsibility ;
(3) investigation of the facilitation of irregular transit and stay, whose responsibility falls on national authorities and Europol agents;
(4) asylum support by channelling refugees into the appropriate procedure, which the UNHCR in conjunction with EASO is supposed to operate; and
(5) return of migrants who do not have the right to stay in the EU legally, with which the national authorities of the Member States concerned are charged.

The main goal of the 'Hotspots' approach is clearly summed up by the Commission: "swiftly identify, register and fingerprint incoming migrants";[11] in other (rather crude) words, the purpose is to separate out a minority of 'good' refugees from what EU ministers want to convince us are a majority of 'bad' (economic) migrants, by considering third country nationals (TCNs) genuinely in need of international protection as irregular migrants. Managing migration by selecting migrants seems to correspond to the position the European Union and its Member States have long adopted and implemented, which the communication the Commission published on 6 April 2016 explicitly confirms as

10 Europol, *Migrant smuggling in the EU*, February 2016.
11 COM(2015)240 final, 13 May 2015, p. 6.

it explicitly refers to a system of selection.[12] This approach further emphasises that the migrants' selection conceals a crueller if possible purpose, which is to admit very few 'refugees' in order to get rid of all the other 'migrants', which reveals how important is the way in which the third country nationals' status is legally defined.

In studying all the documentation (communications, working documents, notes, etc.) the Commission has produced since the publication of the *European Agenda on Migration*, it is clear that the establishment of the 'Hotspots' approach is a key element in the management of the improperly called refugee crisis: the fight against smugglers and traffickers allegedly to disrupt their business model, the relocation programme for refugees, restoration of internal border control, the joint action plan and joint statement concluded between the EU and Turkey, huge pressure and acerbic criticism of Greece. Examining the establishment of the 'Hotspots' approach is henceforward useful for highlighting the way the European Union and its Member States design and apply the reception of refugees and the examination of their claims. Emphasizing the operational purpose of identifying and registering, the EU policy reveals its fundamental intention: categorise, select, reject and return. This was endorsed by the European Council of 25–26 June 2015 within the perspective of "better contain[ing] the growing flows of illegal migration" *inter alia* through the "reinforcement of the management of the Union's external border". The aim of this chapter is to offer some thoughts about the 'Hotspots' approach, and critique the methods and reasons for migrants' selection that its establishment institutionalises. First, the analysis of both the identification process and the fingerprinting registration emphasises the installation of a disturbing hierarchy for the refugees (par. 8.2); second, studying the relocation and resettlement programmes as well as the priority given to improving the effectiveness of return allows us to consider the current European approach to refugees, which is improperly assuming that most of them are undesirable (par. 8.3).

## 8.2 The Methods of Migrants' Selection. Instituting an Upsetting Hierarchy between Refugees

As the European Parliament highlights in its *Report on the situation in the Mediterranean and the need for a holistic EU approach to migration* published on 19 January 2016, "great care needs to be taken to ensure that the categorizing

12 Commission, *Towards a reform of the common European asylum system and enhancing legal avenues to Europe*, COM(2016)167 final, 6 April 2016, p. 19.

of migrants in 'hotspots' is carried out in full respect for the rights of all migrants".[13] The way the 'Hotspots' approach has been designed leads us to think nonetheless that full respect for the rights of all migrants is not and will not be ensured. Among other concerning elements, one must be emphasised here: in the Europol literature, the term 'Hotspots' is employed, accompanied by the adjective 'criminal',[14] indicating some worrying clues concerning the way the European Migrant Smuggling Centre[15] will intervene in the 'Hotspots' via its Europol Mobile Investigation Teams and its Europol Mobile Analysis Teams. Indeed the risk undeniably exists that European agents and national authorities consider incoming migrants to be suspected smugglers who need to be apprehended and convicted, and not as genuine refugees who need to be welcomed and protected.[16] As far as the main and first goal consists in swiftly identifying, registering and fingerprinting incoming migrants, the first subject to explore is the way in which the European Union and its Member States manage the identification process (1.1) and the fingerprinting registration (1.2) that, according to the Commission, "should take place as early as possible in the procedure".[17]

### 8.2.1 *The Identification Process*

According to the UNHCR data, the 856,723 migrants who arrived in the Greek islands in 2015 were Syrian nationals (55%), Afghan nationals (25%) and Iraqi nationals (11%); the 163,114 who arrived by sea in the first eight months of 2016 were from these three countries, though with some changes (48% Syrian, 25% Afghan and 15% Iraqi nationals). The 153,842 migrants who arrived in the Italian islands in 2015 were from: Eritrea (25%), Nigeria (14%) and Somalia (8%), and the 105,628 who arrived in the first eight months of 2016 were: Nigerian

13 EP, LIBE Committee, 2015/2095(INI), 19 01 2016, p. 20, § 74.

14 Europol, *Migrant smuggling in the EU*, February 2016, pp. 6–7.

15 Europol launched on 22 February 2016 the European Migrant Smuggling Centre (EMSC), which is modelled as the European Cybercrime Centre (EC3) or the European Counter Terrorism Centre (ECTC). As Europol asserts, such a Centre tends to support EU Member States in dismantling criminal networks involved in organised migrant smuggling, and consequently focuses its attention and activities on criminal hotspots that "are located along the main migration routes" and that correspond somehow to the "Hotspots" this paper deals with.

16 Commission, *EU action plan against migrant smuggling (2015–2020)*, COM(2015)285 final, 27 May 2015.

17 Commission Staff Working Document on Implementation of the Eurodac Regulation as regards the Obligation to Take Fingerprints, SWD(2015)150 final, 27 May 2015.

nationals (20%), Eritrean nationals (12%) and nationals of equatorial Africa.[18] It seems that the identification process focuses first on determining whether applicants are genuinely of the nationality they claim. The Commission indicates that Europol and Frontex have deployed in all hotspot areas Advance Level Document Experts (ALDO) and dedicated equipment for the detection of fraudulent documents, in order to ascertain whether or not the identity documents the refugees present are forged. This raises some questions. What are the documents to be examined? What does the identity and nationality test entail if the refugees have no documents? How can refugees appeal against the decision denying them the nationality they have pretended to dispose of? As far as none of these questions have obtained a clear answer, the identification process appears disturbing, even more so when its second purpose is examined, which consists in determining whether those migrants are "refugees in clear need of protection". This expression, which is used repeatedly by the Commission, is *per se* not clear at all. It refers in fact to the migrants who are applying for relocation, the migrants who possess a nationality for which the EU-wide recognition rate at first instance is 75% or higher, thus at the moment Syrians, Iraqis and Eritreans.[19] The 'Hotspots' approach consequently creates a distinction between migrants and refugees, and prioritises those who are "in clear need of protection" over those who are not because they are simply in need of protection. Syrians, Iraqis and Eritreans are thus explicitly considered at first glance to have more chance of being recognized as benefitting from international protection, than refugees from Somalia, Afghanistan, Sudan or Nigeria.

Thus a hierarchy which is based on a nationality criterion is set up that affects the very notion of asylum, as it raises, first, the issue of institutionalising discrimination based on nationality, which the Geneva Convention explicitly prohibits, and, second, the question of the obligation of ensuring individual assessment of each refugee's situation. It is well-established and known that the European Union and its Member States have been using for years the notions of 'safe country of origin' and 'safe third country', that establish some ranking between asylum seekers according to their State of origin or transit. Yet the 'Hotspots' approach seems to exacerbate and consolidate this hierarchy, because it induces approval of an implicit very short list of unsafe countries (Syria, Iraq, Eritrea) whose nationals are to be considered as in "clear need of protection". Henceforward all the nationals of all the other countries could

---

18 UNHCR, *Refugees / migrants emergency response – Mediterranean*, last update on 28 August 2016, available at: <data.unhcr.org/mediterranean/regional.php>.

19 Art. 3(2) Decision 2015/1601 of 22 September 2015 establishing provisional measures in the area of international protection for the benefit of Italy and Greece.

be regarded as TCNs who are not clearly in need of protection; Member States could hence be tempted to apply accelerated procedures to them, with shorter deadlines for reaching a decision on the merits of an asylum application, with greater difficulty being recognized as being in a vulnerable situation, with more complexities in applying for international protection when operating on the presumption that the application is unfounded. It should be emphasized here the restrictions the proposal for a regulation establishing an EU common list of safe countries origin has spawned:[20] the European Economic and Social Committee in its opinion asserts that it is "advisable to restrict the use of the concept of safe country of origin";[21] and the Fundamental Rights Agency in its own opinion insists on the indispensable safeguards that must be integrated and deployed at multiple levels as "the concept of safe country of origin may affect different charter rights, including absolute rights which do not allow for exceptions or derogations".[22] And yet the 'Hotspots' approach appears to extend it to all TCNs, except Syrians, Iraqis and Eritreans. Moreover, the strategy for preventing maritime incoming refugees from benefiting from international protection is confirmed by the European Union and its Member States' willingness to regard Turkey as safe:[23] the Commission's proposal to include

20 Proposal for a Regulation of the European Parliament and of the Council establishing an EU common list of safe countries of origin for the purposes of Directive 21013/32/EU of the European Parliament and of the Council on common procedures for granting and withdrawing international protection and amending Directive 2013/32/EU, COM(2015)452 final, 9 September 2015.

21 European Economic and Social Committee, *Opinion on the proposal for a regulation establishing an EU common list of safe countries of origin*, REX/457, 10 December 2015, § 4.2, p. 6.

22 Fundamental Rights Agency, *Opinion concerning an EU common list of safe countries of origin*, 1/2016, 23 March 2016, p. 11.

23 The question of considering Turkey as safe or not is not as simple as it seems. Indeed, the dispute between scholars was harsh particularly on this point at the beginning of 2016, concerning the EU-Turkey deal.
See: Emanuela Roman, Theodore Baird & Talia Radcliffe, "Why Turkey is not a safe country", *Statewatch*, February 2016, available at <www.statewatch.org/analyses/no-283-why-turkey-is-not-a-safe-country.pdf>; Steve Peers & Emanuela Roman, "The EU, Turkey and the refugee crisis: what could possibly go wrong?" *EU Law Analysis*, 5 February 2016, available at <eulawanalysis.blogspot.fr/2016/02/the-eu-turkey-and-refugee-crisis-what.html>.
Daniel Thym, "Why the EU-Turkey deal is legal and a step in the right direction", *Verfassungsblog*, 9 March 2016, available at <verfassungsblog.de/why-the-eu-turkey-deal-is-legal-and-a-step-in-the-right-direction>; James Hathaway, "Three legal requirements of the EU-Turkey deal", *Verfassungsblog*, 9 March 2016, available at <verfassungsblog.de/three-legal-requirements-for-the-eu-turkey-deal-an-interview-with-james-hathaway>.

Turkey in the European common list of safe countries of origin,[24] and to regard Turkey as a safe third country, which is what the EU-Turkey Joint Action has implicitly induced,[25] the so-called 'Samson plan' explicitly considers,[26] and the EU-Turkey Joint Statement published on 18 March 2016 ultimately implies[27] even though the assertion disappeared from the final text. It should be noted here that EU asylum law classifies the 'safe third country' rule as an element determining not the merit but the admissibility of an asylum application, thus allowing national authorities – and particularly the Greek ones – to reject the refugees' asylum applications without examining their substance.

### 8.2.2 *The Fingerprinting Process*

Once the refugees' identification process has been completed, the fingerprinting registration takes place. The emphasis the Commission puts on the effectiveness of such a screening reveals how important it is amongst its ranked priorities. The registration appears to be an imperative whose achievement conditions the refugees' access to their rights and whose non-fulfilment implies negative consequences for them: the principle "no registration, no rights" has been stated, according to which "the registration of migrants (irrespective of their status) is the precondition to appropriately managing flows and setting the rights and duties of migrants";[28] furthermore, the frontline Member States, if facing a refugee who refuses to cooperate being fingerprinted, can use coercion and can even decide to detain him and to examine his asylum

Kay Hailbronner, "Legal requirements for the EU-Turkey refugee agreement", *Verfassungsblog*, 11 March 2016, available at <verfassungsblog.de/legal-requirements-for-the-eu-turkey-refugee-agreement-a-reply-to-j-hathaway>; James Hathaway, "Taking refugee rights seriously", *Verfassungsblog*, 12 March 2016, available at <verfassungsblog.de/taking-refugee-rights-seriously-a-reply-to-professor-hailbronner>.

24 COM(2015)452 final, 9 September 2015.

25 MEMO/15/5777, 6 October 2015 & MEMO/15/5860, 15 October 2015.

26 The 'Samson Plan' called as such because of the position Diederik Samson, leader of the Dutch Labour Party, adopted in January 2016 consists in considering Turkey a safe third country. However, it needs to be explained here that such an idea was previously developed in October 2015 by the European Stability Initiative (ESI), a think tank specialised in Southeast Europe, and was then named the "Merkel Plan", See: ESI, "The Merkel plan: restoring control; retaining compassion – a proposal for the Syrian refugee crisis", 4 October 2015 & "Turkey as a 'safe third country' for Greece", 17 October 2015.

27 Commission, *Next operation steps in EU-Turkey cooperation in the field of migration*, COM(2016)166 final, 16 March 2016, p. 3.

28 Commission, *Report on the follow-up to the leaders meeting on refugee flows along the Western Balkans route*, COM(2015)676 final, 15 December 2015, § 4, p. 7.

application via the accelerated or border procedures.[29] Although the fingerprints of all refugees arriving in Greece and Italy are supposed to be registered in the Eurodac database, the fundamental *rationale* for the screening appears to be clearly aimed at enhancing border migration control and not ensuring due examination of asylum applications. This assertion has been confirmed by the means that have been chosen to and have been provided for achieving the fingerprinting registration of all refugees in the 'Hotspots': the presence of Frontex has been reinforced far more than EASO's in both the Greek 'Hotspots' (419 Frontex agents and 133 EASO experts including 53 interpreters and 21 interim staff) and the Italian ones (370 Frontex agents and 16 EASO experts).[30] Nevertheless, the material means at the disposal of the national authorities do not seem sufficient to allow them to register the fingerprints of the incoming migrants within a reasonable period of time. Greece used 46 Eurodac devices during December 2015.[31] As one machine can process 100 cases in a day, the five Greek hotspots can process some 4,600 refugees. Since 2,000 refugees are reported to be currently arriving in Greece each day (2,175 daily in January 2016, 1,800 daily in February 2016), the number of Eurodac machines appears sufficient. But what will happen in the spring and summer when refugee arrivals could increase to 7,000 a day? One can then easily understand why the national authorities have submitted a request for emergency funding to cover the purchase of an additional 90 fingerprinting stations.[32]

Fingerprinting all the refugees in the Eurodac database raises not only practical and quantitative problems, but also, and more importantly, substantive and qualitative issues. Its premise implies the effectiveness of the Dublin system, while the *European Agenda on Migration* implicitly acknowledges the inefficacy of the system. The European Union and its Member States have, therefore, expressed their clear willingness to stick to this deleterious system which is based on the fiction that national authorities are all receiving asylum seekers in a similar manner and are examining their asylum applications in

29 Commission, *Staff working document on implementation of the eurodac regulation as regards the obligation to take fingerprints*, SWD(2015)150 final, 27 May 2015, § 7 and §§ 2–4 respectively.

30 Commission, *State of play of hotspot capacity*, last update on 26 August 2016.

31 Commission, *Progress report on the implementation of the hotspots in Greece progress*, COM(2015)678 final, 15 December 2015, p. 6.

32 By the beginning of March 2016, only 25 of these devices had been provided, with the remaining 65 other stations being ordered and awaiting delivery. – Commission, *Report on the implementation of the hotspot approach in Greece*, COM(2016)141 final, 4 March 2016, p. 6.

the same way, which is crystallising the lack of solidarity with the countries on the Central and East Mediterranean borders of Europe. The proposal for a modification of the Dublin III regulation that the Commission published in May 2016 is particularly revealing.[33] More generally the position the Commission adopts in its communication on a reform of the Common European Asylum System endorses its support for the Dublin system.[34] Given that the situation of refugees in Greece has been particularly drastic for years and that it is currently deteriorating, the fact that the Commission has announced that it will recommend that the European Council confirm reinstatement of Dublin transfers to Greece seems to be genuinely inadequate and counterproductive.[35] As a matter of fact, the all process the 'Hotspots' approach induces presupposes organising reception for the refugees before identifying and fingerprinting them, during handling the screening process, and after finalizing the registration procedures. The example of Lesbos is interesting, as it reveals the reality of the 'Hotspots' registration environment.[36] Moria, a small village northwest of Mytilene, hosts a pre-screening centre where refugees' origins are determined by personnel from Frontex. Syrian nationals are sent to Kara Tepe, a well-managed camp where the conditions are reported to be quite acceptable, thanks to the well-integrated response the professional NGOs have built up (Oxfam, MDM, MSF, IRC): they have their fingerprints registered in the Eurodac database via a process that can last from some hours up to one day;

33 Commission, *Proposal for a regulation of the European parliament and of the council establishing the criteria and mechanisms for determining the member state responsible for examining an application for international protection lodged in one of the member states by a third-country national or a stateless person*, COM(2016)270 final, 4 May 2016.

34 COM(2016)167 final, 6 April 2016.

35 Commission Recommendation of 10 February 2016 addressed to the Hellenic Republic on the urgent measures to be taken by Greece in view of the resumption of transfers under Regulation (EU) n° 604/2013.

36 For a presentation of the situation in Chios, see Catharina Ziebritzki, "Chaos in Chios: legal questions regarding the administrative procedure in the Greek hotspots", *EU Law Analysis*, 26 July 2016, available at: <eumigrationlawblog.eu/chaos-in-chios-legal-questions-regarding-the-administrative-procedure-in-the-greek-hotspots>.
For a more general presentation of the refugees' situation in the Greek hotspots, see the report "Refugees at risk in Greece", Tineke Strik realised on behalf of the Committee on Migration, Refugees and Displaced Persons of the Parliamentary Assembly of the Council of Europe, Doc. 14082, 7 June 2016, available at: <www.assembly.coe.int/nw/xml/XRef/Xref-DocDetails-EN.asp?FileID=22914&lang=EN>.

they wait one or two days afterwards to receive transit papers allowing them to remain in Greece for up to six months, and to venture onto the mainland. The fate of the refugees who are not Syrians is quite different and worrying, as they remain in Moria: the fingerprinting process usually takes about a week and the official temporary camp (the so-called interior camp) can house some 1,000 refugees, but in conditions that are reported as being deeply concerning for thousands of refugees. The hierarchy between refugees that this thus establishes ultimately reveals the temptation and even the disposition of the European Union and its Member States to institutionalise the perception that most refugees are undesirable.

## 8.3 The Reasons of Migrants' Selection. Installing an Improper Undesirability of Most Refugees

The purpose of fingerprinting all refugees in the Eurodac database can at first glance be explained, as less than 50% of refugees arriving in the Italian Islands and 8% of those arriving in the Greek Islands were registered in 2015. Nevertheless, the genuine aim lies elsewhere: it is to prevent incoming migrants from benefiting from the rights to which they are entitled, by subordinating the access to such rights to the achievement of the screening process. According to the principle "no registration no rights", most of the refugees are, in reality, at first glance regarded as undesirable: refugees who are not registered; refugees who are registered and don't want to apply for asylum in the frontline States; refugees who have been fingerprinted and are applying for but who do not meet the conditions for relocation. The wording in the EU-Turkey Joint Statement published on 18 March 2016 is revealing, as it considers all new TCNs crossing from Turkey to the Greek islands as from 20 March 2016 to be irregular migrants, even though the refusal by EU Member States' national authorities to grant a visa results in their irregularly entering the EU, and even though the Geneva Convention on the status of refugees asserts that refugees who claim international protection do not have to produce any documents when so doing. All incoming refugees are supposed to remain in the frontline States they entered, and those who claim international protection are supposed to accept the right of the national authorities of the States concerned to examine their asylum application, insofar as the Italian and Greek authorities are responsible for organising their reception, examining their claim for international protection if they are not eligible or selected under the relocation mechanism (8.3.1), and organising the return of all the unfortunate ones who have been deemed undesirable (8.3.2).

### 8.3.1 *The Relocation Scheme*

On examining Decision 2015/1601 of 22 September 2015 establishing provisional measures in the area of international protection for the benefit of Italy and Greece, the relocation programme appears disturbing as its scope seems inadequate to cope with the current refugee flow. Member States are clearly wrong about the numbers involved: some 160,000 refugees have been confirmed as having been relocated over two years, while more than 1 million refugees entered the EU in 2015 alone.[37] As the European Parliament emphasizes, "the relocation decisions will affect a relatively small number of people, and will leave the large number of applicants originating from other third countries who cannot be relocated".[38] The scope of the relocation programme seems to be inappropriate not only as the volume appears to be inadequate, but also as its implementation seems to be ineffective. The relocation scheme is not working, Dimitri Avramapoulos admitted. By 26 August 2016, Member States had offered a total number of relocation pledges of 12,990; and they had relocated 4,455 refugees: 1,020 from Italy and 3,434 from Greece.[39] Actually very few refugees are eligible to benefit from the relocation programme. According to Article 3(2) of Decision 2015/1601, the relocation scheme applies only to refugees who satisfy cumulative conditions: they must have been properly fingerprinted, must have applied for asylum in the Italian or Greek State they entered, and must be "in clear need of international protection", that is to say who possess a nationality for which the EU-wide recognition rate at first instance is 75% or higher (so Syrians, Iraqis and Eritreans). Additionally, the responsibility of Italy or Greece for examining the asylum applications of the refugees has to be established under Dublin Regulation rules, in conformity with one of the goals of the scheme which re-establishes Eurodac / Dublin normality in the frontline States, as Articles 3(1) and 5(5) of Decision 2015/1601 enounce. The persistence of the Dublin tradition further appear, as the refugees to be

37 Are concerned 39,500 refugees arrived in Italy, whilst this State registered 153.600 arrivals by sea in 2015; are concerned 66,400 refugees arrived in Greece, whilst this State registered 853,319 arrivals by sea in 2015. The remaining 54,000 initially attributed to Hungary are assigned to be relocated from Italy and Greece unless a proposal is submitted by the Commission to the Council before 26 September 2016 to adapt the relocation scheme (Art 4(3) of Decision 2015/1601).

38 EP, LIBE Committee, *Report on the situation in the Mediterranean and the need for a holistic EU approach to migration*, 2015/2095(INI), 19 January 2016, p. 13, § 16.

39 Consequently, by 26 August 2016, Member States had offered only 8.11% of the 160,000 promised places; and they had relocated only 2.78% of the 160,000 eligible places. – Commission, *First report on relation and resettlement*, COM(2016)165 final, 16 March 2016, pp. 5–6 & *State of Play – Relocation*, last update on 30 August 2016.

relocated have no right to choose the State in which they are relocated or to refuse relocation, whereas the host countries can express a preference for the kinds of asylum seekers they are prepared to take. This restricted eligibility for the relocation programme has some worrying consequences.

As it barely works, Italy and Greece are mainly responsible for tackling the crisis and managing the migrant flows. And yet, the 'Hotspots' approach implies that the *operational and financial* support the other Member States provide to Italy and Greece may be suspended if these beneficiary States fail to comply with the 'Hotspots' roadmap, so the frontline States are condemned for the consequences of their partner States' violations. Moreover, the whole conception of the relocation programme hampers its very implementation, as Italy notably registered a lack of eligible refugees for relocation because incoming migrants were increasingly of the wrong nationalities. Furthermore, the mechanism is particularly worrisome, insofar as it leaves the frontline States to examine all the most sensitive and difficult asylum claims, those that are most likely to give rise to long periods of detention and, if rejected, to removal orders and return operations. The European Parliament has noted that: "The Member States of first arrival will therefore have to handle the more complicated asylum claims (and appeals) – meanwhile their asylum national systems are considered to be affected by structural deficiencies –, will have to organise longer periods of reception, and will have to organise and coordinate returns for those ultimately not entitled to international protection".[40] And yet the question arises of effective respect for the right to asylum, of genuine examination of the asylum claims, in those frontline States overwhelmed by significant refugee arrivals. In particular, the way the Greek authorities consider the international protection claims lodged by TCNs coming from Turkey raises some concern. In order to implement the EU-Turkey Joint Statement published on 18 March 2016, the Greek Parliament adopted Law 4357/2016 on Common procedures for granting and withdrawing international protection which entered into force on 3 April 2016.[41] As Turkey is deemed a 'safe third country',[42] the international protection claim lodged by the migrants coming

40 EP, LIBE Committee, *Report on the situation in the Mediterranean and the need for a holistic EU approach to migration*, 2015/2095(INI), 19 January 2016, p. 13, § 17.

41 The text of Law 4357/2016 is available in Greek at: <www.refworld.org/cgi-bin/texis/vtx/rwmain/opendocpdf.pdf?reldoc=y&docid=573ad4db4>.

42 A 'safe third country' is defined as a country: where the people concerned do not have their life or liberty threatened on grounds of 'race, religion, nationality, membership of a particular social group or political opinion' (reference to the Geneva Convention relative to the Status of Refugees); where there is 'no risk of serious harm' (such as death penalty, torture, civilian risk in wartime) in congruence with the European definition of

from Turkey can be rejected not on its merits but on its admissibility.[43] While it is obviously speedier to examine an asylum claim without scrutinizing its merits, the administrative procedure Greek authorities apply is moreover fast-tracked. If Article 31(8) of the Procedures Directive allows national authorities to develop an accelerated procedure for examining some asylum applications, the text does not consider in its long enumeration the case of refugees coming from a 'safe third country' and claiming asylum. Nevertheless, it is arguable that Article 31(8) enounces a non-exhaustive list. And yet Greece seems to have adopted this approach, as Law 4357/2016 states that new applications for asylum, registered at the borders or in camps, will be examined and processed within seven days (Art. 40), and that appeals against a negative decision will be examined and processed with a final decision within seven days (Art. 60).[44] Hence, behind the relocation scheme for a few eligible refugees, stands the goal of returning all the others, in other words most of the refugees.

### 8.3.2 *The Return Goal*

The leitmotiv that resonates in all the documents published or leaked since the presentation of the *European Agenda on Migration* is the purpose of improving the effectiveness of the return policy. The Commission makes such a goal particularly clear when asserting: "An effective policy of return of migrants, who entered the territory of the host country irregularly and do not qualify for international protection is a necessary component of a coherent strategy to discourage irregular migration".[45] Notwithstanding, it is in the EU *Action Plan on Return* that the theme is the most deployed, as the Commission spends all the communication developing its strategy so much so that "Member States may also apply simplified and swift return procedures to

---

subsidiary protection); where the people concerned won't be sent to another country which is unsafe (the *non-refoulement* principle as stated by the Geneva Convention, and as interpreted by the European Court of Human Rights concerning the ban on removal to face torture); and where 'the possibility exists to request refugee status and, if found to be a refugee, to receive protection in accordance with the Geneva Convention'. See Article 38 of Directive 2013/32/EU of 26 June 2013 on common procedures for granting and withdrawing international protection (recast).

43 Steve Peers, "The EU, Turkey and the refugee crisis: what could possibly go wrong?", *EU Law Analysis*, 5 February 2016.

44 In conformity with Article 25 of Directive 2013/32/EU, Article 45 of Law 4357/2016 excludes unaccompanied children and vulnerable asylum-seekers from such a fast-tracked procedure.

45 Commission, *Joint communication on addressing the refugee crisis in Europe. The role of EU external action*, JOIN(2015)40 final, 9 September 2015, p. 9.

migrants apprehended or intercepted in connection with irregular border crossings, under national law, with respect of certain basic safeguards".[46] This sentence seems odd, as it explicitly recognizes that the effectiveness and the rapidity of the return procedures can be at the price of some migrants' rights violations, as it consequently admits that not all basic safeguards must be respected. And yet the concern arises about the remaining rights the Member States have to guarantee to refugees. The Commission continues: "An effective return policy requires the existence of a functioning asylum system, to ensure that unfounded asylum claims lead to swift removal of the person from the European territory".[47] The implicit reference to the fast-tracked procedure and border procedures that Member States can choose to apply in examining asylum applications is obvious. One question has then to be asked: could not this sentence be understood by some Member States as stating that the best way to ensure an effective return policy is to consider most asylum applications as unfounded? This could be one of the useful means that should "foster and steer the development of an integrated system of return management".[48] Amongst the tools that have to be mobilised, the Commission insists on "the revised proposal on smart borders" that "will help enhance rates of return, by creating a record of all cross-border movements of TCNs", as "this will allow tracing persons who overstay as well as facilitating the identification of those who have destroyed their identity documents".[49] Tracking irregular migrants will also become one of the main goals of Eurodac: according to the Commission, "the possible extension of the scope and purpose of the Eurodac Regulation [will] enable its use for return purposes",[50] the system "will be used as a means to accelerate the identification and re-documentation of migrants and will enable a better assessment of the prospect of absconding, thus enhancing the effectiveness and speed of return and readmission procedures".[51] Additionally, the Commission suggests "setting up a dedicated Frontex Return Office, of Frontex Rapid Return Intervention Teams offering support on identification, consular cooperation with third countries, and organizing return operations for Member States".[52]

46 COM(2015)453 final, 9 September 2015, p. 4.
47 COM(2015)453 final, 9 September 2015, p. 5.
48 COM(2015)453 final, 9 September 2015, p. 9.
49 COM(2015)453 final, 9 September 2015, p. 6.
50 COM(2015)453 final, 9 September 2015, p. 6.
51 COM(2016)167 final, 6 April 2016, p. 9.
52 COM(2015)453 final, 9 September 2015, p. 8.

And yet the insistence of the Commission has been concentrated on calls for improving implementation of the readmission agreements already concluded, and for negotiating and concluding readmission agreements with new third States within the Rabat process and the Khartoum process.[53] Different strategies have been proposed: 1) building synergies between the European Integrated Approach on Return towards Third Countries EURINT and the European Return Liaison Officers network EURLO; 2) scaling up the ability of Frontex to provide operational support and analytical capacity on return and readmission; 3) providing third countries with technical support to assist their efforts to put in place readmission arrangements and agreements with other third countries. This very last point seems to pave the way for institutionalizing indirect violations of the *non-refoulement* principle. Considering extra-European solutions as a key tool for improving the effectiveness of the return policy is of course at the core of the EU-Turkey Joint Statement of 18 March 2016. Its first point states that "all the irregular migrants crossing from Turkey into Greek Islands will be returned to Turkey". Steve Peers comments on the "cynical hypocrisy" of the EU and its Member States, when asserting that such a return policy "will take place in perfect compliance with the EU and international law", while it is obvious that "returning 'all' persons who cross from Turkey to the Greek Islands would contradict the ban on collective expulsion in the EU Charter and the ECHR, as well as EU asylum legislation".[54] Yet European cynicism reaches the paradigm as point 9 of the Joint Statement enounces: "The EU and its Member States will work with Turkey in any joint endeavour to improve humanitarian conditions inside Syria, in particular in certain areas near the Turkish border which would allow for the local population and refugees to live in areas which will be more safe". This aim at creating a 'safe zone' within Syria tends to make unproblematic the return policy Turkey operates, while Amnesty International reveals numerous documented cases of refugees being forcibly returned to Syria and Iraq after being intercepted by Turkish authorities while trying to reach the EU, and others being arbitrarily detained without access to lawyers.[55]

---

53 The Commission indicates Turkey, Lebanon, Jordan, Afghanistan, Niger, Libya, Mali, Nigeria, Central African Republic Somalia, Eritrea, Sudan, Bangladesh, Pakistan.

54 Steve Peers, "The final EU/Turkey refugee deal: a legal assessment", *EU Law Analysis*, 18 March 2016. See also: ECtHR 23 Feb. 2012, 27765/09, *Hirsi v. Italy;* ECtHR 21 Oct. 2014, 16643/09, *Sharifi and others v. Italy and Greece*; ECtHR 1 Sep. 2015, 16483/12, *Khlaifia and others v. Italy*.

55 Amnesty International, "Turkey forcibly returns dozens of refugees to Afghanistan hours after EU deal", 23 March 2016.

## 8.4 Conclusion

The EU-Turkey Joint Statement that establishes a 1:1 scheme – for every Syrian being returned to Turkey from the Greek islands, another Syrian will be resettled from Turkey to the EU – is the exemplification of an industrialised and institutionalised selection of refugees at the EU level, the Member States organising their capacity to pick up the migrants they want to welcome and 'legalizing' their refusal to protect all refugees arriving on European shores. Notwithstanding, less than 40% of the irregular migrants that are ordered to leave the EU depart effectively. And that rate is far away from genuinely increasing as refugees from 20 March 2016 onwards start to apply in large numbers for asylum in Greece. So two different scenarios appear that are both unacceptable: first, the return of large numbers of refugees to unsafe or unviable situations without proper consideration of their asylum claims, which entails obvious violations of the right to asylum, the prohibition of collective expulsion, and the principle of *non-refoulement*; second, the encampment of more and more refugees on Italian and Greek soil as migrants still continue to arrive in large numbers, as the other Member States close their doors, as frontline Member States don't succeed in returning them. These regions could be on the brink of disaster as the Commission has asserted that "Member States confronted with a sudden and unexpected of large number of migrants' arrival are allowed flexibility regarding the conditions of closed detention of migrants",[56] and above all as the 'Hotspots' open facilities are turned into closed detention centres.[57] The 'Hotspots' approach has been allegedly elaborated and adopted as a short term policy response, which should have ensured that the problems were quickly dealt with. But it seems that, conversely, it could generate even more critical issues with worrying domino effects in the long term.[58] The 'Hotspots' express no less than the cold fact of the European States' selfishness: they prefer drowning their fundamental values in the deep blue sea than assuming

56 COM(2015)453 final, 09 September 2015, p. 4.

57 UNHCR, "UNHCR redefines role in Greece as EU-Turkey deal comes into effect", 22 March 2016.

58 The Commission admits these possible side effects of the 'hotspots' approach, when recognizing that this one could "include a risk of a build-up of people stranded at the borders, the possible encouragement of smuggling and a diversion of flows elsewhere". See Report from the Commission on the follow up to the Leaders' meeting on refugee flows along the Western Balkan Route, COM(2015)676 final, 15 December 2015, p. 9.

their legal responsibility to protect *The Wretched of the Earth*,[59] *the wrecked of the earth.*

## References

Basilien-Gainche, M.-L. (2017), 'Leave and let die. The EU *banopticon* approach of migrants at sea', in: V. Moreno-Lax & E. Papastavridis, *Boat refugees' and migrants at sea: a comprehensive approach integrating maritime security in human rights*, Brill.

COM(2015)452 final, 9 September 2015.

COM(2016)167 final, 6 April 2016.

EP, LIBE Committee (2016), *Report on the situation in the Mediterranean and the need for a holistic EU approach to migration*, 2015/2095(INI), 19 January 2016.

European Commission (2013), *Commission recommendation of 10 February 2016 addressed to the hellenic republic on the urgent measures to be taken by Greece in view of the resumption of transfers under regulation (EU) n° 604/2013.*

European Commission (2015a), *Joint communication on addressing the refugee crisis in Europe. The role of EU external action*, JOIN(2015)40 final, 9 September 2015.

European Commission (2015b), *EU action plan against migrant smuggling (2015–2020)*, COM(2015)285 final, 27 May 2015.

European Commission (2015c), *Staff working document on implementation of the eurodac regulation as regards the obligation to take fingerprints*, SWD(2015)150 final, 27 May 2015.

European Commission (2015d), *Progress report on the implementation of the hotspots in Greece progress*, COM(2015)678 final, 15 December 2015.

European Commission (2015e), *Report on the follow-up to the leaders meeting on refugee flows along the Western Balkans route*, COM(2015)676 final, 15 December 2015.

European Commission (2016a), *Report on the implementation of the hotspot approach in Greece*, COM(2016)141 final, 4 March 2016.

European Commission (2016b), *Towards a reform of the common European asylum system and enhancing legal avenues to Europe*, COM(2016)167 final, 6 April 2016.

European Commission (2016c), *Next operation steps in EU-Turkey cooperation in the field of migration*, COM(2016)166 final, 16 March 2016.

European Commission (2016d), *Proposal for a regulation of the European parliament and of the council establishing the criteria and mechanisms for determining the member state responsible for examining an application for international protection*

59 Fanon, F. (1968), *The Wretched of the Earth*, New York: Grove Press.

*lodged in one of the member states by a third-country national or a stateless person*, COM(2016)270 final, 4 May 2016.

European Commission (2016e), *State of play of hotspot capacity*, last update on 26 August 2016.

European Economic and Social Committee (2015), *Opinion on the proposal for a regulation establishing an EU common list of safe countries of origin*, REX/457, 10 December 2015.

European Stability Initiative (ESI) (2015a), *The merkel plan: restoring control; retaining compassion – a proposal for the Syrian refugee crisis"*, 4 October 2015.

European Stability Initiative (ESI) (2015b), *Turkey as a "safe third country" for Greece*, 17 October 2015.

Europol (2016), *Migrant smuggling in the EU*, February 2016,< www.europol.europa.eu/publications-documents/migrant-smuggling-in-eu>.

Fanon, F. (1968), *The wretched of the earth*, New York: Grove Press.

Fundamental Rights Agency (2016), *Opinion concerning an EU common list of safe countries of origin*, 1/2016, 23 March 2016.

Hailbronner, K. (2016), 'Legal requirements for the EU-Turkey refugee agreement', *Verfassungsblog*, 11 March 2016, <verfassungsblog.de/legal-requirements-for-the-eu-turkey-refugee-agreement-a-reply-to-j-hathaway>.

Hathaway, J. (2016a), 'Taking refugee rights seriously', *Verfassungsblog*, 12 March 2016, <verfassungsblog.de/taking-refugee-rights-seriously-a-reply-to-professor-hailbronner>.

Hathaway, J. (2016b), 'Three legal requirements of the EU-Turkey deal', *Verfassungsblog*, 9 March 2016, available at <verfassungsblog.de/three-legal-requirements-for-the-eu-turkey-deal-an-interview-with-james-hathaway>.

Peers, S. (2016), 'The final EU/Turkey refugee deal: a legal assessment', *EU Law Analysis*, 18 March 2016.

Peers, S. & E. Roman (2016), 'The EU, Turkey and the refugee crisis: what could possibly go wrong?', *EU Law Analysis*, 5 February 2016, <eulawanalysis.blogspot.fr/2016/02/the-eu-turkey-and-refugee-crisis-what.html>.

Ricoeur, P. (1992), *Oneself as another*, Chicago: University of Chicago Press.

Roman, E., Th. Baird & T. Radcliffe (2016), 'Why Turkey is not a safe country', *Statewatch*, February 2016, <www.statewatch.org/analyses/no-283-why-turkey-is-not-a-safe-country.pdf>.

Thym, D. (2016), 'Why the EU-Turkey deal is legal and a step in the right direction', *Verfassungsblog*, 9 March 2016, <verfassungsblog.de/why-the-eu-turkey-deal-is-legal-and-a-step-in-the-right-direction>.

UNHCR (2016a), *UNHCR redefines role in Greece as EU-Turkey deal comes into effect*, 22 March 2016.

UNHCR (2016b), *Refugees / migrants emergency response – Mediterranean*, [28 August 2016] <data.unhcr.org/mediterranean/regional.php>.

'Why the EU-Turkey migrant deal is a moral disaster', *Fortune*, 17 March 2016, <fortune.com/2016/03/17/eu-turkey-migrant-crisis-deal-disaster>.

Ziebritzki, C. (2016), 'Chaos in Chios: legal questions regarding the administrative procedure in the Greek hotspots', *EU Law Analysis*, 26 July 2016, <eumigrationlawblog.eu/chaos-in-chios-legal-questions-regarding-the-administrative-procedure-in-the-greek-hotspots>.

CHAPTER 9

# Turkey's Role in EU Migration Law and Policy: Turkeys Voting for Christmas

*Margarite Helena Zoeteweij and Ozan Turhan*

## 9.1 Introduction

Irregular migration to the EU from and through Turkey has been an issue in EU-Turkey relations even before the onset of today's refugee crisis. However, with the number of arrivals through Turkey growing exponentially as of 2010, Turkey has been given a central role to play in the EU's implemented and planned actions to combat irregular migration. This contribution contends that by thus entrusting Turkey with the execution of a significant part of the EU migration policy, the EU does not only deliberately make itself dependent on the goodwill of Turkey (bought with promises of more financial assistance, visa facilitation and accelerated accession talks), it also indirectly takes on responsibility for the migration law and policy of Turkey.

To come to this conclusion, the contribution first briefly discusses the development of EU-Turkey relations in general and in particular with regard to migration, to continue with an analysis of Turkey's position in the recent EU response to the refugee crisis from a general EU and human rights perspective. The analysis will also include an evaluation of the new (2014) Turkish law on foreigners and international protection, by analyzing the types of protection it offers and assessing its compatibility with international and European (human rights) standards. Though at the time of publication the EU-Turkey deal will have become obsolete (since the readmission agreement has come into full force in June 2016), the contribution would not be complete without mentioning this milestone, which supports the conclusion that the EU is willing to relinquish principles of EU law in order to rid itself of the problem of irregular migration.

After the EU-Turkey relation spiraling downwards for almost a decade, Turkey became a welcome guest again at the EU negotiating and dining tables in 2015, when the refugee crisis had reached a height. What these negotiations boiled down to is that Turkey agreed to take over a substantial part of the administration of EU migration law in return for money, visa facilitation and the revival of accession talks. On the face of it, this seems to be a good 'deal' for all

 | DOI 10.1163/9789004330467_010

involved. However, civil society and academia have expressed their concern regarding the capability and suitability of Turkey to cope with the enormous number of displaced people within its borders properly. Furthermore, as research for this chapter is being conducted, particularities of the 'deal' such as the visa-liberalization and accelerated accession talks have already played a role in the campaign of some of Britain's politicians to leave the European Union,[1] and political parties in other Member State threatening to do the same. Last but not least, Turkey's President (and former PM) Erdoğan every so often threatens to end the implementation of the deal in order to put pressure on the EU. It seems therefore only reasonable to call the future of the EU's dealings with Turkey with regard to migration management into question.

This contribution argues however that considering the development of the relations between the EU and Turkey and considering the disinclination of the EU Member States to host larger numbers of people in need of international protection, the EU will continue to rely on Turkey (and other third countries) to manage migration towards to EU – with all the consequences that entails. To sustain this argument, the contribution starts with a review of the developments of EU-Turkey relations, with a particular focus on the issue of migration, to continue with an assessment of the human rights compatibility of recent climaxes in these developments, namely the conclusion of the readmission agreement in 2013, the Turkish Law on Foreigners and International Protection of 2014, the EU Agenda on Migration of 2015, the EU-Turkey deal of March 2016 and the (not) coming into force of the readmission agreement for third country nationals in June 2016. This analysis will show that the EU knowingly and willfully involved Turkey, despite its lack in protecting human rights and despite being an unreliable partner, in the management of migration towards the EU and that there is, unfortunately, no reason to assume that the EU will not continue doing so in future – not only in relation to Turkey, but also to other countries.

## 9.2 The Development of EU-Turkey Relations

It is difficult to decide on the beginning of a timeline for the development of the relation between the EU and Turkey. For the purpose of a contribution to this bundle with its focus on migration law and policy, there are a few events

1 The (then) leader of UKIP, Nigel Farage, called the visa-deal a 'huge error of judgment' that would bring Turkey one step closer to full membership of the EU, see: <www.ukip.org/turkey_visa_deal_a_huge_error_of_judgement_says_farage>.

that stand out and that deserve to be mentioned. One of these events is Turkey's unsuccessful application for membership of the EEC in 1959, which nonetheless resulted in the signing of an association agreement in Ankara in 1963 (the Ankara Agreement) and an Additional Protocol to the Agreement in 1973 providing for a gradual establishment of the free movement of workers.[2] The extent of the rights granted to Turkish citizens under association law were not fully understood, and the Court of Justice of the European Union did not have the chance to shed its light on the practical implications of the association law until 1987, when it was asked for a preliminary ruling in the case of Demirel.[3] This case, in its turn, was an indirect result of the military coup in Turkey in 1980 which give rise to a surge in the number of political asylum seekers from Turkey and consequently, on the request of the Turkish government,[4] the introduction of a visa requirement for its citizens by Germany.[5] The German initiative, which was supposed to be implemented only temporarily and in line with Article 7 of the 1958 Agreement on Regulations governing the Movement of Persons between Member States of the Council of Europe to which Turkey is also a party, was quickly followed by other EU Member States, and remained in place despite the principle of the right to visa-free travel as provided in Article 1 of the Agreement.[6] Turkey's second application for EU Membership in 1987, which originally got rejected in 1990 for economic, democratic and human rights reasons,[7] eventually resulted in the opening of accession negotiations between the EU and Turkey in 2005. Turkey is expected to align its legislation

---

2 Article 12 of the Agreement establishing an Association between the European Economic Community and Turkey, *OJ* 1964, p. 3687/64, and Article 36 of the Additional Protocol, and furthermore Decisions 2/76 and 1/80 of the Council of Association.

3 CJEU 30 September 1987, C-12/86, *Demirel v Stadt Schwäbisch Gmünd,* ECLI:EU:C:1987:400. For an overview of the Court's case law on matters related to the EU-Turkey Association, see: K. Groenendijk (2015), 'The court of justice and the development of EEC-Turkey association law', in: D. Thym & M. Zoeteweij-Turhan, *Rights of third-country nationals under EU association agreements: degrees of citizenship*, Leiden: Brill, p. 39.

4 Toygur, I. & M. Ozsoz (2016), *The good, the bad and the ugly – 5 + 1 steps away from visa-free travel for Turkish nationals*, Heinrich Böll Stiftung – European Union, <eu.boell.org/en> 14 June 2016.

5 Groenendijk and Guild give an overview of the dates of the introduction of the visa requirements for Turkish citizens, in: K. Groenendijk & E. Guild, *Visa policy of member states and EU towards Turkish nationals after soysal*, IKV Publications No. 232, Istanbul 2010.

6 Peers, S. (2013), *EU justice and home affairs law*, p. 247; Turhan, O. (2015), 'The implications of the visa requirements for the EU-Turkey customs union: free movement of products – not the producer', in: D. Thym & M. Zoeteweij, *Rights of third-country nationals under EU association agreements*, Leiden: Brill, p. 250.

7 Bulletin of the EC no. 1/2, 77 (1990); also XXIVth General Report (1990), p. 285.

and the application thereof with the EU acquis, and the progress in the alignment is monitored and reported every year by the European Commission in its Progress Report. The obligation to align includes the Turkish asylum and migration law, with all that it entails, as is analyzed in more detail below. The alignment process and negotiations have very much been a stop and start affair, but overall they advance slowly and have yet to result in a clear roadmap for Turkey's accession to the EU; on both sides many begin to doubt that Turkey will ever be able to join at all.

Though the events and developments referred to above are all related to *Turkish* citizens' right to move to and within the EU (and vice versa for EU citizens to move to and within Turkey, though this has never received much attention), and not to the management of migration of third country nationals, all of these events played an important role in the shaping of the relationship between Turkey and the EU. The outcome of the sum of all these events is an imbalanced association, in which Turkey's progress on the road to Membership is dependent not only on the alignment of its laws with the EU acquis which can be reviewed objectively, but also on the willingness of the EU and its individual Member States to welcome Turkey in their midst. This ambivalent situation is capitalized in a very creative way by politicians on the EU and Turkish side, acerbating the situation and making it very challenging to discuss the EU-Turkish relationship in an academic and impartial way in Europe but even more so in Turkey. But independent of the political views with regard to domestic and foreign policies, the Turks' yearning for visa-free travel into the EU is only fed by the apparent and growing unattainability of it. This may also explain why the role that Turkey has been allocated to play in the execution of the EU's migration law and policy has not caused riots or massive protests in Turkey, whereas the presence of (mostly Syrian) asylum seekers have led to large scale demonstrations and unrest in Member States such as Greece, Hungary, Croatia, Greece, Austria and Slovenia in the second half of 2015 and the first months of 2016. The next paragraph analyzes the role the EU has in mind for Turkey with regard to the management of migration towards the EU.

## 9.3 Turkey's Role in the Management of Migration Towards the EU

Apart from its own citizens moving to and within the EU, it has grown to be predominantly Turkey's role as country of transit for irregular migrants traveling from the east and south to the west that worries the EU. Obtaining reliable date on irregular migration to and through Turkey is very challenging, as most of the irregular migration is never properly charted due to its irregular character. Most of the available statistics are estimates based on data provided by security forces that were until recent changes in the law – which will be discussed below in more detail- the only authority competent to deal with irregular migration.[8] The number of irregular migrants that was apprehended in Turkey between 1995 and 2009 is 797 000, and the nationality of most of the irregular migrants in this period were Pakistani or Afghan. In more recent years this picture has changed. At present, most of the irregular migrants have Syrian nationality, and due to visa liberalization with a number of African countries the share of African irregular migrants is also on the rise.[9] What has not changed is that 68 percent of all irregular migrants in Turkey are considered as (potential) transit migrants that hope to eventually reach the countries of Western Europe. Whereas only one fifth of the total of apprehended irregular migrants was arrested at the eastern borders of Turkey – the eastern external boundary of Turkey with neighboring countries Georgia, Armenia, Azerbaijan, Iran, Iraq and Syria is more than 2000 km long – another two fifth was caught while trying to cross the land and sea borders between Turkey and Greece, whereas the Turkish-Greek land border is just over 200 km. The remaining 40% is apprehended at other places in Turkey. Numbers provided by Frontex are indicating that the actual number of irregular migrants transiting Turkey to reach the EU is higher than those published by the Turkish authorities.[10]

## 9.4 The Turkey-Greece Readmission Agreement

The intense use of the Turkish-Greek border by irregular migrants also affected other Member States of the EU beside Greece, and pressured by the EU a readmission protocol was signed between the two parties 2001,[11] providing the means to speed up the return to Turkey of irregular migrants that had used Turkey as a transit country before being apprehended in Greece. Despite

8 İçduygu, A. & D. Aksel (2012), *Irregular migration in Turkey*, IOM, p. 21; Sirkeci, I. (2009), *Türkiye'de Uluslararası Göç ve Sığınma İstatistiklerinin Geliştirilmesi*, Ankara: Turkish Statistics Institute.

9 Frontex (2015), *Trends and routes: Eastern Mediterranean route*, <frontex.europa.eu/trends-and-routes/eastern-mediterranean-route>.

10 Icduygu, A. (2011), *The irregular migration corridor between the EU and Turkey: is it possible to block it with a readmission agreement?*, Fiesole: Robert Schuman Centre for Advanced Studies, p. 12.

11 Law 2926 of 27 June 2001, Agreement between the Hellenic Republic and the Republic of Turkey on cooperation of the Ministry of Public Order of the Hellenic Republic and the Ministry of the Interior of Turkey on combating crime, especially terrorism, organized crime, illicit drug trafficking and illegal immigration.

the signing of a readmission agreement, in practice the number of irregular migrants returned to Turkey by the Greece police without notification of the Turkish authorities has remained systematically higher than the number of actually returned migrants under the readmission agreement.[12] Notwithstanding the readmission agreement and the ongoing forcible expulsions between Greece and Turkey, the intensity of the use of the Greek-Turkish border by irregular migrants did not relinquish in the years after 2001. On the contrary, whereas in 2007 around 45% of irregular migrants apprehended in the EU were estimated to have used this border, this percentage increased to 75 in 2009.[13] These numbers – those on illegal border crossings and on the use of the readmission agreement between Greece and Turkey – call the effectiveness of readmission agreements as tools of bilateral migration management, intrinsically into question.[14] Furthermore, the Greece-Turkey readmission agreement serves to show that though readmission agreements are framed in a reciprocal context, it was clear from the onset that the parties would not benefit equally from its conclusion and implementation. When incentives to cooperate are not given to the disadvantaged country, or when they cease to offset the disadvantage, readmission agreements will not serve their purpose.[15]

## 9.5 The EU-Turkey Readmission Agreement and Visa Liberalization Roadmap

In the same year as the Greek-Turkish readmission protocol entered into force, and two years before Turkey was officially granted accession candidate status,

12 The Turkish General Staff published a report in 2007 in which it claimed that nearly 12.000 third-country nationals were unlawfully left at the Turkish borders by Greek police and security forces between 2002 and 2007 – an average of over 2000 per year; Yunanistan'in Yasadışı Göçmenlere Ilişkin Tutumu, Turkish General Staff, October 2007. According to a study performed by Içduygu, based on the data from the Turkish Bureau for Foreigners, Borders and Asylum at the Directorate of General Security of the Ministry for the Interior, the number of irregular migrants that was sent by Greece and readmitted by Turkey under the readmission protocol was 2425 in total for the period between 2002 and 2010 – an average of little over 300 per year; A. Içduygu (fn 8), p. 7.

13 Frontex reports for 2007, 2008 and 2009.

14 A leaked Eurojust report, quoted by Strik in a Report to the Parliamentary Assembly of the Council of Europe, mentioned 'the very low number of readmissions to Turkey under its existing agreement with Greece' as recently as 2015; T. Strik, *Human rights of refugees and migrants – the situation in the Western Balkans*, p. 12.

15 Cassarino, J.P. 'Informalising readmission agreements in the EU neighbourhood', *The international spectator*, Vol. 42, No. 2, June 2007, pp. 182–184.

the European Commission was mandated by the Council to negotiate with Turkey for the conclusion of a readmission agreement between the EU and Turkey. Turkey was unwilling to enter into negotiations until the negotiation of a readmission agreement were linked to the opening of accession negotiations in 2005.[16] Both negotiations were effectively started in the early months of 2006, only to stall again in the last months with relations cooling considerably over the ongoing tension between Cyprus and Turkey and the findings of the European Parliament and Commission that the alignment process in Turkey had slowed down, particularly with regard to the implementation of the freedom of expression, protection of religious and minority rights, reform in law enforcement and support for the independence of the judiciary.[17] No real progress was made until 2009, when Turkey appointed its first full-time minister for EU affairs – as the ruling party tried to recover the loss of votes under its more left-oriented voters in the elections of 2009. This step, together with the detachment of Turkey's involvement in the EU migration policy from the dwindling accession negotiations and the shift of Turkey's focus to visa-liberalization instead, created the momentum for the EU and Turkey to officially relaunch negotiations for the conclusion of a readmission agreement in 2010 and to agree upon a draft in January 2011.[18] But whereas Turkey by that time had begun bringing its border management in line with that of the EU and coordination between the two systems had been established, and whereas an arrangement for cooperation with FRONTEX was also in the pipeline,[19] the concessions with regard to visa-liberalization that the Council was willing to make were very few.[20] Turkey therefore refused to sign the agreement, until

16 Wolff, S., 'The politics of negotiating EU readmission agreements: insights from Morocco and Turkey', in: R. Zaiotti (ed.), *Externalizing migration management: Europe, North America and the spread of 'remote control' practices*, p. 101.

17 European Parliament, Committee on Foreign Affairs, Report on Turkey's progress towards accession, 13 September 2006, 2006/2118(INI); European Commission, Commission presents its recommendations on the continuation of Turkey's accession negotiations, November 29, 2006, IP/06/1652.

18 European Parliament, Recommendation on the draft Council decision on the conclusion of the Agreement between the European Union and the Republic of Turkey on the readmission of persons residing without authorization, (10697/2012 – C7-0029/2014 – 2012/0122(NLE)).

19 OECD, International Migration Outlook 2012, p. 278.

20 The JHA Council of 24 and 25 February 2011 only agreed on committing to a 'dialogue on visa, mobility and migration', without the official opening of visa liberalization negotiations, which was far less than other third countries in comparable situations had been

it received assurance that it would be rewarded with a clear perspective of visa-liberalization in exchange. It was therefore only in June 2012, when the Commission was given an official mandate to enter into visa-liberalization negotiations with Turkey that Turkey agreed to consider concluding the readmission agreement. On 16 December 2013 the readmission agreement was signed simultaneously with a roadmap to a visa-free regime with Turkey.[21] The parties agreed on a step-by-step entry into force of the readmission agreement, with the agreement entering into force for EU and Turkish nationals on 1 October 2014. Third country nationals and stateless persons would not be affected by the agreement until three years later.

The roadmap lists 72 requirements that need to be met by Turkey in order to enable the Commission to propose legal steps leading to visa-free travel for Turkish citizens. The Commission reports on progress by Turkey in fulfilling the requirements of its visa liberalization roadmap assess the fulfilment of each of these requirements, organized in five thematic groups: document security, migration management, public order and security, fundamental rights and readmission of irregular migrants. Three central requirements are analyzed in detail below, namely the alignment of the Turkish asylum and migration law to its EU counterpart, the lifting of the geographical limitation to the 1951 Geneva Convention and the respect for fundamental human rights. The choice for these particular requirements is based on the fact that their fulfillment is not only a prerequisite for visa-liberalization, but also for the legality of Turkey's partnership with the EU in migration management matters *per se*.

---

offered, S. Wolff, 'The politics of negotiating EU readmission agreements: insights from Morocco and Turkey', *European Journal of Migration and Law* 16(2014), pp. 86 and 88. See also Commission, communication from the commission to the European parliament and the council, evaluation of EU readmission agreements, COM(2011)76 final, p. 6, under 'Lack of incentives'.

21 Agreement between the European Union and the Republic of Turkey on the readmission of persons residing without authorization, OJ[2014] L134/3, respectively Roadmap towards a visa-free regime with Turkey, consulted on the website of the Commission: http://ec.europa.eu/dgs/home-affairs/what-is-new/news/news/docs/20131216-roadmap_towards_the_visa-free_regime_with_turkey_en.pdf. The roadmap is technically a European Commission document, for the drafting of which Member States are merely consulted. However, the negotiations within the EU to come to the final text of the roadmap with Turkey almost gave the impression that it concerned a formal legal act of the EU; see S. Wolff, (fn 15), p. 102.

## 9.6 Turkish Asylum and Migration Law

In 2005 and 2006, two EU-Turkey Twinning Projects were implemented to start aligning Turkey's asylum and migration practices with the EU acquis. These projects focused predominantly on the Integrated Border Management and the improvement of operational capacity of existing and new administrative structures in Turkey; at the same time, preparations were made to overhaul also the legislation regulating migration, asylum and residence in Turkey.[22] The secondary asylum and migration legislation in force until 2014 consisted of a number administrative decisions and bylaws, creating a haphazard and dysfunctional system, the administration of which was mostly in the hands of the General Staff (armed forces) and Gendarmerie. Furthermore, though Turkey became a party to the Geneva Convention in 1951, it did so reserving the right to limit its application geographically. Displaced persons coming from a non-European country could therefore not be recognized as 'refugee' under the Geneva Convention. For such persons, an Administrative Regulation[23] created a special status in 1994 which allowed them to reside legally in Turkey until permanent relocation by the UNHCR, thus bringing the Turkish law in line with the prohibition of *refoulement* of persons in need of international protection as per the Geneva Convention. This measure and its application in practice however did not substantially improve the rights of those involved,[24] nor did its amendment in 2006. It is safe to say that the Turkish legislation related to migration and asylum before 2013 was clearly below applicable EU and international standards.[25]

The Law on Foreigners and International Protection (*Yabancılar ve Uluslararası Koruma Kanunu*), which was adopted in 2013 and entered in force in 2014, is clearly based on the EU acquis in this policy field. The question of the compatibility of the EU acquis with international and European refugee

22 Geddes, A. & P. Scholten, *The politics of migration and immigration in Europe*, London: Sage, pp. 232–236.

23 6169 sayılı Bakanlar Kurulu Kararı – Türkiye'ye Iltica Eden veya Başka Bir Ülkeye Iltica Etmek Üzere Türkiye'den Ikamet Izni Talep Eden Münferit Yabancılar ile Topluca Sığınma Amacıyla Sınırlarımıza Gelen Yabancılara ve Olabilecek Nüfus Hareketlerine Uygulanacak Usul ve Esaslar Hakkında Yönetmelik.

24 See, for example, with regard to the time limits applicable in the application procedure the ruling of the ECtHR in Jabari v. Turkey, 11.07.2000, Application no. 40035/98, para. 40.

25 There are at least 31 rulings by the ECtHR to this extent made between 1991 (A. and K. v. Turkey, Application no 14401/88) and 2014 (Asalya v. Turkey, Application no. 43875/09) based on the old legal structure; see for an overview until 2013 N. Ekşi, Yabancılar ve Uluslararası Koruma Kanunu (Tasarısı), p. 73.

and human rights standards is dealt with elsewhere in this bundle, and below the focus will therefore be mainly on the particularities in the Turkish law and its application. To begin with positive remarks: the law creates a system with a special civil administration that is bound by its rules – armed and security forces have ceased most of their competences to civil administration. Furthermore, all beneficiaries of international protection in Turkey have the right of access to basic healthcare and primary and secondary education at public schools. Additionally, the scope of the law is relatively broad and covers (almost) all foreigners present in Turkey; the introduction of subsidiary ('secondary') protection for those that do not fall within the scope of Article 1 of the Geneva Convention is a clear step forward, as these persons did not have a clear legal status under the legislation applicable before 2014. Finally, the law was drafted after repeated consultations were held with civil society, relevant NGOs and EU officials and administration. Unfortunately, however, not all suggestions made by civil society were also included in the final draft of the law. It would go too far to mention all aspects in which the law needs improvement, instead the following focuses on a limited number of key issues in order to show that alignment with the EU acquis is not complete nor is it enough to acquit the EU of its responsibility towards readmitted persons.

First of all, since despite urges from the EU and other international organizations to do otherwise, Turkey chose to retain the geographical limitation of the Geneva Convention. Therefore the Law still provides for two protection regimes for those persons who fulfill the conditions of Article 1 of the Geneva Convention, namely refugee status for nationals of European countries and *conditional* refugee status for nationals of other states. Conditional refugees are allowed to await permanent relocation in Turkey, but have lesser rights than recognized refugees during their stay. For example, whereas refugees have access to the labor market after a period of six months from the date of application, conditional refugees do not have access to the labor market – whereas most of them will have to stay in Turkey awaiting relocation for a very long time.[26] Also those granted subsidiary protection status are allowed to work. However, both for the refugee and the holder of the subsidiary protection status the right to work may be restricted in the first three years according to the law.[27] Furthermore, in the same article, the law provides that the principles and procedures governing the employment of applicants or international

26 In 2015, the UNHCR submitted the files of about 134.000 refugees for consideration by resettlement countries – 7577 of them were from Turkey. Turkey hosts 3 million Syrians in 2016.

27 Article 89(4)(c) of the Turkish Law on Foreigners and International Protection.

protection beneficiaries shall be determined by the Ministry of Labor and Social Security in consultation with the Ministry (for the Interior). In case of economic instability, the relevant Ministries may also decide to suspend the access to the labor market for applicants or international protection beneficiaries. Access to the labor market is therefore more problematic in practice than one would assume from a cursory read of the Law. Next to that, whereas 'temporary protection status' (the fourth type of international protection foreseen by the Law) may sound familiar to those dealing with EU asylum law, the catalogue of rights pertaining to this status is not foreseeable, as in each individual case of mass influx the Council of Ministers will decide on what rights should be granted to the holders of this status.[28]

Regardless of the type of international protection, deadlines in the law have been kept very short. For example, when irregular migrants are apprehended while trying to cross the borders of Turkey, their applications for international protection may be evaluated under the accelerated procedure – a procedure which in that case must be finalized within 5 days.[29] Considering that illegal border crossings normally take place in groups, an individual and fair assessment of each individual case within 5 days is hardly feasible. Furthermore, though the law formally makes an end to criminal detention or administrative detention under similar circumstances[30] and for the first time foresees in the possibility to appeal against the detainment decision, practice has often remained unchanged by the new law – the detention practice that has repeatedly led to ECtHR convictions before 2014. To name but one example: in order to file an appeal against any decision negatively affecting the involved foreigner, they are entitled to legal assistance. However, research has shown that it is often impossible for a detained applicant to contact a lawyer – or indeed for a lawyer to see his detained client. In such cases it will be extremely difficult for the applicant to make use of the right to recourse. Next to that, even bar associations in the provinces in the east of Turkey where most refugee camps are built and where most of the refugees are registered for the first time have repeatedly attracted attention to the lack of funds for legal assistance, and the lack of appropriate education.[31] Furthermore, considering the peak in the

28 Articles 91 and 92 of the Turkish Law on Foreigners and International Protection.

29 Article 79 read in conjunction with Articles 54 and 57 of the Turkish Law on Foreigners and International Protection.

30 Armed and security forces were competent for the administration of most of the legislation related to asylum and migration; therefore even 'administrative' detention often took place under the same circumstances as criminal detention.

31 Based on interviews with the board and members of the bar associations in Diyarbakir and Gaziantep provinces.

influx in Turkey of persons in need of international protection coming from Syria in 2015, and again in 2016, it is reasonable to expect that the widespread use of detention and the circumstances of detention have only deteriorated since 2013, when the UNHCR's Special Rapporteur on the human rights of migrants already raised red flags in relation to these issues.

Finally, even if the terminology of the Law may mirror that of the applicable EU legislation, that does not guarantee a similar use and interpretation of these 'outlandish' terms by the Turkish administration and judiciary. One example, the differences in the Turkish and EU regimes pertaining to the 'temporary protection status', was already referred to above. To name another example: according to the law, applicants arriving from a safe third country shall be returned to that country.[32] However, in a country that can hardly be considered as 'safe' by the standards of its own law let alone EU law, the outcome of the assessment of safety and the consequences thereof will very likely be contentious, too. This difference in interpretation of identical terms, combined with the impending entry into force of the readmission agreement and the EU-Turkey deal analyzed below leads to a very high risk of chain *refoulement* of people in need of international protection – for which the EU and Turkey would have shared liability.[33]

The coming into force of the Turkish Law on Foreigners and International Protection in 2014 is therefore in many respects a leap forward. However, such a high number of aspects of the law and its administration in practice still need amendment or adjustment that the EU cannot rely on this law nor its practical application for the assessment of the protection offered by Turkey to people that may be in need of international protection.

## 9.7 Turkey's Role in the EU Migration Management: 2015 and Beyond

2015 saw the publication of the European Agenda on Migration,[34] a document in which the European Commission set out the (legal) actions that it

32 Article 74 of the Law on Foreigners and International Protection.

33 Chetail, V. & C. Bauloz (eds.) (2014), *Research handbook on international law and migration*, Cheltenham: Edward Elgar Publishing, p. 130; A. Zimmermann (ed.) (2011), *The 1951 convention relating to the status of refugees and its 1967 protocol – a commentary*, Oxford: Oxford University Press, p. 1383.

34 European Commission, Communication from the Commission to the European Parliament, the Council, the European Economic and Social Committee and the Committee of the Regions – A European Agenda on Migration, COM(2015)240 final.

will propose in the coming years in order to 'provide the Member States with tools to manage migration better in the medium as well as long term' with 'a new, comprehensive approach grounded in mutual trust and solidarity among Member States'.[35] The Agenda was published in reaction to an exponential increase in the flow of (mostly irregular) migrants coming to the EU, either as economic migrant or fleeing conflict in regions tormented by war and unrest – a flow that the migration management system based on EU legislation existing at that time was unable to handle. Furthermore, persistent media reports about the loss of lives at the Mediterranean Sea, where vessels carrying large numbers of migrants – especially from the west coast of Turkey to nearby Greek islands – would capsize in storms or simply sink, caused protests in the streets of EU countries against legislation and border management that made it almost impossible to reach EU countries legally in order to lodge applications for international protection. The Agenda proposed immediate actions to save lives at sea, to target criminal smuggling networks, to relieve the pressure on frontline EU Member States and third countries by relocation and resettlement, and to cooperate with third countries to tackle migration upstream. The rest of the document is dedicated to recommendations for structural changes in the EU migration management. These recommendations are clustered under four headings, namely the reduction of incentives for irregular migration, border management, a common asylum policy and a new policy on legal migration to the EU. It is especially with regard to the reduction of incentives for irregular migration and border management that the Commission plans to involve third countries. Turkey is mentioned as 'a good example of where there is much to be gained from stepping up cooperation' to help prevent hazardous journeys in the Eastern Mediterranean. The deployment of a Frontex liaison officer is mentioned as one way in which the cooperation will be stepped up.[36] Furthermore, financial and practical assistance in addressing the issue of criminal networks of smugglers, and for the management of external borders will also be offered to third countries, including Turkey. Most of these measures therefore target the role of third countries as transit countries for irregular migrants on their way to the EU, and have the potential of turning them into countries where irregular migrants run aground – with all the consequences that will entail for the human rights of those involved.

---

35 European Commission, website of the DG Migration and Home Affairs: 'Why a new European Agenda on Migration?'

36 Frontex has already been active in Turkey based on a Memorandum of Understanding signed by Turkey and the EU in 2012, and has provided risk analysis, training, research, exchanges of experience and best practice since 2014.

For instance, within the framework of cooperation between Frontex and Turkish authorities, the Regulation establishing rules for maritime operations coordinated by Frontex[37] has been criticized for providing for the interception of boats and the possibility of disembarkation in a non-EU Member State (Turkey). Whereas the intervention in the freedom of navigation in international waters in case of illegal trafficking of migrants *per se* may very well be in line with international law of the sea,[38] as a direct result from these Frontex actions irregular migrants on board of the vessels are de facto deprived of the opportunity to have their request for international protection assessed on its merits in an EU country.[39] Furthermore, the lack of effective remedies, including interpreters, legal advisors and a suspensive effect of the remedy at sea can be mentioned as possible infringements of the human rights of those on the intercepted vessels.[40]

The issue of criminal networks of smugglers will also prove harder to tackle than it seems. It is true that part of the trafficking is done by professional criminal networks. The Turkish police that is responsible for the detection and investigation of these networks is however very often tied up in the investigation of terrorism within Turkey. The volatile internal situation in Turkey obstructs the execution of investigations in other criminal networks, including networks responsible for human trafficking. Next to that, research has also shown that in many cases irregular migrants organize themselves with the use of internet and social media, and use regular transport services to reach the west of Turkey, where fishermen with no ties to any criminal network whatsoever often regard ferrying irregular migrants as a lucrative sideline job. The boats they

37 Parliament and Council Regulation No 656/2014 of 15 May 2014 establishing rules for the surveillance of the external sea borders in the context of operational cooperation coordinated by Frontex at the external borders of the Member States of the EU, *OJ* 2014, L189/93.

38 Art. 8 of the 2000 Palermo Protocol to the United Nations Convention against Transnational Organized Crime foresees in this exception to the freedom of navigation.

39 See to this extent in detail UNHCR comments on the Commission proposal for a Regulation of the European Parliament and of the Council establishing rules for the surveillance of the external sea borders in the context of operational cooperation coordinated by the European Agency for the Management of Operational Cooperation at the External Borders of the Member States of the European Union (Frontex) COM2013(197) final on the website of the UNHCR, <www.unhcr.org/534fd9e99.pdf>.

40 The Meijers Committee pointed out in this regard that the Regulation falls short of a codification of the judgment of the ECtHR 23 February 2012, 27765/09, *Hirsi v. Italy*: Meijers Committee, *Note on the Proposal for a Regulation establishing rules for the surveillance of the external sea borders in the context of operational cooperation coordinated by Frontex*, pp. 2 and 3.

are using are the boats they normally use to earn their living catching fish, and destroying these vessels would leave whole families without source of income. It is difficult to fight this kind of trafficking effectively.

All the same, one can hardly deny that EU and EU-inspired measures in Turkey and on the Turkish sea and land borders have been in so far successful that the use of the eastern Mediterranean route by irregular migrants has decreased dramatically.[41] Recent analyses show however that the use of other, far longer routes to reach the shores of the EU have become more popular with irregular migrants instead.[42] For example, Libyan coast guards noticed an increase in illegal activity on the sea fronts. Thus, EU measures making Turkey unattractive as transit country thus force irregular migrants determined to reach the EU no matter what to take routes that are even more dangerous. It is probable that as a result of EU measures targeting Turkey the location of the departure of the boat journey will have changed, but number of lives lost at sea will not.

## 9.8 The EU-Turkey Deal: A Not so Temporary Solution

One of the EU measures taken in order to stem the flood of irregular migrants from Turkey to the EU was not mentioned in the Agenda, perhaps because in the benevolent atmosphere that prevailed with the general public of the EU in the spring of 2015, perhaps also because the legal status of the measure would be hard to define for the Commission. The EU-Turkey deal, as it is known to most, has by most EU and immigration law experts been categorized as a non-binding political declaration.[43] With numbers of arrivals from Turkey soaring, the readmission agreement with Turkey only fully entering into force in 2017 and Member States unwilling or their asylum systems unable to digest the vast amount of applications for international protection, the EU frantically looked for solutions. The solution was first sought in convincing Turkey to try and keep refugees present in its territory from crossing the border into the EU. For that purpose, the Members of the Council of the European Union

41 European Commission, *Second Report on the progress made in the implementation of the EU-Turkey Statement*, 15 June 2016, COM(2016)349 final.

42 On 22 March 2016, the UNHCR said in 2016 almost 14,500 people had arrived in Italy via Libya, which was 42.5 percent more than in the same period last year.

43 Den Heijer, M. & T. Spijkerboer (2016), *EU law analysis: is the EU-Turkey refugee and migration deal a treaty?*, <eulawanalysis.blogspot.nl> [7 april 2016]. Labayle, H. & P. De Bruycker, *L'accord Union européenne – Turquie : faux semblant ou marché de dupes?* eumigrationlawblog.eu/category/asylum-crisis> [23 March 2016].

called for a meeting with Turkey on 29 November 2015 – a meeting in which 'the vast potential of Turkey-EU relations [was] to be explored', and attempts to 're-energize the accession process' and to 'reinforce the European Project' were discussed.[44] Almost casually, the statement informs that Turkey and the EU decided to activate a 'Joint Action Plan' to step up their cooperation to address the crisis created by the situation in Syria. The action plan boiled down to the EU agreeing to pay a certain amount of money to improve the situation of the Syrian refugees present in Turkey, whereas Turkey would do its best to prevent irregular migrants from crossing the border into the EU.

The statement of 18 March 2016[45] of the Members of the European Council and their Turkish counterparts following their third meeting opened with remarks on the successful implementation of the joint action plan of 29 November 2015; it mentions specifically the security efforts by the Turkish coast guard and police, and the enhanced information sharing. The statement then continues declaring that Turkey agreed on 7 March 2016 to 'accept the rapid return of all migrants not in need of international protection crossing from Turkey into Greece and to take back all irregular migrants intercepted in Turkish waters', and further that 'all new irregular migrants crossing from Turkey into Greece as from 20 March 2016 will be returned to Turkey' as a 'temporary and extraordinary measure… necessary to end the human suffering and restore public order'.[46] Furthermore, Turkey would step up border management in order to prevent the use of new and old illegal migration routes into the EU. In return, Turkey would receive more financial aid, an acceleration of the visa liberalization roadmap and the possibility to send one Syrian to the EU for resettlement per returned Syrian.

Despite condemnation by NGOs, intergovernmental organizations and academics on the plethora of merits of the deal – the missing legal basis, the lack of legal effect, the lack of consultation with relevant actors, the ethical and human rights implications of the execution of the deal -, on 4 April 2016 a group of 197 irregular migrants was returned to Turkey as part of the deal, and a second group was returned four days later. Whereas the first returns received media coverage and attracted numerous protesters, further transports were effected without much commotion and they have become part of the daily

44 Meeting of heads of state or government with Turkey – EU-Turkey statement, 29 November 2015, consulted on the website of the Council of the European Union.

45 EU-Turkey statement, 18 March 2016 <www.consilium.europa.eu/en/press/press-releases/2016/03/18-eu-turkey-statement>.

46 EU-Turkey statement, 18 March 2016 <www.consilium.europa.eu/en/press/press-releases/2016/03/18-eu-turkey-statement>.

routine. The Commission's second report of June 2016 on the implementation of the 'statement' mentions that it has started to deliver, and further that it has provided Greece with all the elements to conclude that Turkey is a safe third country and/or a country of first asylum for the purpose of returning irregular migrants to Turkey – though it does not mention which where the 'elements' provided to Greece.[47] If it would have done so, perhaps it would be more understandable for those opposing the deal, even if only implemented temporarily, why the Commission is so keen on a continuation of a practice that seems to flagrantly infringe all values the EU claims to stand for.

## 9.9 Legalizing the 'deal': The Push for an Early Entry into Force of the Readmission Agreement

That the European Union is fully aware of the illegality of the deal becomes also clear from the EU's efforts to legalize the ongoing return of irregular migrants to Turkey with an advanced entry into force of the Readmission Agreement. As mentioned above, according to Article 24 of the Readmission Agreement, it would not enter into force with regard to third country citizens and stateless persons until 1 October 2017. However, soon after the entry into force of the readmission agreement with regard to EU and Turkish citizens the EU began to press for an advancement of the date of the entry into force of the entire agreement, including third country nationals and stateless persons. Eventually, the EU and Turkey settled on 1 June 2016 as the date on which the readmission agreement would fully enter into effect at a meeting on 29 November 2015. This meeting took place one day after the head of the Bar Association of Diyarbakir was shot and killed on the street during a press conference with which he wanted to attract attention to the state violence against the Kurdish population in the eastern provinces of Turkey. This violence erupted again after the general elections earlier that year and resulted in the ruling party AKP shrinking as the pro-Kurdish HDP passed the 10% threshold for entering parliament with 12% of the votes. What ensued was a period of months in which government forces supposedly purged whole cities in eastern Turkey from PKK cells – instituting a curfew for weeks on end and sharpshooting whatever moved on the streets, including children and elderly people.[48] A group of 1128

47 European Commission (fn 40), pp. 2 and 5.

48 <t24.com.tr/haber/cizrede-oldurulen-miray-bebegin-halasi-kucagimdi-keskin-nisanci-vurdu-agliyordu-olmemisti-daha,321903>; <www.diken.com.tr/cizrede-dort-aylik-bir-bebek-ve-80-yasindaki-dedesi-keskin-nisancilar-tarafindan-olduruldu>. For a report on what

Turkish and non-Turkish academics, protesting against the violence, drafted a public memorandum for peace on 11 January 2016. After being scorned by several Turkish politicians, including President Erdoğan himself,[49] several of them lost their jobs, while others were arrested and more still were prosecuted on charges of terrorism.[50]

Notwithstanding these facts that raise profound questions regarding the state of the democracy and the rule of law in Turkey, the European Commission continued to insist on the advancement of the date of entry into force of the readmission agreement in its entirety. What is more, it could not even wait until the advanced date to begin sending irregular migrants back to Turkey. Therefore it simultaneously brokered the EU-Turkey deal, as can be seen from a proposal for a Council Decision establishing the position the EU would take within the EU-Turkey Joint Readmission Committee dated 10 February 2016.[51] This proposal was adopted by the Council on 23 March 2016,[52] and the relevant decision passed at the meeting of the Joint readmission Committee on 1 April 2016.[53] All that was needed for the Readmission Agreement to enter into effect for third country citizens and stateless persons was the approval of the Turkish legislator.

Interestingly, the proposal for a law approving of the decision was drafted by the Turkish Ministry for Foreign Affairs and sent by the Turkish Council of

happened in Cizre: <hakikatadalethafiza.org/wp-content/uploads/2016/05/2015.09.12_Mazlum Der_CizreOlaylariRaporu.pdf>.

49 In a speech at a conference the day after the publication of the declaration, Erdogan called the academics 'not enlightened but dark'...'dark and ignorant' and traitors; <www.bbc.com/turkce/haberler/2016/01/160111_erdogan_akademisyen_aciklama>.

50 See <barisicinakademisyenler.net/node/266> for a full and updated account of what happened to the academics that signed the declaration.

51 Proposal for a Council Decision establishing the position to be taken on behalf of the European Union within the Joint Readmission Committee on a Decision of the Joint Readmission Committee on implementing arrangements for the application of Articles 4 and 6 of the Agreement between the European Union and the Republic of Turkey on the readmission of persons residing without authorization as of 1 June 2016, COM(2016)72 final.

52 Council Decision (EU) 2016/551 of 23 March 2016 establishing the position to be taken on behalf of the European Union within the Joint Readmission Committee on a Decision of the Joint Readmission Committee on implementing arrangements for the application of Articles 4 and 6 of the Agreement between the European Union and the Republic of Turkey on the readmission of persons residing without authorisation from 1 June 2016, *OJ* L95/9.

53 Scanned version of the Decision, together with the Turkish law ratifying the Decision, available through Refworld: <www.refworld.org/docid/573f0ed04.html>.

Ministers to the parliament on 11 April 2016 as part of the process of alignment with EU law. On 18 April the decision was approved by the Parliament and published in the Turkish Official Gazette.[54] However, according to Article 3 of the Law, the Council of Ministers of Turkey is the body that has competence to apply the law – which actually means that the Turkish Council of Ministers has to take a separate decision to start with the application of the law. The Council of Ministers, referring to the preamble to the Turkish Law, has until now refused to take this decision as it feels the EU does not fulfill its part of the deal: the visa liberalization for Turkish citizens by the end of June. The road to visa liberalization goes through the European Parliament, which insists on the fulfillment of a number of criteria – one of which being the amendment of the Turkish legal framework as regards organized crime and terrorism,[55] so as to ensure the right to liberty and security, the right to a fair trial and freedom of expression, of assembly and association in practice.[56] When the report came out, an outcry ensued in Turkey, and several Turkish politicians including President Erdoğan and MP Yıldırım, voiced their opinion that any amendment of the Law on the Fight against Terrorism (*Terörle Mücadele Kanunu*) was out of the question. Especially after the attempted coup of 15 July 2016, proving president Erdoğan's previous assertions in this respect right, it is highly improbable that this Law will be amended – at least not in a way as to align it with EU human rights standards. Quite the contrary, in the days following the coup, the massive government crackdown on not only those persons with links to the 'Gülen' movement which has been accused of organizing the coup but on all opposition, has confirmed EU views that the Law on Terrorism and its application in practice facilitate to a great extent the infringement of the human rights of those investigated and charged under this law. But in order to be ahead of accusations that Turkey infringes the human rights of those suspected of playing a part in the attempted coup, Turkey announced the state of emergency for at least three months on 21 July 2016, at the same time suspending

54 Law No. 6714 (Kanun No. 6714, Türkiye Cumhuriyeti ile Avrupa Birliği Arasında Izinsiz Ikamet Eden Kişilerin Geri Kabulüne Ilişkin Anlaşma ile Oluşturulan Ortak Geri Kabul Komitesinin 2/2016 Sayılı Kararının Onaylanmasının uygun Bulunduğuna Dair Kanun), 20 Mayıs 2016 Tarihli ve 29717 Sayılı Resmî Gazete.

55 The EU is not alone in its criticism on the Turkish laws regulating the war on terrorism, see for an earlier report of the UN: <www.loc.gov/law/foreign-news/article/turkey-united-nations-criticism-of-anti-terrorism-laws>.

56 Third Report on progress by Turkey in fulfilling the requirements of its visa liberalization roadmap, Report from the Commission to the European Parliament and the Council, 4 May 2016, COM(2016)278 final, p. 8.

its obligations under the ECHR. This decision confirms the deliberateness of further infringements of human rights by the Turkish authorities after the date of the suspension of its obligations – whereas according to applicable European and international human rights law Turkey will indeed still be liable for these infringements, in spite of the suspension.[57] Notwithstanding this fact, the purge of the whole Turkish administration continued at full speed, with the Minister of Justice even announcing the prosecution of all those who claimed on social media that the ruling party could be behind the attempted coup. Furthermore, the debate about the reintroduction in Turkish law of the capital punishment reached such a stage that it seemed possible that such a decision would be taken by the Turkish legislator,[58] which would lead to the Turkish Law on the Fight against Terrorism and the Turkish Criminal Code being even further alienated from EU human rights standards. All these recent developments have not brought the date of an advanced entry into force of the readmission agreement with regard to third country nationals and stateless persons any nearer.

Even in the strictly hypothetical case that Turkey would agree to bring its laws regarding the war on terrorism in line with EU law and international human rights standards, visa liberalization still requires the amendment of Regulation (EC) No 539/2001, which is only possible with a qualified majority in

57 Article 15 of the ECHR stipulates that: 'In time of war or other public emergency threatening the life of the nation any High Contracting Party may take measures derogating from its obligations under this Convention to the extent strictly required by the exigencies of the situation, *provided that such measures are not inconsistent with its other obligations under international law*'. In this regard, The International Covenant on Civil and Political Rights indicated in article 4(1), that derogations are only possible to the extent strictly required by the exigencies of the situation, provided that such measures do not involve discrimination solely on the ground of race, colour, sex, language, religion or social origin. Furthermore, according to the second paragraph of the same article, non-derogable rights are: the right to be free from arbitrary deprivation of life; the prohibition of torture and other ill-treatment; ... retroactive penalty; and freedom of thought, conscience and religion. It is therefore clear that Turkey cannot limit its liability for the treatment of any suspect with the announcement of the state of emergency and the suspension of its obligations under the ECHR.

58 Of the four political parties presently in the Turkish parliament, only the HDP (representing 11% of the total of votes in the last elections of 1 November 2015) immediately opposed the reopening of discussions on the death penalty <t24.com.tr/haber/hdpden-idam-aciklamasi,350596>. Whereas the CHP (25%) does not have an official position yet, MHP (12%) has always been in favor of the capital punishment.

the Council and a positive vote in the European Parliament. A number of EU Member States (Germany, Austria, The Netherlands and Cyprus) have already indicated they will not vote for visa liberalization now – and their number will most certainly rise in case the Syrian migrants legally present in Turkey will receive Turkish nationality as President Erdoğan recently promised.[59] Also the attempted coup of 15 July 2016, which resulted in the declaration of the state of emergency on 21 July, may drive a part of the Turkish population to consider applying for asylum abroad. Visa-liberalization would make it easier for them to leave Turkey and apply for asylum in the EU, and also for this reason many EU Member States will not vote for the necessary amendment of Regulation 539/2001. Thus, it is the second time in the history of the EU-Turkey relation that a coup has deteriorated the rights of Turkish citizens to entry into the Member States of the EU.[60] Without progress on the road to visa-liberalization, Turkey will not enforce the law on the earlier date of entry into force of the whole of the readmission agreement with the EU. Considering these circumstances, it seems to be justified to conclude that a 'legalization' of the EU-Turkey deal is therefore not imminent. The temporary EU-Turkey deal will most probably remain the only basis for return of illegal migrants to Turkey until the full entry into force of the readmission agreement per the originally foreseen date of 1 October 2017 – if by that date the parties still agree on the content of the agreement. However, even if the readmission agreement would fully enter into force and thus provide for a legal basis for the return of illegal migrants to Turkey, considering the state of affairs in Turkey such returns would not be in line with EU and international human rights and refugee law. Efforts of the EU in this direction should therefore be regarded as futile; these

59 On 2 July 2016, during a public Ramadan meal, President Erdogan revealed plans to give Turkish citizenship to 3 million Syrians resident in Turkey. <www.bbc.com/turkce/haberler/2016/07/160703_erdogan_suriyeliler> also: <www.cumhuriyet.com.tr/haber/turkiye/561675/Erdogan__Suriyeli_kardeslerimize_vatandaslik_verecegiz.html>. Law number 5901 on Turkish Citizenship regulates the acquisition of citizenship in Articles 11 (fulfilment of conditions regarding period of residency, knowledge of language, etc.) and 12 (exceptional circumstances). It is clear that most of the Syrians that have been granted international protection in Turkey do not yet fulfil the conditions of Article 11 of Law number 5901. However, Article 12 which regulates acquisition of citizenship in exceptional circumstances can only be applied on a case to case basis, and is not suitable for the naturalization of a large number of persons. It is therefore not clear how the naturalization of 3 million Syrians will be given shape.

60 See reference to the consequences of the military coup in 1980 in this contribution under footnote 4.

efforts can be directed more effectively in finding durable solutions to the failing of the EU migration management within the EU.

## 9.10 Conclusion

The above discourse on the role of Turkey in the EU's new migration management policy serves to show that though Turkey's geopolitical position undeniably makes it a desirable ally for the EU in many respects, past and current political and legal developments in Turkey have made an EU-Turkish partnership with regard to migration management a notorious issue, and rightly so. The EU cannot chose to temporarily ignore the human rights standards and requirements it enforces within the EU, and that it uses as measuring stick with regard to those states that wish to become part of the EU, for the sake of an equally temporary solution to a problem that will persist, without giving permanent damage to its credibility in the world and for its own citizens. Internationally, the EU has worked hard to become not only an economic global power but to also to carve out a role as an international political actor and human rights ambassador. These accomplishments are put at risk if the EU persists in relying on Turkey as partner in the execution of its recent migration management plans.

But also the EU's own citizens and citizens of associated countries, many of which have shown a growing unease with the EU and some of its policies, would prefer to see a Union that is able to manage a difficult situation without transgressing the legal boundaries it previously set and valued. A Union that does not come up with quick fixes but one which leaders are able to produce real solutions even if they involve tough decisions. Only an EU that stands by its own norms inspires trust, confidence and hope, whereas one that measures with two measures only digs its own grave.

Especially in the current political climate, the refugee crisis can be turned into an opportunity for Europe to show its devotion to human rights, and its ability to react effectively and with a heart to crises within and at the borders of the EU. In principle, this does not necessarily mean the end of partnership with third countries in the management of migration flows towards the EU, it only means that these partnerships can only entered into and relied on in case their content and practical application fall within the boundaries of EU human rights and migration law. Where it becomes clear that they do not fulfill this criteria, as argued by the authors of this contribution is presently the case for Turkey, the EU will have to reassess these partnerships and be ready to shoulder its responsibility itself.

## References

Cassarino J.P. (2007), 'Informalising readmission agreements in the EU neighbourhood', *The international spectator*, Vol. 42, No. 2, June.

Chetail, V. & C. Bauloz (eds.) (2014), *Research handbook on international law and migration*, Cheltenham: Edward Elgar Publishing.

European Commission (2015), *Communication from the commission to the European parliament, the council, the European economic and social committee and the committee of the regions – a European agenda on migration*, COM(2015)240 final.

Geddes, A. & P. Scholten (2016), *The politics of migration and immigration in Europe*, London: Sage.

Groenendijk, K. & E. Guild (2010), *Visa policy of member states and EU towards Turkish nationals after soysal*, IKV Publications No. 232, Istanbul.

Icduygu, A. (2011), *The irregular migration corridor between the EU and Turkey: is it possible to block it with a readmission agreement?*, Fiesole: Robert Schuman Centre for Advanced Studies.

Peers, S. (2013), *EU justice and home affairs law* (3rd ed.), Oxford: Oxford University Press.

Thym, D. & M. Zoeteweij-Turhan (eds.) (2015), *Rights of third-country nationals under EU association agreements: degrees of citizenship*, Leiden: Brill.

Zaiotti, R. (ed.) (2016), *Exerternalizing migration management: Europe, North America and the spread of 'remote control' practices*, Routledge.

Zimmermann, A. (ed.) (2011), *The 1951 convention relating to the status of refugees and its 1967 protocol – a commentary*, Oxford: Oxford University Press.

# PART 3

## *People's Europe*

CHAPTER 10

# EU Inclusion and Exclusion: From Workers to Citizens to People

*Elspeth Guild*

## 10.1 Workers

The EEC Treaty of 1957 included as an objective the free movement of persons which was included in Article 3. However, this was only given form in the treaty as regards the economically active – workers, the self employed and service providers. The right of free movement of those who are economically active was extended by the Court of Justice (CJEU) to include those who consume services – service recipients in the 1980s. In today's world where the separation of workers into 'desirable', i.e. the highly skilled, highly qualified and highly paid (the main criteria of the Blue Card Directive) are welcome but the 'undesirable' workers are to be excluded (low skilled, low qualified and low paid) the choice of what is now the EU in 1957 seems unimaginable.[1] However, as many commentators have examined, myself included, in 1957 the priority as regards the work force was to acquire enough workers to fuel industrial development, it was not to exclude workers. Many northern European states had employment recruitment agreements with countries in the south: Germany with Greece and Turkey, the Netherlands with Turkey and Morocco etc. Along the same lines, Germany, the Netherlands and Belgium had bilateral recruitment agreements also with Italy. European countries with colonial territories turned to the people living in those territories to fulfil their labour market needs (France – Algeria, UK Indian sub-continent, Caribbean).[2] Looking backwards over the past 20 years from 2016, one thing which is surprising is how much more rapidly the nationals of those EU States which joined the EU in 2004 have been recognised as full EU citizens in comparison with Italian nationals after the creation of the EEC (as then was). Even in the late 1980s references were being made to the Court of Justice of the EU (CJEU) regarding expulsion of Italian

1 Guild, E. (2002), 'The single market, movement of persons and borders', in: J. Scott & C. Barnard, *The law of the single European market*, Hart: Oxford, pp. 295–310.

2 Guild, E. (2011), *Immigration law in the European community*, The Hague: Kluwer Law International.

 | DOI 10.1163/9789004330467_011

nationals from Germany which exemplified just how limited the sense of these fellow EU nationals were perceived in comparison with own nationals.

There has been some academic work on the degree to which state authorities were directly involved in recruiting migrant workers (common practice of the German labour ministry in the 1960s) or left it open to companies, often owned by the state to carry out recruitment in overseas territories.[3] However, this inquiry often asks a question: whether states have a greater moral obligation to treat the descendants of migrant workers in accordance with principles of equality or not if these states have actively recruited the workers in the first place instead of merely allowing them or failing to prevent them from arriving and settling in. This debate is now in the past. Most of the descendants of migrant workers to EU countries from the 1960s and 1970s have acquired citizenship, usually by birth on the territory in combination with the immigration status of their parents. What seemed even 20 years ago to be an issue of migration is now an issue of citizenship.[4] Those who regret this change of status are usually among those most vocal about the need to have strong laws to deprive people of citizenship when they behave badly in the eyes of the authorities (e.g., the Netherlands, UK and current debate in France).

In 1957 the division between desirable and undesirable workers did not rest on whether they were highly qualified or paid or not. Instead it was calculated on whether the workers were healthy (hence medical checks at various points in the migratory trajectory) and whether they were compliant (e.g., not too active in trade unions and workers' rights – an indication of possible communist tendencies) and with no criminal convictions. The idea which in today's language is expressed as circular migration was very popular – though in the language of the time it was Gastarbeiter. This world of competition for workers on the basis of their health and willingness to work fuelled a very specific approach to free movement in the EU (EEC as it then was). The distance between state control of the migration process or migration as a choice of the individual which is then confirmed by state authorities did not seem so distant. One seemed just to be a flip side of the other. The fixation on migration control and management would arrive in a few decades – around the time that the CMR was established.[5] The gradual control of labour migration began in Europe in

3 Guild, E. (2005), 'Who is entitled to work and who is in charge? Understanding the legal framework of European labour migration', in: E. Guild & D. Bigo (eds), *Controlling frontiers: free movement into and within Europe*, Farnham: Ashgate, pp. 100–139.

4 Guild, E. (1996), 'The legal framework of citizenship of the union', in: D. Cesarani & M. Fulbrook (eds), *Citizenship, nationality and migration in Europe*, London: Routledge.

5 Guild, E. (2001), *Immigration law in the European community*, The Hague: Kluwer Law International.

the late 1960s – the UK which was not yet a Member State was an early advocate of greater state control as de-colonialisation resulted in turbulence in East Africa.[6]

The consequence of the differences in preoccupation of the EU authorities in 1957 and those in 2016 is revealed in the EU's legal regime of free movement of workers, the self employed and service providers and recipients.[7] The idea of free movement of workers bears reflection. It re-sets the clock with a completely different default position from that of migration control and management. It is based on the principle that people know where their best interests lie and should be entitled to choose where to sell their labour or set up their business. It is inimical to the idea that state authorities have a right to decide whether to admit or refuse a foreign national on the basis of criteria which that administration has constructed. Instead the power is in the hands of the person who moves and it is for the state to carry out a test after the fact and in the event that the state authorities decide that they do not actually want the individual to be present on their territory to come up with reasons for this which would justify requiring the person to leave. This reversal of the relationship of power has taken on more and more importance both for those Member States anxious to control movement of persons on their territory but also among those Member States (often the more recent arrivals) who recognise the popularity among their citizens of achieving free movement of workers for them.[8]

The interests of these two groups of Member States often coincide – where in some Member States like the Netherlands and the UK political parties have sprung up which focus on the adverse consequences of being unable to control migration for instance from Poland or Romania[9] – and in other Member States, state authorities and political parties express concern about the loss of young workers in whose hands the future of the country rests (for instance

6 Guild, E. (1990), 'British nationality and East African independence', *I&NL&P*, July.

7 Guild, E. (1998), 'The constitutional consequences of lawmaking in the third pillar of the European Union', in: P. Craig & C. Harlow (eds), *Lawmaking in the European Union*, Dordrecht: Springer, pp. 65–88.

8 Guild, E. (2004), *The legal elements of European identity: EU citizenship and migration law*, The Hague: Kluwer Law International.

9 Van Heerden, S., *et al.* (2014), 'The immigration and integration debate in the Netherlands: discursive and programmatic reactions to the rise of anti-immigration parties', *Journal of Ethnic and Migration Studies* 40(1), pp. 119–136. Davis, A. (2012), *The impact of anti-immigration parties on mainstream parties' immigration positions in the Netherlands, Flanders and the UK 1987–2010: divided electorates, left-right politics and the pull towards restrictionism*, diss. European University Institute (SPS), Florence.

Greece and Spain after the economic slumps of 2008).[10] Yet while various political voices express concern and demand action, the reality of free movement of workers, the self employed and service providers and recipients appears to bring many benefits to everyone in the economy.[11]

This may be reflected by the nature of the challenges and cases which reach the EU's court in the field of free movement of workers. The vast majority of these cases are around social benefits of one kind or another. Hundreds of cases have been referred to the CJEU on Regulation 1408/71 and its successor 883/2004[12] on the coordination of social security systems. Many cases have been referred, though at a less startling rate, on the entitlement of workers to equal treatment in social advantages. What does this tell us about the principle of shifting the burden of proof from the individual to prove he or she fulfils the requirements to enter and work to the state to prove that the individual can be excluded on limited grounds? It would seem that money and profit is very much in question. States seem to be reluctant to enforce equal treatment in wages and working conditions for migrant workers and even more reluctant to treat them in the same way as nationals of the state when it comes to doling out social benefits, even in the case of contributory benefits. What is good enough for workers who are citizens of the state seems to be far too generous when it comes to workers who are not citizens.[13] The CJEU has taken a fairly consistent position (until recently – which I will come back to at the end) to privilege the entitlement of the EU worker to social benefits and to listen, with a healthy degree of scepticism, to the justifications put forward by states for

10 Mrozowicki, A., A. Krasowska & M. Karolak (2015), 'Stop the junk contracts! Young Workers and trade union mobilisation against precarious employment in Poland', in: A. Hodder & L. Ketsos (eds), *HoYoung workers and trade unions*, Palgrave: Macmillan UK, pp. 123–141; Spyridakis, M. (2013), *The liminal worker: an ethnography of work, unemployment and precariousness in contemporary Greece*, Farnham: Ashgate Publishing, Ltd.; Meardi, G. (2013), *Social failures of EU enlargement: a case of workers voting with their feet*, No. 25. New York: Routledge.

11 Minderhoud, P.E. & N. Trimikliniotis (2009), *Rethinking the free movement of workers. The European challenges ahead*, Nijmegen: Wolf Legal Publishers.

12 Fuchs, M. & R. Cornelissen (2015), *EU social security law: a commentary on EU regulations 883/2004 and 987/2009*, Baden-Baden: Beck/Hart/Nomos. Cantillon, B., H. Verschueren & P. Ploscar (eds) (2012), *Social inclusion and social protection in the EU: interactions between law and policy*, Antwerp: Intersentia.

13 Guild, E., S. Carrera Nunez & K. Eisele (2013), *Social benefits and migration: a contested relationship and policy challenge in the EU*, Brussels: CEPS.

the necessity of differential treatment in social benefits between their citizens and workers from other Member States.[14]

The EU approach of establishing a right to equal treatment for workers wherever they are in the Union against which right any Member State wishing to provide worse treatment must justify that choice, has had substantial consequences for the way in which we think about migration of all kinds. The normal position, and one which the trade unions have been eager to support, is that all workers need to have the same rights in respect wages and working conditions.[15] There are a number of reasons for this among them: (1) this is the only way to ensure that employers do not undercut wages and working conditions by hiring cheaper non-national workers and thus freeze out workers from the state; (2) wages and working conditions can only be maintained if everyone in the workplace is able to enjoy the same standards and ensure its enforcement; (3) protection of wages and working conditions have a social purpose which applies to everyone in the labour market irrespective of their status as a citizen or foreigner.[16] The CJEU approved these arguments in its judgment *Tümer*[17] in 2014 when contemplating whether a Turkish worker without permission to reside in the Netherlands should still be entitled to compensation for wages lost as a result of the insolvency of his employer. The outcome was to reinforce the entitlement of everyone in the labour market to wage and working conditions equality and protection[18] – but I am getting ahead of myself here and will come back to this in due course.

The tenacity of EU workers to claim equal treatment in wages and working conditions is also a credit to the original treaty. By giving the power to choice

---

14 Cornelissen, R. & G. Van Limberghen (2015), '14. Social security for mobile workers and labour law', in: F. Pennings & G. Vonk, *Research handbook on European social security law*, Cheltenham: Edward Elgar, pp. 344–384. Pennings, F. (2012), 'EU citizenship: access to social benefits in other EU member states', *International Journal of Comparative Labour Law and Industrial Relations* 28(3), pp. 307–333.

15 Visser, J. (2013), 'ICTWSS: database on institutional characteristics of trade unions, wage setting, state intervention and social pacts, 1960–2011', Amsterdam Institute for Advances Labour Studies (AIAS), University of Amsterdam <www.uva-aias.net/207>.

16 Connolly, H., S. Marino & M. Martinez Lucio (2014), 'Trade union renewal and the challenges of representation: strategies towards migrant and ethnic minority workers in the Netherlands, Spain and the United Kingdom', *European Journal of Industrial Relations*, March 2014, vol 20(1), pp. 5–20.

17 CJEU 5 November 2014, C-311/13, *Tümer*, ECLI:EU:C:2014:2337.

18 Crépeau, F. & B. Hastie (2015), 'The case for "firewall" protections for irregular migrants', *European Journal of Migration and Law* 17(2–3), pp. 157–183.

to the worker against which any state effort to exclude him or her from the labour market or territory requires a great amount of effort and justification, a group of migrant workers came into being with the confidence to make and pursue their claims to equality. As their continued residence and employment did not depend on a state's generosity in extending their work and residence permits every now and then a sense of entitlement to equality could come into existence.[19] Migrant workers whose work and residence status is constantly up for grabs and can be extinguished easily by the state are much less vocal about their rights. The fear that state authorities and employers are working together and any effort to establish a right to equal treatment may result in non-renewal of a residence permit or the curtailment of the right to work is constantly present. Legislation in a number of Member States which requires employers to provide information on third country national workers' immigration status continuously to state authorities creates close relationships between employers and state immigration authorities (such as in the Netherlands and the UK).[20] It becomes easier and easier for employers to get rid of troublesome employees through immigration procedures thus avoiding the nuisance of employment protection legislation.[21]

The second bone of contention among EU workers, self employed and service providers and Member State authorities has been family reunion with third country national family members. This always seems to be a peculiar debate not least as so many international human rights instruments state as the ICCPR does that "The family is the natural and fundamental group unit of society and is entitled to protection by society and the State" (Article 23(1) ICCPR).[22] Yet, for some EU States, national law is constructed so that the family entitled to protection means the family composed exclusively of nationals of the state.[23] Those citizens who acquire third country national family members

19 Collett, E. (2013), *The integration needs of mobile EU citizens: impediments and opportunities*, Brussels: Migration Policy Institute Europe.

20 Anderson, B. (2015), 'Precarious work, immigration, and governance', in: C.-U. Schierup, R. Munck, B. Likic-Brbobic & A. Neergaard (eds), *Migration, precarity, and global governance: challenges and opportunities for labour*, Oxford: Oxford University Press, p. 68.

21 Guild, E., C. Gortázar Rotaeche & D. Kostakopoulou (eds) (2013), *The reconceptualization of European Union citizenship*, The Hague: Martinus Nijhoff Publishers.

22 Desmond, A. (2015), 'The triangle that could square the circle? The UN international convention on the protection of the rights of all migrant workers and members of their families, the EU and the universal periodic review', *European Journal of Migration and Law* 17(1), pp. 39–69.

23 Heinemann, T. & Th. Lemke (2012), 'Suspect families: DNA kinship testing in German immigration policy', *Sociology* 47(4), pp. 810–826.

appear to be excluded from the entitlement to protection. But not only is protection of the family not on offer, but in these cases some states seem to being falling over themselves to think up ever greater obstacles to family life where one or more members of the family is a third country national. One only needs to reflect on the development of language requirements, income thresholds, integration tests, age limits and the like to recognise this restrictive tendency, the volition to create obstacles ever more insurmountable for their citizens.[24] This is a form of punishment by the state of citizens for acquiring the wrong sort of family members.[25]

EU workers are protected by EU law against these tendencies – first in the form of secondary legislation dating from the 1960s and only ever extended not reduced, setting out the right to family reunion with their family members (defined in the EU secondary legislation not left to Member States' imagination) and secondly by the CJEU's interpretation of the worker's right to family reunion as an inherent part of the internal market.[26] The consequence of various struggles between Member States and EU workers from other Member States regarding the entitlement to family reunion has taken unexpected paths. The first has been regarding constitutional issues in some Member States where citizens must always have the best rights available to anyone on the territory (e.g., Austria).[27] As national immigration laws regarding family reunion for citizens of the state became increasingly hostile to third country national family members, the right of EU workers to these family rights became ever more incongruent.[28] State authorities had an increasingly complicated time of it to explain to their citizens why they could not have the same generous family reunion rights as those which their EU worker neighbours from another Member

24 Van Oers, R., E. Ersbøll & D. Kostakopoulou (eds) (2010), *A re-definition of belonging?: language and integration tests in Europe*, The Hague: Brill.

25 Groenendijk notes that in the parliamentary debates on the Dutch integration abroad test, the government sought to justify the new obstacles on the grounds that the children of Moroccan and Turkish immigrants to the Netherlands should marry someone already in the Netherlands rather than someone from their parents' country of origin. Groenendijk, K. (2011), 'Pre-departure integration strategies in the European Union: integration or immigration policy?', *European Journal of Migration and Law* 13(1), pp. 1–30.

26 CJEU 25 July 2008, C-127/08 *Metock*, ECLI:EU:C:2008:449. Wiesbrock, A. (2012), 'Granting citizenship-related rights to third-country nationals: an alternative to the full extension of European Union citizenship?', *European Journal of Migration and Law* 14(1), pp. 63–94.

27 Messinger, I. (2013), 'There is something about marrying... The case of human rights vs. migration regimes using the example of Austria', *Laws* 2(4), pp. 376–391.

28 Lenaerts, K. (2015), 'EU citizenship and the European court of justice's "stone-by-stone" approach', *International Comparative Jurisprudence* 1(1), pp. 1–10.

State were entitled to enjoy. The second has been a rear-guard action by some Member States, the Netherlands and the UK among them, to roll back EU family reunion rights for EU workers both in law and practice.[29] When one examines the number of cases which have come before the CJEU on this subject, a predominant number of them involve the Netherlands and the UK and in almost all of them (though with some surprising exceptions) these two states if not immediately party have intervened against the EU worker.[30]

The third field in respect of which the CJEU has reined in Member States' enthusiasm to limit EU workers' rights has been in respect of expulsion. Very much an issue of the early days of free movement of workers in the EU, the temptation of Member States to expel EU workers when they became unemployed was great. This ground of expulsion was specifically prohibited by the secondary legislation so particularly as unemployment rose in the 1970 Member States began to examine the grounds on which they could expel EU workers and to test their residual powers. Once again the position of the CJEU was central.[31] Doing no more than interpreting the Treaty and subsidiary legislation faithfully it pointed out to the Member States that they had agreed a high level of protection for EU workers which could only be displaced by a real danger to public policy or public security. As far as public policy is concerned this requires a conviction by a criminal court in addition to evidence of a future threat to public policy on the basis of the individual's continued residence. Efforts to diminish this standard have not so far been successful – but at the time of writing in Spring 2016 are back on the table in the context of the UK government's demands for revision of the EU.[32]

As workers, nationals of the Member States have gradually extended and consolidated their rights entering into prolonged struggles with some Member States. The three fields which are outstanding in this regard are social security and benefit rights, third country national family members and protection from expulsion.

29 Groenendijk, K. (2004), 'Legal concepts of integration in EU migration law', *European Journal of Migration and Law* 6(2), pp. 111–126.

30 Explicitly, this policy seems to have been motivated in both countries by concerns about their nationals who have an immigrant background and thus in the eyes of the authorities too many links with countries abroad. Guild, E., C.A. Groenendijk & S. Carrera (eds) (2009), *Illiberal liberal states: immigration, citizenship, and integration in the EU*, London: Ashgate Publishing.

31 Guild, E. (2014), *The social impact of migration and the notion of citizenship for the EU. Ensuing challenges and opportunities for the Union*, CEPS Commentaries, 13 March 2014.

32 Kostakopoulou, D. (2014), 'When EU citizens become foreigners', *European Law Journal* 20(4), pp. 447–463.

## 10.2 Citizens

Enlargement of the EU has had a profound impact on the rights of EU nationals. The enlargement in 1973 to include Denmark, Ireland and the UK took place amid concerns about migration from the UK in particular to the continent which would include workers with no history of minimum wages (which did not exist in the UK at that time).[33] At that time in the Dutch parliament fears were expressed explicitly about the risks of allowing free movement to the Netherlands to Black British workers. The 1980 enlargements (Greece, Portugal and Spain) had a more profound impact on the rights of people – first in a negative manner – for the first time transitional restrictions were applied to free movement of workers for periods of up to seven years from accession of each of the countries.[34] For Portugal and Spain there was an adjustment of the transitional restrictions lifting them a year before the end date on account of German reunification.[35] On the positive side, Spain championed the creation of citizenship of the Union introduced in the Maastricht Treaty in 1991 – a new dimension of free movement which according to the treaty provision swept up all the rights of movement and residence into the new status of citizen.

When the Maastricht Treaty came into force and all nationals of the Member States became citizens of the Union there was joy in some countries and dismay in others.[36] According to an anecdote of a Commission official at the time, a number of British (and other national) citizens wrote to the Commission advising that they did not want this new citizenship. The automatic acquisition of a second citizenship by everyone who was a Member State national also undermined the principle of only one citizenship – a dearly held principle in some Member States. It was no longer possible for any national of a Member State to remain other than a dual citizen. Economically inactive Member States nationals had already won the right to move and reside elsewhere in the

33 Bohning, R. (1972), 'The problems of immigrant workers in West Germany', in: N. Deakin (ed), *Immigrant in Europe*, London: Fabian Society, pp. 18–29. Wallace, H. (2013), 'The UK: 40 years of EU membership', *Journal of Contemporary European Research* 8(4), pp. 531–546.

34 Preston, Chr. (1995), 'Obstacles to EU enlargement: the classical community method and the prospects for a wider Europe', *JCMS: Journal of Common Market Studies* 33(3), pp. 451–463.

35 Royo, S. & P. Chr. Manuel (eds) (2003), *Spain and Portugal in the European Union: the first fifteen years*, Oxford: Taylor & Francis.

36 Wiener, A. & V. Della Sala (1997), 'Constitution making and citizenship practice–bridging the democracy gap in the EU?', *Journal of Common Market Studies* 35(4), pp. 595–614.

EU by virtue of a series of three directives in 1990.[37] The consolidation of rights in the new citizenship brought together under one heading all nationals of the Member States irrespective of whether they had exercised a free movement right and where they had exercised such a right irrespective of the basis on which they had done so.[38]

But what did these new citizens want from their citizenship? For about ten years it was not entirely clear as the CJEU consistently resisted interpreting the meaning of the new citizenship provision.[39] A number of these new citizens sought to use their new status to claim rights that they would acquire only through the exercise of a free movement right without actually doing the free movement act. But either these cases never went to the CJEU or the CJEU found no link to EU law.[40]

Citizenship of the Union as a new status began to take hold just as a number of cases about marginal movement and the escape from national citizenship were favourably considered by the CJEU.[41] In the marginal movement cases, *Chen* stands out – a Chinese woman resident in the UK who went to Northern Ireland to give birth so that her daughter would be an EU citizen (At the time, Irish citizenship was accorded to all people born on the territory of the island or Ireland, not just the Republic of Ireland, this was changed following the decision of the CJEU).[42] The decision in 2004 recognised that the baby Chen was entitled as an Irish national (although never having set foot in Ireland) to reside in the UK as an EU citizen and in order to exercise this right was entitled to have her third country national mother live with her. That the family was economically self-sufficient and had health insurance was a factor (the economically inactive right of residence directives all require health insurance and sufficient resources not to become a burden on the social assistance system of the host Member State). Citizens apparently want to live in the state where they

37 Guild, E. (1996), 'The right to travel: three new directives from the European Commission', *I&NL&P* Vol 10(2).

38 Mantu, S. (2008), *The boundaries of European social citizenship,* Nijmegen: Wolf Legal Publishers.

39 Fries, S. (1998), 'Citizenship of the union: first steps in the European Court of justice', *European Public Law* 4(4), pp. 533–559.

40 Shuibhne, N.N. (2002), 'Free movement of persons and the wholly internal rule: time to move on?', *Common Market Law Review* 39(4), pp. 731–771.

41 Berneri, C. (2014), 'Protection of families composed by EU citizens and third-country nationals: some suggestions to tackle reverse discrimination', *European Journal of Migration and Law* 16(2), pp. 249–275.

42 Ryan, B. (2004), 'The celtic cubs: the controversy over birthright citizenship in Ireland', *European Journal of Migration and Law* 6(3), pp. 173–193.

are born enjoying EU rights. They no longer wanted to exercise a free movement right in order to enjoy the flanking rights such as family reunion, which come into existence through the exercise of a treaty free movement right. This new demand, to enjoy EU rights without moving would become something of a clarion call from EU citizens. By 2011 the demand was recognised by the CJEU as valid in *Zambrano* a particularly important case about moving from national of a Member State to citizen of the Union without having to exercise a free movement right for more than three months.[43] Once again it revolved around a child who had acquired citizenship of the country where he lived (Belgium) but whose parents were third country nationals subject to expulsion procedures (which had been stopped by a court and over the effective period of 10 years had not been carried out). The CJEU found that the child had a right to have his parents live with him in Belgium and those parents had the right to work. These rights even extended to the right of a third country national older sister to remain with him in the host Member State. It looked as if citizenship of the Union might be about to acquire the key characteristics of citizenship in international law – the right to enter and live in the country of one's nationality, though these indications were quickly scotched. In a series of cases which have followed *Zambrano* and have been fully discussed in the legal literature, the CJEU withdrew somewhat from its position which seems at the moment to apply specifically to children, taking into account their vulnerable position. For adults the only solution is to exercise a free movement right to go and live in another Member State.[44]

Another development of the power of EU status to counter national citizenship came early in the 1990s in the *Surinder Singh* judgment though it was not argued on the basis of EU citizenship as the provision had not come into force yet.[45] Here a British citizen exercised her free movement right and worked in Germany then returned to the UK with her third country national husband. The UK authorities sought to apply national UK immigration law to the husband. He claimed that EU law must continue to apply to him even though he and his wife had now returned to her country of underlying citizenship – the UK. The UK authorities claimed Mrs Singh as their national and with that claim the entitlement to treat just as disadvantageously as they treated all their other citizens in respect of family reunion. The CJEU found against the UK

43 Tryfonidou, A. (2012), 'Redefining the outer boundaries of EU law: the Zambrano, McCarthy and Dereci trilogy', *European Public Law* 18(3), pp. 493–526.

44 Lenaerts, K. (2015), 'EU citizenship and the European Court of justice's "stone-by-stone" approach', *International Comparative Jurisprudence* 1(1), pp. 1–10.

45 CJEU 7 July 1992, C-370/90 *Surinder Singh*, ECLI:EU:C:1992:296, *ECR* [1992] I-04265.

authorities. Effectively the Singh family which had set out from the UK as British citizens had become EU citizens while working in Germany and retained that status and all its consequential rights on their return to the UK. Mrs Singh did not revert back to her British citizen status on returning to the UK with her third country national husband. She remained an EU citizen and he remained protected by EU family reunion law, which was much more generous than its British counterpart.[46]

While the claim was specifically about rights to family life it can also be seen as a sign of emancipation of EU status from nationality of a Member State. Although the latter was and continues to be an necessary characteristic to enjoy EU citizenship, once an EU citizen has started to acquire EU based rights through the exercise of a free movement right he or she is entitled to continue to enjoy the benefits of that EU status when returning to his or her state of underlying nationality. The starting place is the same – a national of a Member State at home cannot access rights attached to free movement but once they have been accessed then they can be enjoyed back in the state of nationality.[47]

Further citizens of the Union appear to want equal treatment in respect of social rights.[48] The reluctance of Member States to afford real equality to EU workers as regards benefits available to their own nationals has been even more pronounced when it comes to EU citizens. The claim to the right to move and reside for more than three months has been carefully restricted in EU secondary legislation to apply only to those who have rights as workers or self employed or those who are self sufficient and have health insurance. Member States really object to extending their social benefits to EU citizens on the basis of their common citizenship (see *Dano, Alimanovic* etc).[49] While there is a grudging acceptance of states' obligation to extend such rights to workers, citizens are certainly not considered equal enough for this purpose.[50]

46 Groenendijk, K. (2006), 'Family reunification as a right under community law', *European Journal of Migration and Law* 8(2), pp. 215.

47 Oosterom-Staples, H. (2012), 'To what extent has reverse discrimination been reversed?', *European Journal of Migration and Law* 14(2), pp. 151–172.

48 Guild, E. (2013), 'Does European citizenship blur the borders of solidarity?', in: E. Guild, C. Gortazar & D. Kostakopoulou (eds), *The reconceptualization of European Union citizenship,* The Hague: Brill, pp. 189.

49 CJEU 11 November 2014, C-333/13 *Dano*, ECLI:EU:C:2014:2358. CJEU 15 September 2015, C-67/14 *Alimanovic*, ECLI:EU:C:2015:597. Verschueren, H. (2015), 'Preventing "benefit tourism" in the EU: a narrow or broad interpretation of the possibilities offered by the ECJ in Dano?', *Common Market Law Review* 52(2), pp. 363–390.

50 Peers, S. (2015), 'Benefits for EU-citizens: a u-turn by the court of justice?', *The Cambridge Law Journal* 74(2) pp. 195–198. Van der Mei, A.P. (2015), 'Overview of recent cases

The question also remains whether EU citizenship is a real citizenship. The fact that EU citizens can still be expelled from one Member State to their state of underlying nationality and the limitations on their voting rights[51] are indications that this citizenship is incomplete as regards international law. I have argued elsewhere that the only way around this problem is to suggest that expulsion from one part of the EU to another is the equivalent of an internal residence restriction. But the EU law still calls expulsion 'expulsion' not a residence order.[52] The violence inherent in expulsion still applies to EU citizens when they are being pushed back to their country of underlying nationality by the authorities of a host Member State. It would be difficult, in good faith, to suggest that this is anything but expulsion.[53] As the expression goes, if it quacks like a duck and it walks like a duck it probably is a duck.

The EU legislator attempted to reduce the power of Member States to expel EU citizens from their territory in the negotiations which led to Directive 2004/38. The Member States insisted on retaining the expulsion power but they did agree to the creation of a new status of permanent residence and the limitation of expulsion powers by ever increasingly strict requirements with the passage of time. Serious reasons of public policy must be established by the Member State to expel an EU citizen with a right of permanent residence, after ten years residence or in respect of a child imperative grounds of public security are need to justify expulsion. Sadly, the CJEU saw fit to interpret these two new protections in a vague manner not particularly conducive to the intention of additional protection.[54] The creation of a right of permanent residence for a citizen is a very odd idea in itself. Citizens are entitled to residence

before the court of justice of the European Union (October–December 2014)', *European Journal of Social Security* 17(1), pp. 103.

51 In EU law, EU citizens living in a member state other than that of their underlying nationality can only vote and stand for election in municipal and European parliament elections. Groenendijk, K. (2008), *Local voting rights for non-nationals in Europe: what we know and what we need to learn*, Brussels: Migration Policy Institute.

52 Guild, E. (2004), *The legal elements of European identity: EU citizenship and migration law*, The Hague: Kluwer Law International.

53 Genova, N. De & N. Peutz (eds) (2010), *The deportation regime: sovereignty, space, and the freedom of movement*, Duke University Press. Guild, E. (2016), 'Understanding immigration detention in the UK and Europe', in: M.J. Guia, R. Koulish & V. Mitsilegas (eds), *Immigration detention, risk and human rights*. Springer International Publishing, pp. 141–155.

54 Kostakopoulou, D. (2014), 'When EU citizens become foreigners', *European Law Journal* 20(4), pp. 447–463. Kochenov, D. (2012), 'A real European citizenship: the court of justice opening a new chapter in the development of the union in Europe', *Columbia Journal of European Law* 18(1), pp. 55–109.

by their citizenship – how odd that they should be able to acquire a more permanent form of it by residing in their territory of citizenship for five years.[55]

So the EU has citizens who lack an essential characteristic of the international law status of a citizen.[56] But, on the other hand, they have acquired a whole series of rights which are highly portable and can be taken 'home' when the EU citizen goes back to his or her state of nationality.[57]

Perhaps the most important aspect of the move to citizenship of the Union is the shift away from an economic conceptualisation of rights for people in the EU. However, in widening the concept of citizenship to include a *supra* national entity which is not a state, it may be that the EU has also weakened the concept.[58] While at Member State level, citizenship is based on the idea of allegiance between the citizen and the state what is the link at the EU level? It may be that the new ways of thinking about citizenship have been relevant to its increasing fragility. In 1999 eight years after nationals of the Member States obtained their new status as EU citizens they lost a right in international law which is tied to 'real' citizenship – the right to seek international protection in any country as soon as one is outside one's state of nationality.[59] By virtue of the Aznar Protocol to the Amsterdam Treaty EU citizens are presumed not to be in need of international protection (though in theory the presumption can be rebutted).[60] The logic goes that EU Member States respect human rights and do not create refugees. Thus citizens of the Union do not need a right to seek asylum elsewhere in the EU. The consequence has been that EU citizens seek (and receive) asylum outside the EU, notably but not only in Canada.[61] While EU citizens can be expelled back to their countries of underlying

55 Kochenov, D. (2013), 'The right to have what rights? EU citizenship in need of clarification', *European Law Journal* 19(4), pp. 502–516.

56 Guild, E. (2007), 'Citizens without a constitution, borders without a state: EU free movement of persons', in: A. Baldaccini, E. Guild & H. Toner, *Whose freedom, security and justice? EU immigration and asylum law and policy*, Oxford: Hart, pp. 25–56.

57 Douglas-Scott, S. (2014), 'A tale of two courts: Luxembourg, Strasbourg and the growing European human rights acquis', *CML Review* 43, p. 629.

58 Askola, H. (2012), 'Tale of two citizenships? Citizenship, migration and care in the European Union', *Social & Legal Studies* 21(3), pp. 341–356.

59 Guild, E, and K. Zwaan (2014), 'Does Europe still create refugees-examining the situation of the Roma', *Queen's LJ* 40, pp. 141.

60 Guild, E. & M. Garlick (2010), 'Refugee protection, counter-terrorism, and exclusion in the European Union', *Refugee Survey Quarterly* 4, pp. 63–82.

61 Carrera, S., E. Guild & M. Merlino (2011), *The Canada-Czech Republic visa dispute two years on: implications for the EU's migration and asylum policies*, Brussels: Centre for European Policy Studies.

nationality they cannot seek asylum on the basis of a fear of persecution, real risk of torture, inhuman or degrading treatment or punishment in another Member State.[62]

An increasing number of Member States like the Netherlands and the UK have passed legislation which permits them to withdraw citizenship from unsatisfactory citizens, usually described as those involved in terrorism though the UK legislation permits this on the basis that their continued citizenship is not conducive to the public good.[63] The idea that citizenship is difficult to get rid of and states are responsible for the citizens they have has been changing.[64] That citizenship might be a privilege which the state can take away from anyone is a complicated way of defining the polity. In EU law, the protection of the EU citizen from the coercive state has taken numerous forms, some set out above. That the EU citizen always has the right to enter the territory of the EU has been a given. The CJEU refused to permit Member States to include EU citizens among the people whose details are entered on the Schengen Information System for the purpose of excluding them from the territory (refusal of entry).[65] The reason for this was that Article 96 of the Schengen Implementing Agreement (CISA) when read in conjunction with Article 1 defining an 'alien' prohibits the registration of EU citizens for the purposes of exclusion from the territory of the Member States. EU citizens can be registered for other purposes such as for surveillance.

But some states, such as the UK, Belgium, have passed legislation which permits the authorities to withdraw the privileges of citizenship granted by international law, i.e. the right to enter one's state. The UK legislation permits this exclusion of citizens for periods of up to two years (The Counter Terrorism and Security Act 2015 – temporary exclusion orders). Thus it would seem that ideas which have seemed permanent are actually changing. The use of the term 'foreign fighters' to describe EU citizens who have gone to the Middle East to engage in the regional war there seems an anomaly. How foreign are these fighters if they are British, French, Belgium, Dutch citizens? Is their

62 Byrne, R., G. Noll & J. Vedsted-Hansen (2004), 'Understanding refugee law in an enlarged European Union', *European Journal of International Law* 15(2), pp. 355–379.

63 Mantu, S. (2015), *Contingent citizenship: the law and practice of citizenship deprivation in international, European and national perspectives,* The Hague: Brill.

64 Mantu, S. (2015), 'Citizenship in times of terror: citizenship deprivation in the UK', *Change* 36(5), pp. 735–751. Baldaccini, A. (2008), 'Counter-terrorism and the EU strategy for border security: framing suspects with biometric documents and databases', *European Journal of Migration and Law* 10(1), pp. 31–49.

65 Brouwer, E. (2008), *Digital borders and real rights: effective remedies for third-country nationals in the Schengen information system,* Den Haag: Brill.

foreignness somehow an attribute associated with the deep characteristic of citizenship – allegiance? Also in the terminology of foreign fighters may be embedded the assumption that these people are dual nationals – the children of migrant workers from elsewhere and so their EU citizenship is somehow an extra, or a luxury acquired by reason of accident of birth and immigration status of their parents. In the debates around citizenship from the 1980s and before particularly in Germany, one of the key arguments for refusing to permit dual nationality was that in the event of hostilities between the two countries of nationality the dual national would find him or herself in a position of treason in respect of one of them and this should be avoided at all costs.[66] The loyalty of the dual national is the matter in issue – can a state really rely on the allegiance of a dual national? States with long colonial pasts have often been less concerned about dual nationality as the assumption of links between the independent former colonial state and the former master state is only reluctantly abandoned. However, the changing world of disaffected young people appears to be changing that assumption. These young people are now framed as the problem of their 'other' citizenship and country not the EU Member State where they have often been born and lived most of their lives.

There are some indications that in discussions among EU working groups on counter-terrorism and organised crime there are efforts afoot to find ways to use the SIS system to signal which EU citizens should be excluded from entering the EU altogether even if, formally, they still hold the nationality of a Member State.

## 10.3 People

The division of the world into citizens and foreigners depends on a profound belief in the magic which borders perform. International borders can transform people from citizens in their own state to foreigners in some one else's state and the reverse.[67] This extraordinary capacity of an international border is determinant of the rights of those who cross it – to stay, to work to enjoy

66 Hailbronner, K. (1989), 'Citizenship and nationhood in Germany', in: R. Brubaker (ed), *Immigration and the politics of citizenship in Europe and North America*, American University Press, pp. 67.

67 Guild, E. (2006), 'Danger – borders under construction: assessing the first five years of border policy in an area of freedom, security and justice', in: J. de Zwaan & F. Goudappel, *Freedom, security and justice in the European Union: implementation of the Hague programme*, Asser Press, The Hague, pp. 45–72.

equal treatment etc. It is founded in the idea of the citizen as the legitimate participant in the polity and the foreigner as someone who might be tolerated.[68] It is in constitutions and constitutional settlements that this relationship of the citizen and the state is inscribed.

Yet, there is a parallel universe of rights which is based not on citizenship but on human rights.[69] This universe has developed rapidly in the post WWII period moving from aspirational declarations (UDHR) to binding commitments and increasingly binding supranational adjudication of rights (ICCPR etc).[70] The regional form of this is the ECHR and as a late comer the EU Charter of Fundamental Rights. What is common to these obligations is that they are cast in the form of universal duties to people, not limited to citizens. Thus while the standard is often lower than that which national constitutions provide to their own citizens, human rights set a threshold below which the actions of no signatory state should fall. Where human rights are at stake the beneficiaries are everyone and anyone. There are few human rights which are limited by a nationality restriction, usually around voting and electoral rights.[71] Even the right to enter one's country in Protocol 4 ECHR is not defined in terms of citizens and there has been a lively academic debate about whether long term resident foreigners can claim a country as their own.

The EU was slow in developing its Charter of Fundamental Rights, the consequence of its traditional task as being the creation and completion of an internal market (not protecting human rights).[72] The road to the creation of the convention mandated to write the Charter began in the 1990s and the work commenced seriously in 2000.[73] Yet, the Charter did not acquire legal binding

---

68 Guild, E. (2011), 'Equivocal claims? Ambivalent controls? Labour migration regimes in the European Union', in: E. Guild & S. Mantu (eds), *Constructing and imagining labour migration: perspectives of control from five continents*, Farnham: Ashgate, pp. 207–228.

69 Falk, R.A. (2000), *Human rights horizons: the pursuit of justice in a globalizing world*, New York: Routledge. Donnelly, J. (1998), 'Human rights: a new standard of civilization?', *International Affairs* 74(1), pp. 1–23.

70 Baldinger, D. (2015), *Vertical judicial dialogues in asylum cases: standards on judicial scrutiny and evidence in international and European asylum law*, Den Haag: Martinus Nijhoff.

71 Groenendijk, K. (2008), *Local voting rights for non-nationals in Europe: what we know and what we need to learn*, Migration Policy Institute.

72 Von Bogdandy, A. (2000), 'The European Union as a human rights organization? Human rights and the core of the European Union', *Common Market Law Review* 37(6), pp. 1307–1338.

73 Peers, S., *et al.* (eds) (2004), *The EU charter of fundamental rights: a commentary*, Oxford: Hart Publishing.

effect as a tool capable of providing rights to individuals until the entry into force of the Lisbon Treaty in 2009.

The language of the Charter is that of human rights applicable to everyone with few exceptions. These exceptions are: Article 12 which provides that political parties express the political will of EU citizens. Article 15 provides a right to employment for EU citizens; Articles 39 and 40 entitled EU citizens to stand for election and vote in European Parliament and municipal elections wherever they live in the EU. Articles 42, 43, 44 and 45 set out the rights to access to documents, to use the services of the Ombudsman and to petition the European Parliament but all of them are expressly stated to be available to any natural or legal person residing or having its registered office in the EU. Article 45 extends the right of free movement only to EU citizens (though extendable to third country nationals). Article 46 entitles only EU citizens to diplomatic and consular protection when in third countries. The rest of the fifty articles creating rights apply to everyone (within the jurisdiction of a Member State).[74] For the moment the pressing legal conundrum in respect of the Charter relates to its scope – what exactly is covered by the Charter as within the scope of EU law and what is excluded as within the competence of the Member States. This is a perennial fixation of EU law which has nothing particularly revelatory about it in this field. However, in respect of people, those who have been most discussed in the decisions of the Court of Justice which rely on the Charter have been migrants, refugees and asylum seekers, by definition not citizens of the Union.[75]

On the scope issue, so long as the action comes within the scope of EU law then an individual whether a citizen or third country national is entitled to claim Charter rights in respect of it.[76] It seems apparent that the Charter does not affect the right of Member States to expel from their territory nationals of other Member States. The Charter includes a right to asylum but all the EU secondary legislation on international protection exclude from their scope nationals of the Member States hence the scope issue might be at play. So, for instance, it is not clear whether the Charter reinstates the right of EU citizens to seek asylum in another Member State.

---

74 Guild, E. (2004), 'The variable subject of the EU constitution, civil liberties and human rights', *European Journal of Migration and Law* 6(4), pp. 381–394.

75 Ippolito, F. (2015), 'Migration and asylum cases before the court of justice of the European Union: putting the EU charter of fundamental rights to test?', *European Journal of Migration and Law* 17(1), pp. 1–38.

76 Dougan, M. (2015), 'Judicial review of member state action under the general principles and the charter: defining the "scope of union law"', *Common Market Law Review* 52(5), pp. 1201–1245.

The Charter only resolves issues of EU citizens right to respect to family life in so far as this is covered by the ECHR and its jurisprudence. In one recent CJEU judgment an Advocate General (Sharpston)[77] suggested that the rights of EU citizens returning to their home Member States after working in another and having acquired third country national family members should only have Charter and ECHR family life rights regarding taking their family members home with them. This would have diminished dramatically the family reunion rights of EU citizens. The CJEU did not follow the A-G in this regard. Similarly, the Charter does not provide EU citizens with better rights as regards equality in access to social benefits. However, it does set a floor which applies to everyone including in its social chapter.[78] Increasingly the CJEU has invoked the charter to examine claims to equality of third country nationals resident in the EU with EU citizens – often with positive outcomes.[79]

The sequence of developments which have taken place in the EU from 1961 (when the first directive on rights of EU workers including regarding family members) to 2016 in family reunion law has revealed only movement in one direction – the widening of rights. No EU right has yet been reduced though national family reunion laws have been dramatically restricted. This has left an increasingly wide gap between what is available to EU citizens who move to another Member State and the offer of their home state makes to them. Such a bifurcation may also take place in respect of the Charter though only time will tell. This same process is also evident in the protection of Turkish workers and self employed under the EC Turkey Association Agreement in comparison with the treatment of other third country nationals in the EU. What seemed normal for migrant workers and self employed in the 1970s and 1980s and was thus included in the EC Turkey Association Agreement and the secondary legislation made under it now seems extremely generous in relation to national legislation of many Member States.[80]

77 CJEU 12 March 2014, C-456/12, *O & B*, ECLI:EU:C:2014:135.

78 Prassl, J. (2012), 'Book review of: N. Bruun, K. Lörcher & I. Schömann (eds), The Lisbon treaty and social Europe, (Oxford: Hart Publishing, 2012)', *Common Market Law Review* 52(1), pp. 310–311.

79 Minderhoud, P.E. (2015), 'Nr. 61. Kamberaj. Equal treatment of long-term resident for housing benefit and Article 34 Charter; annotation with CJEU 24 April 2012, C-571/10', in: S.G. Kok, C.H. Slingenberg & K.M. Zwaan (eds), *Landmark cases on asylum and immigration law,* Nijmegen: Ars Aequi Libri. Acosta Arcarazo, D. (2015), 'Civic citizenship reintroduced? The long term residence directive as a post national form of membership', *European Law Journal* 21(2), pp. 200–219.

80 Rogers, N. (1999), *A practitioner's guide to the EC-Turkey association agreement,* The Hague: Martinus Nijhoff Publishers.

With time, the Charter may come into its own increasingly providing a common threshold of rights valuable not only to third country nationals but also to EU citizens. The 'everyone' of the Charter may in fact become everyone if the rights of EU citizens continue to be interpreted in a restrictive manner and the rights of third country nationals catch up.

## 10.4 Conclusions

In this chapter I have examined the development of the status of people in EU law from workers with rights to EU citizens with rights to everyone irrespective of nationality or status as economically active or self sufficient. This process appears to have been fairly fluid, a continuous movement of rights acquired and retained with each revision of the Treaties. However, things may now be changing. From the 2015 general election in the UK, the government there has been committed to holding a referendum on the UK's membership of the EU. The date was set for 23 June 2016. In anticipation of this referendum the UK government sought concessions from the other Member States in a variety of areas including free movement of persons, an issue of some political salience in the UK.[81] Among those concessions agreed at the European Council meeting 18–19 February 2016[82] four stand out as particularly relevant to the discussion of this chapter. All of the concessions with which I will finish here would result in a reversal of the process of acquisition of rights by people in the EU moving from one Member State to another. Not all of the concessions agreed are of immediate interest to the UK so there is some scepticism that some other Member States have slipped in their pet concerns particularly in the social benefits area.[83] Should the UK vote to remain in the EU then these concessions will be implemented. Should the vote go the other way then there is no obligation on the remaining EU to go ahead with the measures, indeed, considering the controversial nature of some of them which appear to require the reversal of decisions of the CJEU, it might be contrary to EU law to do so. The four areas

81 Geddes, A. (2016), *Britain and the European Union*, Basingstoke (UK): Palgrave Macmillan. Koutrakos, P. (2016), 'Brexit and international treaty-making', *European Law Review* 1, pp. 1–2.

82 <www.consilium.europa.eu/en/press/press-releases/2016/02/19-euco-conclusions> [1 April 2016].

83 Steve Peers: <eulawanalysis.blogspot.com/2016/02/the-draft-renegotiation-deal-eu.html> [1 April 2016].

also reveal the concerns and anxieties of some Member States as regards the current state of rights of people in the EU.

Four areas stand out as specifically revelatory the February 2016 European Council Agreement on a new relationship with the UK:

(1) Equality in social benefits
EU workers even in 2016 are better protected in a host Member State as regards equality in treatment on social benefits than anyone else. This has been a sticking point for the UK Government in its 2016 demands for a new relationship between the EU and the UK – the UK has insisted on the right to an emergency break to exclude EU workers from access to in work benefits for at least four years from their arrival and succeeded in getting an assurance for this from the Council. But this agreement may be particularly welcome for a number of other Member States such as the Netherlands and Germany.

(2) Family reunion with third country national family members
A handful of Member States have a problem with third country national family members of EU citizens, both those of other Member States and their own nationals returning home. This point of friction has also arisen in the UK Government's demands for a new relationship with the EU where it has demanded that third country national family members of EU citizens must enter a Member State in the first instance via its national immigration rules on family reunion not on the basis of EU rules.[84] Further British citizens coming back to the UK after working in another Member State must fulfil UK national rules on family reunification even if this means leaving in the former host Member State their third country national family members. These demands appear to have been accepted by the Council.

(3) Expulsion
The Member States have resolutely hung on to the right to expel EU citizens from their territory. In the UK Government's negotiations on a new relationship with the EU again it has insisted that it has the right to expel EU citizens on less robust grounds than currently apply in EU secondary legislation and its interpretation by the CJEU. The UK does not want to be bothered with having to check whether an EU citizen is a future risk to public policy after completing a prison sentence, it wants to be able to

84 Tryfonidou, A. (2016) <eulawanalysis.blogspot.com/2016/03/whats-wrong-with-uk-immigration-rules.html> [1 April 2016].

expel them automatically on general preventive grounds. In fact it wants to be able to expel EU citizens even without a criminal conviction. Once again, the Council appears to have accepted this demand.

(4) Bad Boys
Finally there is the issue of the EU citizens which Member States no longer want – the 'bad boys' they have designated as foreign fighters.[85] For the moment it remains unclear how various measures which fall short of full deprivation of citizenship (such as the UK measures on temporary exclusion from the territory for up to two years and the like) will be reconciled with EU citizenship. Will the Member States once again ceded to demands by the UK (and other Member States) that British citizens in respect of whom the UK has placed a temporary exclusion order are excluded from the whole of the EU even though they continue to be EU citizens?

EU inclusion and exclusion of people has a trajectory very different from that of immigration law in most Member States. Instead of the story being one of increasing exclusion and the application of ever more exclusionary rules and tests on foreigners seeking to move to their territory, as has happened in many Member States, it is one of opening up ever more to nationals of other Member States. Nationals of the Member States have moved from being workers to being citizens but retained their rights as workers. People (EU citizens and everyone else) have acquired status and rights in EU law beyond the scope of the Member States' national rules. Some have even gained access to the whole of the EU territory and labour market.[86] The outcome of this steady line of ever increasing liberalisation of movement of persons in the EU has been that the percentage of the EU population which lives in a Member State other than that of their underlying citizenship has remained fairly constant between 2.5 and 3% of the total EU population (according to the EU's statistical agency EUROSTAT).[87] Although the EU has got larger from six Member States in 1957 to 28 in 2016, the percentage of people who move to live in another Member

---

85 Mantu, S. & E. Guild (2013), 'Acts of citizenship deprivation: ruptures between citizen and state', in: E.F. Isin, (ed), *Enacting European citizenship*, Cambridge: Cambridge University Press, pp. 111–131.

86 Guild, E. (2014), 'The EU's internal market and the fragmentary nature of EU labour migration' in: C. Costello & M. Freedland (eds), *Migrants at work. Immigration and vulnerability in labour law*, Oxford: Oxford University Press, pp. 98–118.

87 http://ec.europa.eu/eurostat/statistics-explained/index.php/Migration_and_migrant_population_statistics#Migrant_population [1 April 2016].

State has remained remarkably stable. Yet, free movement of persons is one of the rights most cherished by those who enjoy it.[88] The idea and practice of freedom is most easily lived and understood by people in Europe through their entitlement to travel, reside and work anywhere they want in the 28 Member States.

## References

Acosta Arcarazo, D. (2015), 'Civic citizenship reintroduced? The long term residence directive as a post national form of membership', *European Law Journal* 21(2), pp. 200–219.

Anderson, B. (2015), 'Precarious work, immigration, and governance', in: C.-U. Schierup, R. Munck, B. Likic-Brbobic & A. Neergaard (eds), *Migration, precarity, and global governance: challenges and opportunities for labour*, Oxford: Oxford University Press.

Askola, H. (2012), 'Tale of two citizenships? Citizenship, migration and care in the European Union', *Social & Legal Studies* 21(3), pp. 341–356.

Baldaccini, A. (2008), 'Counter-terrorism and the EU strategy for border security: framing suspects with biometric documents and databases', *European Journal of Migration and Law* 10(1), pp. 31–49.

Baldinger, D. (2015), *Vertical judicial dialogues in asylum cases: standards on judicial scrutiny and evidence in international and European asylum law*, Den Haag: Martinus Nijhoff.

Berneri, C. (2014), 'Protection of families composed by EU citizens and third-country nationals: some suggestions to tackle reverse discrimination', *European Journal of Migration and Law* 16(2), pp. 249–275.

Bohning, R.(1972), 'The problems of immigrant workers in West Germany', in: N. Deakin (ed), *Immigrant in Europe*, London: Fabian Society, pp. 18–29.

Brouwer, E. (2008), *Digital borders and real rights: effective remedies for third-country nationals in the Schengen information system,* Den Haag: Brill.

Byrne, R., G. Noll & J. Vedsted-Hansen (2004), 'Understanding refugee law in an enlarged European Union', *European Journal of International Law* 15(2), pp. 355–379.

Cantillon, B., H. Verschueren & P. Ploscar (eds) (2012), *Social inclusion and social protection in the EU: interactions between law and policy*, Antwerp: Intersentia.

88 http://ec.europa.eu/COMMFrontOffice/PublicOpinion/index.cfm/ Survey/getSurvey Detail/instruments/FLASH/surveyKy/2101 [1 April 2016].

Carrera, S., E. Guild & M. Merlino (2011), *The Canada-Czech Republic visa dispute two years on: implications for the EU's migration and asylum policies*, Brussels: Centre for European Policy Studies.

Collett, E. (2013), *The integration needs of mobile EU citizens: impediments and opportunities*, Brussels: Migration Policy Institute Europe.

Connolly, H., S. Marino & M. Martinez Lucio (2014), 'Trade union renewal and the challenges of representation: strategies towards migrant and ethnic minority workers in the Netherlands, Spain and the United Kingdom', *European Journal of Industrial Relations*, March 2014, vol 20(1), pp. 5–20.

Cornelissen, R. & G. Van Limberghen (2015), '14. Social security for mobile workers and labour law', in: F. Pennings & G. Vonk, *Research handbook on European social security law*, Cheltenham: Edward Elgar, pp. 344–384.

Crépeau, F. & B. Hastie (2015), 'The case for "firewall" protections for irregular migrants', *European Journal of Migration and Law* 17(2–3), pp. 157–183.

Davis, A. (2012), *The impact of anti-immigration parties on mainstream parties' immigration positions in the Netherlands, Flanders and the UK 1987–2010: divided electorates, left-right politics and the pull towards restrictionism*, diss. European University Institute (SPS), Florence.

Desmond, A. (2015), 'The triangle that could square the circle? The UN international convention on the protection of the rights of all migrant workers and members of their families, the EU and the universal periodic review', *European Journal of Migration and Law* 17(1), pp. 39–69.

Donnelly, J. (1998), 'Human rights: a new standard of civilization?', *International Affairs* 74(1), pp. 1–23.

Dougan, M. (2015), 'Judicial review of member state action under the general principles and the charter: defining the "scope of union law"', *Common Market Law Review* 52(5), pp. 1201–1245.

Douglas-Scott, S. (2014), 'A tale of two courts: Luxembourg, Strasbourg and the growing European human rights acquis', *CML Review* 43, p. 629.

Falk, R.A. (2000), *Human rights horizons: the pursuit of justice in a globalizing world.* New York: Routledge.

Fries, S. (1998), 'Citizenship of the union: first steps in the European Court of justice', *European Public Law* 4(4), pp. 533–559.

Fuchs, M. & R. Cornelissen (2015), *EU social security law: a commentary on EU regulations 883/2004 and 987/2009*, Baden-Baden: Beck/Hart/Nomos.

Geddes, A. (2016), *Britain and the European Union*, Basingstoke (UK): Palgrave Macmillan.

Genova N. De & N. Peutz (2016), *The deportation regime: sovereignty, space, and the freedom of movement*, Duke University Press, 2010.

Groenendijk, K. (2004), 'Legal concepts of integration in EU migration law', *European Journal of Migration and Law* 6(2), pp. 111–126.

Groenendijk, K. (2006), 'Family reunification as a right under community law', *European Journal of Migration and Law* 8(2), p. 215.

Groenendijk, K. (2008), *Local voting rights for non-nationals in Europe: what we know and what we need to learn*, Brussels: Migration Policy Institute.

Groenendijk, K. (2011), 'Pre-departure integration strategies in the European Union: integration or immigration policy?', *European Journal of Migration and Law* 13(1), pp. 1–30.

Guild, E. (1990), 'British nationality and East African independence', *I&NL&*P, July.

Guild, E. (1996), 'The legal framework of citizenship of the union', in: D. Cesarani & M. Fulbrook (eds), *Citizenship, nationality and migration in Europe*, London: Routledge.

Guild, E. (1996), 'The right to travel: three new directives from the European Commission', *I&NL&P*.

Guild, E. (1998), 'The constitutional consequences of lawmaking in the third pillar of the European Union', in: P. Craig & C. Harlow (eds), *Lawmaking in the European Union*, Dordrecht: Springer, pp. 65–88.

Guild, E. (2001), *Immigration law in the European Community*, The Hague: Kluwer Law International.

Guild, E. (2002), 'The single market, movement of persons and borders', in: J. Scott & C. Barnard, *The law of the single European market*, Hart: Oxford, pp. 295–310.

Guild, E. (2004), 'The variable subject of the EU constitution, civil liberties and human rights', *European Journal of Migration and Law* 6(4), pp. 381–394.

Guild, E. (2004), *The legal elements of European identity: EU citizenship and migration law* Elspeth Guild, Kluwer Law International, The Hague, 2004.

Guild, E. (2004), *The legal elements of European identity: EU citizenship and migration law*, The Hague: Kluwer Law International.

Guild, E. (2005), 'Who is entitled to work and who is in charge? Understanding the legal framework of European labour migration', in: E. Guild & D. Bigo (eds), *Controlling frontiers: free movement into and within Europe*, Farnham: Ashgate, pp. 100–139.

Guild, E. (2006), 'Danger – borders under construction: assessing the first five years of border policy in an area of freedom, security and justice', in: J. de Zwaan & F. Goudappel (eds), *Freedom, security and justice in the European Union: implementation of the Hague programme* Asser Press, The Hague, 2006, pp. 45–72.

Guild, E. (2007), 'Citizens without a constitution, borders without a state: EU free movement of persons', in: A. Baldaccini, E. Guild & H. Toner (eds), *Whose freedom, security and justice? EU immigration and asylum law and policy*, Oxford: Hart, pp. 25–56.

Guild, E. (2011), 'Equivocal claims? Ambivalent controls? Labour migration regimes in the European Union', in: E. Guild & S. Mantu (eds), *Constructing and imagining labour migration: perspectives of control from five continents,* Farnham: Ashgate, pp. 207–228.

Guild, E. (2011), *Immigration law in the European Community*, The Hague: Kluwer Law International.

Guild, E. (2013), 'Does European citizenship blur the borders of solidarity?', in: E. Guild, C. Gortazar & D. Kostakopoulou (eds), *The reconceptualization of European Union citizenship,* The Hague: Brill, p. 189.

Guild, E. (2014), 'The EU's internal market and the fragmentary nature of EU labour migration', in: C. Costello & M. Freedland (eds), *Migrants at work. Immigration and vulnerability in labour law*, Oxford: Oxford University Press, pp. 98–118.

Guild, E. (2014), *The social impact of migration and the notion of citizenship for the EU. Ensuing challenges and opportunities for the Union*, CEPS Commentaries.

Guild, E. (2016), 'Understanding immigration detention in the UK and Europe', in: M.J. Guia, R. Koulish & V. Mitsilegas (eds), *Immigration detention, risk and human rights.* Springer International Publishing, pp. 141–155.

Guild, E., C. Gortázar Rotaeche & D. Kostakopoulou (eds) (2013), *The reconceptualization of European Union citizenship*, The Hague: Martinus Nijhoff Publishers.

Guild, E., C.A. Groenendijk & S. Carrera (eds) (2009), *Illiberal liberal states: immigration, citizenship, and integration in the EU*, London: Ashgate Publishing.

Guild, E. & K. Zwaan (2014), 'Does Europe still create refugees-examining the situation of the Roma', *Queen's LJ* 40, p. 141.

Guild, E. & M. Garlick (2010), 'Refugee protection, counter-terrorism, and exclusion in the European Union', *Refugee Survey Quarterly* 4, pp. 63–82.

Guild, E., S. Carrera Nunez & K. Eisele (2013), *Social benefits and migration: a contested relationship and policy challenge in the EU*, Brussels: CEPS

Hailbronner, K. (1989), 'Citizenship and nationhood in Germany', in: R. Brubaker (ed), *Immigration and the politics of citizenship in Europe and North America,* University Press of America, p. 67.

Heinemann, T., & Th. Lemke (2012), 'Suspect families: DNA kinship testing in German immigration policy', *Sociology* 47(4), pp. 810–826.

Ippolito, F. (2015), 'Migration and asylum cases before the court of justice of the European Union: putting the EU charter of fundamental rights to test?', *European Journal of Migration and Law* 17(1), pp. 1–38.

Kochenov, D. (2012), 'A real European citizenship: the court of justice opening a new chapter in the development of the union in Europe', *Columbia Journal of European Law* 18(1), pp. 55–109.

Kochenov, D. (2013), 'The right to have what rights? EU citizenship in need of clarification', *European Law Journal* 19(4), pp. 502–516.

Kostakopoulou, D. (2014), 'When EU citizens become foreigners', *European Law Journal* 20(4), pp. 447–463.

Koutrakos, P. (2016), 'Brexit and international treaty-making', *European Law Review* 1, pp. 1–2.

Lenaerts, K. (2015), 'EU citizenship and the European Court of justice's "stone-by-stone" approach', *International Comparative Jurisprudence* 1(1), pp. 1–10.

Mantu, S. (2008), 'The boundaries of European social citizenship', Nijmegen: Wolf Legal Publishers.

Mantu, S. (2015), 'Citizenship in times of terror: citizenship deprivation in the UK', *Change* 36(5), pp. 735–751.

Mantu, S. (2015), *Contingent citizenship: the law and practice of citizenship deprivation in international, European and national perspectives,* The Hague: Brill.

Mantu, S. & E. Guild (2013), 'Acts of citizenship deprivation: ruptures between citizen and state', in: E.F. Isin (ed), *Enacting European citizenship*, Cambridge: Cambridge University Press, pp. 111–131.

Meardi, G. (2013), *Social failures of EU enlargement: a case of workers voting with their feet*, Vol. 25, New York: Routledge.

Messinger, I. (2013), 'There is something about marrying... The case of human rights vs. migration regimes using the example of Austria', *Laws* 2(4), pp. 376–391.

Minderhoud, P.E. (2015), 'Nr. 61. Kamberaj. Equal treatment of long-term resident for housing benefit and Article 34 Charter; annotation with CJEU 24 April 2012, C-571/10', in: S.G. Kok, C.H. Slingenberg & K.M. Zwaan (eds), *Landmark cases on asylum and immigration law,* Nijmegen: Ars Aequi Libri.

Minderhoud, P.E. & N. Trimikliniotis (2009), *Rethinking the free movement of workers. The European challenges ahead,* Nijmegen: Wolf Legal Publishers.

Mrozowicki, A., A. Krasowska & M. Karolak (2015), 'Stop the junk contracts! Young workers and trade union mobilisation against precarious employment in Poland', in: A. Hodder & L. Ketsos (eds), *HoYoung workers and trade unions*, Palgrave: Macmillan UK, pp. 123–141.

Oosterom-Staples, H. (2012), 'To what extent has reverse discrimination been reversed?', *European Journal of Migration and Law* 14(2), pp. 151–172.

Peers, S. *et al.* (eds) (2014), *The EU charter of fundamental rights: a commentary*, Oxford: Hart Publishing.

Peers, S. (2015), 'Benefits For Eu citizens: a u-turn by the court of justice?', *The Cambridge Law Journal* 74(2), pp. 195–198.

Pennings, F. (2012), 'EU citizenship: access to social benefits in other EU member states', *International Journal of Comparative Labour Law and Industrial Relations* 28(3), pp. 307–333.

Prassl, J. (2012), 'Book review of: N. Bruun, K. Lörcher & I. Schömann (eds), The Lisbon treaty and social Europe, (Oxford: Hart Publishing, 2012)', *Common Market Law Review* 52(1), pp. 310–311.

Preston, Chr. (1995), 'Obstacles to EU enlargement: the classical community method and the prospects for a wider Europe', *JCMS: Journal of Common Market Studies* 33(3), pp. 451–463.

Rogers, N. (1999), *A practitioner's guide to the EC-Turkey association agreement*, The Hague: Martinus Nijhoff Publishers.

Royo, S. & P. Chr. Manuel (eds) (2003), *Spain and Portugal in the European Union: the first fifteen years*, Oxford: Taylor & Francis.

Ryan, B. (2004), 'The celtic cubs: the controversy over birthright citizenship in Ireland', *European Journal of Migration and Law* 6(3), pp. 173–193.

Shuibhne, N.N. (2002), 'Free movement of persons and the wholly internal rule: time to move on?', *Common Market Law Review* 39(4), pp. 731–771.

Spyridakis, M. (2013), *The liminal worker: an ethnography of work, unemployment and precariousness in contemporary Greece*, Farnham: Ashgate Publishing.

Tryfonidou, A. (2012), 'Redefining the outer boundaries of EU law: the Zambrano, McCarthy and Dereci trilogy', *European Public Law* 18(3), pp. 493–526.

Van Heerden, S., *et al.* (2014), 'The immigration and integration debate in the Netherlands: discursive and programmatic reactions to the rise of anti-immigration parties', *Journal of Ethnic and Migration Studies* 40(1), pp. 119–136.

Van Oers, R., Eva Ersbøll & D. Kostakopoulou (eds) (2010), *A re-definition of belonging?: language and integration tests in Europe*, The Hague: Brill.

Verschueren, H. (2015), 'Preventing "benefit tourism" in the EU: a narrow or broad interpretation of the possibilities offered by the ECJ in Dano?', *Common Market Law Review* 52(2), pp. 363–390.

Visser, J. (2013), *ICTWSS: database on institutional characteristics of trade unions, wage setting, state intervention and social pacts, 1960–2011*, Amsterdam Institute for Advances Labour Studies (AIAS), University of Amsterdam <www.uva-aias.net/207>.

Van der Mei, A.P. (2015), 'Overview of recent cases before the court of justice of the European Union (October–December 2014)', *European Journal of Social Security* 17(1), p. 103.

Von Bogdandy, A. (2000), 'The European Union as a human rights organization? Human rights and the core of the European Union', *Common Market Law Review* 37(6), pp. 1307–1338.

Wallace, H. (2013), 'The UK: 40 years of EU membership', *Journal of Contemporary European Research* 8(4), pp. 531–546.

Wiener, A. & V. Della Sala (1997), 'Constitution making and citizenship practice–bridging the democracy gap in the EU?', *Journal of Common Market Studies* 35(4), pp. 595–614.

Wiesbrock, A. (2012), 'Granting citizenship-related rights to third-country nationals: an alternative to the full extension of European Union citizenship?', *European Journal of Migration and Law* 14(1), pp. 63–94.

CHAPTER 11

# Alternative Views on EU Citizenship

*Sandra Mantu*

## 11.1 Introduction

The direction in which EU citizenship is heading has been a matter of debate for some time, although there is little agreement as to whether the interpretation given to the rights of mobile EU citizens is too restrictive, or too generous. 2016, as the year in which a majority of the British people voted to leave the European Union (EU) and, consequently, renounce their status as EU citizens, may turn out to play an important role in shaping the future of EU citizenship. In this context, the extent to which EU citizenship will live up to the expectations derived from its characterization by the EU Court of Justice as destined to become the fundamental status of the nationals of the Member States seems to be an open question. Brexit is a reminder that at least a sufficient number of British citizens failed to see the benefits associated with EU citizenship. If the political campaign preceding the vote on leaving the EU is anything to go by, the main legal right associated with EU citizenship, namely the right to move and reside freely within the territory of the Member States, proved to be a divisive matter in assessing the benefits of UK's EU membership.

Against this background, the aim of this contribution is to flag out a series of aspects concerning EU citizenship that could serve as a basis for reflection on its potential to act as a fundamental status. My starting point is the increasing politicization of the right to free movement as evidenced by debates on the (negative) effects of free movement that are taking place in a number of Member States.[1] The decision of the British people to leave the EU was partly fuelled by discontent towards free movement and accompanied by the message that the mobility of certain EU citizens is undesirable and should be limited. In other Member States, such as Germany, while support for free movement remains politically the main message, 'poverty migration' and 'welfare tourism' are branded as problematic cases of EU mobility.[2] Who exactly is

1 Mantu, S. & P. Minderhoud (2016), 'Exploring the limits of social solidarity: welfare tourism and EU citizenship', *UNIO-EU Law Journal* 2, pp. 4–19.

2 Nowrot, K. & B. Struckmeyer-Öner (2014), 'Sozialtourismus in Europa?: unions-und sozialrechtliche Anmerkungen zu einer aktuellen Debatte', *Policy Papers on Transnational Economic*

 | DOI 10.1163/9789004330467_012

targeted by such notions is not always clear, since from a legal perspective such discourses seem to involve a combination and conflation of mobile poor EU citizens, economically inactive EU citizens, EU citizens who engage in poorly paid work, citizens from poorer Member States etc. I want to suggest a number of alternative perspectives on EU citizenship that may inform discussions on how EU citizenship can achieve its 'radical' and 'transformative potential'.[3] While I agree that it is necessary to problematize EU citizenship, its meaning and potential, I want to suggest that this can be done without recurring to racialized discourses such as those relying on 'poverty migration', which castigate some EU citizens as unworthy of mobility and EU citizenship. While these discourses proved popular with voters, as shown by Brexit, they deflect our attention from questioning to what extent and how EU citizenship can achieve its potential and function as a fundamental status, with all the consequences and expectations attached to such a label.

The discussion below builds upon the idea that EU citizenship can be explored as a 'momentum concept'[4] that must be continuously reworked in a way that realizes more and more of its egalitarian and anti-hierarchical potential. As Lister points out, this means engaging with citizenship's exclusionary-inclusionary nexus to deal with marginalized groups' calls for social justice.[5] The analytical lenses through which EU citizenship and mobility are examined in this chapter depart from the traditional frames of constitutionalism or European integration and offer a critique of EU citizenship that builds on: the figure of the 'Other'; the notion of biopolitics, and questions of difference and embodiment. These alternative ways of thinking about EU citizenship and its relevance are an attempt to break out of the mould of EU law as the main disciplinary frame through which EU citizenship is approached and naturalized as producing knowledge on and of EU citizens' mobility.

---

*Law* 40, Transnational Economic Law Research Centre. Bräuningerd, D. (2015), 'Debate on free movement – does the EU need new rules on social security coordination?', Deutsche Bank Research Briefing.

3 Kostakopoulou, D. (2014), European Union citizenship rights and duties: civil, political and social, in: E. Isin & P. Nyers (eds) *Routledge handbook of global citizenship studies*, Abingdon, Oxon: Routledge, pp. 487–488.

4 John Hoffmann quoted in R. Lister (2007), 'Inclusive citizenship: realizing the potential', *Citizenship Studies* 11(1), p. 49.

5 Lister (2007) p. 49.

## 11.2 To Whom Does EU Citizenship Belong? Who is the 'Other' of EU Citizenship?

According to Mezzadra, the very discourse of citizenship is historically and theoretically based upon the distinction between an inside and an outside, which is not easily escaped while remaining within the discourse of citizenship itself.[6] Moreover, national citizenship is usually understood to be a bounded category, closely associated with the development of the nation-state as the main political unit and container of people within delimited territorial units. If EU citizenship is built upon the image of national citizenship, as Article 20 TFEU seems to suggest,[7] one can ask to what extent it implies a similar closure and boundary making exercise in determining its reach and the people it embraces. Through the lens of citizenship as an exercise into 'othering', one can start to articulate whether EU citizenship, similar to national citizenship, requires the existence of an 'Other' in opposition to which it is defined. Who is caught by the personal scope of EU citizenship has been a vexing issue since the introduction of EU citizenship by the Maastricht Treaty.[8] This issue has been raised in relation to the exclusion of third-country nationals (TCNs) from the personal scope of EU citizenship, which was seen as confirmation of EU citizenship's exclusionary nature (similar to the exclusionary nature of national citizenship). Groenendijk feared that this distinction between '*us*' (EU citizens) and '*them*' (TCNs) would have a detrimental effect upon the legal position of the latter group, although he later acknowledged that the Court's jurisprudence did much to alleviate this sort of concerns by interpreting the secondary EU legislation dealing with TCNs in a positive manner and by trying to approximate their rights to those of EU citizens.[9] In his contribution to this

6 Mezzadra, S. (2011), 'The gaze of autonomy – capitalism, migration and social struggles', in: V. Squire (ed), *The contested politics of mobility. Borderzones and irregularity*, Abingdon, Oxon: Routledge, p. 24.

7 Article 20(1) TFEU states 'Citizenship of the union is hereby established. Every person holding the nationality of a member state shall be a citizen of the union. Citizenship of the union shall be additional to and not replace national citizenship'.

8 Føllesdal, A. (2000), 'Third country nationals as European citizens: the case defended', *The Sociological Review* 48(1), pp. 104–122. Hansen, R. (1998), 'A European citizenship or a Europe of citizens? Third country nationals in the EU', *Journal of Ethnic and Migration Studies* 24(4), pp. 751–768.

9 Groenendijk, K. (2009), 'Forty years of free movement of workers: has it been a success and why?', in: P. Minderhoud & N. Trimikliniotis (eds), *Rethinking the free movement of workers: the European challenges ahead*, Nijmegen: Wolf Legal Publishers, pp. 11–25; Groenendijk, K.

volume, he again voices concerns about the impact that Brexit will have on the rights of TCNs, showing that the issue is still salient and unresolved. A different set of criticisms relating to EU citizenship's reach concerns the position of those EU citizens who never move. Besides having the nationality of one of the Member States, the other condition for being able to exercise what the Treaty labels EU citizenship rights, is to physically move to another EU Member State.[10] Although the Court's jurisprudence is making a series of inroads into this condition in cases such as *Zambrano*[11] or *Rendón Marín*,[12] its implications remain limited to exceptional situations that involve minor EU citizens whose genuine enjoyment of the substance of their rights as EU citizens would be violated should they not come within the protective scope of EU law.

From a legal perspective, Articles 20–25 TFEU detail to whom EU citizenship belongs and what this citizenship entails. As such, every person holding the nationality of a Member State is a citizen of the Union and in this capacity she has a series of rights: the right to move and reside freely within the territory of the Member States, electoral rights, the right to diplomatic protection while outside of the EU, the right to petition the European Parliament and the Ombudsman, the right to petition EU institutions, and the right to access EU documents. In addition, Article 18 TFEU establishes a right to non-discrimination on the basis of nationality. Despite this panoply of rights, EU citizenship remains associated primarily with the right to move and reside freely in another Member State. Opinion polls confirm that free movement is the most visible achievement of EU citizenship and a right most cherished by EU citizens themselves.[13] Without repeating the history of EU citizenship and its coming into being upon the already existing provisions concerning the free movement of workers, it is nevertheless important to stress that the transformation of EU citizenship into a meaningful legal status is intrinsically connected with the incorporation of economically inactive citizens into the legal framework of EU free movement of persons. This process was driven by the case law of the Court of Justice that relied on the joint reading of the provisions on EU citizenship and the principle of non-discrimination on the basis of nationality

---

(2006), 'Citizens and third country nationals: differential treatment or discrimination?', in: J.Y Carlier & E. Guild (eds), *The future of free movement of persons in the EU*, Brussels: Bruylant, pp. 79–101.

10 Guild, E. (2014), Migration, security and European citizenship, in: E. Isin & P. Nyers (eds) *Routledge handbook of global citizenship studies*, Abingdon, Oxon: Routledge, p. 421.

11 CJEU 8 March 2011, C-34/09, *Zambrano*, ECLI:EU:C:2011:124.

12 CJEU 13 September 2016, C-165/14, *Rendón Marín*, ECLI:EU:C:2016:675.

13 Flash Eurobarometer 43, 2016; Standard Eurobarometer 83, 2015.

in order to bring economically inactive citizens within the scope of application of the Treaty. Tomkin describes EU citizenship as the '*dedicated legal home*' for non-economically active EU citizens.[14] In his view, this explains why after its introduction, the Court stopped squeezing certain categories of economically inactive citizens into the scope of Article 45 TFEU that deals with EU workers and '*then perform conceptual gymnastics in order to distinguish their rights from the rights of economically active workers*'.[15]

A combined reading of Articles 20, 21 and of the Court's citizenship case law, suggests that in theory, every national of a Member State is a EU citizen who has a subjective and enforceable right to move. However, if we start deconstructing the idea that EU citizenship is a universal status or as the Court of Justice states '*the fundamental status of nationals of the Member States when exercising free movement rights*',[16] it becomes clear that not all EU citizens enjoy free movements rights in the same way. Conditions and restrictions can be placed through secondary legislation, such as those enacted through Directive 2004/38, also known as the Citizens' Directive. Different legal categories of citizens enjoy different rights when they want to reside in a host Member State for longer than 3 months, while the performance of an economic activity remains the main axis of differentiation between the rights of mobile EU citizens. This differential treatment is meant to end once a mobile EU citizen has resided legally in a host state for 5 continuous years, after which she is entitled to acquire permanent residence. However, clocking the 5 years of continuous residence is going to be more difficult for some EU citizens: economically inactive citizens who find themselves temporarily without resources or become unemployed may find it difficult to meet the conditions set by the Directive.

It can be argued that the conditional nature of the right to reside for longer than 3 months means that only those nationals who meet the criteria of self-sufficiency or performance of an economic activity will be able to enjoy their EU citizenship rights, and that EU mobility has a set of inbuilt filtering mechanisms. Yet, the mobility of some categories of EU citizens is described as problematic and in need of control. Calls to restrict the free movement of EU citizens focus on citizens from poor EU states exercising free movement rights, EU citizens who circumvent restrictive family reunification rules in

14 Tomkin, J. (2009), 'The worker, the citizen, their families and the court of justice: tales of free movement from Luxembourg', in: P. Minderhoud & N. Trimikliniotis (eds), *Rethinking the free movement of workers: the European challenges ahead,* Nijmegen: Wolf Legal Publishers, p. 56.

15 Tomkin (2009).

16 CJEU 20 September 2001, C-184/99 *Grzelczyk,* ECLI:EU:C:2001:458.

their own state of nationality by exercising free movement rights as EU citizens, and criminal EU citizens, whom their state of residence cannot expel as easily as non-EU migrants. Focusing on what is termed 'poverty migration' alone, the underlying message is that citizens from poor Member States move to benefit from the generous welfare systems of the richer EU States and that this movement is somehow abusive – both an abuse of free movement rights and an abuse of the host state's welfare system that ultimately endangers the prosperity of the host state and of its national citizens. Traces of such thinking are present in the demands put forward by David Cameron in relation to Brexit and the amendment of EU free movement rules. Similar ideas were underpinning the letter sent by the ministers of interior Austria, Netherlands, UK and Germany to the president of the EU Commission in 2013 prior to the end of transitional arrangements for Bulgaria and Romania, two of the EU's poorest Member States, claiming that the end of the transitional measures would see an increase in free movement from these two Member States that would implode their welfare systems.[17] According to the critics of EU mobility, the only persons who should be able to move within the EU are workers, students if they have enough resources, and persons looking to set up a business in a host Member State. Unemployed citizens, those who perform atypical work or have patchy employment histories, and citizens who lack resources do not seem to have any place in such visions of EU citizenship. Their mobility is to be regulated, not least by denying them access to the host state's welfare system.

The data that exists on the mobility of EU citizens shows that the number of mobile EU citizens remains low (under 3% of the entire EU population is mobile) and, while, most migration takes place from EU10 to EU15, the main reason for which people move in the EU is work. The popular theme of migrants moving to draw welfare benefits is not supported by empirical data. Since 2013, a host of studies were published in an effort to collect data to understand the impact of intra-EU mobility on host states. Most of these studies show that the number of economically inactive citizens who draw welfare in their host states is small, that benefit tourism is not taking place on a large scale and, that generally, EU migrants have positive effects upon the economies of their host states.[18] A comprehensive study commissioned by the European Commission concluded that the share of non-active intra-EU migrants is small; such migrants account for a very small share of special non-contributory benefits

17 Mantu & Minderhoud (2016), p. 10.

18 ECAS (2014) *Fiscal impact of EU migrants in Austria, Germany, the Netherlands and UK*, Brussels; Guild, E., S. Carrera & K. Eisele (2013), *Social benefits and migration: a contested relationship and policy challenge in the EU*, CEPS: Brussels.

(SNCB) recipients whereas the budgetary impact of SNCB claims made by non-active EU citizens is low; moreover, costs associated with the take-up of healthcare by non-active intra-EU migrants is equally small.[19]

Based on existing empirical data, one is tempted to argue that the main beneficiaries of EU citizenship are persons who engage in an economic activity. Qualitative sociological studies looking at the mobility patterns of Romanian citizens in Southern Europe depict these mobile EU citizens as: '*mobile labour force that is willing to change countries in times of economic hardship*' while their response '*to changes in the labour market is further migration and not reliance on the welfare state*'.[20]

The patterns of their migration are described as '*an adaptation to the structural opportunities inherent in economic and political systems*', while the choice of destination relates to the possibility to integrate into the labour market or educational system, depending on the reason for migration.[21] Studies focusing on how EU citizens perceive their mobility, highlight the transformational impact of EU citizenship based mobility for Eastern European citizens:

> in the wider EU, human mobility will help cross-border liberalisation, because mobility has the ability to liberate localities from central authority and encourage new dynamics of connectivity in such a way as to confound both core/periphery expectations and conventional models of growth and competitiveness.[22]

These accounts highlight the positive role that EU citizenship and the model of free movement associated with it can have on citizens seen as individuals who have dreams and aspirations. This is not to deny that there may be individual cases of EU citizens drawing social welfare benefits without entitlement, but the overall picture one gets from empirical studies is not one of abuse or fraud.

---

19 Fóti, K. (2015), *Social dimension of intra-EU mobility: impact on social services*, Eurofound report EF1546; ICF/GHK (2013), *A fact finding analysis on the impact on the member States' social security systems of the entitlements of non-active intra-EU migrants to special non-contributory cash benefits and healthcare granted on the basis of residence*, Brussels <ec.europa.eu/social/BlobServlet?docId=10972>.

20 Ciobanu, R.O. (2015), 'Multiple migration flows of Romanians', *Mobilities* 10(3), p. 482.

21 Ciobanu (2015), p. 469 and p. 471.

22 Marcu, S. (2016), 'Learning mobility challenging borders: cross-border experiences of Eastern European immigrants in Spain', *Mobilities* 11(3), p. 358.

One can approach the question of who are the addressees of EU citizenship in a variety of ways– legally, socially, culturally etc. Although in this section the starting point in answering this question was EU law, one can argue that the 'Other' of EU citizenship is not only the legal 'Other' of citizenship status, namely, the third country national (TCN) or the asylum seeker. The 'Other' appears as a fluid category that covers an undetermined number of possibilities – different persons can be classified as the 'Other' at different moments in time, drawing on different rationales. It is the 'poor Other' that haunts EU citizenship at the moment. To paraphrase Bridget Anderson,[23] it becomes increasingly clear that the EU citizen in law and in data is not the same as the EU citizen of popular and political discourse. The gap between these different constructions of EU citizenship is difficult to close which, in turn, has consequences for public perceptions of EU citizenship. To question who are meant to be the beneficiaries of EU citizenship involves delving into a discussion about the normative assumptions upon which EU citizenship was built and continues to be developed legally through existing legislation, its application by the Member States and its interpretation by the courts, including the European Court of Justice. What the discussion on EU 'poverty migration' shows is that those who are legally included, may nevertheless find themselves symbolically excluded. The undoing of EU citizenship at a symbolic level and through discursive practices may constitute the first steps towards the legal reconfiguration of EU citizenship. Prior to the British referendum on leaving the EU, the European Commission negotiated a series of amendments to the current rules on EU citizenship and free movement as a way of appeasing British concerns on these topics. As Groenedijk discusses in his contribution, if adopted, they would have implied a reduction in the rights of EU citizens and affected the position of TCNs. Even if such proposals seem abandoned as a result of the Brexit vote, the precedent is set.

## 11.3 Dangerous 'Others': Towards a Biopolitics of EU Citizenship?

Claims that the mobility of some EU citizens is, in the words of David Cameron 'too free' and needs to be controlled,[24] can equally be examined through the lens of studies that analyse the links between citizenship, security, and the

---

23 Anderson, B. (2012), *What does 'the migrant' tell us about the (Good) citizen?*, Working Paper 12–94, Oxford: University of Oxford.

24 Cameron, D. (2013), 'Free movement in Europe needs to be less free', in: *Financial Times*, 26 November 2013.

development of forms of governance that are connected to notions of risk, fear, anxieties and insecurity in the population.[25] These studies explore how discourses about migration conflate a plurality of threats (terrorism, crime, disease, unemployment) with the image of the migrant. Some of them rely on M. Foucault's notion of 'biopolitics' to capture state practices of power that rely on processes of organization and categorization aimed at the selection of migrants by filtering out the deserving from the undeserving ones. In this section, the use of the term is influenced by the work of Imogen Tyler who has shown how British citizenship law can be examined as 'biopolitics', namely, a field of biopolitical techniques and practices (legal, social, moral) through which populations are controlled and fashioned.[26]

We can ask whether in the EU context, we are moving towards a biopolitics of EU citizenship that rests on framing certain groups of EU citizens as problematic and risky since their exercise of free movement rights threatens 'our' security and prosperity. In turn, this requires legal practices to control the free movement of EU citizens and make it manageable. The framing of EU mobility as 'poverty migration' can be seen as playing on 'our' fears of poverty and of losing the sense of security that the welfare state brings along. During the Brexit debate, parts of the UK government presented EU mobility as a threat to public services, employment, and the general wellbeing and prosperity of the national community.[27] Likewise, UK political parties argued that EU mobility needs to be controlled since most of these EU citizens come here to claim 'our' benefits and 'our' jobs.[28] For the same part, the UK could be substituted for a number of EU Member States – Austria, Belgium, Germany or the Netherlands. To the framing of EU mobility as 'poverty migration', one can add the prevalent negative depiction of Roma EU citizens exercising their mobility

25 Guillaume, X. & J. Huysmans (2013), *Citizenship and security: the constitution of political being*, Abingdon, Oxon: Routledge, pp. 1–18; Rygiel, K. (2010), *Globalizing citizenship*, UBC Press: Vancouver, esp. pp. 92–113; Nyers, P. (2004), 'Introduction: what's left of citizenship?', *Citizenship Studies* 8(3), pp. 203–215; Isin, E. (2004), 'The neurotic citizen', *Citizenship Studies* 8(3), pp. 217–235.

26 Tyler, I. (2010), 'Designed to fail: a biopolitics of British citizenship', *Citizenship Studies* 14(1), pp. 61–74.

27 Cameron, D. (2015), *The future of Britain's relationship with the UK*, Chatham House 10 November 2015.

28 Geddes, A. (2014), 'The EU, UKIP, and the politics of immigration in Britain', *The Political Quarterly* 85(3), pp. 289–295; Vicol, D.O. & W. Allen (2014), *Bulgarians and Romanians in the British national press: 1 Dec 2012–1 Dec 2013*, Migration Observatory report, COMPAS, Oxford: University of Oxford.

rights as disruptive and a threat to the security of the host state.[29] In a number of EU States, the 'poor Other' is inscribed within a racialized discourse about the mobility of EU citizens from the Eastern states. Parker highlights how mobile Roma are designated or produced as 'delinquent citizens' and subjected to two different logics:

> a political realist logic of security, which seeks to eliminate the existential threat to community or citizenry, and a liberal logic, which seeks to manage risks to the internal market as a space of mobility and economic freedoms.[30]

The situation of Bulgarian and Romanian mobile Roma and their difficulties in exercising EU citizenship rights is illustrative of EU citizenship's limits, which stem from the securitizing and exclusionary potential hidden within EU citizenship and free movement law.[31]

In her work on sovereignty and the building of (physical) walls to keep out migrants, Wendy Brown asks what makes efforts of walling parts of a country so popular and desired by late modern subjects.[32] Whereas in the EU, attempts to build walls are primarily targeting non-EU economic migrants disguised as 'bogus' asylum seekers, bearing in mind the conflation that exists in migration management discourse between non-desirable TCN economic migrants and EU 'poverty migration', the answer Brown gives to this question is significant for understanding what is at stake in relation to claims that EU mobility needs to be controlled. The conflation I refer to is best observed in the UK, where part of the public debate on EU migration concerned the need to regain control over EU migration in order to bring it more in line with UK's sovereign powers over non-EU migration. Although during the pre-Brexit debates it was never proposed to build a wall to seal off the UK from the rest of the EU, several ideas about limiting rights were being deployed as ways of managing EU migration. They went further than simply limiting mobility rights for economically inactive EU citizens and included proposals to limit access to social rights for EU workers.[33] After the vote in favour of Brexit and, at the moment inevitable

29 Pallida, S. (2016), *Governance of security and ignored insecurities in contemporary Europe*, Abingdon, Oxon: Routledge, pp. 151–152.

30 Parker, O. (2012), 'Roma and the politics of EU citizenship in France: everyday security and resistance', *Journal of Common Market Studies* 50(3), p. 477.

31 Parker (2012), p. 488.

32 Brown, W. (2014), *Walled states, waning sovereignty*, Zone Books: New York.

33 Cameron (2015).

conclusion that the UK will no longer be an EU Member State in the foreseeable future, it seems that there will be some form of migration control involving EU citizens migrating to the UK – in a post-Brexit world, those EU citizens will no longer enter an EU Member State, thus their EU free movement rights will no longer be legally relevant in that territory. The same will be true for British citizens (no longer EU citizens) when entering an EU state. The exact solution that will be reached after Brexit in relation to free movement of persons is at the moment of writing unclear (see Groenendijk in this volume), but the political signals coming from both London and Brussels suggest that future arrangements will depart from the mobility framework championed by EU citizenship. We seem to be moving away from the notion of a borderless space of freedom in which people move freely and uninhibited by regular border controls. Similarly, the idea of labour circulating freely where it is most needed, which was the building block of the free movement of persons in the first stages of European integration, also appears to have lost its sheen.

While Brexit is not the equivalent of building a wall (along the lines of the U.S.-Mexico wall, for example), it can be read as a desire to extricate the country from the transnational space created by EU citizenship and re-inscribe it within a national space, defended by a wall of sovereign power. In her work, Brown notes that although (physical) walls are in fact icons of faltering sovereignty and failure, they are nevertheless strongly desired and imbued with popular passions.[34] Using Freud's psychoanalytical theory of defense, she argues that:

> walls facilitate a psychic defense against recognition of a set of internal or systemic failures that are relocated to the outside and against recognition of a set of unacceptable facts of dependency, unprotected vulnerability, or even responsibility for colonial violence in the context of declining sovereign power.[35]

Though it is illusionary to believe that walls can stem off transnational migration flows, from the perspective of a modern subject (a citizen) who faces a loss of horizons and identity as well as being faced with the decline of state sovereignty, walls offer psychic reassurances. Brown's 'diagnosis' of the underlying causes for desiring walls, containment and security in the familiar space of the nation state is relevant for discussions on EU citizenship and its capacity to deliver a unifying supranational project of peace and economic prosperity that

34 Brown (2014), p. 114.
35 Brown (2014), p. 125.

places the (EU) citizen at the centre of its design. As such, '... *declining protective capacities of the state, diluted nationhood, and the increasing vulnerability of subjects everywhere to global economic vicissitudes and transnational violence*'[36] fuel the search for protection mechanisms which may take the form of a physical wall or, as in the context of increasing migration, more restrictive migration policies and practices. It does not seem accidental that in the EU, the contestation of EU citizens' mobility started to build momentum as the effects of the global economic crisis were starting to be felt in various EU countries, and as EU governments started to adopt restrictive welfare policies designed to implement austerity measures. It is at this moment of (economic) crisis that national solidarity towards mobile EU citizens starts to show its cracks, as welfare rights are reinforced as the hallmark of national belonging and worthiness. Thus, it becomes possible not only to politically rally voters around cries for regaining sovereignty and limiting EU migration, but also to legitimately shift the boundaries of social solidarity to which mobile EU citizens are entitled to in their host states.[37]

According to T.H. Marshall's definition of citizenship, social rights are the hallmark of being a full member of a community.[38] In the context of EU citizenship, this reading of citizenship has always been problematic for labelling EU citizenship as real 'citizenship' (see Guild this volume) since economically inactive citizens enjoy a much more restricted notion of social solidarity than economically active citizens. Directive 2004/38 and the Court's case law that advanced the social rights of economically inactive EU citizens were seen as part of EU citizenship's development towards citizenship in the Marshallian understanding of this term. The Directive introduced the legal status of permanent residence, which effectively means that a EU citizen who is a permanent resident in a host EU state enjoys in that state equal treatment with nationals in respect of social rights, without having to fulfil other conditions. The Court's case law that proclaimed that EU citizens may expect a certain amount of financial solidarity from their host state, if they find themselves in difficulties finds expression in the preamble of the Directive 2004/38 and Article 14 that states that expulsion should not be the automatic consequences of having access to social rights in the host state as far as economically inactive citizens

36 Brown (2014), p. 114.

37 O'Brien, C. (2015), 'The pillory, the precipice and the slippery slope: the profound effects of the UK's legal reform programme targeting EU migrants', *Journal of Social Welfare and Family Law* 37(1), pp. 116–136.

38 Marshall, T.H. (1950), *Citizenship and social class and other essays*, Cambridge: Cambridge University Press.

are concerned. Although poor citizens are not necessarily economically inactive from the perspective of EU law, the emblematic figure of the intersection between poverty and economic inactivity is Ms Dano,[39] a Romanian Roma single mother who lived with her two children in Germany in the apartment of her sister. In the judgment of the Court of Justice, Ms Dano is described as not working, nor looking for a job and, almost illiterate. Ms Dano was already receiving allowances for her two children, when she asked for a social benefit to supplement her resources. The German authorities refused her the benefit arguing that Ms Dano had moved to Germany with the sole aim of claiming benefits, which excluded her from entitlement to receive social assistance benefits. Based on the applicable national law, it can be argued that social solidarity in the form of social assistance benefits was not available to EU citizens who, in the eyes of the law, moved to Germany in order to seek benefits, but only to those who moved to perform activities as workers or self-employed EU citizens or if economically inactive, had enough resources not to need benefits. As Minderhoud has pointed out, applicants like Ms Dano find themselves in a 'catch-22' situation: they are entitled to social solidarity as economically inactive EU citizen only when they have enough resources not to need it.[40] The Court decided that since Ms Dano did not fulfil the conditions of self-sufficiency set out in Article 7(1) of Directive 2004/38, her residence was not in line with EU law and thus not entitled to equal treatment on the basis of EU law.

It is nevertheless important to highlight that, at both discursive and legal levels, the move is not towards a complete denial of the benefits of EU free movement. Similar to contemporary migration management regimes developed by liberal economies, the aim is to manage migration and filter out the legitimate from the illegitimate,[41] and intervene where the market logic breaks down and leads to unemployment, atypical work, zero hours contracts and precarity.[42] Law is called to uphold the narrative of freedom associated with EU citizenship but also to intervene when the market disrupts that narrative by reinforcing the different treatment awarded by Directive 2004/38 to those

39 CJEU 11 November 2014, C-333/13, *Dano*, ECLI:EU:C:2014:2358.

40 Minderhoud, P. (2016), 'Sufficient resources and residence rights under Directive 2004/38', in: H. Verschueren (ed), *Where do I belong? EU law and adjudication on the link between individuals and member states*, Antwerp: Intersentia, p. 61.

41 Bigo, D. (2011), 'Freedom and speed in enlarged borderzones', in: V. Squire (ed), *The contested politics of mobility. Borderzones and irregularity*, Abingdon: Routledge, p. 46.

42 Mezzadra, S. (2011), 'The gaze of autonomy – capitalism, migration and social struggles', in: V. Squire (ed), *The contested politics of mobility. Borderzones and irregularity*, Abingdon: Routledge, p. 130; C.U. Schierup *et al.* (2015), *Migration, precarity and global governance – challenges and opportunities for labour*, Oxford: Oxford University Press.

who fail to engage with the market via performance of economic activities or via self-sufficiency and self-reliance. It is at this juncture that the case law of the European Court of Justice concerning mobile EU citizens and their claims to social solidarity is worth bringing into the discussion. Cases such as *Brey, Dano, Alimanovic, Garcia Nieto* or *Commission v. UK*[43] put forward a specific reading of free movement rights that affects the link between EU citizenship and non-discrimination in the social field – that is, the tenet upon which EU citizenship has developed as a status that transcends the free movement of workers and self-employed persons. The above mentioned cases question the extent to which an EU citizen who is not a worker or no longer a worker can in cases where she faces financial difficulties due to unemployment or lack of sufficient resources ask her host Member State for social benefits of a financial nature to help meet the costs of daily life. The Court has gradually and increasingly started to answer 'no' to such questions by relying on the argument that Member States have a right to refuse social benefits to mobile EU citizens who cannot or no longer fulfil the requirements of self-sufficiency. This right to refuse social benefits stems from the fact that self-sufficiency is a prerequisite for exercising free movement rights for longer than 3 months, in accordance with the provisions of Article 7 of Directive 2004/38.

The trend has been not only towards a more restrictive view of social solidarity and who is entitled to share in a nation's welfare, but also towards dismantling one of the legal mechanisms through which social solidarity has been pursued in the Court's previous case law, namely, the principle of proportionality. In the general economy of EU law and EU free movement of persons, state interferences with an EU citizen's right to move and reside freely can be justified if they are proportional, an exercise which relies on the individual assessment of each case based on its merits. In the more specific field of equality and social rights, Directive 2004/38 introduces the idea that, although prior to the acquisition of the right to permanent residence, a host EU state may refuse economically inactive citizens and jobseekers social assistance benefits (which are needs based and funded through general taxation as opposed to personal contribution into the welfare system), the state should nevertheless undertake an individual examination of the case and perform a proportionality assessment. At the same time, in line with neoliberal trends concerning the contraction of the welfare state,

43 CJEU 19 September 2013, C-140/12, *Brey*, ECLI:EU:C:2013:565; CJEU 11 November 2014, C-333/13 *Dano*, ECLI:EU:C:2014:2358; CJEU 15 September 2015, C-67/14 *Alimanovic*, ECLI:EU:C:2015:597; CJEU 25 February 2016, C-299/14, *Garcia Nieto*, ECLI:EU:C:2015:366; CJEU 14 June 2016, C-308/14 *Commission v. UK*, ECLI:EU:C:2016:436.

the Court of Justice has increasingly relabelled benefits social assistance, as opposed to social security,[44] thus hollowing out the content of the welfare state.

The 'poor Other' of EU citizenship can be described as an object of biopolitics because of its dangerousness for the nation as the species-body[45] that needs to be secured through governmental practices that emphasize the need to control mobility by sorting out deserving EU citizens from undeserving ones. Law plays an important role in this process as the mechanism through which legitimate claims of mobility are recognized. The case law of the Court of Justice shows a clear move towards giving value as a source of rights, protection, and equal treatment, only to residence that fulfils the conditions of Directive 2004/38. Deservingness is increasingly viewed through the lens of financial self-sufficiency and coupled with a restrictive interpretation of welfare rights. More radical readings of Marshalls' citizenship theory suggest that the extension of welfare rights was meant to incorporate the working poor into the community and pacify them, while equally ensuring the smooth functioning of the capitalist market.[46] The continued saliency of questions about social inclusion and exclusion in the context of EU citizenship case law points towards the failure of EU citizenship to act as an equalizer of the different social and economic conditions of EU citizens. The current legal tools contained by the citizenship and free movement provisions in the Treaty and the Citizens Directive do not seem sufficient to address how the transformation of welfare rights from citizenship rights (as in the Marshallian definition of citizenship) into conditional rights under neoliberalism and the rise of the precariat are played out at the EU level and, more specifically, in the context of EU citizenship.

The figure of the poor and dangerous 'Other' as an 'internal Other'[47] and as an object of biopolitics confronts us with a vision of EU citizenship that is far removed from the initial optimism associated with it but which, nevertheless, reflects the mobility experiences of some EU citizens. One can interpret this development as connected with the fact that after more than 20 years, the legal implications of EU citizenship finally start to bite, as the Member States need to implement them. The economic crisis has not helped this process as it exacerbated a number of contradictions that exist within national citizenship itself,

44 CJEU 11 November 2014, C-333/13 *Dano*, ECLI:EU:C:2014:2358.

45 Isin, E. (2004), 'The neurotic citizen', *Citizenship Studies* 8(3), p. 230.

46 Tyler, I. (2010), 'Designed to fail: a biopolitics of British citizenship', *Citizenship Studies* 14(1), pp. 61–74.

47 Pullano, T. (2014), 'How European citizenship produces a differential political space', in: E. Isin & P. Nyers (eds), *Routledge handbook of global citizenship studies*, Abingdon: Routledge, p. 441.

especially in relation to social rights.[48] And yet, the 'poverty migration' debate highlights the tension that is in-built in EU citizenship's reach and its failure to move entirely away from has been labelled the 'market' model of citizenship.[49] While the economic crisis will eventually ease out and the Member States will get better at implementing the legal rights of EU citizens, the latter tension is not that easily resolved without sustained political and legal commitment to a supranational model of membership.

## 11.4 EU Citizenship and Difference

The previous two sub-sections have discussed how the 'poor Other' is the imagine that haunts political discourses and legal practices of EU citizenship, to an extent where it becomes plausible to interrogate discourses such as 'poverty migration' through the lens of biopolitics or, at the very least, a politics of fear and insecurity. In this final part, I want to propose a different take on the Court's case law concerning mobile EU citizens by having a closer look at who claims EU citizenship rights. To put it differently, who is behind the legal fiction of the EU citizen? There are certain dangers in trying to understand the social aspects of EU citizenship by focusing on rights' claiming and jurisprudence alone. The Court's case law can offer a limited understanding of EU citizenship: it tells us where tensions and difficulties exist in relation to claiming EU citizenship rights, but fails to say anything about the mobility of EU citizens who do not encounter obstacles when moving or about the mobility of those citizens who lack resources to make legal claims. Equally, jurisprudence has little to say in terms of why people move or fail to do so.

With this caveat in mind, I still think it is important to ask who makes legal claims in their capacity as mobile EU citizens and what this means for our understanding of EU citizenship's potential. A bird's eye view of the Court's recent case law suggests that economically inactive citizens, unemployed or job-seeking EU citizens encounter problems when seeking equal treatment with nationals of their host states in relation to welfare rights (see also Guild, this volume Chapter 10). Mobile citizens with a criminal past are also targeted

---

48 Anderson, B. (2013), *Us and them – the dangerous politics of immigration control*, Oxford: Oxford University Press.

49 Shuibhne, N. (2010), 'The resilience of EU market citizenship', *Common Market Law Review 476*, pp. 1597–1628; Everson, M. (1995), 'The legacy of the market citizen', in: J. Shaw & G. More (eds), *New legal dynamics of the European Union*, Oxford: Clarendon Press, pp. 73–89.

by host Member States as problematic migrants who should be expelled from state territory, and ideally prevented from returning.[50] Mobile Roma citizens, most of who are from Eastern Europe, are one group of EU citizens who encounter a whole range of difficulties when attempting to exercise their rights as EU citizens,[51] but their struggles are not well reflected by EU citizenship case law. It can be argued that some of the persons who were supposed to find a legal home in EU citizenship continue to have difficulties in asserting their rights as EU citizens. In the introduction I suggested that EU citizenship could be approached as a 'momentum concept' that needs to be constantly reworked to achieve its inclusionary potential. To understand why some citizens are left out and have difficulties in exercising their EU citizenship rights, it may be useful to look beyond economic activity as the only axis of differentiation in the economy of EU citizenship provisions. This section draws on feminist concerns with embodiment and positionality to raise a series of questions about the manner in which EU citizenship incorporates difference in its legal provisions dealing with free movement rights.

Lister (2007) has examined the important role played by feminist scholars in questioning the reach of citizenship's claims of universalism in the face of its failure to include marginalized groups in its theory and practice.[52] Much of this work is doubled by feminist critiques of liberal legalism and law's use of neutral and genderless notions of personhood that are nevertheless built upon a male template, thus making it difficult for women to claim legal subjectivity and recognition. Hunter examines how feminist scholars have consistently questioned the tenet of liberal legalism that views the legal person as '*rational, autonomous, self-contained, self-possessed, self-sufficient and formally equal before the law*'.[53] The link with citizenship comes from the fact that modern citizens are understood as modern legal subjects, thus the superimposition of a gendered template of legal subjectivity inevitably leads to gendered citizenship. It is worth exploring the implications of this process for EU citizenship,

50 CJEU 13 September 2016, C-165/14, *Rendón Marín*, ECLI:EU:C:2016:675.

51 Parker (2012). There is no CJEU case law concerning the expulsion of Roma citizens from Italy or France, for example. The *Dano* case which deals with access to social rights is one of the few cases involving a Roma applicant ascertain a violation of her EU citizenship rights.

52 Lister, R. (2007), 'Inclusive citizenship: realizing the potential', *Citizenship Studies*, 11(1), pp. 49–61.

53 Hunter, R. (2013), 'Contesting the dominant paradigm: feminist critiques of liberal legalism', in: M. Davies & V. Munro (eds), *The Ashgate Research Companion to Feminist Legal Theory*, Abingdon: Routledge, p. 13.

since as a legal status it does not abandon the language of national citizenship and legal personhood with its claims of universality and neutrality.

According to Rygiel feminist scholarship underlines the relational aspect of mobility by highlighting how one's access and ability to move relate to one's positionality or the body one is in.[54] The recognition of the importance of the biological body in the economy of mobility makes 'embodied mobility' the frame through which mobility and its politics are investigated. Bodies are not neutral, they are gendered and produced through relations and hierarchies of power that rest on gender, race, class, sexuality etc.[55] The lesson to be taken from feminist critiques of citizenship is the need to think of how bodies are differentially included into the body politic, despite being legally included as citizens. Beyond the fiction of the legal person enjoying the legal status of EU citizenship there is a physical body whose characteristics influence one's experiences of (EU) citizenship, the possibility of moving and the manner in which movement is legally captured. To put this into a personal perspective, although I share the same nationality as the applicant in the *Dano* case my experience of free movement as an EU citizen is miles apart from hers. This remains true even if, in the legal framework of EU law, it is traditionally our nationality that singles us out for different treatment as mobile EU citizens in a host state. EU citizenship does not depart from the liberal understanding of citizenship that exists at the national level according to which all citizens are equal before the law as ideal-type legal subjects. Since in an EU context, EU citizens have different nationalities this is dealt with by making the principle of non-discrimination on the basis of nationality an instrument to neutralize difference as well as the building block of the internal market.

Once we attempt to go beyond the legal categories used by the Citizens' Directive to capture the mobility of EU citizens, it becomes clear that terms such as 'worker', 'economically inactive' or 'jobseeker' fail to reveal the personal stories and characteristics of the bodies that exercise mobility. From the vantage point of embodied practices of mobility, some of the Court's case law can be described as comprising women, single mothers, sometimes with a foreign spouse with an immigration problem,[56] pensioners with low incomes,[57]

54 Rygiel, K. (2011), 'Governing borderzones of mobility through e-borders', in: V. Squire (ed), *The contested politics of mobility. Borderzones and irregularity*, Abingdon: Routledge, pp. 143–168.

55 Rygiel (2011) p. 144.

56 CJEU 5 May 2011, C-434/09, *McCarthy*, ECLI:EU:C:2011:277; CJEU 6 December 2012, C-356/11, *O. & S.*, ECLI:EU:C:2012:776.

57 CJEU 19 September 2013, C-140/12 *Brey*, ECLI:EU:C:2013:565.

poor people,[58] low-skilled workers,[59] people with a criminal background,[60] or Roma making claims based on their EU citizenship status.[61] This alternative view posits gender, class, social origin, ethnicity, age etc as relevant factors for understanding EU citizenship and its differentiated meaning. Despite EU citizenship's claim to universality that posits that every EU citizen has a right to move, it is possible to speak of a logic of exclusion that maps onto gender, age, class etc. In turn, this raises questions as to how categories of citizens who are marginalized at the national level can assert supranational rights at the EU level and to what extent EU citizenship is a mechanism through which agency can be exercised. EU citizenship can be approached as a strategy to negotiate access to rights at various levels. This is shown by the line of case law opened by *Zambrano* that brought within the scope of EU law citizens who have never moved and who were traditionally viewed as outside the reach of EU citizenship rights. This new direction is encouraging when thinking of EU citizenship as a work in progress since it highlights its transformative potential. Yet, this line of case law is difficult to square with that on social rights as EU citizenship rights which at the moment is moving into a more restrictive direction.[62] We need critical engagement with the tensions that EU citizenship has to address in order to become a transformative status for all EU citizens and achieve its inclusionary potential. Economic activity or lack thereof is not the only factor that can lead to a different experience of EU citizenship and of the right to move. Differences based on age, gender, ethnicity, social class are equally important in structuring the mobility of EU citizens and they deserve a more prominent place in (legal) analyses of EU citizenship.

## 11.5 Concluding Remarks

This chapter has tried to sketch some alternative ways of thinking about EU citizenship that incorporate socio-political aspects of EU mobility and citizenship. The aim is to broaden the analysis of EU citizenship and the frames of

58 CJEU 10 October 2013, C-86/12, *Alokpa & Moudoulou*, ECLI:EU:C:2013:645.

59 CJEU 15 September 2015, C-67/14, *Alimanovic*, ECLI:EU:C:2015:597; CJEU 25 February 2016, C-299/14 *García Nieto*, ECLI:EU:C:2016:114.

60 CJEU 23 November 2010, C-145/09 *Tsakouridis*, ECLI:EU:C:2010:708; CJEU 16 January 2014, C-400/12 *G.*, ECLI:EU:C:2014:9.

61 CJEU 11 November 2014, C-333/13 *Dano*, ECLI:EU:C:2014:2358.

62 Shuibhne, N. (2015), 'Limits rising, duties ascending: the changing legal shape of union citizenship', *Common Market Law Review* 52, pp. 889–938.

reference beyond the legal rules contained in the Treaty, secondary legislation, and their interpretation by the EU Court of Justice. If EU citizenship is indeed to become a fundamental status for EU citizens, a number of contradictions that are inbuilt in the notion of citizenship itself need to be articulated and confronted at the EU level. The area of social rights is one where the inclusionary-exclusionary nexus of citizenship has been most visible, as claims about 'poverty migration' show very well. Public and political debates concerning EU citizens and their mobility have shown that there is a danger that some EU citizens will be labelled 'poor' and 'dangerous' Others and left outside the scope of EU citizenship. The capacity of EU citizenship law to deal with differences based on other categories besides nationality is an equally problematic aspect of how law frames the mobility of EU citizens. The tensions and difficulties discussed in this chapter are intended as a critique of EU citizenship and as a reminder that the legal expression of this status and of the rights associated with it has exclusionary consequences that are difficult to square with the proclaimed universality and neutrality of EU citizenship. EU citizens use their status and make claims in their capacity as EU citizens, to which national and EU authorities must respond. These encounters are constitutive of the process through which EU citizenship gains weight and materiality, and hopefully reaches its inclusionary potential.

## References

Anderson, B. (2012), *What does 'the migrant' tell us about the (good) citizen?*, Working Paper 12–94, Oxford: University of Oxford.

Anderson, B. (2013), *Us and them – the dangerous politics of immigration control*, Oxford: Oxford University Press.

Bigo, D. (2011), 'Freedom and speed in enlarged borderzones', in: V. Squire (ed), *The contested politics of mobility. Borderzones and irregularity*, Abingdon: Routledge, pp. 31–50.

Bräuninger, D. (2015), *Debate on free movement – does the EU need new rules on social security coordination?*, Deutsche Bank Research Briefing.

Brown, W. (2014), *Walled states, waning sovereignty*, New York: Zone Books.

Cameron, D. (2013), 'Free movement in Europe needs to be less free', *Financial Times*, 26 November 2013.

Cameron, D. (2015), *The future of Britain's relationship with the UK*, Chatham House 10 November 2015.

Ciobanu, R.O. (2015), 'Multiple migration flows of Romanians', *Mobilities* 10(3), pp. 466–485.

ECAS (2014), *Fiscal impact of EU migrants in Austria, Germany, the Netherlands and UK*, Brussels: ECAS.

Everson, M. (1995), 'The legacy of the market citizen', in: J. Shaw & G. More (eds), *New legal dynamics of the European Union*, Oxford: Clarendon Press, pp. 73–89.

Føllesdal, A. (2000), 'Third country nationals as European citizens: the case defended', *The Sociological Review* 48(1), pp. 104–122.

Fóti, K. (2015), *Social dimension of intra-EU mobility: impact on social services*, Eurofound report (EF1546).

Geddes, A. (2014), 'The EU, UKIP, and the politics of immigration in Britain', *The Political Quarterly* 85(3), pp. 289–295.

Groenendijk, K., (2006), 'Citizens and third country nationals: differential treatment or discrimination?', in: J.Y. Carlier & E. Guild (eds), *The future of free movement of persons in the EU*, Brussels: Bruylant, pp. 79–101.

Groenendijk, K. (2009), 'Forty years of free movement of workers: has it been a success and why?', in: P. Minderhoud & N. Trimikliniotis (eds), *Rethinking the free movement of workers: the European challenges ahead*, Nijmegen: Wolf Legal Publishers, pp. 11–25.

Guild, E. (2014), 'Migration, security and European citizenship', in: E. Isin & P. Nyers (eds), *Routledge handbook of global citizenship studies*, Abingdon: Routledge, pp. 418–425.

Guild, E., S. Carrera & K. Eisele (2013), *Social benefits and migration: a contested relationship and policy challenge in the EU*, Brussels: CEPS.

Guillaume, X. & J. Huysmans (2013), *Citizenship and security: the constitution of political being*, Abingdon: Routledge.

Hansen, R. (1998), 'A European citizenship or a Europe of citizens? Third country nationals in the EU', *Journal of Ethnic and Migration Studies* 24(4), pp. 751–768.

Hunter, R. (2013), 'Contesting the dominant paradigm: feminist critiques of liberal legalism', in: M. Davies & V. Munro (eds), *The ashgate research companion to feminist legal theory*, Abingdon: Routledge, pp. 13–27.

ICF/GHK (2013), *A fact finding analysis on the impact on the member states' social security systems of the entitlements of non-active intra-EU migrants to special non-contributory cash benefits and healthcare granted on the basis of residence*, Final report submitted by ICF GHK in association with Milieu Ltd., DG Employment, Social Affairs and Inclusion via DG Justice Framework contract.

Isin, E. (2004), 'The neurotic citizen', *Citizenship Studies* 8(3), pp. 217–235.

Kostakopoulou, D. (2014), 'European Union citizenship rights and duties: civil, political and social', in: E. Isin & P. Nyers (eds), *Routledge handbook of global citizenship studies. Routledge international handbooks*, Abingdon: Routledge, pp. 427–436.

Lister, R. (2007), 'Inclusive citizenship: realizing the potential', *Citizenship Studies*, 11(1), pp. 49–61.

Mantu, S. & Minderhoud, P. (2016), 'Exploring the limits of social solidarity: welfare tourism and EU citizenship', *UNIO – EU Law Journal* 2, pp. 4–19.

Marcu, S. (2016), 'Learning mobility challenging borders: cross-border experiences of Eastern European immigrants in Spain', *Mobilities* 11(3), pp. 343–361.

Marshall, T.H. (1950), *Citizenship and social class and other essays*, Cambridge: Cambridge University Press.

Mezzadra, S. (2011), 'The gaze of autonomy – capitalism, migration and social struggles', in: V. Squire (ed), *The contested politics of mobility. Borderzones and irregularity*, Abingdon: Routledge, pp. 121–142.

Minderhoud, P. (2016), 'Sufficient resources and residence rights under directive 2004/38', in: H. Verschueren (ed), *Where do I belong? EU law and adjudication on the link between individuals and member states*, Antwerp: Intersentia, pp. 47–74.

Nic Shuibhne, N. (2010), 'The resilience of EU market citizenship, *Common Market Law Review*', 47(6), pp. 1597–1628.

Nic Shuibhne, N. (2015), 'Limits rising, duties ascending: the changing legal shape of union citizenship', *Common Market Law Review*, 52, pp. 889–938.

Nowrot, K. & Struckmeyer-Öner, B (2014), *Sozialtourismus in Europa?: Unions- und sozialrechtliche Anmerkungen zu einer aktuellen Debatte*, Policy Papers on Transnational Economic Law 40, Transnational Economic Law Research Centre.

Nyers, P. (2004), 'Introduction: what's left of citizenship?', *Citizenship Studies* 8(3), pp. 203–215.

O'Brien, C. (2015), 'The pillory, the precipice and the slippery slope: the profound effects of the UK's legal reform programme targeting EU migrants', *Journal of Social Welfare and Family Law*, 37(1), pp. 116–136.

Pallida, S. (2016), *Governance of security and ignored insecurities in contemporary Europe*, Abingdon: Routledge.

Parker, O. (2012), 'Roma and the politics of EU citizenship in France: everyday security and resistance', *Journal of Common Market Studies*, 50(3), pp. 475–491.

Rygiel, K. (2010), *Globalizing citizenship*, Vancouver: UBC Press.

Rygiel, K. (2011), 'Governing borderzones of mobility through e-borders', in: V. Squire (ed), *The contested politics of mobility. Borderzones and irregularity*, Abingdon: Routledge, pp. 143–168.

Schierup, C.U. *et al.* (2015), *Migration, precarity and global governance – challenges and opportunities for labour*, Oxford: Oxford University Press.

Tomkin, J. (2009), 'The worker, the citizen, their families and the court of justice: tales of free movement from Luxembourg', in: P. Minderhoud & N. Trimikliniotis (eds), *Rethinking the free movement of workers: the European challenges ahead*, Nijmegen: Wolf Legal Publishers, pp. 39–59.

Tyler, I. (2010), 'Designed to fail: a biopolitics of British citizenship', *Citizenship Studies* 14(1), pp. 61–74

CHAPTER 12

# Access to Justice for Asylum Seekers

## *Is the Right to Seek and Enjoy Asylum Only Black Letter Law?*

*Ashley Terlouw*

### 12.1 Introduction

The subject access to justice for asylum seekers is very topical.[1] Many asylum seekers try to reach Europe in order to be recognised as refugees and to find protection from injustice in their countries of origin. However, at the moment the focus is on the interest of European States. After more than one million asylum seekers crossed the Aegean Sea in 2015, EU Member States responded by closing their borders thus displaying a lack of solidarity with the frontline States and finally on 19 March 2016 by concluding the so called EU-Turkey deal in order to prevent asylum seekers leaving Turkey for Greece and obliging Turkey to take asylum seekers back. In effect, after building the Common European Asylum System, which confirms obligations under the Refugee Convention, and consists of, among other legal requirements, the Procedures Directive guaranteeing fair and efficient procedures to asylum seekers, the legal pathways to Europe have become more and more restricted.

The important issues at stake are reception capacity, solidarity between EU States, between the EU and other European States and solidarity with asylum seekers,[2] the right to seek asylum and the concept of safe third country or first country of asylum.[3] But for the EU it seems to come down to the following three questions:

(1) How do we deal with more than one million asylum seekers?
(2) How can we prevent asylum seekers crossing the external borders?
(3) How can we oblige third countries to take back asylum seekers who have passed through their countries on their way to the EU?

1 The text of this chapter has been updated until August 2016.

2 Compare Madeline Garlick (2016), *Solidarity under strain. Solidarity and fair sharing of responsibility in law and practice for the international protection of refugees in the European Union*, (diss. Nijmegen), Mont-St-Guibert, Belgium: McPlan.

3 Proposal for a common EU list of safe countries of origin, 9 September 2015, COM(2015)452 final and Amendment of the recast of the Procedures Directive (Directive 2013/32/EU).

 | DOI 10.1163/9789004330467_013

In this atmosphere the asylum seekers' perspective is often missing. For asylum seekers access to justice is the central issue. Access to justice is a broad term with different layers. Firstly, the term is used to express the right of *access to a court of law*, which includes all elements of a fair trial, such as access to an independent judge and an effective remedy and it assumes that this access is financially affordable. Affordable legal aid is also part of access to justice within the meaning of access to a court of law. Secondly, access to justice may encompass *access to the law*, the formal law as it is laid down in legislation and jurisprudence. This not only presupposes knowledge of the law and of the rights it grants and of the possibilities to claim these rights, but also that the law functions, that it is effective, that the formal law is not just black letter law. Thirdly, access to justice may be used to express that everybody should have the right to a *fair solution*, to justice in a very broad sense. Justice in the sense of a fair solution may be required by law but it may be understood as rights that are not or not yet recognised by law: such as 'the right to shelter and health care' for illegally residing migrants. The ideas about justice may not be in conformity with formal law. Asylum seekers whose claims have been rejected and who have lost their appeal before an independent judge may still feel that they have not found access to justice.

## 12.2 Sociology of Law

In the sociology of law it is known that there are many obstacles to attaining justice in the first sense (access to the courts). As a result, only a very small portion of all legal problems is solved through the legal system and an even smaller portion leads to a court case. According to Felstiner, Abel & Sarat, this is due to the transformation of law that must be made before a problem can be solved by the legal system.[4] This transformation leads to problems of naming, blaming and claiming. In short: people have to recognise that their problem is a legal problem (naming), they have to know whom they can hold responsible (blaming) and after that they have to find out how to use the legal system (claiming).

This is all different when we look at asylum seekers. They don't have difficulty naming and blaming. Naming and blaming happens in the country of origin at the moment the asylum seekers realise that they have to flee from persecution and that their government is to blame. Their main problem is claiming;

4 Felstiner, W.F.L., R.L. Abel & A. Sarat (1981), 'The emergence and transformation of disputes: naming, blaming, claiming', *Law & Society Review*, pp. 613–654.

they all have to find a country of refuge where they can claim to be recognised as refugees and obtain a residence permit. The obstacles to attaining access to justice with which asylum seekers are confronted are, therefore, of a different order. Even if there were full transposition of EU law into national laws – which is not the case: we do not yet have a harmonised system of norms – even if there were fair implementation of norms in practice – which is not the case: the law in the statute books, the Procedures and Reception Directives, and the Dublin Regulation, are often not applied in practice – even if transposition and implementation and harmonisation were realised, we could hardly speak about access to justice as long as there is no access to the territory.

It might be useful to develop a specific access to justice theory for asylum seekers and to recognise that instead of naming, blaming and claiming, asylum seekers are confronted with the following three other obstacles to attaining justice: the obstacles of access to the territory, access to the asylum procedure and access to a fair and durable solution. I will elaborate on each of these obstacles below.

## 12.3 Access to the Territory

The first and most important obstacle is getting *access to the territory*: If we imagine a legal iceberg in the field of asylum, the tip of the iceberg would not represent the few cases that reach the courts, but would represent the difficulties with which asylum seekers are confronted when they try to reach Europe safely.

For years Member States have more and more openly tried to close the doors of the Fortress of Europe. For a long time there have been prolonged gate checks, visa requirements,[5] carrier sanctions,[6] readmission agreements, etc. It is difficult if not impossible for asylum seekers to legally enter the EU without a valid visa. And the new policies and proposals go even further. Member States on their own initiative have closed their borders. Barbed wire has appeared around Member State after Member State. Instead of criticising Hungary for closing its border, the example has been followed. Safe zones have been built

5 Regulation 539/2001.

6 Art. 26 of the Schengen Implementation Agreement and Art. 4 of Directive 2001/51. See also: Scholten, S. (2014), *Privatisation of immigration control? A socio-legal study on the role of private transport companies in the Netherlands and the United Kingdom*, (diss. Nijmegen), Ipskamp Drukkers.

and quotas established (Austria 37,500 a year).[7] The idea of open borders within the EU seems to have been abolished. The EU is divided: only 17 of the 27 countries have taken any responsibility for asylum seekers, 10 Member States have refused to cooperate. The solution found has not been to put pressure on these countries – although the European Commission has proposed the imposition of a fine of 250,000 euro on the unwilling countries for each person they refuse[8] – or to help them by relieving them of some of the burdens, but to conclude the EU-Turkey deal.

And at sea, Frontex has been in action, officially to save asylum seekers from drowning but also to push back the loaded boats and return them to where they came from, without access to justice for the asylum seekers being guaranteed.[9] Since 25 February 2016 NATO has also been helping with surveillance in the Aegean Sea, outside the territorial zone of the EU. In fact NATO is helping to guard the Turkish borders in this way and to prevent asylum seekers from entering Europe without any guarantee of non-refoulement.

## 12.4 So How to Reach Europe?

By land, in a closed truck through Hungary[10] or on a bicycle via the Russian-Norwegian border?[11] By air, deep frozen and hidden in the landing

7 'Migrant crisis: Austria to slash asylum claims', *BBC News*, 20 January 2016.

8 The proposal formulates it as a choice: 'The member state which temporarily does not take part in the corrective allocation must make a solidarity contribution of EUR 250,000 per applicant to the member states that were determined as responsible for examining those applications'. Regulation of the European Parliament and of the Council establishing the criteria and mechanisms for determining the Member State responsible for examining an application for international protection lodged in one of the Member States by a third-country national or a stateless person, 4 May 2016, COM(2016)270; <eur-ex.europa.eu/procedure/NL/2016_133?qid=1462976943745&rid=1>.

9 Ruben te Molder & Laurie Kampkuiper, 'Frontex: is de grens bereikt?', *A&MR* 2016, nr. 1, pp. 10–15; M.H.A. Strik, 'Frontex de grenzen van zijn mandaat', *Justitiële verkenningen* 2015, (3), pp. 47–56.

10 On 28 August 2015, 71 dead asylum seekers were found in a truck at the Hungarian-Austrian border.

11 According to Norwegian law, it is prohibited to cross the Russian-Norwegian border on foot or to take a hitch hiker across this border without the necessary documents. However, the Norwegian laws do not mention bicycles. So apparently many asylum seekers buy bicycles to cross the border at Storskog, close to Kirkenes, the only border crossing between Russia and Norway.

gear?[12] By sea, together with 40 other asylum seekers, dressed in fake life jackets in a rubber vessel crossing the Mediterranean?[13]

Where are the necessary legal pathways? For years the UNHCR pointed out that legal pathways to Europe would be necessary to prevent destabilisation of the regions.[14] It stressed the necessity for resettlement, humanitarian visas, improvement of the possibilities for family reunification and scholarships and sponsorships. Nothing of this has happened and, indeed, the regions have been destabilised with, as a result, more than a million asylum seekers entering in 2015.

The reaction of the EU Member States has been painfully lacking in any solidarity. There has been no solidarity with the overburdened regions, no solidarity between the Member States, let alone with the asylum seekers seeking access to justice. The plans by the European Commission to enhance legal avenues into Europe have so far remained nothing but good intentions.[15]

EU Member States are reluctant to take responsibility for people intercepted or rescued in international waters. However, since the ECHR condemned the push backs and collective expulsions by Italy to Libya in the important *Hirsi* judgment[16] more asylum seekers than before have been saved in the Mediterranean and brought to Italy. Still, it remains nearly impossible for asylum seekers who have been pushed back to get access to the EU. In practice it is of course very difficult for refused asylum seekers to have a Member State convicted for not fulfilling its responsibilities. Member States at the borders of the Mediterranean are still shamelessly pushing them back. For example Spain

12 The official possibilities to flee by air diminish. In the Netherlands for example currently hardly any asylum seeker enters via Schiphol airport. According to the Dutch Refugee Council AC Schiphol registered (Art. 6 Aliens Act) 619 asylum seekers in 2015.

13 'Over 5,400 people are estimated to have lost their lives on migratory routes around the world in 2015, and the first half of 2016 has only seen the numbers increase. The Mediterranean alone witnessed a record number of at least 3,770 deaths in 2015, with numbers climbing in 2016. The International Organization for Migration (IOM) estimates that over the last two decades, more than 60,000 migrants have died trying to reach their destinations, and this only includes deaths for which there is some record. Often occurring far from the public eye, an unknown number of deaths go unrecorded'. IOM, *Fatal Journeys Volume 2: Identification and tracing of dead and missing migrants*, 2016.

14 Recent UNHCR EXCOM 2 March 2016, 65th meeting p. 4.

15 Communication from the Commission to the European Parliament and the Council, Brussels 6 April COM(2016)197 final: towards a reform of the common European asylum system and enhancing legal avenues to Europe. See also: COM(2015)240 final and COM(2016)270 final.

16 EHRM 23 February 2012, appl. no. 27765/09, *Hirsi Jamaa a.o. v. Italy*, ECLI:CE:ECHR:2012:0223JUD002776509.

has concluded agreements with Mauritania and Senegal to have coastguards preventing asylum seekers fleeing to the Canary Islands; and there are the so-called hot returns by Spain to Morocco and Hungary to Serbia.[17] This might also be an indirect consequence of, or a response to, the lack of solidarity from other Member States and their resistance to reforming the Dublin system.

The most recent and far reaching obstacle is the much contested EU-Turkey deal. In exchange for money, skipping visa restrictions for Turkish citizens, and reopening the negotiations for the accession of Turkey to the EU, Turkey has promised to take back all asylum seekers (Syrians and others) and to prevent them fleeing to the EU. The deal also foresees possibilities for resettlement. For each Syrian refugee returned to Turkey, from the Greek islands, the EU will resettle another Syrian refugee from Turkey (the so-called 'one for one' approach), to a maximum of 72,000 Syrian refugees (including the 18,000 already promised). Priority will be given to those who have not tried to enter the EU illegally. So far, the expectations are not high. The EU will start larger humanitarian resettlement programmes (the Voluntary Humanitarian Admission Scheme) only after there has been a structural decrease in the number of arrivals and only if the number reaches 72,000, but there has been no agreement so far on when there will be a structural decrease. Furthermore there has been disagreement over which refugees should be resettled. The UNHCR has urged that it should be vulnerable people, while the EU would prefer to accept the highly educated.[18]

And what are the criteria for resettlement? We know that higher educated people are not brought in under the resettlement programme for Europe.[19] There is hardly any control on the way the authorities deal with requests for resettlement by Syrian refugees. With regard to these questions and these small numbers one cannot say that there are realistic legal pathways.

There are serious questions about the legality of the EU-Turkey deal. According to the deal some Syrians will be resettled (however not those who have been sent back from Greece to Turkey[20]) but what will happen to other returned asylum seekers, refused by Greece? This aspect of the deal seems to

---

17 Margarita Martínez Escamilla *et al.*, 'Hot returns: when the state acts outside the law' Legal report, <eprints.ucm.es/27221> 27 June 2014.

18 Compare Parliamentary Assembly, Doc. 14028, 19 April 2016, *The situation of refugees and migrants under the EU-Turkey, agreement of 18 March 2016*, rapporteur Tineke Strik.

19 Wilmer Heck, 'Erdogan: "EU komt deal niet na"', klopt dat?', *NRC Handelsblad* 28 juli 2016.

20 The latter do receive residence permits upon return if they were not yet in possession of such a permit.

be discrimination based on nationality. But the main problem is that Turkey is regarded as a safe third country and as a first country of origin. Both of these assumptions can be and are contested.[21] Turkey didn't sign the 1967 New York Protocol to the Refugee Convention, which means that it retained the geographical limitation that exempts it from extending the Convention to cover non-European refugees. According to Amnesty International, Turkey refoules asylum seekers at the Syrian border.[22] Human Rights Watch even reported that Turkey's border guards shot asylum seekers at the borders.[23]

And what about the current situation in Turkey after the failed coup, in which the principle of a free press was abolished and judges and university professors were dismissed?[24] After the failed 15 July coup, Turkey's Government declared a state of emergency and subsequently on 21 July notified the Council of Europe that it might derogate from the European Convention on Human Rights.[25] President Erdogan even suggested that the death penalty should be introduced for the coup leaders. Since the EU-Turkey deal and now that the western Balkan route has been closed, refugees are increasingly trying to reach the EU via more dangerous routes, for example via Libya to Italy and via Bulgaria's eastern border, where they meet more and more fences.[26]

---

21 See for example: UNHCR High Commissioner for Refugees, Legal considerations on the return of asylum-seekers and refugees from Greece to Turkey as part of the EU-Turkey Cooperation in Tackling the Migration Crisis under the safe third country and first country of asylum concept, 23 March 2016; Sergio Carrera & Elspeth Guild, EU-Turkey plan for handling refugees is fraught with legal and procedural challenges, 10 March 2016, CEPS Thinking ahead for Europe; Den Heijer *et al.*, 'Coercion, prohibition, and great expectations', *CMLR* June 2016 (translated in Dutch: *NJB* 2016, nr. 24, p. 1672 ff.). See also: DRC/ECRE, *Desk research on application of a safe third country and first country of asylum concepts to Turkey*, May 2016.

22 Amnesty International 31 March 2016: <www.amnesty.nl/nieuwsportaal/nieuws/turkije-stuurt-op-grote-schaal-vluchtelingen-terug-naar-syrie>.

23 Human Rights Watch: *Turkey: border guards kill and injure asylum seekers*, 10 May 2016.

24 According to Amnesty International there is 'credible evidence that detainees in Turkey are being subjected to beatings and torture, including rape, in official and unofficial detention centres in the country. The organization is calling for independent monitors to be given immediate access to detainees in all facilities in the wake of the coup attempt, which include police headquarters, sports centres and courthouses. More than 10,000 people have been detained since the failed coup'. Amnesty international 24 July 2016.

25 It is according to Art. 15 ECHR possible to derogate from the obligations of this Convention in emergency situations.

26 Read for example: Slovenians faith in a fence, Deutsche Welle, 4 August 2016-10-21: <www.dw.com/en/slovenians-faith-in-a-fence/a-19450017>.

We can without any hesitation conclude that there are major obstacles to accessing justice in the sense of access to the territory for asylum seekers. Member States do not even hide that they do everything to prevent asylum seekers gaining access to EU territory. We must protect our external borders is the ever repeated message. Many asylum seekers do not survive the dangerous journey to Europe. Nevertheless they keep coming. In the first seven months of 2016, 250,000 asylum seekers managed to reach the EU, since the EU-Turkey deal, mainly to Italy. This number is remarkably lower than the one million asylum seekers in 2015. One could say that (August 2016) the argument of the high numbers can no longer be an argument for the EU for not organising the legal pathways for which the UNHCR has urged. Besides, legal pathways will probably contribute to further lowering the number of spontaneous arrivals.

## 12.5 Access to the Asylum Procedure

The second burden is obtaining *access to the asylum procedure*: Lack of access to the territory also means lack of access to an asylum procedure. But even if asylum seekers reach the EU access to an asylum procedure is problematic. Of course we have the important recast of the Procedures Directive[27] and Art. 47 of the Charter which require fair procedures for every asylum seeker. The purpose of the recast of the Procedures Directive is to establish common standards for Member States' procedures for granting and withdrawing refugee status. It guarantees, for example, access to procedures, the right to appeal an asylum decision, the right to remain in the country during appeal procedures and the right to legal aid.[28] However, this Directive also contains many derogation clauses and many optional clauses and a part of it is still black letter law. Not every Member State has implemented the Directive but even if it has the law in the statute books is not always law in action. For example in Germany the recast of the Procedures Directive has not yet been implemented. The European

27 Recast procedures Directive (Directive 2013/32/EU).

28 American research shows that nationwide only 37 percent of all immigrants in the U.S. had legal representation, and only 14 percent of immigrants had a lawyer (Michelle Waslin, 'Access to Legal Representaion is Unequal and the Consequences are serious' in Immigration Courts, Right to Council Immigrants', Paper submitted 28 September 2016: <immigrationimpact.com/2016/09/28/immigrants-access-legal-representation-unequal-consequences-serious>). I am not aware of European research with regard to legal representation of asylum seekers, but regarding the consequences of not having access to legal representation, such research would be useful.

Commission has started an infringement procedure. Besides, there are signs that in other countries the Procedures Directive has been implemented in the most minimal way. There is, at the very least, reluctance to implement the Directive in a full and positive way.[29]

The Dublin system is aimed at sharing responsibilities, preventing refugees in orbit and preventing forum shopping, but in practice seems to have turned out to be contra productive as Member States are reluctant to take responsibility for refugees.[30] The Dublin responsibility rules are based on the idea of a harmonised asylum system but the situation for asylum seekers in the EU is far from harmonised and the responsibility division rules, which are primarily based on the idea that the country of first entry or where the asylum claim is first lodged, leads to frustration on the part of both asylum seekers and the countries at the external borders.[31] For the asylum seekers this leads to non-registration in the first country of arrival and throwing away any documents that can prove that they entered the EU. The Member States of first asylum entry close their eyes to this and are tempted to keep their asylum system below the EU norms in order to prevent returns from other Member States (or prevent Dublin claims). Other Member States close their borders[32] in order to

---

29 The European Commission evaluation report on the application of the Directive on minimum standards on procedures for granting and withdrawing refugee status: <ec.europa.eu/dgs/home-affairs/news/intro/docs/com_2010_465_en.pdf>. From the conclusion (be aware: concerns *first* Procedures Directive): 'This evaluation confirms that some of the Directive's optional provisions and derogation clauses have contributed to the proliferation of divergent arrangements across the EU, and that procedural guarantees vary considerably between Member States. This is notably the case with respect to the provisions on accelerated procedures, 'safe country of origin', 'safe third country', personal interviews, legal assistance, and access to an effective remedy. Thus, important disparities subsist. A number of cases of incomplete and/or incorrect transposition and flaws in the implementation of the Directive have also been identified. The cumulative effect of these deficiencies may make procedures susceptible to administrative error. It is noteworthy, in this regard, that a significant share of first instance decisions is overturned on appeal. The present report shows that the objective of creating a level playing field with respect to fair and efficient asylum procedures has not been fully achieved'.

30 René Bruin, Stefan Kok & Ashley Terlouw, 'Dublin, Interstatelijk vertrouwen is een fictie', *Justitiële Verkenningen*, 3–15; Stefan Kok (2016), 'Hoe functioneert het Dublinsysteem? Over de weerbarstige praktijk', *A&MR*, nr. 6/7, p. 291–301.

31 Compare Den Heijer *et al.* (2016), 'Coercion, prohibition, and great expectations', *CMLR* June 2016 (in Dutch: *NJB*, nr. 24, p. 1672).

32 Art. 26 Schengen Border Code. Regulation 562/2006 allows for reintroduction of internal border controls for periods of two years.

prevent secondary movements or to be held responsible if they cannot return the refugees.[33] In short, the Dublin system has failed.[34]

But the main problem of access to an asylum procedure at the moment exists for the around 50,000 asylum seekers who are in Greece. So far 'the total number of pledges remains low at 7,463 – only 11% of the total target of 66,400 to be relocated from Greece to other EU Member States by September 2017'.[35] After the closure of the borders between Macedonia and Greece in 2015 they found themselves between the Scylla of the Mediterranean and a possible return to Turkey and the Charybdis of the closed Macedonian borders and the reception camps without a real prospect of an asylum procedure. Due to the EU-Turkey deal the new arrivals in Greece diminished in April 2016. Nevertheless, according to the Parliamentary Assembly report refugees at risk: 'as a result of the co-ordinated closure of borders along the western Balkans route, there are now 46,000 refugees and migrants blocked in mainland of Greece and a further 8,500 on the islands. Those on the mainland who qualify for international protection will be forced to stay in Greece, whose reception and integration capacity remains seriously insufficient, until relocated to another country participating in the European Union's relocation scheme – or until they find a clandestine way to continue their journey north, most probably in the hands of migrant smugglers. Those on the islands are for the most part detained in inadequate conditions, and in all cases subject to the vagaries of the dysfunctional Greek asylum system for assessment of whether or not they will be returned to Turkey. In 2016, 89% of arrivals were from Syria, Afghanistan or Iraq but the asylum seekers who arrived after the closing of the Macedonian border in February, were stuck over in Greece'.[36]

Refugees on the mainland do not fall within the EU-Turkey deal, but Greece has to offer them a fair asylum procedure in accordance with the Procedures Directive. These procedures have hardly started, as the Greek Government first had to organise the reception of tens of thousands of refugees. Nevertheless, this is of course not a good reason for not organising access to the procedure.

---

33 Compare: Guild *et al.* (2015), 'Enhancing CEAS and alternatives for Dublin', Study for the LIBE Committee.

34 DG Migration and Home Affairs, Evaluation of the implementation of the Dublin III regulation, 18 March 2016.

35 See: <data.unhcr.org/mediterranean/documents.php?page=1&view=grid> consulted 14 August 2016.

36 As of June 10th there were 57,000 asylum seekers stranded in Greece. See COM(2016)817. More than 8,500 of them remained on the Islands with hotspots.

Besides, the other Member States should, to reduce the burden on Greece, comply with their promise to relocate 66,000 refugees.

Since 2011, both European Courts have regarded the procedures and the reception of asylum seekers in Greece as insufficiently fair.[37] At the time of writing, August 2016, the situation seems to be even worse. Until 20 March 2016 the asylum seekers and other migrants could freely enter and leave the hotspots on the islands of Lesbos and Chios; since then this has no longer been possible and the hotspots have been turned into detention centres. Procedures have gradually been established, but according to the Parliamentary Assembly the Greek asylum system lacks, among other things the capacity to ensure timely registration of asylum applications, issue first instance decisions or determination of appeals. Furthermore, remedies against decisions to return asylum seekers to Turkey do not always have automatic suspensive effect.[38] Moreover, the Assembly warns that the detention of asylum seekers in the hotspots on the Aegean Islands may be incompatible with the requirements of Art. 5 of the ECHR, due notably to procedural failures undermining the legal grounds for detention and adequate detention conditions. On 19 April 2016, three Afghan refugees lodged a complaint with the ECtHR against Greece: they considered their detention in the hotspot on Chios to be a violation of Art. 5 ECHR, because of the duration and the circumstances of their detention and the lack of information on the reason for the detention.[39] On 26 May, the Court asked the parties if the detention circumstances in the hotspot in Chios had led to a violation of Arts. 3 or 5 and if the length of the detention had been reasonable, taking into account the (lack of) progress in the processing of the asylum claims, and if the detainees had been informed in an understandable language about the reasons for their detention, in conformity with Art. 5(2) ECHR.

According to the European Commission, by 12 June 2016 the Appeals Committees had decided in 70 cases of Syrian refugees that Turkey was not a safe country.[40] On 16 June, the Greek parliament adopted an amendment to the new Greek Law (Law 4375, entered into force in April 2016) with a view to introducing a new Appeals Body. This happened after the Greek Government

37 ECHR 21 January 2011, appl. no. 30696/09, *M.S.S. v. Belgium and Greece* ECLI:CE:ECHR:2011:0121JUD003069609; CJEU 21 December 2011, C-411/10 *N.S.* and C-493/10 *M.E.* ECLI:EU:C:2011:865.

38 See the Resolution of the Parliamentary Assembly of 19 April 2016. Doc. 14028 Report; Tineke Strik, 'Gestrand in Griekenland', *A&MR* 2016, nr. 6/7, p. 311 ff.

39 ECHR introduite 19 avril 2016, 22696/16, *Javid Raoufi v. Greece.*

40 Second Report on the progress made in the implementation of the EU-Turkey; Brussels, 15.6.2016 COM(2016)349. And: ECRE 17 June 2016: The Lesvos hotspot: refugees stuck on the island, <www.ecre.org/the-lesvos-hotspot/>.

disagreed with the outcome of these appeals, and decided to review the composition of the Appeals Committees). The Appeals Committees had decided in almost all appeals that the claims could not be declared inadmissible; they were not convinced that Turkey would be a safe third country within the sense of Article 38 APD. Two appeals have been rejected so far: in these cases the applicants have filed a complaint with the ECHR. In one of the two cases, the Court has already decided not to take an interim measure.[41]

Moreover, on 22 March and 19 May, three similar applications for annulment of the EU-Turkey deal were lodged with the General of the EU Court of Justice under Article 263 TFEU. Two cases were brought on behalf of nationals from Pakistan residing in Lesbos, the third one was launched by an Afghan national staying in Athens. The applicants stated that the EU-Turkey deal exposed them to the risks of refoulement to Turkey or indirect refoulement to Pakistan or Afghanistan. Besides they complained that they were, in this way, obliged to apply for international protection in Greece, against their will. The applicants have requested that the case proceed under an expedited procedure.[42]

So far the Greek asylum procedure can still not be regarded as a real and functioning fair procedure. Nevertheless a start has been made. Although incomparable to the Greek disaster, all over Europe asylum seekers are confronted with long waiting periods sometimes in dreadful conditions. This is also the case in the Netherlands. In the company of some Macedonian lawyers I visited the reception centre in the former prison in de Havenstraat Amsterdam. I was shocked by the detention-like situation in which some 350 men had been living for five months. But the Macedonians were impressed and compared it to the situation of refugees at their borders, waiting in containers in the snow.

We can conclude that although the differences in this respect within the EU are enormous, access to justice for asylum seekers in the sense of access to an asylum procedure is problematic; even if they overcome the obstacle of access to the territory and manage to reach Europe, access to an asylum procedure is far from guaranteed.

## 12.6 Access to a Fair and Durable Solution

The third obstacle is getting access to *a fair and durable solution*. It sometimes seems to be forgotten that asylum seekers do not only have the immediate

41 ECtHR 3181/16, *Maliki v. Greece*.

42 CJEU (pending), T-192/16 *NF v. European Council*; CJEU (pending), T-193/16 *N.G. v. European Council*; CJEU (pending), T-257/16, *N.M. v. European Council*.

right to non-refoulement as long as their claims have not been processed in a fair and efficient procedure, but that if they are refugees, they also have other kinds of rights, the right to safety and perspective in the long term. They have the right to access to justice in the widest sense: access to a fair and durable solution (*the right to enjoy asylum*). The Refugee Convention is not only about protection but also about full participation in the host country. In fact the Refugee Convention is mainly about these other kinds of rights. It requires for example in Arts. 23 and 24 equal treatment with citizens with regard to elementary education, social security and health care and in Art. 21 with regard to housing treatment as favourable as possible and, in any event, not less favourable than that accorded to aliens generally in the same circumstances.

According to the UNHCR, 65.3 million individuals have been forcibly displaced worldwide as a result of persecution, conflict, generalized violence, or human rights violations. It estimates that 41% of those under the UNHCR's mandate were in a protracted situation by the end of 2015.[43] As far as the Syrian refugees in Turkey are concerned, Mr. Hanno van Gemund, Protection Officer at the UNHCR with responsibility for developing and implementing programmes for refugees in Turkey, writes that Turkey houses 2.7 million Syrian refugees of whom 260,000 are in refugee camps. The living conditions of the latter are good: there is education for the children, shops, medical care. However the situation for the 90% of the other refugees, living outside the camps, is much more difficult. According to the World Food Programme, 90% of them live below the poverty line. Only 40% of the Syrian children attend school.[44]

Within the EU, durable solutions and material rights are not always offered.

Apart from the situation in Greece, in other better equipped Member States, like Germany and the Netherlands, asylum seekers are also confronted with several problems with regard to their reception and material situation.

The European Commission, which always seemed to be in favour of equal treatment for refugees and persons eligible for subsidiary protection, announced that it would investigate whether differentiation was necessary in order to prevent secondary movement.[45] In the most recent proposal to replace the Qualification Directive by a Regulation, the Commission concluded (fortunately) that support for differentiation is lacking and some Member States even stressed 'the importance of not unduly undermining integration

---

43 UNHCR Global trends. Forced displacement in 2015.

44 Hanno van Gemund (2016), 'Medeverantwoordelijk voor meer dan 2,7 miljoen vluchtelingen, Europese column', *A&MR*, nr. 6/7, p. 351.

45 COM(2016)197 final.

prospects via the perception that the protection may only be temporary'.[46] So we may assume that equal treatment for refugees and those persons with subsidiary protection will be required.

The right for a third country national to accept work in another Member State is only permitted with conditions after five years' legal stay.[47] Art. 34 of the Refugee Convention prescribes that the Contracting States shall as far as possible facilitate the assimilation and naturalization of refugees and in particular that they shall make every effort to expedite naturalization proceedings and to reduce as far as possible the charges and costs of such proceedings. How does this relate to the integration requirements Member States more and more also impose on refugees[48] and to the requirements of longer and longer periods of legal stay before a refugee may be naturalized?

The 1951 Convention Relating to the Status of Refugees is silent on the issue of family reunification. And although Article 8(1) ECHR grants everyone 'the right to respect for his private life and family life', Article 8 ECHR does not grant a right to family reunification. Nevertheless according to steady jurisprudence of the European Court of Human Rights (ECtHR) Article 8 ECHR does protect the family life of refugees if the interruption of family life was solely a result of the decision to flee the country of origin out of a genuine fear of persecution within the meaning of the Refugee Convention. In such cases there are insurmountable obstacles to re-establishing family life in the country of origin and family reunification in the country of refuge should be granted.[49] In 2003, the Family Reunification Directive was adopted.[50] More favourable rules for family reunification for refugees (but not for those persons with subsidiary protection) are laid down in Articles 9–12, exempting refugees from the waiting period and from complying with income, housing and integration requirements. However

46 Proposal for a regulation on standards for the qualification of third-country nationals or stateless persons as beneficiaries of international protection, for a uniform status for refugees or for persons eligible for subsidiary protection and for the content of the protection granted and amending Council Directive 2003/109/EC of 25 November 2003 concerning the status of third-country nationals who are long-term residents, explanatory memorandum, p. 10 "On the level of rights granted to beneficiaries, Member States did not generally support the idea of further differentiating between the two international protection statuses".

47 Art. 14 Directive 2011/51/EU (Long-term residence).

48 In the Netherlands asylum seekers have the obligation to integrate as soon as they are recognized as refugees and have to do an integration exam within three years. Sanctions are primarily financial (a fine of 1250 euro) but failing the test can also lead to refusal of permanent status (Art. 34(1) Dutch Aliens Act.

49 For example ECtHR 1 March 2006, 60665/00, *Tuquabo-Tekle a.o. v. the Netherlands*.

50 Directive 2003/86 on the right to Family Reunification.

since the number of refugees has risen, Member States are giving an increasingly minimalistic interpretation of the requirements of Art. 8 ECHR and the Family Reunification Directive, some of them by making a distinction between family reunification for refugees and those persons with subsidiary protection. Germany and Sweden, for example, are suspending the right to family reunification for the latter group.[51] But there are also proposals to make the conditions for family reunification for refugees more restrictive. For example in Belgium, the special treatment given to family members of refugees will be reduced from twelve to three months after the status has been granted, and in Norway waiting periods of four years have been proposed and Sweden wants to allow family reunification only if both spouses are 21 years of age. According to Groenendijk, in several countries the waiting period has or will be introduced or existing periods extended. In Norway the government proposed to allow family reunification only after persons with international protection have worked and studied for four years in Norway. In Denmark a waiting period of three years has been introduced for beneficiaries of temporary or subsidiary protection. In Austria, a bill with a similar restriction has recently passed.[52] In February 2016, Germany introduced a two-year waiting period for persons with subsidiary protection.[53] The Swedish government proposed to suspend the family reunification for all protection categories suggesting that the suspension might be lifted for convention refugees after three years'.[54]

As there was no common definition of subsidiary protection at the moment of adoption of the Family Reunification Directive, this group doesn't fall within

51 See Mark Klaassen & Jorrit Rijpma, 'Vluchtelingencrisis, gezinsleven en het risico van een race to the bottom', *A&MR* 2016, nr. 6/7, p. 316 e.v. The CJEU in its recent judgment in the *Alo and Osso* case observed that from the recitals of Directive 2011/95 it is clear that "the EU legislature intended, in responding to the call of the Stockholm Programme, to establish a uniform status for all beneficiaries of international protection and that it accordingly chose to afford beneficiaries of subsidiary protection the same rights and benefits as those enjoyed by refugees, with the exception of derogations which are necessary and objectively justified". CJEU 1 March 2016, C-443/14, *Alo* and C-444/14, *Osso*, par. 32, ECLI:EU:C:2016:127.

52 996 der Beilagen zu den Stenographischen Protokollen des Nationalrates XXV. GP: <www.parlament.gv.at/PAKT/VHG/XXV/I/I_00996/fname_498905.pdf> [18 August 2016].

53 Migrationsverket, Legislative changes that will effect asylum seekers, 16 April 2016; Die Bundesregierung, Asylpakket II in Kraft: Kürzere Verfahren, weniger Familiennachzung, 17 March 2016.

54 Commissioner for Human Rights, Concept Note in the view of the Expert Brainstorming meeting on Family reunification for refugees, beneficiaries of other forms of international protection and asylum seekers, Strasbourg, 1 April 2016, prepared by Professor Kees Groenendijk.

its scope. And as the Directive has never been reviewed, this exclusion has not yet been lifted. But what could be the justification for treating those with subsidiary protection (among them many Syrians) in this regard differently from Convention Refugees? It seems as if the Member States are simply taking advantage of this legal loophole.

In the Netherlands, the total waiting period for family reunification may amount to two years. At the end of 2015, the Secretary of State announced that, it might take fifteen months before a decision on the asylum application was given. Moreover the Dutch Government decided to extend the time limit for deciding on family reunification for refugees to the maximum time limit in the Directive, which is nine months.[55] This race to the bottom with regard to the possibilities for family reunification is in contradiction with the harmonisation, equal treatment and protection aims of the CEAS. As a result it may take an unacceptably long time before the families of the refugees can join them. Some asylum seekers even return to dangerous situations out of concern for their family members left behind.

In the meantime, asylum seekers are more and more confronted with the anti-migrant actions of the extreme right and xenophobic and racist reactions. As the UN Secretary General stated in his report of 21 April 2016: 'I note with grave concern that xenophobic and racist responses to refugees and migrants seem to be reaching new levels of stridency, frequency and public acceptance…'.[56] So even after eventual access to the country of reception is granted to the refugees, it is far from guaranteed that they will be able to integrate within a friendly climate.

To conclude, even if there is access to the EU territory and even if there is access to an asylum procedure, access to justice in the sense of access to a fair and durable solution is not guaranteed at all.

## 12.7 How Can Access to Justice be Improved?

Firstly there should be access to the territory, which means a safe and, thus, legal pathway to Europe. This has been stressed by the UNHCR for years.[57]

---

55 Letter of the Dutch Secretary of State for Safety and Justice, Dijkhof, 27 November 2015, *TK* 2015–2016, nr. 19637, nr. 2086.

56 United Nations, General Assembly 21 April 2016, Seventieth session, In safety and dignity: addressing large movements of refugees and migrants, report of the Secretary-General, p. 11.

57 For example by António Guterres, Geneva 10 December 2014: High Commissioner's Dialogue on Protection Challenges, Protection at Sea. Opening remarks. See also UNHCR

It has subsequently been underlined by many others who also stress that this is the only way to combat human smuggling. Eduard Nazarski, director of the Dutch Section of Amnesty International has asked us to remember the Comprehensive Plan of Action, by which in 1989, 1.6 million Vietnamese boat refugees were saved. Why can't we make such a Comprehensive Plan of Action for the Syrians? It is not impossible, but it is a lack of will and solidarity and the fear that this will attract more asylum seekers to the EU than would otherwise come.[58] And why do we only focus on Syrians? We should not forget all the other asylum seekers. At least we should accept that people will keep coming and open the possibility for asylum seekers to apply for a visa to the EU and strive for resettlement of people who are staying in the overloaded camps in the region[59] and in third countries at the borders of the EU.

Secondly, access to a fair procedure should be guaranteed. As full implementation of the Procedures Directive was not achieved, it seems to be a good idea to replace it with a directly applicable Regulation (COM(2016)467 final). It can however be questioned whether the content of this Regulation will really contribute to improving access to justice for asylum seekers, if the proposed further acceleration of the procedures and the obligatory safe country provisions are accepted.

An improvement in access to justice for asylum seekers cannot be expected from the proposal of the European Commission for a new recast of the Dublin regulation.[60] The proposal is not based on solidarity; it sticks with the status quo and even contains an obligation to return and negative stimuli for asylum seekers as rights will be withheld if they decide to travel onward to another Member State. Furthermore it aims to conclude other agreements with transit countries comparable with the EU-Turkey deal without taking sufficiently into account the asylum seekers' perspective.[61]

The EU should also take the *Hirsi* judgment seriously and take responsibility if there is causality between a violation of the fundamental rights of asylum

---

General Assembly 21 April 2016 A/70/59: In safety and dignity: addressing large movements of refugees and migrants. Report of the Secretary-General.

58 Nazarski, E. (2016), 'De Vietnamezen gingen bijna zonder wanklank op in hun nieuwe landen', *Wordt Vervolgd*, maart, nr. 3.

59 Strik, T. (2016), Resettlement Report Council of Europe, UNHCR Projected Global resettlement Needs 2016: www.unhcr.org/53408c4fda.htlm.

60 Proposal for a Regulation establishing the criteria and mechanisms for determining the Member State responsible for examining an application for international protection lodged in one of the Member States by a third-country national or a stateless person (recast) Brussels, 4.5.2016 COM(2016)270 final.

61 COM(2016)270 final.

seekers in a third country, like Libya, or Turkey or Serbia, on the one hand, and a readmission agreement or other forms of push backs on the other hand. The proposal by the European Commission to make Union law applicable in cases of extraterritorial action by Frontex is hopeful.[62] Moreover, Europe should invest in research for alternatives in order to offer fair procedures. In my view, the proposals on joint processing within the EU are rather promising: the establishment of a migration protection agency at EU level with joint teams of officials (asylum expert teams) who have the power to take decisions on claims submitted to Member States (or to the EU as such).[63] This joint processing could be combined with the idea of hotspots. This, of course, requires a real, uniform and common procedure which includes lawyers and judges present at the hotspots, as well as adequate reception standards in open centres. It also requires that the EU takes responsibility for providing durable solutions to relocation for those whose requests have been positively decided, which means social inclusion and access to family reunification, education, work and free movement; and return of those whose requests have been refused, in order to avoid their staying in orbit around the hotspots.

The idea of joint processing in Europe is so much better than ideas about reception and eventual processing in the region. In the regions access to justice is a fairy tale. The idea of joint processing is not new. The UNHCR proposed it in 2003[64] and the EASO even started eight joint processing pilots in 2014.[65] But there still seems to be a lack of political will to join forces and competences.

---

62 European Commission, Strasbourg, 15.12.2015 COM(2015)671 final 2015/0310 (COD); Proposal for a regulation of the European Parliament and the Council on the European Border and Coast Guard and repealing Regulation (EC) No 2007/2004, Regulation (EC) No 863/2007 and Council Decision 2005/267/EC. Preambles 28 and 29.

63 Goodwinn Gill (2015), 'Regulating irregular' migration: international obligations and international responsibilities': keynote address at an international workshop, National and Kapodistrian University of Athens Faculty of Law, 20 March 2015, in: Goodwinn-Gill The Mediterranean Papers. See also Stockholm Programme 2009, 6.2.1.: the Council (…) invites the Commission to finalise its study on the feasibility and legal and practical implications to establish joint processing of asylum applications'.; Urth, H., M. Heegarard Bausager, H.M. Kuhn & J. Van Selm, 'Study on the legal and practical implications of establishing a mechanism for joint processing of asylum applications on the territory of the European Union', Rammboll and Eurasylum February 2013, HOME/2011?ERFX/FW/04; ACVZ 2016, *Delen in verantwoordelijkheid* (Sharing responsibilities; A proposal for a European Asylum System based on solidarity).

64 See UNHCR Working Paper 'UNHCR'S three-pronged proposal', UNHCR Geneva June 2003.

65 EASO Newsletter September 2015, 'establishment of 'hotspots'.

Finally, as the UN Secretary General stressed, migration and development are linked. There is therefore 'a need to strengthen the nexus between humanitarian and development assistance in responding to large movements of refugees and migrants. Humanitarian and development actors must work together towards achieving collective outcomes over multi-year periods on the basis of comparative advantage, particularly in situations of protracted displacement'. He also points to the need for changing the tenor of policy and public discourse on migrants and refugees.

> The tenor (…) must be shifted from one of threat to one of international solidarity, protection of dignity and recognition of positive contributions. Such efforts need to take address the fears and concerns of host communities, and they must be based on facts rather than assumptions and misinformation. Given the overwhelming evidence that personal contact significantly reduces prejudice, more creative ways of fostering contacts between host communities on the one hand and refugees and migrants on the other, are urgently needed.[66]

## 12.8 Conclusion

In conclusion, with regard to access to justice for asylum seekers in the EU, the problem is of course that in order to realise any alternative closer collaboration, more solidarity and acceptance of responsibilities for the externalisation of EU policies will be needed. And the EU is not in the mood for this. That is not only a pity, it is very unwise. In order to succeed, the Common European Asylum System should not remain black letter law, for law in action a true asylum seekers' perspective will be needed.

The conclusions above are all rather normative. With regard to my earlier remark that there should be a specific access to justice theory for asylum seekers I do not aim at a normative theory but at a theory based on the empirical findings that access to justice for asylum seekers is – in contrast with other fields of law – not a question of naming, blaming and claiming. Asylum seekers are confronted with other obstacles on the road to access to justice. The theory should seek to analyse and understand these obstacles. One of the explanations could be that asylum seekers are seen as a burden and that obstacles

66 United Nations, General Assembly 21 April 2016, Seventieth session, in safety and dignity: addressing large movements of refugees and migrants, report of the Secretary-General, p. 11.

are raised on purpose in order to prevent asylum seekers access to justice in Europe. Another explanation could be that asylum seekers are more and more regarded as a group instead of as individuals. Finally these obstacles could be understood by realising that asylum seekers who have not yet reached the EU are not seen as people with rights but as outsiders, not falling within the responsibilities of the EU. This is only meant as a starting point for a sociology of law theory of access to justice for asylum seekers, but it is clear that the current theories on access to justice can insufficiently explain the obstacles asylum seekers are confronted with if they seek protection against persecution.

## References

ACVZ 2016, *Delen in verantwoordelijkheid* (Sharing responsibilities; a proposal for a European asylum system based on solidarity), The Hague (NL): ACVZ.

BBC (2016), 'Migrant crisis: Austria to slash asylum claims', *BBC News*, 20 January.

Bruin, R., S. Kok & A. Terlouw (2016), 'Dublin, Interstatelijk vertrouwen is een fictie', *Justitiële Verkenningen*, pp. 3–15.

Carrera, S. & E. Guild (2016), 'EU-Turkey plan for handling refugees is fraught with legal and procedural challenges', *Thinking ahead for Europe*, CEPS 10 March.

Den Heijer, M. *et al.* (2016), 'Coercion, prohibition, and great expectations', *CMLR* June 2016 (translated in Dutch: *NJB*, nr. 24, p. 1672).

ECRE (2016), *Desk research on application of a safe third country and first country of asylum concepts to Turkey*, ECRE May.

Felstiner, W.F.L., R.L. Abel & A. Sarat (1981), 'The emergence and transformation of disputes: naming, blaming, claiming', *Law & Society Review* 1981, pp. 613–654.

Garlick, M. (2016), *Solidarity under strain. Solidarity and fair sharing of responsibility in law and practice for the international protection of refugees in the European Union*, (diss. Nijmegen), Mont-St-Guibert, (B): McPlan.

Gemund, H. van (2016), 'Medeverantwoordelijk voor meer dan 2,7 miljoen vluchtelingen, Europese column', *A&MR*, nr. 6/7, p. 351.

Goodwinn Gill, G. (2016), 'Regulating "irregular" migration: international obligations and international responsibilities': keynote address at an international workshop, National and Kapodistrian University of Athens Faculty of Law, 20 March 2015, in: G. Goodwinn-Gill, 'The Mediterranean Papers: Athens, Naples and Istanbul', *International Journal of Refugee Law* 28(2), pp. 276–309.

Guild, E. *et al.* (2015), *Enhancing CEAS and alternatives for Dublin*, Study for the LIBE Committee, July.

Heck, W. (2016), 'Erdogan: "EU komt deal niet na", klopt dat?', *NRC Handelsblad* 28 juli.

IOM (2016), *Fatal journeys volume 2: identification and tracing of dead and missing migrants*, IOM.

Klaassen, M. & J. Rijpma (2016), 'Vluchtelingencrisis, gezinsleven en het risico van een race to the bottom', *A&MR*, nr. 6/7, p. 316.

Kok, S. (2016), 'Hoe functioneert het Dublinsysteem? Over de weerbarstige praktijk', *A&MR*, nr. 6/7, p. 291–301.

Martínez, E.M. *et al.* (2014), 'Hot returns: when the state acts outside the law', Legal report <eprints.uc.es/27221>, 27 June.

Molder, R. te & L. Kampkuiper (2016), 'Frontex: is de grens bereikt?', *A&MR*, nr. 1, pp. 10–15.

Nazarski, E. (2016), 'De Vietnamezen gingen bijna zonder wanklank op in hun nieuwe landen', *Wordt Vervolgd*, maart, nr. 3.

Scholten, S. (2014), *Privatisation of immigration control? A socio-legal study on the role of private transport companies in the Netherlands and the United Kingdom*, (diss. Nijmegen), Ipskamp Drukkers.

Strik, M.H.A. (2015), 'Frontex de grenzen van zijn mandaat', *Justitiële Verkenningen*, nr. 3, pp. 47–56.

Strik, M.H.A. (2016), 'Gestrand in Griekenland', *A&MR*, nr. 6/7, p. 311.

UNHCR (2003), *UNHCR'S three-pronged proposal*, Working Paper, June, Geneva: UNHCR.

UNHCR (2016), *Legal considerations on the return of asylum-seekers and refugees from Greece to Turkey as part of the EU-Turkey cooperation in tackling the migration crisis under the safe third country and first country of asylum concept*, Geneva: UNHCR 23 March.

Urth, H., M. Heegarard Bausager, H.M. Kuhn & J. Van Selm (2013), *Study on the legal and practical implications of establishing a mechanism for joint processing of asylum applications on the territory of the European Union*, HOME/2011/ERFX/FW/04, Brussels: European Commsion.

Waslin, M. (2016), 'Access to legal representation is unequal and the consequences are serious' in: *immigration courts, right to council immigrants*, Paper submitted 28 September 2016.

CHAPTER 13

# Navigating Migration Policies in Europe: Insights from the Field

*Asuncion Fresnoza-Flot*

## 13.1 Introduction

In 2015, more than one million migrants arrived in Europe by crossing the Mediterranean Sea.[1] Most of them came from Syria, but there were also a considerable number of migrants who originated from Iraq and Afghanistan.[2] In the same year, more than 3,000 people lost their life in the sea during their crossing on the way to Europe.[3] Despite the dangers present in their paths, the high financial cost of their cross-border movement, and the tightened border controls in their desired country of destination, many people from war-stricken, politically unstable, and developing countries continue to embark on a migration journey towards Europe. How do these migrants succeed in overcoming the macro-level hurdles to their spatial mobility, notably the restrictive migration policies of many European countries? What are the impacts of these hurdles on their individual and familial lives?

The present chapter addresses these questions by examining the micro dimension of migration in Europe, that is, migrants' experiences of and interactions with state policies. Focusing on the perspectives of these social actors, this chapter aims to shed light on the governmentality of the state, i.e. the way it manages its population through the 'ensemble formed by the institutions, procedures, analyses and reflections, the calculations and tactics, that allow the exercise of this specific albeit complex form of power'.[4] It also intends to highlight the subjectivities that the governmentality of the state creates as well as the agency it entails among its subjects. Informed by the phenomenological approach to the study of social phenomena, this chapter argues that to grasp

1 UNHCR (2016), Refugees/migrants emergency response – Mediterranean. Regional overview, <data.unhcr.org/mediterranean/regional.php> [12 August 2016].

2 UNHCR (2016).

3 IOM (2016), *IOM Counts 3,771 Migrant Fatalities in Mediterranean in 2015*,<www.iom.int/news/iom-counts-3771-migrant-fatalities-mediterranean-2015> [12 August 2016].

4 Foucault, 1991, p. 102.

 | DOI 10.1163/9789004330467_014

state's power, logics, and limitations, it is important to look at not only the impact of state's actions on its subjects, but also how they respond to its instruments of governmentality such as policies. The idea behind this argument is that the relationship between the state and the people inhabiting its territory is neither static nor straightforward, but is continuously in the making and is mutually constructed.

To attain the objectives of this chapter, I scrutinize three types of movements from South-east Asia to Europe, namely maternal migration, marriage migration, and children migration.[5] I specifically examine the experiences of Filipino and Thai migrants residing in France and in Belgium, respectively. Contrary to refugees and asylum seekers from the Middle East and in Africa, who enter Europe by boat or by foot, these Southeast Asian migrants arrived by plane, as is the case of many migrants in the region. As Frontex data of 2016 show, international airports serve as 'one of the biggest entry routes for migrants into the European Union'. This is notably the case for Filipino and Thai migrants, given the geographical distance between their region of origin and Europe. These migrants are predominantly women, which sets them apart from asylum seekers in the region who are mostly young men.[6]

The ethnographic data presented in this chapter originated from three different studies that I conducted between 2004 and 2015: a doctoral research on Filipino migrant mothers in France and on their transnational families (2005–2008), a collaborative study on 1.5-generation Filipinos in France (2009–2015), and a postdoctoral project on children of Filipino and Thai migrants growing up in ethnically mixed families in Belgium (2012–2015). These qualitative studies were mainly based on observations and interviews of migrants and their family members. During the first study, 35 migrant mothers and 40 members of their families left in their country of origin were interviewed. For the second study, I interviewed 52 persons including 21 young people of the '1.5 generation' who migrated to their receiving country before reaching majority.[7] The third study relied on 142 interviews, including 19 Thai women. Despite their varying focus and objectives, these researches provide complementary insights about the power of state policies in structuring individual lives and aspirations as well as about the way individuals respond to its intricacies.

5 I refer here to the following countries that are members of the Association of Southeast Asian Nations (ASEAN): Brunei, Cambodia, Indonesia, Laos, Malaysia, Myanmar, Philippines, Singa-pore, Thailand, and Vietnam.

6 Eurostat, 2016.

7 Nagasaka & Fresnoza-Flot, 2015.

Before investigating the migration cases of Filipino and Thai migrants in Europe, I first position the present chapter within the migration studies literature focusing on how migrants respond to the governmentality of the state. After this, I explain the analytical framework of the chapter, and then describe the context within which the spatial movements of Southeast Asians take place. I conclude by reflecting on the emerging views of migrants about Europe, their agency as subjects of the state, and the importance of their perspectives.

## 13.2 Migrants' Agency in the Face of the State

Migration studies scholarship has documented through time the different phases, dimensions, and processes of life of migrants from varying viewpoints and perspectives. One of the most widely held approaches is one that values migrants' points of view and examines their lived experiences of migration.[8] The works in this line of thought reveal how migrants interact with the states of their country of origin and/or immigration[9] by living with, navigating, or contesting their policies, notably migration-related ones.

Living with migration policies means not attempting to counter them, although it does not imply accepting them or agreeing with them. For instance, under the sponsorship (*kafala*) system in many countries in the Middle East, employers keep the travel documents of migrant domestic workers, thereby restricting their spatial and professional mobilities.[10] Despite being tied to their labour contract, many migrants find a way to survive with-in this system. However, when their working and living conditions become intolerable for them, they escape their employers and look for another employment in the domestic service sector.[11] Others escape when they are brought abroad during their employer's travel and become undocumented migrants.[12] In both cases, the *kafala* system remains unaffected. Migrants in these cases may appear as 'powerless victims', but their way of living with migration policies is often a strategy in itself to attain their personal objectives, such as supporting economically their families in their countries of origin. We can also cite the example of people

8 E.g., the classic work of Thomas & Znaniecki, 1958.

9 Basch *et al.*, 1994; Sayad, 1999.

10 Bajracharya & Sijapati, 2012.

11 Pande, 2013.

12 Anderson, 2000; Fresnoza-Flot, 2009.

who 'settled in mobility'[13] due to their legal statuses in two or more countries.[14] They learn to live with the migration policies of these countries, thereby gaining mobility and economic opportunities.

Navigating the law is another response of migrants to state policies, notably restrictive ones. Similar to the first approach, it does not involve contestations. Nevertheless, it is about following and using policies to realize one's personal aims. One example is the case of irregular migrants in Europe. They are well aware that they do not have the 'legal right' to stay in their receiving countries, and they follow this line of thought by staying away as much as possible from the eyes of the authorities while waiting an amnesty or a possibility to regularize their situation. Many work in the domestic service sector[15] and do not participate in undocumented migrants' movement.[16] Making themselves socially invisible is how they navigate the law. Another example is marriage migrant Filipinas in Japan, whose legal status depends on their marriage with their Japanese husband, or if they divorce, on their Japanese children. Many of these women are able to continue staying legally in the country by deciding not to divorce their husbands but instead to run away from their problematic conjugal relationships.[17]

Finally, migrants react to policies by contesting them, mostly through collective mobilizations and protests. A rich literature on this topic shows its transnational character. For instance, migrant domestic workers' activism has challenged many discriminatory policies concerning their labour and living conditions.[18] One of its successes is the signing of the Domestic Workers Convention (no. 189) in 2011 by the International Labour Organisation, which specifies the rights of domestic workers and provides them legal protection. At the national level, domestic workers in Hong Kong remain very active in their associations. The Internet offers possibilities to these migrants to communicate their grievances, reveals their predicament, and call for a change in policies affecting their lives. Contesting the state is the obvious way of responding to state policies, its power, and hegemony. While many migrants are living with or navigating policies, at some point of the migratory process some of them become tired and start to be vocal and fight for their rights. We observe

13 Morokvasic, 2004.
14 See also Michalon, 2003.
15 Kilkey, Lutz & Palenga-Möllenbeck, 2010; Shinozaki, 2015.
16 Fresnoza-Flot, 2010.
17 Faier, 2009.
18 E.g., Anderson, 2001; Schwenken, 2003; Sim, 2009.

this among migrant Filipinas in France (notably irregular migrants) who have started to join labour unions in the country.[19]

Based on these migrants' responses to the state, it is evident that they do have different ways of expressing their agency. Their living with, navigating, or contesting policies may take place one at a time or overlap with one another during the migration process. Nonetheless, it is unclear how connected these responses are to migrants' views about the state and family lives, which this chapter attempts to elucidate.

## 13.3 The State and Its Subjects: A Phenomenological Approach[20]

A social phenomenon such as migration is imbedded in unequal power relationships. In order to understand it, we need to identify the key players concerned and the dynamics of their interactions. In the context of migration, these key actors are the state and (potential) migrants, the interconnectedness of which can be highlighted using a phenomenological approach stressing the links between individuals and their 'life world' as well as the latter's subjective experiences.[21] This implies looking at what and how the top (the *state*) thinks about or does concerning the bottom (the *people*), and the other way around.

Starting from the top, we observe at least two tendencies among European states. On the one hand, the tendency to establish and reinforce an 'immobility regime' generally characterizes the so-called 'enclave societies'.[22] 'Enclavement' in this regime is a state's 'primary expression of sovereignty in excluding aliens without and undesirables within'.[23] In the European 'immobility regime', it takes the form of segregation (e.g., refugee camps), containment, and detention. As states exercise their power through their respective regime of immobility, they create what the Italian philosopher Giorgio Agamben calls 'spaces of exception',[24] in which people with 'bare life' are treated as not worthy of basic human rights and of the privilege of being recognized as one of 'us'. 'Bare life' implies being excluded from all forms of life (the *bios*) and of the natural

19 Ito, 2015.

20 Some parts of this section are drawn from a paper that I presented during the international seminar "Towards a European theological ethics of migration and its implications for Catholic social thought" at the Katholieke Universiteit Leuven (Belgium) on 31 October 2015.

21 Ritzer & Goodman, 2004.

22 Turner, 2007.

23 Turner, 2007, p. 295.

24 Agamben, 1998.

life (the *zoë*). The deaths of those migrants during their attempts to cross the Mediterranean Sea to reach Europe illustrate what 'bare life' means. On the other hand, the states also tend to engage in the 'disciplining of mobility'.[25] Through their governmentality, they attempt to create 'ideal' subjects who control themselves and conform to what is legally expected from them.[26] From this perspective, we can say that a system of 'compensation' and 'punishment' is put in place to reinforce such disciplining.[27] For those who abide and become disciplined subjects, the reward comes in the form of entry visa, residence permits, access to citizenship, and other entitlements. On the contrary, those who disobey and are caught become often criminalized for their lack of legal migration documents (e.g., detention and imprisonment), barred from access to many social entitlements, or kicked out of the political community (e.g., deportation).

Alongside these two tendencies, we also observe in Europe how migrants as legal subjects face different migration and 'immobility' regimes and find alternative routes (notably irregular) to realize their migration projects. This behaviour of migrants does not appear out of the blue, but is rather fashioned by their knowledge of how the system in place works and what are the gaps within it that may serve as spaces of contestation and empowerment. In short, these migrants possess 'legal consciousness', that is, are able to understand and interpret the laws governing them.[28] This consciousness shapes human 'tactics', called la *perruque* (the wig) by the French philosopher Michel de Certeau.[29] Tactics are individual moves and actions seen from the outside as non-deviant and obeying the established rules and norms. They are means to dance with the flow but with an objective different from what outsiders believe. In this chapter, I pay attention to migrants' legal consciousness and to their tactics to illuminate the relationality between their behaviour and the actions of the state.

## 13.4 The Southeast Asia-Europe Migration Corridor

Dynamic migratory waves from Southeast Asia to Europe have taken place since the breakdown of the European colonial power in the region. Many

25 Pécoud, 2012.
26 Pécoud, 2012.
27 Foucault, 1997.
28 Ewick & Silbey, 1998.
29 De Certeau, 1988.

Vietnamese, Indonesians, and Filipinos mi-grated to their countries' former colonial administrators: France, the Netherlands, and Spain, respectively. During the Cold War years, Vietnamese refugees settled in European countries, particularly the UK and the Czech Republic. Since the 1980s, a feminine migratory wave has started to reinforce the links between Southeast Asia and Europe.

This women-dominated movement has been oriented towards the reproductive markets (labour and marriage),[30] wherein Filipino and Thai women occupy important places and play a key role in their reinforcement. In 2012, there were 768,326 Filipinos in Europe, which represents 7.3% of the total Filipino migrant population in the world (CFO, 2013). On the same year, the Thai Ministry of Foreign Affairs reported 249,855 Thais living or working in Europe, representing 24% of the 1,039,032 Thais abroad.[31] Filipino women usually arrived in the region to look for work and other economic opportunities. They are mainly concentrated in the service sector where they work as nannies, caregivers, and health professionals. On the other hand, Thai women generally migrated to Europe as brides or spouses of European men.[32] There are also women who entered Europe to work in massage parlours, bars, or restaurants. The movement of Filipino and Thai women to Europe has been part of their respective countries' migration regimes, which focus on the exportation of labour. These migration regimes became explicit in the Philippines in early 1970s when a labour migration programme was introduced and in Thailand in early 1980s when a similar programme was put forth in the country's Fifth Economic Development Plan. In the 1980s the Philippines observed the feminisation of its migration outflows, whereas Thailand experienced the same thing in the 1990s.[33] Unlike Thailand, the Philippine state established different agencies to promote, manage, facilitate, and control the outflow of its migrant workers. The state has also liberalized the labour exportation market, which has led to the emergence of the so-called 'black market of emigration' composed of private migration agencies.[34] These actors play an important role in concretizing the migration projects of individuals and families in the Philippines.

Concerning marriage migration, Germany and the UK are the leading destinations of Filipinos,[35] whereas Germany is the major receiving country of

30 There is also a dynamic student migration from Southeast Asia to Europe, and the United Kingdom is one of its popular destination countries.

31 Kanchanachitra *et al.*, 2014.

32 Suksomboon, 2009; Ruenkaew, 2003.

33 Kang, 2012.

34 Massey *et al.*, 2005.

35 CFO, 2014.

Thais.[36] Meeting and marriages between these women and men of economically developed countries (such as in Europe) are facilitated by their social networks, by technological means of communication such as the Internet, by the increased availability of low-cost ways of transportation, and by matchmaking agencies.[37] In the Philippines, the state regulates its citizens' international marriages and relationships by prohibiting the so-called 'Mail-Order Bride' (MOB) marriages, by its anti-trafficking measures, and by organizing Pre-Departure Orientation Seminars (PDOS)[38] for departing Filipino brides and spouses of foreign nationals. In Thailand, there is no law prohibiting specific MOB marriages, but the government has adopted anti-trafficking measures to protect women and children. Although there is no such thing as PDOS in Thailand, the government in collaboration with non-governmental organisations and Thai migrant women abroad has held awareness-raising activities about the possible difficulties of getting married with a *farang* (foreigner).[39] With the aim of discouraging young girls and women who are wishing to marry one day a *farang*, these activities mainly take place in the Northeast of Thailand, where many marriage migrants originate from.

Furthermore, the Southeast Asia-Europe migration corridor does not only involve one directional movement from the former to the latter, but also include a reverse flow. In the Philippines and Thailand, British and German nationals are more numerous than nationals of other countries.[40] Although these migration flows are also dynamic and display interesting characteristics, the present chapter concentrates on the Southeast Asia-to-Europe migration direction.

## 13.5 Accessing Europe: The Ways and Means of the Subaltern

The regimes of immobility and the disciplining of mobility in Europe do not automatically create immobile subjects. As shown below, Filipino and Thai

36 Kanchanachitra *et al.*, 2014.

37 Fresnoza-Flot & Ricordeau, forthcoming.

38 This pre-departure orientation seminar is country-specific and departing migrant domestic workers are obliged to take part in it to obtain socio-cultural knowledge about their receiving country and other practical information. Young migrants aged between 13 and 19, on the other hand, are required to attend the Peer Counselling Seminar instead.

39 Information about these awareness-raising activities came from my interview in 2014 with one Thai migrant woman from the Netherlands who actively took part in it.

40 Asis & Battistella, 2014; Kanchanachitra *et al.*, 2014.

migrants mostly navigate the law rather than living with or contesting it. This response to state policies requires both legal consciousness and tactics.

### 13.5.1 *The Tourist Visa Route via the 'black market of migration': The Case of Filipino Mothers*

Maternal migration is one of the dynamic migratory outflows from Southeast Asia (specifically from the Philippines) to Europe. It is composed of lone mothers who left their families (children and husband) in their countries of origin and came to work in the domestic service sector, generally to fulfil the basic needs of their family and to support the schooling of their children.[41]

This is for example the case of Francisca, 60 years old and mother of four. I met her in Paris where she was working as a home cleaner and she told me during her interview the reason why she had decided to migrate to France.

> Because of the eruption of the Pinatubo, I decided to go abroad at that time [1991]. I told to myself 'if I don't go abroad [to work], nothing will happen to us' [...] I said 'how about my children? They will not be able to study if I don't go abroad.

Francisca arrived in Paris in 1991 with a tourist visa through the help of an illegal migration agency disguised as a travel agency in the Philippines. She knew that there was no other way to reach France than through a tourist visa. Like other Filipino migrants, Francisca sought assistance from the 'black market of migration'.[42] She paid 80,000 pesos (about 1,500 euros) to a disguised travel agency that took care of her visa, airplane tickets, and accommodation on her way to France. She was part of a group that first did tourism in Casablanca, then went to Germany, and finally to Amsterdam from where they proceeded to their final destination country. Francisca chose France and took the train to go to Paris to meet a Filipino friend there who offered her place to stay and later helped her find a job. Francisca's reliance on a travel agency facilitated her legal entry in Europe, a tactic that helped her overcome the bureaucratic hurdles to migration. What facilitated Francisca's settlement in France were her ethnic networks, a social capital that provided her with housing and employment opportunities. In France, once her visa expired Francisca became an irregular migrant. Because of her status, she was not able to visit her children

41 Fresnoza-Flot, 2013; see also Mozère, 2005.

42 Massey *et al.*, 2005.

back home during ten years. She shared with me her experience with the French migration regime:

> My [regularization] application was not granted in 1998 because I lacked some papers. Since I just needed a few more years to reach my ten years [of residence in France], I decided not to return yet but to wait for the ten years.

What she meant here by 'ten years' was the required length of residence in France to be able to apply for regularization under the former Chevènement Law. During my fieldworks in France between 2005 and 2013, I met many Filipino migrant mothers who had adopted this tactic of staying without going back for ten years or more in order to be regularized, at which time they became able to work legally and to visit their family regularly in their home country. The emerging pattern of their responses to state policies is that they navigate them through the tourist visa route and via the tactic of staying for years without ever going back to their country, in the hope of being regularised. The lives of these migrants were shaped by the migration policy of their receiving country in Europe. Maternal migration results in longer family separation because of this state policy that influences migrant mothers' decision to prolong their stay in order to secure economic resources.

### 13.5.2 *The 'intimate' Route: The Case of Thai Migrant Women*

As explained earlier, another strong migratory wave from Southeast Asia to Europe is marriage migration. Aside from Filipino women, many Thais come to this region to look for a partner, to get married, or to legally cohabit with their European partner. The two tales below of Thai migrant women in Belgium demonstrate the role of this 'intimate route' to enter and settle in Europe.

The first tale narrates how Thai women use binational union, in the form of marriage or legal co-residence, to stay in migration. Migrating to Europe through the work channel appears difficult for Thais. According to Kanchanachitra and colleagues,[43] 'the proportion of Thai workers' in Europe compared to that in Asia 'is not high due to laws and regulations and labour demand of the destination countries as well as the mismatch between available work and the workers' qualifications'. Binational union before or after one's entry to Europe has become a popular migration channel these days for Thai women. For example, Pailin (60 years old at the time of the interview) arrived

43 Kanchanachitra *et al.*, 2014.

as a tourist in Belgium in 1989 to meet a Belgian man that her Thai friend had sent her a picture of:

> I came with my [Thai woman] friend here. […] I only saw his [her present husband's] photo. My friend showed it to me. She said 'he's a good man' and yeah I believed her.

Though Pailin did not know well the man, she decided to tie the knot with him as her Thai friend vouched for the man's good character. Thanks to her marriage with this man, Pailin did not need to return to Thailand after her tourist visa expired. Pailin's story is not exceptional, as more and more Thai women are arriving in Europe with a tourist visa then look for a prospective partner to extend their stay in the country. This tactic of using first the tourist visa channel resembles that of Filipino migrant mothers in France. What differentiates the two groups from each other is that Thais tend to adopt the tactic of immediately looking for a partner in order to prolong their legal stay in Belgium, whereas Filipinos, notably adults, become irregular mi-grants then try to avoid police arrest and deportation by concentrating in the domestic service sector. Their paid work in this sector invisibilizes them in some way, as they exercise it in the home of their employers. They then wait for regularization opportunities to legalize their migration status.

A Thai friend of mine narrated to me a second tale when we were talking about Thai women's migration to Belgium. It tells the story of a Thai woman married to a Belgian who went to Finland to meet a prospective 'next' partner through the matchmaking effort of her Thai friend who was already living there. The arrangement was that she would date the man during three days and at the end she would decide whether to pursue a relationship with him or not. This story suggests how binational union formation has become an effective means of not only prolonging one's migration in Europe, but also of legitimizing one's presence in the region. This practice is shaped by the awareness of Thai women of the difficulty to uphold their legal status in Europe, particularly when their binational union on which this status depends breaks down. As Williams remarks:[44]

> local policies set the tone for the interaction of migrant spouses with the general population. The attitudes of society in general are influenced by the citizenship policies of the state, and most spouses crossing borders experience a probationary period short of citizenship during

44 Williams, 2010, p. 191.

> which their connection to their citizen partners and families grants them their rights.

Thai women's experience of this 'probationary period' made them conscious of their un-stable legal status in their receiving country and of the importance of being closely connected to an insider citizen to gain stability in one's status. Living together with an insider citizen appears to be a viable solution for these migrants to address the legal insecurity they are feeling. Besides, the relationship between insider men citizen and migrant women are most often seen by the court as less risky that that between a woman citizen and a migrant man.[45] Taking the 'intimate' route to access and settle in Europe represents Thai women's way to navigate the strict migration policies in the region.

### 13.5.3 *The Tourist Visa Route via the Schengen Space: The Case of Filipino Migrant Children*

Migration of children from Southeast Asia to Europe takes place side-by-side with the migratory movements of adults. These young people usually migrate with or following their parents. This is the case of 1.5-generation Filipino children who experienced 'mobile childhoods',[46] meaning spatial, temporal and contextual movements during their child-hood years due to the migration of one or more members of their family or due to their own migration. Movements across contexts refer to migrant children's experiences of changes from one familial arrangement to another, from one school system to another, or from one legal framework to another.

This happened to Tina, a 20-year-old university student in Paris. She was five years old when her mother went to France using the tourist visa route, and it was her father who took care of her and her sister. Three years after, her father decided to follow her mother to France, again through the tourist visa channel. This time, her maternal grandparents acted as caregivers for her and her sister. When Tina was diagnosed with a congenital heart disease, her parents decided to make her come to France to be treated there. Since her parents were irregular migrants, they used the tourist visa route in Schengen space for their daughter to come to France:

> What I knew is that my parents had no papers at that time [2004]. So, my mother's friend in Sweden who had I think Swedish nationality was

45 De Hart, 2009.

46 Fresnoza-Flot & Nagasaka, 2015.

> the one who invited me. I arrived in Sweden and after that I came here to France by airplane. It was legal because I had a Schengen visa.

The difficulty to regularize one's migration status in France for undocumented migrants and to meet the requirements of the family reunion program for regular migrants leads many Filipino parents like Tina's to choose the tourist visa route via the Schengen space for their children.[47] Migrant parents hope that by using this route, their children will be able to legally enter in France and live with them there. Knowing how difficult it is to obtain a tourist visa at the French embassy in the Philippines, many Filipino parents turn to other Schengen country to realize their family reunion project. This tactic obviously stems from their legal consciousness that one can travel easily within the Schengen area using a tourist visa obtained in one Schengen country. At that time when she arrived in France at the age of fifteen, Tina had been separated for ten years from her migrant mother and for seven years from her migrant father. Asked whether she was happy about the family reunification, she confided that she actually did not like to migrate to France:

> I actually didn't like to come here, because all of my friends were in the Philippines. My grandmother was also there with me. I was used to be with her. I didn't like to leave her. That's why when I arrived here, my parents really had a hard time with me.

Tina's involuntary migration can partly explain her conflictual relation with her parents, notably with her mother. Filipino migrant parents' decision to make their children follow them in France is shaped by their legal consciousness that in their receiving country minors can access schooling and health care without fearing deportation, unlike undocumented adult migrants. However, when children reach majority, they experience the same feeling of insecurity as their parents due to their irregular migration status. In the migration of Filipino 1.5-generation children, familial-context mobility takes place as children find themselves in a new family arrangement, being reunited with their parents after long years of separation. These children also experience political-context mobility, as they be-come aware of what visa, residence permits, citizenship, and irregularity mean when they migrate to their receiving country. They also undergo downward social class mobility, as they lived in a comfortable life in the Philippines thanks to their parents' remittances and then suddenly find

47 This area is composed of 26 European countries including France and Belgium (see: <ec.europa.eu/dgs/home-affairs/what-we-do/policies/borders-and-visas/schengen>).

themselves living in the small apartment of their parents who are working in the domestic service sector in France. Generational irregularity is common among Filipino migrants in this country, attesting to the structuring power of state's governmentality across generations of migrants.

What is interesting in the case of Filipino migrant children is that it is their parents and not them who prepared and chose the route to take to enter Europe. It is their parents who navigate the law for them, which can be attributed to their desire for family reunification and to their awareness of the legal framework in Europe, how it works, and how to use it to their advantage. De facto tourism is a sort of camouflage of their real intention, which is family reunification. Through their adopted tactics, Filipino migrants are able to navigate the law but cannot avoid the undesirable consequences of their migration such as family separation and long-term irregular migration status.

## 13.6 Discussion and Conclusion

The cases examined in this chapter provide interesting insights on how Filipino and Thai migrants succeed in overcoming the hurdles imposed by migration policies to their movement to Europe and the way those obstacles affect their lives. This suggests that migrants and the state are closely interlinked and the way they behave appear to result from their dynamic interactions.

As their response to migration policies, the migrants in this chapter adopt tactics to navigate them but not to contest or live with them. This can be partly explained by the logic of their migration, which is mostly family-related as it aims to support their family back home (in the case of Filipinos) or to form their own family (in the case of Thais). By navigating the law, they maximize their chance to attain their desired objectives in a minimal amount of time. Their legal consciousness guide them how to do so, which results in different tactics such as using the tourist visa route to access Europe and getting involved in binational union with an insider citizen. The behaviour of Filipino and Thai migrants vis-à-vis migration policies suggests that they view the state as a powerful entity with a system of rewards and punishments. Their chosen response of navigating the law is their discrete way to turn the governmentality of the state to their own advantage. However, they could not impede its strong impact on their familial lives such as long family separation, parent-child emotional gap, and mobile childhoods among their children. This represents the limitation of their capacity to deal with the state and its policies that continuously structure their possibilities, aspirations, and tactics.

At the macro-level, the case studies presented here show that the countries of origin and of destination of migrants such as Filipinos and Thais play very important roles in shaping the Southeast Asian migration corridor. The influence of state policies 'here' and 'there' is well illustrated by the alternative channels, tourist visa, or binational union formation that potential migrants or migrants' family members take to reach Europe. Restrictions 'here' and 'there' often collide with labour market demands in the domestic service sector, which creates spaces of opportunities for migrants such as Filipinos who despite their irregular migration status are able to remain in Europe and later have their children reunite with them. The cases of Filipino and Thai migrants are examples of how the 'disciplining of mobility'[48] in Europe creates certain groups of obedient subjects who take legal migration routes to enter Europe. These routes entail expensive migration fees, family separation, and long periods of irregular status in the receiving country, and are continuously alimented by the 'black market of migration',[49] the existence of which attests to the power of human agency over constraining structures.

Nowadays, states in the EU are responding back to migrants' tactics as we can observe from their actions to prevent irregular migration and how they deal with the present refugee crisis. Taking into account voices from below or the voices of those De Certeau calls 'ordinary people' appears important in policy-making. The states and their subjects are in a continuous positioning in relation to each other, a repeated and dynamic process during which ethical, human rights, and security issues may collide. The question is what happens next when migrants (regular or irregular) settle in their receiving country in Europe. Some migrants do succeed to socially integrate themselves in their country of immigration through labour market participation or 'mixed' family formation with their European partners. Nevertheless, in terms of political participation, some migrants remain 'lost in integration', as they struggle to obtain residence permits, master the language of their receiving country, or confront negative stereotypes and discriminatory attitudes of the majority population. The challenge to be socially incorporated is obviously different from that to enter their destination country, but the repercussions on migrants' well-being appear the same. The case studies examined in this paper suggest that the success of the state's 'disciplining of mobility'[50] and its 'regime of immobility'[51] lies not in creating and reinforcing borders and control, but in understanding the way its subjects react to such disciplining, how it affects their lives (notably in the long term), and how they respond to it.

48 Pécoud, 2012.
49 Massey *et al.*, 2005.
50 Pécoud, 2012.
51 Turner, 2007.

## References

Agamben, G. (1998), *Homo sacer: sovereign power and bare life*, Stanford (Cal.): Stanford California Press.

Anderson, B. (2000), *Doing the dirty work? The global politics of domestic labour*, London: Zed Books.

Anderson, B. (2001), 'Different roots in common ground: transnationalism and migrant domestic workers in London', *Journal of Ethnic and Migration Studies*, 27(4), pp. 673–683.

Asis, M. & G. Battistella (2014), 'Flows and patterns of temporary transnational migration: the Philippine case', in: P. Pitkänen & M. Korpela (eds), *Characteristics of temporary transnational migration. Collected working papers from the EURA-NET project*, Tampere, Finland: University of Tampere, pp. 267–296.

Bajracharya, R. & B. Sijapati (2012), *The kafala system and its implications for Nepali domestic workers*, Policy Brief 2012/1, Kathmandu (Nepal): Centre for the study of labour and mobility.

Basch, L.G., N. Glick Schiller & C. Szanton Blanc (1994), *Nations unbound. Transnational projects, postcolonial predicaments, and deterritorialized nation-states*, Langhorne (Phi.): Gordon and Breach.

De Hart, B. (2009), 'Love thy neighbour: family reunification and the rights of insiders', *European Journal of Migration and Law*, 11(3), pp. 235–252.

CFO (2014), 'Number of Filipino spouses and other partners of foreign nationals by sex: 1989–2013', <www.cfo.gov.ph/images/stories/pdf/gender8913.pdf> [30 November 2014].

CFO (2013), 'Stock estimate of overseas Filipinos as of December 2012', <www.cfo.gov.ph/images/statistics/stock_estimate/StockEstimate2012.pdf> [12 August 2016].

De Certeau, M. (1988), *The practice of everyday life*, Berkeley: University of California Press.

Ewick, P. & S. Silbey (1998), *The common place of law: stories from everyday life*, Chicago: University of Chicago Press.

Eurostat (2016), 'Asylum statistics', <ec.europa.eu/eurostat/statistics-explained/index.php/Asylum_statistics> [12 August 2016].

Faier, L. (2009), *Intimate encounters: Filipina migrants remake rural Japan*, Berkeley: University of California Press.

Fresnoza-Flot, A. (2009), 'Le rôle de l'Église et des associations dans la structuration de la population immigrée philippine en France' [The role of the Church and associations in structuring the Filipino immigrant population in France], *Migrations Société*, 21(123–124), pp. 65–82.

Fresnoza-Flot, A. (2013), *Mères migrantes sans frontières. La dimension invisible de l'immigration philippine en France* [Migrant mothers without borders. The invisible dimension of Filipino immigration to France], Paris: L'Harmattan.

Fresnoza-Flot, A. (2010), 'The catholic church in the lives of irregular migrant Filipinas in France: identity formation, empowerment and social control', *The Asia Pacific Journal of Anthropology*, 11(3–4), pp. 345–336.

Fresnoza-Flot, A. (2015), 'A secular viewpoint on the expert seminar', Paper presented at the seminar *Towards a European theological ethics of migration and its implications for Catholic social thought,* Katholieke Universiteit Leuven, 31 October.

Fresnoza-Flot, A. & I. Nagasaka (2015), 'Conceptualizing childhoods in transnational families: the 'mobile childhoods' lens', in: I. Nagasaka & A. Fresnoza-Flot (eds), *Mobile childhoods in Filipino transnational families. Children of immigrants with similar roots in different routes*, Basingstoke: Palgrave Macmillan, pp. 23–41.

Fresnoza-Flot, A. & G. Ricordeau (forthcoming), *International marriages and marital citizenship: Southeast Asian women on the move*, Abingdon: Routledge.

Foucault, M. (1991), 'Governmentality', in: G. Burchell, C. Gordon & P. Miller (eds), *The foucault effect: studies in governmentality*, Chicago: The University of Chicago Press, pp. 87–104.

Foucault M. (1997), *'Il faut défendre la société', Cours au Collège de France 1975–1976* ['We must defend the society', Lectures at the College of France], Paris: Seuil/Gallimard.

Frontex (2016), *Migratory routes map 26 January*, <frontex.europa.eu/trends-and-routes/migratory-routes-map> [15 February 2016].

IOM (2016), *IOM Counts 3,771 Migrant Fatalities in Mediterranean in 2015*, <www.iom.int/news/iom-counts-3771-migrant-fatalities-mediterranean-2015> [12 August 2016].

Ito, R. (2015), 'Negotiating partial citizenship under neoliberalism: regularization struggles among Filipino domestic workers in France (2008–2012)', *International Journal of Japanese Sociology*, 25, pp. 69–84.

Kanchanachitra, M., N. Sakkarin & P. Sureeporn (2014), 'Characteristic features of temporary migration to and from Thailand', in: P. Pitkänen & M. Korpela (eds), *Characteristics of temporary transnational migration. Collected working papers from the EURA-NET project*, Tampere, Finland: University of Tampere, pp. 270–291.

Kang, X. (2012), 'Migration policies of Thai nationals abroad and evaluation of migration policy effect', First Thai-Chinese strategic research seminar, 24–26 August, Bangkok.

Kilkey, M., H. Lutz & E. Palenga-Möllenbeck (2010), 'Introduction: domestic and care work at the intersection of welfare, gender and migration regimes: some European experiences', *Social Policy and Society*, 9(3), pp. 379–384.

Massey, D., J. Durand & N.J. Malone (2005), 'Principles of operation: theories of international migration', M. Suárez-Orozco, C. Suárez-Orozco & D.B. Qin (eds), *The new immigration. An interdisciplinary reader*, New York and East Sussex: Brunner-Routledge, pp. 21–33.

Michalon, B. (2003), 'Circuler entre Roumanie et Allemagne' Les Saxons de Transylvanie, de l'émigration ethnique au va-et-vient. *Balkanologie*, VII(1): pp. 19–42.

Morokvasic, M. (2004), 'Settled in mobility: engendering post-wall migration in Europe', *Feminist Review*, 77, pp. 7–25.

Mozère, L. (2005), 'Filipina women as domestic workers in Paris. A transnational labour market enabling the fulfilment of a life project?', in: E. Spaan, F. Hillmann & T. van Naerssen (eds), *Asian migrants and European labour markets. Patterns and processes of immigrant labour market insertion in Europe*, Oxon: Routledge, pp. 177–194.

Pande, A. (2013), '"The paper that you have in your hand is my freedom": migrants domestic work and the sponsorhip (kafala) system in Lebanon', *International Migration Review*, 47(2), pp. 414–441.

Pécoud, A. (2012), 'Introduction: disciplining the transnational mobility of people', in: M. Geiger & A. Pécoud (eds), *Disciplining the transnational mobility of people*, Basingstoke: Palgrave Macmillan, pp. 1–14.

Ritzer, G. & D.J. Goodman (2004), *Modern sociological theory*, New York: McGraw-Hill.

Ruenkaew, P. (2003), *Heirat nach Deutschland. Motive und Hintergründe thäiländisch-deutscher Eheschließungen* [Marriage to Germany. Motives and backgrounds of Thai-German marriages], Frankfurt: Campus Verlag.

Sayad, A. (1999), *La double absence: des illusions de l'émigré aux souffrances de l'immigré* [The double absence: From emigrant's illusions to immigrant's sufferings], Paris: Seuil.

Schwenken, H. (2003), 'RESPECT for all: female migrant domestic workers in the European Union', *Refuge*, 21(3), pp. 45–52.

Shinozaki, K. (2015), *Migrant citizenship from below. Family, domestic work, and social activism in irregular migration,* New York: Palgrave Macmillan.

Sim, A. (2009), 'Women versus the state: organizing resistance and contesting exploitation in Indonesian labor migration to Hong Kong', *Asian and Pacific Migration Journal*, 18(1), pp. 47–75.

Suksomboon, P. (2009), Thai migrant women in the Netherlands: cross cultural marriages and families, dissertation Leiden, Ede: Ponsen & Looijen.

Thomas, W.I. & F. Znaniecki (1958), *The Polish peasant in Europe and America,* New York: Dover Publications.

Turner, B. (2007), 'The enclave society: towards a sociology of immobility', *European Journal of Social Theory*, 10(2), pp. 287–303.

UNHCR (2016), *Refugees/migrants emergency response – Mediterranean. Regional overview*, <data.unhcr.org/mediterranean/regional.php> [12 August 2016].

Williams, L. (2010), *Global marriage. Cross-border marriage migration in global context*, London: Palgrave Macmillan.

CHAPTER 14

# Brexit: Free Movement of Union Citizens and the Rights of Third-Country Nationals under Threat?

*Kees Groenendijk*

## 14.1 Introduction

The outcome of the Brexit referendum on 23 June 2016 created a shock in the UK and in other Member States. The immediate and long-term effects on the capacity of nationals of all 28 current Member States to move to and stay in other Member States became the subject of personal worries and public debate. Suddenly, free movement to and from Britain was no longer self-evident. The outcome of the forthcoming negotiations on the conditions of the Brexit will remain unknown for months or years. The outcome of the negotiations between the UK and the other Member States and the dubious position of several EU institutions during those negotiations, all intended to avoid a Brexit, most probably will never achieve the force of law. Nevertheless, the texts agreed may well influence the development of free movement law in the years to come.

On 19 February 2016 the Heads of State and Government of the 28 Member States, "meeting within the European Council", agreed on a Decision concerning "a new settlement for the United Kingdom within in the EU". The text of the Decision was published as an Annex to the conclusions of the European Council.[1] The Decision is an informal agreement between the 28 Member States aiming at changing elements of Union law without amending the Treaties. The Decision is a piece of international law not an instrument of Union law. Hence, the Court of Justice cannot rule on the validity of the Decision, but it may be asked to rule on the compatibility of some of the changes agreed with the Treaties. The Decision provides in Section E that it "shall take effect on the same date as the Government of the United Kingdom informs the Secretary-General of the Council that the United Kingdom has decided to remain a member of the European Union". Considering that a majority of the British voters in the referendum on 23 June 2016 voted to leave the EU, it is highly unlikely that this condition will be fulfilled. Most probably, the agreement formulated in the February 2016 Decision will never enter into force. Nevertheless, the Decision

1 EUCO (European Council document) 10/16 of 19 February 2016, pp. 8–37.

 | DOI 10.1163/9789004330467_015

may have far-reaching political, constitutional, legal and practical consequences within the Union and its remaining Member States. In this contribution I will describe and comment on the elements of the Decision concerning free movement of Union citizens, deal with the potential effects for Union citizens and for nationals from countries outside the EU and conclude with some remarks on the wider implications of the Decision.

## 14.2 The Democratic Deficit of Intergovernmental Cooperation

Before I embark on that programme, it should be noted that the preparation of the Decision was not an example of democratic decision making. UK Prime Minister David Cameron in 2013 announced the referendum and in 2014 outlined his wishes for reform of Union law in public speeches. In 2015 he twice spoke briefly in the European Council about his desire to start negotiations on this issue without further specification.[2] It was only after being pressured by his colleagues that Cameron wrote a letter to the President of the European Council in November 2015 outlining the areas in which he was seeking reform "to address the concerns of the British people over our membership of the European Union".[3] From the summer of 2015, UK officials held "technical discussions" with officials of the European Commission. During these discussions three wishes formulated by Cameron in his speeches in 2014, were, apparently, dropped: EU workers should have a confirmed job offer before admission in another Member State, no social benefits and social housing for EU nationals from other Member States during the first four years and the introduction of long-term re-entry bans in cases of begging or fraud. These demands did not appear in the November 2015 letter. Negotiations between the Member States with the participation of the European Commission started only after the December 2015 European Council. They resulted in a draft Decision published on 2 February 2016.[4] Two weeks later the Decision was adopted. Thus, the European Parliament, national parliaments and the general public in the Member States were effectively given only two weeks to read, comment on the draft and try to influence the content of the Decision. According to press reports, the European Parliament's (EP) President and leaders of the three main political factions in the EP were invited by Donald Tusk to his office on 19 February 2016

2 EUCO 22/15, p. 8 and EUCO 26/15, p. 6.

3 Letter of 10 November 2015 to Donald Tusk.

4 EUCO 4/16 of 2 February 2016.

to give their opinion on or, possibly, their informal consent to the text of the Decision.[5]

The ordinary procedure for amending the Treaties in Article 48 TEU provides that the national parliaments shall be informed about the proposals for amendment before a decision is made to amend the Treaties and that a decision to amend comes into effect after national approval according to the Member States' constitutional procedures, often involving their parliaments. Even the ordinary legislative process of the EU provides for far more and longer opportunities for public and parliamentary participation than the negotiations between Member States on the Decision of 19 February 2016.[6] The Legal Service of the Council assured the European Council that the Decision "does not require any formality for the parties to express their consent to be bound. It does not require any formality such as signing or notification of having accomplished a formal ratification or any other procedure in accordance with constitutional requirements".[7] The Legal Service's opinion was sought after publication of the Draft Decision within three days of being requested. Following this advice, the consent of the national parliaments was not made a requirement for the entry into force of the Decision, although enhancing the role of national parliaments was one of the explicit aims of the Decision (see Section C). Politicians who criticize the democratic deficit of the EU and propose intergovernmental cooperation as an attractive alternative for EU membership, often forget that that intergovernmental cooperation has far fewer guarantees for democratic participation in the legislative process than provided by the current, admittedly imperfect, law making in the EU.

## 14.3 What Did Member State Agree on Free Movement and Social Security?

The Decision has four main sections entitled Economic Governance, Competitiveness, Sovereignty and, finally, "Social Benefits and Free Movement". This chapter focuses on the last section (Section D). This section is by far the longest and most detailed section of the Decision. Moreover, three detailed

5 *Volkskrant*, 27 February 2016.

6 For more details see: Meijers Committee, *Accommodating British EU-demands and democratic change of the Treaties*, CM 1516 of 27 October 2015.

7 EUCO 15/16 of 8 February 2016, par. 5; for a critical discussion of the role of the Council's Legal Service see E. Guild, *Brexit and its consequences for the UK and EU citizenship or monstrous citizenship*, inaugural lecture at Queen Mary University of London, 27 September 2016.

declarations of the Commission with respect to the issues dealt with in Section D are attached to the Decision. This may reflect the level of agreement between some Member States and the centrality of these issues during the negotiations. In this section Member States for the first time since the beginning of free movement in the EEC agreed on major restrictions of three central elements of the right to free movement of Union citizens: their security of residence, their right to family reunification and the equal treatment of EU workers. The agreed changes in Section D of the Decision are presented as new interpretations of existing primary and secondary EU rules (under the heading "Interpretation of current EU rules") or as amendments to existing Union law ("Changes to EU secondary legislation"). Further amendments of secondary EU law are to be found in the three Declarations annexed to the Decision in which the Commission promises to propose changes in all three central secondary law instruments in this field: Directive 2004/38 on free movement of Union citizens, Regulation 492/2011 on free movement of workers and Regulation 883/2004 on the coordination of social security systems.

According to the Decision and the relevant European Council Conclusions, the "arrangements" of the Decision "are fully compatible with the Treaties". The Treaties are not amended. But whether the agreed amendments and interpretations are compatible with the Treaties is subject to considerable doubt.

### 14.3.1 *The Emergency Brake and the Reduced Exportation of Child Benefits for EU Workers*

With regard to social benefits two major changes were agreed: the introduction of the "emergency brake" on non-contributory in-work benefits and the "indexation" (read: reduction) of the child benefits to children of EU workers who do not accompany the worker. The Commission promised to make a proposal to introduce a "safeguard mechanism" in Regulation 492/2011 allowing the Council in cases of exceptional inflow of workers from other Member States to decide on a proposal from the Commission to authorise a Member State to limit the access of newly arriving EU workers to non-contributory in-work benefits for the first seven years of employment in that Member State. The Commission in advance of the possible entry into force of the Decision stated that the UK would be fully justified in triggering this safeguard mechanism considering the information provided by the UK and "in particular as it has not made full use of the transitional periods on free movement of workers which were provided for in recent Accession Acts".[8] This early green light for the UK was justified

8 EUCO 10/16, p. 23 and Annex VI on p. 34.

as retroactive compensation for having allowed free movement workers from new Member States during the transitional periods, disregarding the benefits from their employment.

The Commission also promised the Member States to propose amendments to Regulation 883/2004 in order to allow Member States to reduce the child benefits paid for children of EU workers who remained in the Member State of origin or another Member State, taking into account the standard of living and the level of child benefits applicable in that Member State.[9] Until 2020 this indexation would only apply to "new" workers. The EU workers under the new rules would pay social contributions and taxes according to the (higher) level of the Member State where he or she was employed and receive the lower child benefits applicable in the Member State of origin. The Court of Justice in 1986 and again in 1989 had held a similar rule in Regulation 1408/71 to be a typical example of indirect discrimination, incompatible with the equal treatment clause in Article 48 EEC Treaty, since national workers would rarely be confronted with a reduction in benefits.[10] Would the Court interpret the prohibition on discrimination on the ground of nationality in Article 18 TFEU of the same Treaty differently 30 years later, because the benefits would now be only reduced to the level in the Member State of origin, rather than not being paid abroad at all?[11] The Member States in the Decision promised that they would do their best to ensure a rapid adoption of both proposals.[12]

### 14.3.2 *Limiting Security of Residence of EU Citizens*

In the Decision the Member States also agreed to expand the interpretation of the public policy exception allowing for expulsion of Union citizens in cases where that expulsion would not be allowed under the current interpretation of primary and secondary Union law (Article 45 TFEU and Articles 27 and 28 of Directive 2004/38) by the Court of Justice. The Decision states that Member States may take "the necessary restrictive measures to protect themselves against individuals whose personal conduct is likely to represent a genuine and serious threat to public policy or security. In determining whether the conduct of an individual poses a present threat to public policy or security, Member States may take into account past conduct of the individual concerned and the threat may not always need to be imminent. Even in the absence of a previous

---

9 EUCO 10/16, p. 22 and Annex V on p. 33.

10 CJEU 15 January 1986, C-41/84, *Pinna I*, ECLI:EU:C:1986:1, ECR I-17, par. 23–24; CJEU 2 March 1987, C-359/87, *Pinna II*, ECLI:EU:C:1986:1, ECR I-610.

11 See also the contribution of Minderhoud: Chapter 4 in this volume.

12 EUCO 10/16, p. 23.

criminal conviction, Member States may act on preventative grounds, so long as they are specific to the individual concerned".[13] This formulation departs on at least two grounds from the constant interpretation of the public policy exception in the EEC/EC/EU Treaty and the current TFEU by the Court of Justice since the 1977 *Bouchereau* judgment[14] until today, an interpretation which the Member States unanimously codified in 2004 in Article 27 of Directive 2004/38. Firstly, the requirement that threat to public policy needs to be actual or present has been implicitly deleted. Secondly, Member States and the Commission explicitly agreed that the important guarantee that Union citizens can only be expelled on the ground of serious criminal offences for which they have been convicted by a court would disappear. The procedural guarantees of criminal law, which, generally, offer citizens far more protection than immigration law procedures can be circumvented if Member States want to expel Union citizens.

The European Commission in Annex VII further declared that it would "clarify that Member States may take into account past conduct of an individual in the determination of whether a Union citizen's conduct poses a 'present' threat to public policy or security. They may act on grounds of public policy or public security even in the absence of a previous criminal conviction on preventative grounds but specific to the individual concerned". The Commission also promised to clarify the notions of "serious grounds of public policy or public security" and "imperative grounds of public security". How, the Commission imagined that it had the power to depart from the constant case law of the Court and the text of a Directive in guidelines remains unclear.

Apparently, Member States and the Commission considered that guidelines might not be sufficient to amend Union law and they agreed that amendment of the secondary law was necessary to reach the desired goal. This explains the final and rather vague declaration that "on the occasion of a future revision of Directive 2004/38 on free movement of Union citizens, the Commission will examine the thresholds to which these notions are connected".[15] This implies amending Article 28 of Directive 2004/38. That occasion could have been present on short notice, since on the previous page of the same declaration the Commission promised to introduce a proposal to amend Directive 2004/38 in order to severely restrict the right to family reunification of mobile Union citizens.

13 EUCO 10/16, p. 21.

14 CJEU 27 October 1977, C-30/77, *Regina*, ECLI:EU:C:1977:172.

15 EUCO 10/16, Annex VII on p. 36.

### 14.3.3 *Reduction of the Right to Family Reunification*

The most far-reaching change in free movement law is not mentioned in the Decision at all, but only in a declaration by the Commission in Annex VII. In the Decision the Member States under the heading "Interpretation of current EU rules" stated: "In accordance with Union law, Member States are able to take action to prevent abuse of rights or fraud, such as the presentation of forged documents, and address cases of contracting or maintaining marriages of convenience with third country nationals for the purpose of making use of free movement as a route for regularising unlawful stay in a Member State or address cases of making use of free movement as a route for bypassing national immigration rules applying to third country nationals".[16]

The Commission, accordingly, promised to clarify (read: publish guidelines) that: "Member States can address specific cases of abuse of free movement rights by Union citizens returning to their Member State of nationality with a non-EU family member where residence in the host Member State has not been sufficiently genuine to create or strengthen family life and had the purpose of evading the application of national immigration rules".[17] Moreover, the Commission redefined the concept of marriage of convenience, now covering "a marriage which is maintained for the purpose of enjoying a right of residence by a family member who is not a national of a Member State". According to the Commission this concept is not protected under Union law, although the concept is explicitly mentioned in Article 35 of Directive 2004/38 and Article 16 of Directive 2003/86. The Commission's declaration further disregards the far more restrictive definition in the latter Article: "the marriage, partnership or adoption was contracted for the sole purpose of enabling the person concerned to enter or reside in a Member State".

The Commission's declaration on reunification with third-country national family members goes far beyond the text of Decision of the Heads of Governments. The Commission in Annex VII expressed its intention "to adopt a proposal to complement [sic] Directive 2004/38 on free movement of Union citizens in order to exclude, from the scope of free movement rights, third country nationals who had no prior lawful residence in a Member State before marrying a Union citizen or who marry a Union citizen only after the Union citizen has established residence in the host Member State. Accordingly, in such cases, the host Member State's immigration law will apply to the third country national".[18] This last amendment would overrule the constant case

16 EUCO 10/16, p. 21.

17 EUCO 10/16, Annex VII on p. 35.

18 EUCO 10/16, Annex VII on p. 35.

law of the Court of Justice on EU nationals returning to their own Member State after having used their free movement rights in *Surinder Singh* (1992), *Eind* (2007) and *O & B* (2014).[19] The effect of this amendment would be that Union citizens would have to choose between remaining with their spouse in the host Member State or returning to the home Member State without his or her spouse, who would then remain alone in the host Member State or be obliged to return to a third country.

The right of workers (later Union citizens) to live in the host Member State with their third-country national family members was granted in 1961 in the first Regulation on the free movement of workers and was confirmed by the Court in its case law. In the *Metock* judgment the Court rejected the plea of several Member States that family reunification should no longer be a right of the EU national but subject to national immigration law.[20] The Court rejected that plea among others as contrary to the idea of an Internal Market with common rules, different rules on family reunification would then apply in each Member State and because the Union legislator could not reasonably have had in mind to place Union nationals in a worse position than lawfully resident third-country nationals whose right to family reunification had been granted in Directive 2004/86. After the *Metock* judgment some Member States (Ireland, Denmark, and the UK) in 2008 proposed to amend Union law in order to overrule this judgment, arguing "significant misuse" of the rules on family reunification. But France and other Member States voiced opposition and the proposal was dropped after the Commission's promise to issue Guidelines on the application of the Directive.[21] In 2011 the Dutch minority government published a position paper advocating reduction of the right to family reunification of Union citizens in Directive 2004/38 to the level of the far more restricted right to family reunification of lawfully resident third-country nationals under Directive 2003/86. That government depended on a formal agreement on immigration issues with Geert Wilders and on the votes of the MPs of his one-member political party for its majority in parliament. This Dutch proposal received little support from other Member States. But in 2016 in its Declaration in Annex VII, the Commission promised to go much further, by proposing complete abolishment of the right to family reunification

19 CJEU 7 July 1992, C-370/90 *Surinder Singh*, ECLI:EU:C:1992:296; CJEU 11 December 2007, C-291/05, *Eind*, ECLI:EU:C:2007:771; CJEU 12 March 2014, C-456/12, *O & B*, ECLI:EU:C:2014:135.

20 CJEU 25 July 2008, C-127/08, *Metock*, ECLI:EU:C:2008:449.

21 See the report on the September 2008 JHA Council and Council documents nos. 15903/08, 16151/08, 16483/08, 10551/09 and 13467/09.

in Union law for Union citizens moving to other Member States. This would mean a return to the situation before the beginning of the first transitional phase of free movement in 1961. Did the Commission really think that the Court would no longer adhere to the arguments it mentioned in the *Metock* judgment in 2008?

## 14.4 Wider Implications of the Decision

In the Decision the Member States for the first time since 1961 agreed to reduce the right to free movement of Union citizens. In the five decades after 1961 the Member States in the Council (until 2004 the main Union legislator) and the Court gradually extended the personal scope of free movement and the material and procedural rights attached to it. Moreover, the personal and geographical scope of free movement was extended with the accession of new Member States in 2004, 2007 and 2013. Only on a few occasions was free movement somewhat reduced by the introduction of a new restriction or the abolishment of a protective rule. The 2003 *Akrich* judgment,[22] requiring admission of TCN family members under national law, which was explicitly overruled by the Grand Chamber of the Court five years later in *Metock* and the abolishment in Directive 2004/38 of the automatic suspensive effect of an appeal against a decision to end the residence right of a Union citizen which was part of free movement law since 1964 are examples of such rare regressions. Until recently, the general line of development extended free movement of EU citizens.

### 14.4.1 *A Better Deal for Britain, but also for other Member States?*

The Decision was presented as a "better deal" for Britain, but the new rules and new interpretations would apply, generally, to all 28 Member States. On the four issues discussed above, the Decision reflected not only British wishes but also old wishes of at least three other Member States. Three of the four issues (restriction of access of EU nationals to social benefits, wider possibilities for expulsion and restriction of reunification with TCN family members) were raised by the Ministers of Interior of Austria, Germany, the Netherlands and the UK in a letter to the EU Council in April 2013.[23] The European Commission in 2013 reacted with a letter pointing to the absence of data on the postulated abuse, fraud and benefits tourism of nationals of other Member

22 CJEU 23 September 2003, C-109/01, *Akrich*, ECLI:EU:C:2003:491.

23 Published in council document 10313/13 of 31 May 2013.

States. This effort to give the debate a more rational basis failed as the authors of the letter did not provide serious data. The four Member States did not get much support in the Council and the letter gradually disappeared from the agenda of the Council.[24] Three years later the same Member States were able to get more support from other Member States and the Commission, apparently, changed its position. The initial opposition changed to cooperation with Member States' wishes to an extent that at certain points were hardly compatible with the Commission's role as guardian of the Treaties in question.

The issue of reduction of child benefits for children of EU workers remaining in another Member State was not mentioned in the 2013 letter from the four Ministers. But reducing child benefits for children living abroad has been a recurrent issue in several Member States. The two *Pinna* judgments in the 1980s concerned the exception in the original Regulation 1408/71 allowing France not to pay child benefits for the children of Italian workers who remained in Italy. The German and the Austrian chancellor immediately after the adoption of the Decision on 19 February 2016 announced a reduction of child benefits for children living elsewhere in the EU and the Dutch authorities published the total amount of benefits paid to Polish nationals employed in the Netherlands for their children living in Poland (16 million euro in 2015).[25]

### 14.4.2 *Who Can Overrule the Court?*

Several elements of the Decision clearly intended to overrule established jurisprudence of the Court of Justice either by amending secondary law or by giving a (new) interpretation to existing primary and secondary Union law that clearly departs from or is hardly compatible with interpretations given by the Court. This concerns not only old and established judgments (*Bouchereau* 1977, *Pinna I* 1986, *Pinna II* 1989 and *Singh* 1992) but also more recent judgments such as *Eind* 2007, *Metock* 2008 and *O & B 2014*. In the EU just as in Member States the democratically legitimated legislator can overrule case law of the courts, within the limits set by the constitution or Treaties. But the legislator has to play by the rules in changing the law. He cannot simply dictate binding new interpretations without changing the law. This also applies in the EU: neither a consensus among Member States nor a statement by the Commission is sufficient for changing Union law. The case law interpreting the current law remains in force, until the Union legislator changes the

24 Groenendijk, K., 'Recent developments in the EU law on migration: the legislative patchwork and the court's approach', *EJML* 2014, pp. 313–335, at p. 318 ff.

25 *Suddeutsche Zeitung* 20 February 2016; *Die Presse* 20 February 2016; *Volkskrant* 16 April 2016. See also the contribution of Minderhoud: Chapter 4 in this volume.

rules or the Court decides that its previous case law is no longer valid. The Member States are Masters of the Treaties. With consensus they can amend the Treaties, but in February 2016 on paper they decided to leave the Treaties unchanged. The European Council Conclusions state that the "arrangements" of the Decision "are fully compatible with the Treaties". The first recital of the Decision states that Member States settled issues raised by the United Kingdom in its letter of 10 November 2015 "in conformity with the Treaties".[26] But Member States cannot authoritatively declare that their new interpretations of the unchanged Articles 45 and 48 TFEU are correct, nor do they have the power to declare that the amendments of secondary law sketched in the Decision, if adopted by the legislator, are in conformity with the Treaties. That power resides with the Court of Justice only. The European Council is a political institution not a legislator. Member States only make primary Union law. Secondary union law is made by the Council and the Parliament upon a proposal of the Commission.

## 14.5 Possible Effects of the Decision

The Decision of 19 February 2016 will probably never become legally binding on the Member States. As long as the Decision does not enter into force, none of the EU institutions will be bound by it. Nevertheless, the Decision may still be politically relevant and have real effects in the practice of EU institutions and Member States' authorities.

The *Commission* in three declarations attached to the Decision agreed to introduce proposals to amend Directive 2004/38, Regulation 883/2004 and Regulation 492/2011 and to publish new guidelines concerning the interpretation and application of Directive 2004/38. The Commission is not bound by its declaration when the Decision does not enter into force. Certainly, Commission guidelines cannot overrule the case law of the Court of Justice, however much Member States agree with the content of such guidelines. Most probably, between February and July 2016, Commission officials were busy preparing drafts of those documents, which are now stored in the files. Actually, the Commission and its officials may feel relieved, if after the negotiations with Member States' officials on the 2009 Guidelines for better application of the Directive and on its 2014 Handbook on marriages of convenience,[27] they do not have to

26 See point 2 at p. 1 of conclusions EUCO 1/16 and p. 8.

27 COM(2009)313 and COM(2014)604.

negotiate and publish yet another document with different interpretations on the same issues. But the Commission may be asked to draft texts on the same issues during the negotiations on Brexit. There may well be demand for new rules on those issues on both sides of the negotiation table again.

The *Court of Justice* in pending or new cases may be confronted by Member States with the argument that the content of the Decision represents a consensus between Member States on how the current Union law on free movement should be interpreted. The Court may feel political pressure to depart from its case law and implement some of the agreed changes in the Decision. The recent judgments in *Dano,*[28] *Alimanovic,*[29] *Garcia Nieto*[30] and *Commission/UK*[31] on the entitlement of Union citizens to social benefits are perceived as a similar response by the Court to the prolonged debate in several Member States on the so-called benefits tourism.[32] But departing from long-standing case law interpreting Treaty provisions on free movement or equal treatment of EU workers on the basis of a political decision that did not enter into force is quite another matter. As long as the outcome of the negotiations between the 27 Member States and the UK is unknown, it will be difficult and unattractive for the Court to anticipate that outcome.

In the Member States which in recent years have been lobbying in Brussels for similar restrictions of free movement as formulated in the Decision, *politicians and national immigration authorities* may be inclined to consider the consent of other Member States in February 2016 as a sign of support for their views and start to apply the new interpretations of the existing EU free movement law concerning the public policy exception or family reunification at national level through changes in national law or administrative practices. Member States are bound to apply Union law as interpreted by the Court, but it may take years before a case on such premature application of the standards formulated in the Decision reaches the Court.

Finally, the *remaining 27 Member States*, especially the ones that for many years have been campaigning for these changes, could be inclined to use the negotiations with the UK on the consequences of the forthcoming Brexit as

---

28 CJEU 11 November 2014, C-333/13, *Dano*, ECLI:EU:C:2014:2358.

29 CJEU 15 September 2015, C-67/14, *Alimanovic*, ECLI:EU:2015:597.

30 CJEU 25 February 2016, C-299/14, *Garcia-Nieto*, ECLI:EU:C:2016:114.

31 CJEU 14 June 2016, C-308/14, *Com/UK*, ECLI:EU:C:2016:436.

32 See: Sandra Mantu & Paul Minderhoud, *Social rights as a case of Europeanization through law. The role of CJEU jurisprudence*, Nijmegen Migration Law Working Papers Series, no 2016/01, Nijmegen: Radboud University Nijmegen.

an opportunity to introduce some of the changes formulated in the Decision into Union law as part of the new deal with the UK. This may be the case, if the UK opts to become an EEA State (the "Norwegian model"); amending certain EU/EEA rules in order to restrict free movement could be attractive also in selling this outcome in the UK to those who voted to leave the EU. In February 2016 Member States tried to address the wishes of the UK government without amending the Treaties. The departure of the UK from the Union will make amendment of the Treaties unavoidable and thus create an opportunity to amend the Treaties on other issues as well. It is a political question whether the 27 Member States will be prepared to grant the UK more room to restrict the movement of their nationals to and from the UK, once the UK is no longer an EU Member State, than they granted the UK in February 2016 with the aim of avoiding the Brexit.

## 14.6 Union Citizens and Third-Country Nationals will be Affected

Who will be affected if the changes in EU free movement law formulated in the Decision in one way or another come into force some day in the future? The categories primarily affected will be workers from Member States that recently acceded to the Union, EU workers with little education and income, EU citizens of immigrant origin and nationals of third countries. Most students and highly educated or well paid workers, irrespective of their nationality, will only be marginally affected.

The exclusion from social and tax benefits and the reduction of child benefits will primarily affect workers and the self-employed with a low income. The benefits are designed especially to assist low income groups. For those with a higher income child benefits represent only a small proportion of their income. Workers from "new" Member States, employed in "old" Member States, tend to be employed in low paid jobs. Moreover, they will, on average, have shorter periods of residence than mobile workers from "old" Member States and thus will rarely be affected by the "emergency brake". Replacement of EU free movement rules on family reunification by the national rules of Member States will put an additional burden on low income workers unable to meet the national income requirement without taking an additional job. Several Member States in recent years have raised the income requirement in order to reduce family migration. Under the current UK rules persons with an income below the national median de facto are excluded from reunification with their non-EU family members. In the Netherlands almost half of the refusals of family reunification with non-EU family members are founded on the sponsor not meeting the income requirement.[33]

Union citizens of immigrant origin clearly will be affected more often than other ("native") Union citizens by the abolition of the right to family reunification with third-country national family members, since the first group will more often have relationships with third-country nationals and more often marry third-country nationals than "native" Union citizens. EU citizens of immigrant origin, generally, will be more mobile within the EU than "native" EU citizens, if only because they will have more often family members, friends or co-ethnics in other Member States than the "native" Union citizen. Hence, they, arguably, will also be more often affected by the other three restrictions formulated in the Decision.

The Decision of February 2016 deals almost exclusively with the rights of Union citizens. Only the abolishment of the EU right to live together with third-country family members and of the right to accompany the EU spouse or parent returning to his or her home Member State will clearly have direct negative effects for those non-EU family members. But the changes in free movement law, if actually implemented, will in several ways have far-reaching indirect effects for the rights of third-country nationals.

Firstly, abolishment of the right of EU nationals to live with their non-EU family members in another Member State, as provided in Community and EU law since 1961, and making their family reunification dependent on national law, will raise the question of whether EU nationals in this respect can be treated less favourably than lawfully resident third-country nationals who have a right to family reunification granted by Directive 2003/86. It will be hard to justify this difference in treatment under Articles 8 and 14 ECHR. This will then in turn result in pressure by Member States to reduce the level of rights granted to third-country nationals in that Directive.

Secondly, in several Directives and other instruments on third-country nationals the Union legislator used the rules of free movement as a model or used the same concept as in instruments on free movement of Union citizens. In a series of recent judgments the Court of Justice interpreted those concepts in instruments on third-country nationals as having the same or a similar meaning. For instance, the Court held that the concept of "risk to public policy" in the Returns Directive, the Refugee Qualification Directive and the Reception

33 Kulu-Glasgow, I. *et al.* (2016), *Schijn bedriegt, Een onderzoek naar de prevalentie en verschijningsvormen van schijnrelaties*, WODC cahier 2016–6, The Hague: Ministry of Security and Justice, p. 79.

Conditions Directive presupposes the existence, in addition to the perturbation of the social order which any infringement of the law involves, of a genuine, present and sufficiently serious threat affecting one of the fundamental interests of by way of analogy with its case law on the public policy exception in the rules on free movement of Union citizens.[34] If the current interpretation of the concept of public policy in rules on Union citizens is amended in a restrictive way, because of the analogous interpretation by the Court, this will most probably have the effect of reducing the rights and protection of third-country nationals under Union law as well. The same will apply to Turkish nationals, since the Court has interpreted the public policy exception in Association Council Decision 1/80 as having (almost) the same meaning as the similar exception in the rules on EU workers.[35]

Thirdly, the rights of certain categories of third-country nationals are explicitly linked to those of EU nationals in a similar position. Article 59 of the Additional Protocol to the EEC-Turkey Association Agreement provides: "In the fields covered by this Protocol Turkey shall not receive more favourable treatment than that which Member States grant to one another pursuant to the Treaty establishing the Community". According to the non-discrimination clause in Article 3 of Association Council Decision 3/80 Turkish workers employed in the EU are entitled to full child benefits for their children living in Turkey. If the rights of EU workers to child benefits for children living outside the host Member State are reduced, a similar reduction will automatically apply for Turkish workers as well.

## 14.7 Conclusions

Until now the ordinary legislative procedure in the EU has functioned as a brake on demands from Member States to amend the rules on free movement of Union citizens in order to restrict free movement and de facto exclude certain categories of EU citizens. Over the last decade, the UK and some other Member States, with respect to three of the four main elements of the Decision

34 CJEU 11 June 2015, C-554/13, *Zh & O*, ECLI:EU:C:2015:377, point 60 with regard to Article 7(4) of Directive 2008/115; CJEU 24 June 2015, C-373/13, *H.T.*, ECLI:EU:C:2015:413, point 79, with regard to Article 24(1) of Directive 2004/83 (now Directive 2011/95); CJEU 15 February 2016, C-601/15 PPU, *J.N.*, ECLI:EU:C:2016:284, points 64 ff with regard to Article 8(3) of Directive 2013/32.

35 CJEU 10 February 2000, C-340/97, *Nazli*, ECLI:EU:C:2000:77 with a restriction in CJEU 24 September 2013, C-221/11, *Demirkan*, ECLI:EU:C:2013:583.

relating to free movement, have tabled suggestions or concrete proposals for amendments to the EU rules. Only the "emergency brake" was a completely new and British issue. The negotiations with the UK provided these Member States with the opportunity to realise old wishes without having to respond to the European Commission's demand for facts instead of sentiments supporting the desired changes.

By choosing the form of an intergovernmental agreement and by convincing the Commission to propose amendments in secondary law and to make declarations that amounted to new interpretations of primary and secondary Union law departing from settled interpretations of the relevant instruments by the Court of Justice, the Member States tried to circumvent the constitutional arrangement of the EU and minimize the role of the European Parliament and the national parliaments. This road was paved and legitimized by the Council's Legal Service. The Decision of 19 February 2016 is a clear example that intergovernmental cooperation is not an attractive alternative for cooperation within the EU. Intergovernmental cooperation provides far fewer guarantees for democratic participation in the legislative process than the current rules on law making in the EU, provided that those rules are observed.

The UK and other Western European Member States in the Decision agreed to reduce the rights of workers from Central European Member States and of unskilled workers from other Member States. The Decision illustrates the lack of solidarity of the richer Member States with the less rich ones. In this respect the position of the Visegrad countries in the forthcoming negotiations on Brexit will be of interest. Those negotiations, probably, will take more time and be more visible than the negotiations on the Decision.

The Decision constituted a clear effort by Member States to shift competence from EU level to national level. It is a clear example of renationalization ("repatriation of sovereignty") with respect to one of the four central freedoms of the Treaties. The Decision would have made the EU a less social and more economic undertaking. The decrease in equal treatment with regard to basic social rights, the abolishment of the right to family reunification and the reduction of the security of residence would have removed three essential elements of Union citizenship. EU nationals residing in another Member State were to become more "foreigners" and less citizens. The agreed reduction of rights of EU nationals would have reduced rights of third-country nationals as well. This side effect did not get any visible attention during the negotiation process. Would this reduction have enhanced the integration of the large majority of EU nationals and TCNs lawfully residing in the Member States or would it have created new barriers to that integration?

The Decision most probably will never enter into force. But it has to be seen how the 27 remaining Member States will approach the same issues during the forthcoming negotiations on Brexit. Will the governments of some Member States use these negotiations as another opportunity to reduce the rights of Union citizens, in the hope of appeasing and re-attracting their citizens voting for populist or anti-immigrant parties?

## References

*Die Presse*, 20 February 2016

EUCO (European Council document) 22/15.

EUCO 10/16.

EUCO 15/16.

EUCO 26/15.

EUCO 4/16.

Groenendijk, K. (2014), 'Recent developments in the EU law on migration: the legislative patchwork and the court's approach', *EJML* 2014, pp. 313–335.

Guild, E. (2016), *Brexit and its consequences for the UK and EU citizenship or monstrous citizenship*, inaugural lecture at Queen Mary University of London, 27 September 2016.

Kulu-Glasgow, I. *et al.* (2016), *Schijn bedriegt, Een onderzoek naar de prevalentie en verschijningsvormen van schijnrelaties*, (WODC cahier 2016–6), The Hague: Ministry of Security and Justice.

Mantu S. & P. Minderhoud, *Social rights as a case of Europeanization through law. The role of CJEU jurisprudence,* Nijmegen Migration Law Working Papers Series, no 2016/01, Nijmegen: Radboud University Nijmegen.

Meijers Committee (2015), *Accommodating British EU-demands and democratic change of the Treaties*, CM 1516 of 27 October.

Report on the September 2008 JHA Council.

*Suddeutsche Zeitung,* 20 February 2016

*Volkskrant*, 16 April 2016.

*Volkskrant*, 27 February 2016.

# Index

www.ingramcontent.com/pod-product-compliance
Lightning Source LLC
LaVergne TN
LVHW010625300926
849162LV00001B/61